Faith and Order in Moshi

Edited by Alan Falconer

Faith and Order in Moshi

The 1996 Commission Meeting

Faith and Order Paper No. 177

WCC Publications, Geneva

Cover design: Edwin Hassink
Cover Photo: Dagmar Heller

ISBN 2-8254-1233-3

© 1998 WCC Publications, World Council of Churches,
150 route de Ferney, 1211 Geneva 2, Switzerland

Printed in the Netherlands

Table of Contents

Preface

ALAN D. FALCONER

In August 1996, the commission on Faith and Order of the World Council of Churches met at the Uhuru Hostel in Moshi, at the foot of Mount Kilimanjaro. With its 120 members representing the member churches of the World Council and several non-member churches, especially the Roman Catholic Church, the commission seeks "to proclaim the oneness of the Church of Jesus Christ and to call the churches to the goal of visible unity in one faith and one eucharistic fellowship, expressed in worship and in common life in Christ, in order that the world may believe". This mandate is pursued through studies on questions both doctrinal and non-doctrinal which have been a source or occasion for church division; the studies are undertaken by commission members themselves, and in connection with initiatives undertaken with other church instruments seeking the unity of the church. The meeting of the full plenary commission has the specific task of examining and appraising the work undertaken on its behalf, and initiating the programme, laying down general guidelines for it and communicating the results of the studies to the churches.

This was the first full meeting of the commission since Budapest in 1989. Normally the commission has gathered every four years. However, with the decision at Budapest to hold a fifth world conference on Faith and Order in 1993, the commission was able to meet for only a limited period immediately after the world conference at Santiago de Compostela.

At the Moshi meeting, therefore, some 42 percent of the delegates or proxies were attending their first commission meeting. Some ten younger theologians (under 35 years) participated fully, while the commission membership included a greater number of theologians from Africa, Asia, Latin America, the Caribbean and the Pacific, and more women theologians.

The basic agenda of the meeting was the review of work which had been put in place as a result of the recommendations of the fifth world conference.

The programme at Moshi

There were three main sections to the programme. The first part focused on the reception of work produced by Faith and Order. Delegates had been asked in the preparatory material to come to Moshi prepared to share how the work of Faith and Order had been received in their churches and regions. Does the work address the issues around unity being faced by the churches? What are the processes of discussion and appropriation of the work? How can the commission engage in its studies in ways which are faithful to the insights, questions and experiences of churches in all regions of the world? The reflections of the delegates were shared in group discussions and plenary sessions. But what is the nature of reception? What are the theological issues and ecclesiological implications of reception? What are the processes of reception? These questions were addressed through presentations and discussions in plenary sessions. They continued to undergird the discussions throughout the meeting.

The second part of the meeting focused on the studies being undertaken by Faith and Order – ecclesiology, ecumenical hermeneutics, worship, and ecclesiology and ethics. For each of these topics, three plenary commission members who had not been involved in the drafting processes and who represented different ecclesial traditions, regions and genders, had been invited to initiate discussion and raise questions. All the commissioners then discussed the texts in small groups which, in a final plenary discussion on each theme, presented some key points of guidance to the board of Faith and Order for further work on that theme. After this, the drafting group on each topic brought proposals for adoption in relation to the further work in the light of the directions received. The full and detailed comments of each group were given to each of the drafting groups but were not the subject of a formal presentation to the commission. In this way the commission was able to give direction to and general guidance for each study, and also play a positive role in the further drafting of each text.

The commission also received work which had been published since the fifth world conference, e. g. *Towards Sharing the One Faith* (a study guide on the apostolic faith), and work undertaken in collaboration with other bodies, e. g. the Week of Prayer for Christian Unity, the Bilateral Forum and the Joint Working Group.

The third part of the commission meeting focused on the future. How is the work to be communicated in the different churches and contexts? What is the continuing agenda of BEM, the Faith and Order report which had been most widely received by the churches? What is the task and role of Faith and Order at the WCC assembly in Harare? What is the nature of the World Council of Churches, and how might it order its life and work in appropriate ways?

Each day began with Bible study, designed to inform the discussion on the theme of the day. At the centre of each day, the commission came together for worship.

In this volume, the major presentations to the commission are published. These are followed by a record of the main points raised in plenary discussion sessions. The recommendations and actions of the commission are also published. This is not simply to serve the function of a minute of the meeting, but also as a measure of accountability to the World Council of Churches and to the churches represented on the commission of Faith and Order. For its future work, the Faith and Order board considers seriously the recommendations and insights of the commission for the development of the studies. So that the discussion can be made transparent, the volume includes the draft texts discussed at Moshi on ecclesiology and ecumenical hermeneutics. Since the other studies under discussion have been published in their Moshi form in separate publications they do not appear in this volume. The full group reports and the reports of the regional meetings have been transmitted directly to the Faith and Order board and its drafting groups, and therefore do not appear here. The Bible studies have all been included in the publication since they directly and indirectly influenced the discussions.

Undoubtedly presentation of a report such as this can only indicate general directions. It cannot convey the passion with which insights were communicated, nor the subtly nuanced argumentation of positions espoused. Nor can it convey the pain and struggle involved in the attempt to reach convergence. Clearly, the commission meeting at Moshi provided occasions of misunderstanding, frustration, tension and hurt. Due to a number of last-minute cancellations, the balance of speakers which had been sought was not always achieved. The relation between insights from different Christian traditions and different contexts, between inductive and deductive methods of doing theology, was not always easy to moderate. And yet there was a clear and continuing commitment to maintain the fellowship while differences were faced.

At the foot of Kilimanjaro

Meeting in Tanzania proved to be a unique opportunity to enter dialogue with Africa. While the commission had met in Accra in 1974 where the context made an immense impact on the commissioners, only a limited number of meetings of Faith and Order study groups and regional meetings had taken place on the continent since that time. The commission met in Moshi at the invitation of the Tanzanian churches and in particular of the Evangelical Lutheran Church in Tanzania (ELCT). To prepare for the meeting, a joint local committee of Lutheran, Anglian and Roman Catholic representatives had planned worship, presentations on Tanzanian church life and witness, performances by choirs, local schools and dancers, and had arranged for the commissioners to join local churches for worship. It was the first time that such cooperation by these churches had been evident and at the end of the commission meeting, in a very moving declaration, they committed themselves to continue to work together.

The reality of the African situation was movingly presented in a major address at the beginning of the plenary commission meeting by His Excellency Benjamin Mkapa, president of Tanzania. The issues being faced by the nation, the interdependence of all nations, and the vision of unity in diversity were clearly and thoughtfully articulated by the president. So important was this keynote address that the decision was taken to devote a plenary session to discussion of it at a later point in the meeting. Subsequent to the meeting in Tanzania, a number of commissioners entered dialogue with their own governments to seek the remission of indebtedness with respect to Tanzania. The president, however, also challenged the churches urgently to place unity as a priority on their agenda.

The Uhuru Hostel itself presented a wonderful and memorable setting for the meeting. The plenary hall had been completed days before our gathering. The variety of birds and flowers in the gardens presented a colourful tapestry of unity in diversity. The exuberance of the youth choirs, the swaying of the dancers and the rhythms of the music brought vitality and effervescence to our meeting.

Yet it was Kilimanjaro that provided a parable for the commission. The commission met at the base of the mountain for ten days. We all believed it to exist. We had been told of its majesty, its dominance and of the shelter it gave to animal and human life on its slopes. Yet, day after day, it remained unseen, shrouded in mist. Suddenly, the mist lifted during a plenary session of the meeting. Commissioners drifted from their seats, cameras in hand, until such time as business had to be suspended so that the whole commission could glimpse its stature and majesty. No photograph could capture its stature. All accounts of the mountain can only give a partial glimpse of its fullness. The moment had to be seized, because all too quickly it passed – the mountain was again cloaked in mist.

Throughout its meeting the commission and the commissioners were challenged to seize the moment for the reception of the results of studies, for reception of one another, and for the manifestation of visible unity. Glimpses of convergence and understanding strengthened the commitment to strive together for the unity of the church as a sign of God's intention for the unity of humankind. The fullness of the vision was glimpsed. The continuing challenge is to work for its implementation.

The commission at its concluding sessions gave thanks to those whose hospitality and welcome enhanced the meeting. Bishop Erasto Kweka and the leaders of the churches, including the Roman Catholic Church, in Moshi and Arusha who helped us appreciate the life and witness of the churches in northern Tanzania; Nigel Rooms and the local worship committee; Mrs E. Mshomi, Mr E. Malekia and the staff of the Uhuru Hostel, the International School and Masoka Training Institute; the local church choirs and schools.

This was the first occasion on which I myself have participated in a meeting of the commission of Faith and Order. I am very grateful to my colleagues who shared with me in the planning and the running of the meeting, and to Mary Tanner, the moderator of the commission, for her constant advice and inspiration. I would also like to express my gratitude to Konrad Raiser, the general secretary of the World Council of Churches, for his support and encouragement. The commission greatly appreciated his presence among us for over half the meeting, and his thoughtful and challenging presentations and engagement in dialogue. We were also pleased that the Unit I director, Thomas F. FitzGerald, was able to join us for a substantial period of our meeting and to make an important presentation to our commission.

Finally it remains to thank the publications department of the WCC for their skill and patience. It had been planned that we would be able to return from Moshi with the completed text of this report. Unfortunately, a week before the meeting our minute-taker had to withdraw, due to unforeseen circumstances. The report has therefore had to be constructed from tapes of the meeting. I am indebted to my colleagues for the additional burden that has been placed on them in sharing in the recording of our commission meeting. I hope that those not present at Moshi will manage to catch a glimpse of its discussions and concerns and will join us in seeking to seize the moment to call the churches to manifest the visible unity of the church as a sign of God's intention for the unity of humankind.

Message from the Plenary Commission of Faith and Order

Moshi, Tanzania, August 1996

We the members of the Faith and Order plenary commission of the World Council of Churches, assembled in Moshi, Tanzania, 10-24 August 1996, send greetings to our brothers and sisters in all the churches and in all parts of the world. The Faith and Order commission comprises over 120 members, drawn from among the member churches of the WCC and from the Roman Catholic Church, Pentecostals and Seventh-Day Adventists. At the end of our meeting we wish to share some of its fruits with you.

The fact that our meeting took place in Africa made more relevant many critical issues which unfortunately are also found in other parts of the world: the stark poverty of the vast majority of the people, while the riches of the continent are drained away through the international debt; the horrific violence of ethnic conflicts, like those of Rwanda and Burundi, stimulated by economic interests; the threat to cultural identity and values from a growing individualism that sharpens social fragmentation.

At the same time we were privileged to get a glimpse of the gift of our African context: the profound sense of community, expressed in the Tanzanian concept of *Utu*; the joyous spirit manifested in songs, dance, hospitality in a growing and vital Christianity; the solidarity and collaboration among churches and between churches and government, in a concern for peace and in caring for refugees. In all these and in many other actions and attitudes, we hear a call to unity which embraces the whole of humankind.

As this century draws to a close, we as churches committed to the ecumenical movement are invited to evaluate our achievements and shortcomings in the quest for Christian unity. Our task as the plenary commission of Faith and Order was undertaken within this context. As we dealt with specific studies we became conscious of the progress made and convergence reached in many fields, but also of the difficulties that are preventing us from moving ahead. We affirm our commitment to the goal of visible Christian unity for we plainly trust in the love of God that brought us together and which we experienced in the blessing of mutual encounter, in dialogue and in prayer. At the same time however we are aware of the tensions created among us by our different ecclesiologies, our diverse appreciations of the social, economic and political realities of the world and their significance for our theological vision, and our various ways of doing theology, related to ecclesial traditions and/or cultural contexts.

Nevertheless we are committed to continue working on the themes that are central to our task. We wish to intensify our work on worship because it is through worship that we best appropriate the unity that we have so far reached by God's grace. Further, we need to continue our studies on the nature and mission of the church as well as to assess their relationship to ethical and hermeneutical questions. We reaffirm our commitment to seek together the full visible unity of the church, believing that this primary purpose is indeed the heartbeat of the World Council of Churches. We look with hope to the provisional results of our efforts confident that through honest dialogue and fidelity to the word of God, in a renewed spirituality of commitment and, above all, under the guidance of the Holy Spirit, we will be able to grow and be built in unity and communion.

Our churches are divided across confessional and denominational lines, but also because of tensions created by political options, ethical issues and social and economic inequalities. As we enter a new millennium these challenges require a new approach to the quest for the unity of the church. Only with realism and humility will we be able to face the coming task. The wounds to be healed, inflicted on one another through history, as well as the present state of human relations which endanger the lives of many and even the integrity of the created world, demand an attitude of repentance and a will for repairment that can only be inspired by the gracious gift of God.

Our experiences of unity and our desire for full communion, inspired in us by the presence and action of the Triune God, allow us to live in freedom and diversity in these times of grief and uncertainty. "We are afflicted in every way but not crushed; perplexed but not driven to despair; persecuted but not forsaken, struck down but not destroyed, always carrying in the body the death of Jesus so that the life of Jesus may also be made visible in our bodies" (2 Cor. 4:8-9). With that mission and in that hope we ask the churches to continue in prayer and commitment to unity. God's will for the church and for the whole of creation is not in vain, and God's continuous love renews in us the strength and desire to live in a growing koinonia with the Trinity and with one another.

Report from the Plenary Commission of Faith and Order to the Churches

Introduction

1. Greetings: From the Faith and Order commission of the World Council of Churches, to the churches of the world: greetings in the name of Christ Jesus our Saviour. The Faith and Order plenary commission has concluded its meeting in Moshi, Tanzania, at the foot of Mount Kilimanjaro (10-24 August 1996). It wishes to share with the churches the content and future direction of its work, together with reflections on how the churches may be encouraged in their work towards full visible unity among themselves, the task in which Faith and Order has been engaged on behalf of the churches for nearly seventy years. The Faith and Order plenary commission is made up of 120 people drawn from among the member churches of the WCC, and from the Roman Catholic Church, Pentecostals and Seventh Day Adventists. In our meeting we have sought to become a community of prayer and theological reflection, attempting to model a unity in diversity in our life together.

Context

2. Africa: the context of our meeting: It was highly appropriate that the plenary commission met in Africa, and the setting has influenced our lives and our work. Christianity in Africa is in many places jubilant, musical, flourishing with young life; the church is growing faster here than on any other continent, growing every day in number and in spirit. Christians here are also, in some places, troubled minorities. In Rwanda and Burundi, next door to our host country, complex ethnic, historic, political and demonic forces, not to mention outside interests exploiting the situation, have combined to produce a horrific scene in which neighbours slay neighbours, Christians slay Christians, while the international community appears helpless. We pray that the churches of the region may be able to do all that is possible to bring the bloodshed to an end and to work for a peaceful solution for the reconciling of peoples in the Spirit of Jesus Christ, who "is our peace" (Eph. 2:14).

3. *Utu, an African expression of koinonia:* Here in Tanzania, which has taken concrete steps in helping its neighbours in conflict, both the enthusiasm of the people of God and their material poverty stand as reminders that the gospel's promise of life abundant is not what the world understands by success. The African understanding of community, of extended family, of *Utu*, is a profound image of koinonia, and is a gift to be received by those who have been tempted by the spirit of egocentrism. We have also been powerfully reminded that, in contrast to *Utu*, there are forces and structures of greed at work in this continent which impoverish whole nations and peoples, and which allow practices of environmental destruction to continue so long as they are far from the homes of those who profit. In Tanzania we are vividly called back to the truth that faith in Jesus Christ brings freedom, wholeness and salvation, and commits us to work for the building of a community of love and reconciliation throughout the world.

4. *For the unity of all:* At the beginning of our meeting, we were honoured in being welcomed by the president of Tanzania, His Excellency Benjamin William Mkapa. He reminded us that the search for unity is not just about the unity of the church, but about "the unity and universality of humankind in its entirety". Here in Africa, where the extremes of the division of rich and poor are seen in such contrast, where such beauty in creation and such exploitation and despoliation both abound, we are reminded that the church's calling to proclaim the gospel on every continent and island is always to be accompanied by the requirement to live by the values of the gospel in every aspect of our life together, and to call the world to a gospel quality of life for all. As one of our members observed, one cannot have true koinonia, true unity and communion, among unequal partners.

5. *Partnership for mission:* We invite the churches who are engaged in mission in Africa and elsewhere to cooperate with, and take their cues from, the churches already flourishing on the local soil. We invite the churches to model partnership in mission, allowing church to speak to church in prophetic ways which call us all back to the values of the gospel. We remind all churches that St Paul invited the diverse Christian communities of his time to share their resources, both material and spiritual. Churches have opportunities, as very few institutions do, to remind the world that we are one world, that the indebtedness of one impoverishes us all, that the greed of one corrupts us all. The church has a divine mandate to be and to be seen to be a community of love, a community of blessing.

Unity and diversity

6. Many voices, one faith: The Faith and Order movement is itself learning to listen to and speak with more and more voices, from many different contexts. The voices of African Christians here have spoken of their experience of disunity sown in families by competing denominations, and have shared new articulations of theology forged in persecution and oppression, in extreme poverty and in isolation. They have spoken through cultures which are ancient and yet new in their Christian expression. We are reminded that those committed to unity need to find ways of speaking, understanding and sharing across the human boundaries of regions, cultures, languages, race and gender, as well as among the families of Christian churches. We invite all our churches to learn "to listen to what the Spirit is saying to the churches" (Rev. 2:7) through their own languages.

7. Called to be one: Diversity is a joyous gift, yet it needs to "be united in the same mind and the same purpose" (1 Cor. 1:10) by the God who is three and yet one. Diversity today can and does raise new and difficult questions of theology and ethics which the churches need to find ways to address together, within and among themselves. Faith and Order, and the churches, are searching for models and methods for achieving unity without uniformity, diversity without division. If the churches engage wholeheartedly in their quest for unity in diversity, they might provide models of hope for a divided humanity.

The ecumenical movement

8. A century of ecumenism: The century which is drawing to a close has been called the "ecumenical century". As we begin to reflect on what this period of growth together as churches has meant, it is important to recall that the modern ecumenical movement was initiated by Christians who had learned in their missionary experience that a divided church cannot effectively preach and advance the one gospel. As in so many other parts of the world, the missionary movement brought the great blessing of the Christian message to Africa, where it has been received with joy, in spite of the hurt which the human failings of its agents have at times caused. The ecumenical movement which was born from the missionary movement has been transformed from an alliance of northern churches into a truly global community. It has become a process of mutual understanding among churches, among women and men, among people from all the diverse regions of the planet. The ecumenical agenda now includes more than the search for reuniting divided church communions, though that, in itself, is the central goal for which we are still striving.

9. *Common understanding and vision of the WCC:* At its meeting, Faith and Order was conscious of the process currently underway in the World Council of Churches, the "Common Understanding and Vision" process, which has sought afresh to express the intention of the churches in working together in a World Council of Churches. The meeting welcomed Dr Konrad Raiser, general secretary of the WCC, who expressed the hope that the assembly in Harare in 1998, which will mark the 50th anniversary of the founding of the WCC, would reaffirm that "the primary purpose of the World Council of Churches is for the churches together to call each other to the goal of visible unity in one faith and in one eucharistic fellowship expressed in worship and in common life, and to advance towards that unity in order that the world may believe". Faith and Order believes that this purpose is, indeed, the heartbeat of the World Council of Churches.

The work of Faith and Order

10. *The harvest of Faith and Order:* This is the first full-length meeting of the plenary commission since the Canberra assembly of the World Council of Churches, which adopted the Canberra statement on unity: "The Koinonia of the Church: Gift and Calling". It is also the first meeting since the fifth world conference on Faith and Order held in Santiago de Compostela, which "harvested" the work of Faith and Order over the past thirty years. Santiago affirmed the many ecumenical achievements in bilateral and multilateral dialogues among our Christian traditions, invited the churches to make concrete the convergences identified in the "Baptism, Eucharist and Ministry" study, and underlined the importance of confessing together the one apostolic faith as well as sharing in mission and service. It stressed that "there is no turning back either from the goal of visible unity or from the single ecumenical movement that unites concern for the unity of the church and concern for engagement in the struggles of the world" (Message, Santiago, para. 3).

11. *A time for discernment:* As the 21st century dawns, much of the harvest of this century's ecumenical endeavours is still waiting to be turned into bread for the life of the churches and the world. Many expressions and instruments of the ecumenical movement, including the World Council of Churches, are struggling to be faithful to their mandate in a time of new challenges. This is a time for discernment, a time which many are calling a crisis, even a spiritual crisis: the churches and the world face new and diverse threats to unity; the enthusiasm of ecumenical discovery has turned more measured and sober; financial resources are scarcer (or given elsewhere). Faith and Order is at a crossroads. It has offered much ecumenical convergence to the churches, but knows that

there is much more yet to be done, both in making convergence concrete and in trying to achieve convergence on many difficult issues. Do we have the courage and the will to address together deep and complex questions related to authority and interpretation which not only separate churches from one another, but which are also being debated within churches?

12. Our study projects: Faith and Order, in this context, has been engaged in some specific studies building on the foundation of BEM, which are all intended, under grace, to contribute to the task of building for unity:

a) ecclesiology: the ongoing study on the nature and purpose of the church will be asked to consider issues of conciliarity, primacy and the ministry of unity, oversight, authority, laity, the ministries of women, reconciliation of memories, the four marks of the church, the visible and invisible nature of the church, the trinity as source of the koinonia of the church, as well as the insights and challenges of the other major studies;

b) ecumenical hermeneutics: a study asked for by Santiago, which focuses on the way in which texts, symbols and practices of the various Christian churches may be interpreted, communicated and received accurately by each other as they engage in dialogue;

c) ecclesiology and ethics: this ongoing work on the relationship between the nature of the church and its ethical witness in and for the sake of the world will be asked to include work on the unity of the church in relation to ethnic identity and nationalism;

d) worship: work on worship in the search for unity will continue, with consideration of the question of unity and diversity in worship and its relationship to the search for visible unity in the church; a consultation on baptism is planned for January 1997 to address baptismal ordo, inculturation of baptism, and ethical and ecclesiological implications of baptism;

e) apostolic faith: a study guide *Towards Sharing the One Faith* was warmly received and will be sent to the churches; it is intended to engage Christians everywhere on the issues addressed in the important study "Confessing the One Faith", which was sent to the churches in 1990; the study guide offers a flexible resource for use as locally appropriate.

13. Reception: Agreed statements are wonderful gifts, born of the Spirit who calls us together in dialogue and mutual learning, but they will pile up in libraries and be of little use in achieving the goal of full visible unity unless the churches make them their own. The texts, but also the spirit in which ecumenical texts are written, are offered for reception and action by the churches. We have learned that such reception will be furthered by Christians from different contexts and regions engaging in a dynamic process of building unity and mutual understanding in and among local churches. We call on churches to find ways to commit themselves concretely, not only to agreed statements (most of which have still to be received) but also to living out the implications of agreement in the faith. Reception will involve being much more open to receiving one another, as persons and as churches.

14. Some specific steps: There are many steps towards unity which the churches are taking, and we invite them to learn from one another's rich experience as they take further steps. The Canberra statement on unity included a number of concrete proposals, all of which are achievable if the will is there. In addition, this plenary commission has been reminded of additional possibilities: youth exchanges among churches and regions; undertaking journeys of pilgrimage together; publicly asking for forgiveness from and forgiving one another; using the apostolic faith study guide ecumenically; finding more ways of worshipping together more often, including a broader observance of the Week of Prayer for Christian Unity; finding ways of sharing their ecumenical learnings and insights.

Conclusion

15. One ecumenical movement: There is one ecumenical movement, a movement born of the Spirit of Christ, the Spirit of reconciling love. The plenary commission of Faith and Order affirms, and invites all churches to affirm, that the church of God, one, holy, catholic and apostolic, is evangelical, ecumenical, biblical, sacramental, orthodox, charismatic, diverse yet united in the koinonia of the divine Trinity. It is our hope that all churches may find fresh ways to enable all believers to tell their own stories, to sing their own songs of praise, to share their own experience of the Spirit, and to claim them all as our common heritage in the expression of the one faith. It is our prayer that all Christians everywhere may begin the new century, the new millennium, in a spirit of humility, repentance and open-hearted discovery, ready to be led by the Spirit, together where God wills and, if God wills, into a new life which will bring gladness and hope to the whole earth.

16. Conclusion: We also gladly proclaim that, although we invite all to try their best to reconcile their divisions, to heal the hurts of the past, to learn from many more contexts, to seek together the truth of the gospel, and to live as true brothers and sisters with each other around the globe, we will not achieve the visible unity of the church by our own efforts. The church is God's church, as the world is God's world, and to that God we give glory and praise and thanksgiving, in a song new and old, the song of all creatures under heaven: to the holy trinity be glory, three in one and one in three, diversity perfectly united, and we pray: *Mungu abariki watu wote, awape uhuru na umoja!* ("May God grant everyone freedom and unity", based on the Tanzanian national anthem).

Welcome to the President of Tanzania

ERASTO N. KWEKA

I have been given the honour and privilege, on behalf of the churches of the area and the host churches under the umbrella of the Christian Council of Tanzania and the Tanzania Episcopal Conference, to welcome you all to Tanzania, the land of Kilimanjaro. We are glad that God has brought you safely to this place from around the world and it is our hope and prayer that you will enjoy your stay here and that your deliberations will be fruitful and to God's glory.

The decision of the plenary commission of Faith and Order of the World Council of Churches to hold this session in Africa gives the world an opportunity to focus fresh attention on Africa-related issues, and to find out how churches here live their faith and work together in common witness to their faith.

The major task of the commission on Faith and Order is "to bring all churches together to proclaim the oneness of the church of Jesus Christ and to call the churches to the goal of visible unity in one faith and one eucharistic fellowship, expressed in worship and in common life in Christ, in order that the world may believe".

The Faith and Order commission is the only church body worldwide which benefits from the participation of the Roman Catholic Church as full member, not observer, as well as of other churches which are not members of the World Council of Churches. This unity has been visibly demonstrated in local planning for this meeting: the Roman Catholic, Anglican and Lutheran churches have worked in very close cooperation. This has given us all a foretaste of the joy to come from greater unity. We know we have a long way to go to achieve such unity. But, as the Chinese proverb reminds us, the thousand-mile journey begins with the first short step.

I would like here to express my profound dismay at the endless fragmentation of the church through splinter groups, mostly in impoverished nations of the so-called third world. The emergence of most of these groups is hardly justifiable theologically. Such divisions not only weaken the common witness of the church; they also are a waste of the limited resources at our disposal.

To demonstrate the commission's commitment to unity, a message should be sent out from this venue calling on all churches and church bodies to reaffirm their pledge and to redouble their efforts towards "visible unity in one faith and one eucharistic fellowship, expressed in worship and in common life in Christ".

My heart overflows with joy because our president, Mr Benjamin William Mkapa, has honoured us all with his presence. It is about ten months since Mr Mkapa assumed the nation's highest office. He is the third president in the nation's history of nearly 35 years. All Tanzania's presidents have been democratically elected and the two former presidents are alive and well, just like him – only a little older!

So I respectfully take this opportunity, on behalf of all of us, to congratulate him heartily on his election and to assure him of our support and prayers as he shoulders this heavy responsibility. Mr President, thank you very much for putting aside much of your pressing work to come to Moshi and to this conference.

We are gathered in this small town in one of the world's least industrialized nations. There are dozens of churches and communities, just like us, who are represented here, who know first-hand what injustice, war and disunity mean. Many communities have been torn apart by ethnic unrest. The quality of life is low because of unspeakable poverty, disabling diseases and lack of technical know-how, among other major problems. All this despite the fact that the world has enough resources to guarantee happiness, health and home to all.

This is why churches in developing nations join hands with governments and other agencies to ensure that the limited life-saving resources available are efficiently and effectively used to alleviate human suffering. Your presence here, Mr President, is a good testimony to this cooperation between the church and the state in Tanzania and other developing countries.

The church in Tanzania, in cooperation with your government and non-governmental and international agencies, has a long history and good track record in service to hundreds of thousands of refugees. We deeply sympathize with all the displaced people. However, Mr President, we believe that efforts to address the root causes of this human suffering are much more appropriate. That is why we would like to encourage you to step up your efforts in the sub-region and throughout the African continent to promote justice, peace and unity.

Mr President, the churches represented here are deeply concerned about the state of the economy of most of the developing world, where the majority of the people are said to be poorer today than they were at the dawn of political independence. The servicing of the external debt is breaking the backs of too many nations. The International Monetary Fund and Western funding agencies are making confusing demands on our fragile economies. We have serious problems in paying the bills for our social services. Youth without jobs or hopes are increasingly becoming addicted to drugs and alcoholism, and prostitution and all forms of corruption are on the increase. No nation can single-handedly tackle these and other equally pressing problems adequately. Our churches want to encourage you to take the necessary initiatives both at home and abroad in cooperation with other leaders of political goodwill to tackle these issues aggressively.

Mr President, welcome, once again. On behalf of all of us gathered here, I have the privilege and the honour to request you to address this meeting of the plenary commission on Faith and Order.

Karibu Sana!

Address of Welcome

H.E. BENJAMIN WILLIAM MKAPA

Welcome to Tanzania and to Moshi! For those of you who have been to our country before, we are very glad to see you again. And for those who are making their first visit to Tanzania, I extend to you a particularly warm welcome. I do hope that all of you will find the will and opportunity to visit us again in the future, even in a private capacity. We pride ourselves on having a beautiful and peaceful country, and we try to be friendly and hospitable. I trust that you will have the opportunity to see a little of the country and to meet some of the people. Above all, I hope you will not find us wanting as your hosts for this particular meeting.

After receiving your invitation to be with you at the opening of your meeting, I took time to educate myself on the Faith and Order commission of the World Council of Churches and its aims, and to reflect on what I could say to such a distinguished audience. I hope I have learned something about the commission and chosen wisely the theme of my discourse. You will be the better judges when I am done.

Unity in Tanzania

You have done us a great honour in choosing our country as the venue for the pursuit of your worthy objectives. I hope that you will not regret the decision to meet in Moshi and that you will be spiritually enriched by your encounter with Tanzanians at this conference.

Forgive me if I sound as though I am boasting, but instinctively I consider your choice of Tanzania as a venue most appropriate. You are a community of churches in search of practical Christian unity – unity in diversity. On our part, we are a country that perhaps more than any other on our continent has shown in practice a high degree of unity, in a context of diverse tribes, cultures, races, religions and denominations. You and we have, I think, a lot in common in our aspirations, and a lot to learn from our different experiences.

As a country and a people we took heed of the imperative need for unity very early in our nationhood. Indeed, even our struggle for independence was based on one and only one aim: unity. We did not use guns. We did not engage in the sabotage of vital installations. We relied on peaceful agitation, and representation, confident of the strength of our arguments and points of view, and on the unwavering assertion of our right to liberty and dignity. But such strategies would never have succeeded if we had allowed our differences to be exploited by the colonialists in order to undermine our resolve to independent nationhood. I wish, therefore, to pay tribute to those early leaders of this country for having championed the cause of unity across our diverse religious faiths, tribes, races and cultures.

To us unity is a national virtue, a phenomenon that distinguishes Tanzania from many other African countries. The union between the mainland part of Tanzania (formerly known as Tanganyika) and the Islands of Zanzibar stands out as the only successful African endeavour towards unity through the union of two independent, sovereign states. Other attempts did not succeed so well. Ours has stood the test of time for over 32 years now. Yet in Zanzibar 98 percent of the population are Muslims, and on the mainland a third of the people are Christians, of various denominations, a third are Muslims, of various denominations, and the rest adhere to various traditional faiths and beliefs.

We recognize fully that this exemplary unity did not come of its own but is a product of political foresight, and of the desire to put national interests first rather than personal ones based on history, religion, tribe or race. We have, therefore, vowed not to take the present unity for granted, but to continue nurturing and promoting it in our multifaith society. And here I do not mean simply co-existence, but the nurturing of a social union that cuts across all faiths.

The freedom of religious belief, worship and practice is enshrined in our constitution. We even encourage our people to be religious, in the knowledge that religious people are usually good citizens. Yet we proscribe the establishment of any political party based on religious faith. This is a non-partisan issue among all our registered political parties. We all know the dangers that would lie ahead were we to permit such political parties in a multi-religious society.

To us, freedom of religion goes far beyond an expression and the legal protection of one's right to faith and worship. We also wish to encourage dialogue between various faiths and religions – a dialogue that will help to develop an understanding of the faith and religious beliefs of others. We are free to differ in our manner of worship and faith, but at least we should differ from a point of knowledge – not ignorance.

For ignorance is the seed of religious bigotry and intolerance, but mutual understanding breeds respect for each other. Hence the imperative need for interfaith and interdenominational dialogue within the wider Christian family, as well as inter-religious dialogue.

There is much common ground among various religions and denominations, especially on social issues and the edifying role of religious living. There are in our society clearly interfaith concerns, such as on economic development and the upholding of societal values, that call for interfaith solutions and approaches. But such cooperation need not only be problem-solving. We should also hold interfaith and interdenominational celebrations and feasts.

Apart from dialogue, we also need to encourage cooperation in social welfare issues and projects. The churches in Tanzania have a long and laudable history of investing in social welfare projects. Many of our secondary schools and hospitals were built by churches. With an area of 945,000 square kilometres Tanzania is a vast country, and a poor one. Tremendous resources are needed to put up the necessary economic and social infrastructure. The government has no capacity to raise sufficient resources to deal with the problems of development. We need and encourage the participation of the churches knowing that they address both the spiritual and physical needs of God's people.

We remain grateful for what the churches have done and we encourage their greater participation in our social services delivery system. But we also do not want to break up our country into distinct religious or denominational spheres of influence. That is why we encourage interfaith and interdenominational cooperation, rather than mutual exclusion, in putting up social services such as schools and hospitals. A good example of such cooperation is what is happening in the refugee camps in Tanzania where different faiths and denominations have cooperated very well in tending to the needs of refugees. We wish to see an extension of such cooperation to other fields. All these will, I hope, also contribute to greater Christian unity and faster social development in our country.

Government in Tanzania

The present government in Tanzania is a product of our first multi-party elections for over thirty years. God was merciful to us and we had a peaceful election, contrary to what has happened in other African countries during their transition from military or one-party systems to multi-party political systems. Examples are many of countries that ended up in chaos, civil conflict, or even reversion to dictatorships. Proceeding from our solid foundation of unity we have embarked upon political diversity that does not threaten unity and our sense of nationalism.

As in religion, we encourage dialogue between the various political parties. We encourage constructive dialogue in the pursuit of faster social and economic progress. We frown upon endless electioneering and vituperative attacks and denunciations across party lines turning into a common feature of our politics even in the intervening period between elections. We exhort our people not to make acrimonious language and invective a permanent feature or style of politics.

This includes the basic democratic requirement for all political parties to recognize and accept the will of the people as expressed through free and fair elections. In the continent's political evolution of democracy, we must respect the competitive system for electoral office we have established for ourselves.

Failure to do so is in part responsible for what we see now in Burundi. In 1993 an election was held in that country that was witnessed by international observers, and which was subsequently declared free and fair. Yet the people who lost in the election set out almost immediately to emasculate the government put in power by the will of the people. The president who had won a 60 percent mandate in the election was killed in military barracks. Subsequently the constitution was sidelined. It was replaced by an unworkable so-called convention of government that produced an ineffective government.

The coup d'etat of 25 July 1996 was, therefore, only the culmination of a process set in motion in 1993 to emasculate a legally elected government and create conditions for the resumption of power by the very person who lost in a free and fair election. In other words, what the people put in power through the ballot box was taken away by the bullet. The time has come for such illegal and unconstitutional changes of government to end in Africa. This is why the government of Tanzania and other regional governments could not reconcile themselves to doing business as usual with the new regime in Bujumbura, and that is the rationale for the regional sanctions on it.

Taken in perspective, the situation in Tanzania as far as the union government is concerned is a matter of great satisfaction. The transition from a single to a multi-party system was smooth and peaceful. The union parliament in which the opposition political parties have 20 percent of the electoral seats works perfectly well within acceptable bounds of political competition. As I speak to you, I am in the middle of a tour of the Kilimanjaro region, a large part of which is a stronghold of opposition parties. Yet, everywhere I go, and contrary to expectations, I am always received very warmly by huge crowds of citizens and well-wishers. No one has so far shouted me down or thrown tomatoes in my face. On the contrary I have moved from place to place, in the company of opposition members of parliament, in a manner suggesting not the slightest hint of opposition save for the many flags of opposition political parties flapping in the gentle winds of Kilimanjaro. All this has reinforced my belief in the political maturity and civility of the people of Tanzania.

We who won the elections recognize very well that our victory is not only a matter of being installed in political authority, but also one of applying this political authority to engender greater and wider nationalism. Furthermore, we recognize our responsibility to address the concerns of our society and the expectations of the electorate even as each political party seeks to attract people to its own political philosophy. From our political opponents we expect understanding and cooperation. We call on them to resist the temptation to spend all their time looking for errors or dirt in us, rather than recognizing our virtues and being inspired by them in making their own contribution to the political maturity and the development of our country.

From the Lord Jesus Christ we learn that "any kingdom divided against itself will be ruined, and a house divided against itself will fall" (Luke 11:17). Likewise the advice given by St Paul to the Romans almost 2000 years ago was as valid to them as it is to us today. He said:

> Just as each of us has one body with many members, and these members do not all have the same function, so in Christ we who are many form one body, and each member belongs to all the others... Live in harmony with one another (Rom. 12:4-5,16).

What is good for the body spiritual must surely be good for the body politic.

The future for Tanzania

As we work towards entrenching a strong political culture of tolerance, and unity in diversity, we need also to look to the future. A very large proportion of our population is below 18 years of age. This poses a huge challenge to the polity in terms of developing the capacity to satisfy the social and economic needs of the youth of this country. Their future prosperity depends on our making sufficient investments in developing their human capital today by giving them a good education, good health care and good nutrition.

We recognize the need to increase investments in these areas especially in the face of the emerging phenomenon of globalization of knowledge, jobs, markets and investments. Tanzania is currently on a very strict budget that has resulted in the reduction of expenditure in many sectors. But we managed to increase, albeit in small percentages, the budgetary appropriation to the health, education and water sectors. Only yesterday I participated in the national efforts on child immunization against polio. We will do all we can, in cooperation with churches, NGOs and the donor community in contributing to the health and education of the future generation of our country. I say this because we try our best to address these urgent issues from a shrunken resource base. As I said, the churches in Tanzania are a great help. They are genuine partners to the government. We also recognize that quite a large proportion of the social sector investments made by the local churches originates from outside, including from the churches some of you represent. We thank you on behalf of the many beneficiaries whose lives have been made better through your assistance. Please continue to extend a helping hand to Tanzanian churches in the full knowledge that they make a great impact on the social development of our country, that they use your assistance wisely, and that we greatly appreciate their work in our communities.

This brings me to the imperative need to extend the theme of unity beyond national confines and involve the entire humanity. As in internal politics and interfaith relations, international cooperation and unity can only be achieved first by mutual understanding and respect, and second by reaching out to each other. Our youth are less polluted with the prejudices and stereotypes of their parents and hence more amenable to the initiative to reach out. I am convinced that churches can help to create better international relations by encouraging and facilitating all-round links between the youth of the world. We need to encourage them to reach out to each other, to understand each other better, and to learn from each other. We should not pass on to them our prejudices which can foreclose the chances for better international relations for them. It is their future: we should contribute to making it better for them. Exchange programmes between religious youth groups lasting about three weeks each year would go a long way in realizing this goal. There was a time when such programmes were common. We need to revive and encourage them.

There is a challenge facing humanity that is an offshoot of the unprecedented human freedoms and prosperity that characterize present and future generations. This applies to both rich and poor countries. In Tanzania, for instance, we used to be known for our egalitarian principles and the collective concern we felt for justice and equality in our societies. It is no secret that it is the adherence to such principles that contributed to the unity for which Tanzania has become famous. Today, the government is holding on to those virtues, but as the horizon of freedoms and prosperity expands further, a growing sense of individualism is taking root. We need to address this problem before it plants the seed of disunity in our country. We are a society with common interests and obligations. But with increasing democracy, the betterment of our lives and freedoms may be propelling us headlong into egocentrism and unprecedented individualism. What is more, we now have people who would rather use our legal system to pursue and protect their individual rights at the expense of clearly spelt-out community rights. I do not consider it a fair judicial system that promotes and protects the interests of one individual at the expense of the interests of an entire community.

Family and societal values which are the pillars that should hold our nation together are also increasingly under threat. It is, therefore, important to work for the moral edification of our societies from the individual level – by giving greater importance to the needs and interests of our families, our neighbourhoods, our societies and our nations. Individual interests must be balanced by societal and national interests. Churches and faiths have a critical role to play in this. The problems of the heart and of our consciences cannot be resolved only by the state or through political means. The problems of the heart need love, faith and compassion – the kind of love, faith and compassion of which the Lord Jesus Christ was such an eloquent exponent and practitioner.

The future for humanity

This problem of bloated individualism extends also to the sphere of international relations whereby the single-minded pursuit of national interests leaves no room for our common humanity – our concern for the welfare of the entire humanity – to come out. Christian beliefs and values to which many world Christian leaders subscribe are not always translated into action in the conduct of their relations especially with the weaker and poorer members of the international system. Yet as Christians we know that our faith is not much use unless we translate it into action.

The sense of obligation towards helping the weak and poor which appeared in the 1960s and 1970s is now disappearing fast. The gap between the rich and poor grows wider day by day while traditional values, including egalitarian principles, are being abandoned in favour of bigotry, selfishness and material incontinence. The universality and unity of humanity is under great threat. *The Economist* magazine of 25 May 1996 aptly described this phenomenon in the following concise terms:

> For years the North wrung its hands about poverty in the developing countries, and asked what could be done to relieve those countries' misery. Now, for the most part, the North no longer feels guilty about its wealth, or anxious to see the South do better; rather, it feels anxious about its wealth, and would prefer on the whole (but off the record) that the South stayed poor.

This increasing division between the rich and the poor is one of the greatest moral challenges facing humanity as we approach the next millennium. But the world is not sufficiently agitated by this trend. Yet as Christians we should strive to guide our international relations not only from an economic and technological standpoint, but from a moral one as well. It is a fact that the wealth of the rich is not totally unconnected with the poverty of the poor. It is as if the poor must get poorer so that the rich can get richer or at least sustain their levels of affluence. Unfortunately, the unprecedented advances of this century in science and technology have not solved the problem of poverty – often extreme poverty – in the world. We must, therefore, have the moral decency to tame our pride at these scientific and material advances with our shame for the poverty that still characterizes the lives of thousands of millions of our fellow human beings on the eve of the 21st century.

It is at times like these that the role and obligation of the churches, and of all religions, to stand out and speak loudly and clearly for the preservation of unity and the universality of humankind is needed most. As I said before, these are issues of the heart, not just of politics or economics. As Christian leaders we must factor in moral decency in the calculus of our domestic and international obligations. For we may represent different political parties, different faiths, different cultures and different nationalities, but we are all God's children and surely God would wish us to live and work together as brothers and sisters.

Jesus has taught us to love our neighbours as we love ourselves. And when asked by a Jewish lawyer who really qualifies to be a neighbour, Jesus responds with the parable of the Good Samaritan – a total stranger providing succour to a person in need. Today's world is correctly described as a global village. What a better place such a global village would be if all nations were to interact on the basis of good neighbourly relations!

The external debt
One of the millstones around the neck of Africa is the debt burden. External debt for sub-Saharan Africa rose from $84.3 billion in 1980 and the projection for 1994 was a staggering $313 billion. Tanzania, for example, has an external debt of over $7 billion. If we were to apportion this debt to every man, woman and child, each of them would be indebted to the magnitude of their total earnings for two and a half years. And if we were to spend all our national foreign exchange earnings to pay off this debt it would still take us over 12 years to do so.

Eventually, we have to ask: shall we let our children die of curable or preventable diseases, prevent them from going to school, let people drink polluted water, just to pay off this debt? For this is indeed what is happening. We in Tanzania now spend about 30 percent of our budget to service only a part of our debt obligations. In the 1995-96 financial year, we spent shs 135.8 billion to service our national debt, an amount sufficient to meet the budgeted expenditures of *seven* major government ministries: home affairs, defence, agriculture, education, health, finance and science and technology.

Surely there must be something churches and like-minded institutions can do to exert pressure on creditor nations and institutions to write off this unpayable debt, or at least reschedule most of it so that we have breathing space to address the enormous problem of poverty in our countries. For as William Penn said: "It is a reproach to religion and government to suffer so much poverty and excess."

There is a perception that all Africa wants is aid and, as long as aid is forthcoming, there is no need to give Africa further attention. This is wrong. Our relationship must be based on much more than aid – after all, aid keeps on declining. British aid to Africa has dropped in the last five years from £417.6 million to £386.1 million. Their aid budget has been cut this year by 5.4 percent. British diplomatic representation in Africa has been cut by 10 percent since 1990. The same trend applies to most donor countries.

In 1987, Margaret Thatcher is reported to have said: "The ANC is a typical terrorist organization... Anyone who thinks it is going to run the government in South Africa is living in cloud-cuckoo land." Well, last month, Nelson Mandela, president of the ANC and a truly free South Africa, was received in state in the United Kingdom and given the highest state and academic accolades of the land. I have great hopes for Africa and those who think Africa will forever remain the tail of human progress and advancement are mistaken.

Africa needs genuine and all-round friendship, partnership and cooperation with Europe and other developed countries. It is not only Africa that needs Europe; we need each other. Yet Africa gets almost negligible attention in major world capitals. How often does Africa feature in the speeches of world leaders or the parliaments of those countries? What and how much coverage does Africa get in the media of the developed world?

In conclusion

The African countries know all too well that the task of developing their economies is their own. They subscribe to the wisdom of Suleiman in his pithy assertion: "Lazy hands make a man poor, but diligent hands bring wealth" (Prov. 10:4). They also know that it is necessary to have good governance that will result in political stability and hence the sustainability of development and economic growth. They know how important it is to pursue prudent economic policies. But sustained growth cannot be ensured without the participation of our development partners. Foreign capital is not a substitute for domestic resources, but in the transition it is an essential component which should be forthcoming because of current circumstances.

You have come to Moshi to work, among other things, for Christian unity. I wish you great success in this noble undertaking. But I am impelled also to raise with you the need to go beyond unity in matters of faith to the unity and universality of humankind in its entirety. For we are all God's children, and as such we need to work for unity in our diversity. The humanity of each society is measured by the way it treats its more vulnerable members. On the international plane the humanity of a nation should be measured according to the attention it pays to Africa and other least developed countries.

I wish to end my speech, therefore, by urging you to persevere in your quest for Christian unity, as you also take note of the need to be the moral crusaders for the unity and universality of humankind and the needs of its disadvantaged. Poverty amid affluence should be considered unacceptable to each and every human being. As custodians and repositories of Christian values and charity, I challenge you to work and agitate for greater unity and cooperation in our world as we come to the end of this century. The Lord Jesus Christ says:

> "No one lights a lamp and puts it in a place where it will be hidden or under a bowl. Instead he puts it on its stand, so that those who come in may see the light" (Luke 11:33).

The church is such a lamp, and as such it should stand up for the moral rearmament of our societies and of our nations.

The mission of Jesus Christ was to bring human beings closer to their Maker through the path of love – including love for the weak, vulnerable, sinners and rejected people. His mission was all-inclusive, and he taught us to love our neighbours as we love ourselves. He told us that the good deeds we do to our fellow human beings will be considered good deeds to him. This should inspire us as we face the challenges I have outlined today.

I thank you for your kind attention and I wish you great success in your meeting.

Reply of the Moderator

MARY TANNER

On behalf of the members of the Faith and Order plenary commission of the World Council of Churches, let me express to you our heartfelt thanks for being with us at the opening of this meeting. I thank you for your words of welcome to your country and for your message to us. It is a great encouragement as we begin our work that you, as president of your country with all the responsibility that entails, have graced us with your presence. You have indeed given us a keynote address for our meeting. You have spoken of dialogue, collaboration, celebration, unity and diversity – all themes which are close to the themes of this meeting.

You see gathered in this room Christians from many different churches and countries. We are often described as the most comprehensive ecumenical forum that exists. In a very real sense our director was right when he said that the world church has come to Tanzania. I think perhaps you can sense something of the joy we all feel at being gathered together here in your dazzlingly beautiful country, in the shadow of Mount Kilimanjaro. I wish you could have seen the commission members arriving tired after long journeys across the world, but the tiredness forgotten with the delight of arriving in such a beautiful place, a garden of Eden.

In preparation for our meeting I read a number of books on Tanzania. I came across your national anthem and I was struck by the sentiments of its two verses. The first prays for wisdom, unity and peace – *Hekima, umoja na mani hizi ni ngao zetu.* The second prays for eternal freedom and unity for the sons and daughters of Tanzania: *Dumisha, uhuru na umoja wake kwa waume na watoto.* How very appropriate for us is this theme of unity of which your national anthem speaks! Having heard your address I now know that these are not just words on a page but sentiments which live in the heart of the president of Tanzania.

Our time here will be dedicated to helping overcome those things that keep Christians apart, to working for a unity, a communion in faith, life and witness, so that Christians together, wherever they live and work in families, in villages, in towns across the world may be reconciled to each other and together become the reconciling community. I assure you that our vision of unity is not a narrow one. Our vision is not of churches knocked together in some sort of ecclesiastical joinery but a unity of men and women amongst whom the barriers of race and class and wealth and gender have been broken down. We are concerned with a unity which will speak to the world of a better way of living and loving.

I know that you will understand this. You yourself are committed to the reconciliation of divisions of all sorts in this country and have been praised in the press in my own country for your success in bringing together the presidents of Kenya and Uganda and enabling the establishment of the new East African secretariat.

But more than this, I am told that you are a Roman Catholic married to a Lutheran. Those in interchurch families bear in perhaps the most acute way the consequence of the scandalous divisions of the churches. You will understand the importance of the task that we have been given and our work here.

Again our thanks for your presence here with us, for making this a very special and memorable occasion for us. And our heartfelt thanks for your inspiring address, which I have no doubt will echo through the days of our meeting here and have a lasting effect on our work. May God bless you as you face the challenges and possibilities before you and as you work for that eternal freedom and unity for the sons and daughters of Tanzania of which your national anthem speaks.

Life and Witness
of the Tanzanian Churches

VICTUS MROSSO

There were traces of Christianity along the coast of Tanzania, or Tanganyika as it was then called, in the 15th and 16th centuries already. However, it never took root in the interior and it finally disappeared in the 17th century. It was reintroduced, with its different denominations, in the 19th century.

Almost all the denominations were at loggerheads, partly because there was cut-throat competition to win areas and followers, and partly because the missionaries came from different backgrounds. After they had established themselves, there were clear lines of demarcation among the denominations, with very little interaction or interference among them. Occasionally, however, there was conflict of interests, and to avoid religious wars the colonial administration had to intervene and divide the country into territories of evangelization. For instance, in the region of Kilimanjaro Captain Johannes, the German administrator in Moshi, was obliged to divide it into areas of evangelization. As time went on, such sharp distinctions and divisions gave way to peaceful co-existence. In many parts of Tanzania people now live happily and peacefully regardless of tribe, language or religious denomination. A number of factors have contributed to such a situation.

In the title of this paper, "life" means the sum total of human activities from the point of view of one's faith; "witness" means readiness to give a testimony of what we believe. Our concern here is to find out what we have in common in life and witness as Christians.

At the beginning, we had very little in common to witness to what we believed. The reason is that when the Christian missionaries arrived in Tanzania, they found mainly African traditional believers and a few Muslims on the trade routes to the interior and along the coast. As the early converts were few, the missionaries of different denominations kept their followers separate from the traditional believers and Christians of other denominations. However, within a very short time, Christianity won many converts; thus it was not easy to keep people separate from each other. The African traditional believers had much in common with the growing number of Christian converts. Moreover, due to the concept of extended families in Africa, it was not easy to keep clear boundaries for long.

The pattern Tanzania followed in nation-building helped considerably in breaking down the barriers among denominations. In 1929 the Tanganyika African Association (TAA) was formed which defined the territory within which the new nation was to be born. The TAA had a unique character: it was non-tribal and non-religious. It bequeathed this unique character to the TANU, the CCM and all the other mass movements in Tanzania. So it was not easy to create boundaries within the frontiers of the nation.

Also contributing to the situation was the policy of Ujamaa, which succeeded in bringing together people of different denominations and tribes. People therefore thought more as Tanzanians and not as members of a particular denomination. Religions and denominations were secondary.

Tanzania is also blessed with a supra-tribal Swahili culture. Kiswahili is our national language. This has enabled people from various corners of the country to come together, and has given rise to a number of other factors which has made it possible for people from different denominations to come together also. Kiswahili has meant that people from different tribes and denominations intermarry, and through intermarriage they have found themselves living under the same roof.

The economic set-up of the country has also helped to reduce tensions, and people from different denominations work happily and peacefully together in the same office or factory.

There are also many occasions which bring adherents of different denominations together; the birth of a child, a baptism, the celebration of a wedding, the death of a relative or friend. In all these activities there is usually either a mass or Bible service where people witness to what they believe.

As well as the above-mentioned activities, interdenominational aid, the social services, education and medical relief play an important role in uniting people. Hospitals, dispensaries and many schools in Tanzania are used by everyone, regardless of tribe, religion or denomination. All this shows that there are countless possibilities for members of different denominations to live together. Of course, living together does not rule out the fact that people attend their respective denominations in ordinary times.

We are convinced that Tanzania has gone a long way in the direction of common life and witness. In most cases Tanzanians do not discuss their denomination – they simply live and witness to what they believe. It is as if they follow unknowingly what Jesus said in St Luke: "Anyone who is not against you is for you" (Luke 9:50b). For a good number of ordinary people, a friendly neighbourhood means more than doctrines and denominations. The principle "scratch my back and I'll scratch yours" is applied here. Nobody likes to live as an island; we need each other regardless of our denomination.

Nevertheless, it is not enough to remain at the level of simply living together; we have to move a step further. We are going in the right direction. Now we need genuine dialogue among the denominations; most of our people do not know the essential differences between one denomination and the other.

What do we mean by genuine dialogue? It is very clear in scripture that God wills that every human person be saved and reach full knowledge of truth (1 Tim. 2:4; 1 John 2:2; John 3:16-17; 4:42). If everyone is destined for salvation according to God's will, then the best way of conducting our dialogue should be based on love. God so loved the world that he sent his only Son to save us (John 3:16). This Son of God commanded us to love one another. He says: "By this love you have for one another, everyone will know that you are my disciples" (John 13:35). This kind of love can only be shown in our daily life experience, through which we can give witness to our discipleship. Tanzanian churches are already in the stage of giving witness through their daily life experience.

Here let us borrow the words of Fitzgerald and Caspar:

> Dialogue is not just discussion, it is an attitude, a spirit of friendship, a wish to meet the other, to listen and learn from the other... We can sometimes witness best by being ready to listen...[1]

The people are ready to listen to each other. Let us, through meetings of this kind, help to deepen their friendship and readiness to listen. Let us encourage them to continue with a life in dialogue, help them to remove all mutual distrust through love, to pray together especially during the week of prayer, and assist each other in love. When this is fully accepted, then we can gradually talk of doctrines.

The prayer of Jesus that they may all be one (John 17:21) is still our motto. It is our sincere hope that one day this prayer will be realized. We have already come a very long way. There are traces of light which show a bright future. Let us keep on praying and struggling. Filling the gaps, healing the wounds and building the broken bridges to unity and love is not an easy task but hope should be the last thing we lose.

Let us continue to concentrate on the service we can render to humanity regardless of denomination. This is the opportune moment as everybody seeks to be ecumenical. It is our conviction that the unity of the church can be possible through life and witness as the starting point. No matter how hard the journey becomes, we must never give up. The beautiful words of Pope John XXIII will be a fair summary of our discussion:

> At the judgment day, we will not be asked whether we have achieved or realized the unity, but rather whether we sacrificed, prayed, worked and suffered for it.

What have you personally done apart from mere talk?

NOTE

[1] Michael L. Fitzgerald and Robert Caspar, *Signs of Dialogue: Christian Encounter with Muslims*, Zaniboaga City, Philippines, Silsilah Publications, 1992, p.60.

Continuity and Newness:
From Budapest to Moshi

MARY TANNER

It seems to me from my twenty or more years of membership of the Faith and Order commission that one of Faith and Order's greatest strengths has been its commitment to develop in a continuous way the work for visible unity which was outlined at Lausanne in 1927. Yet Faith and Order has been open to fresh insights and understandings brought by the increasingly inclusive community around the Faith and Order table. There have of course been times when we have been dangerously close to weakening continuity or deaf to new voices from other ecclesial traditions and cultural contexts or from those outside the church. Perhaps the most creative times have come from moments of struggle to remain faithful to the insights we have inherited while open to new ones. For me, an example of that was the breaking open of Faith and Order's work to some of the radical insights of the study on the "Community of Women and Men", and more recently the attempts to take into our view of unity the work on ecclesiology and ethics.

It is with the ideas of continuity and newness in mind that I want to reflect on the work from Budapest to Moshi and beyond. But first, a word about the plenary commission of Faith and Order and its particular role in relationship to the board of Faith and Order and the World Council of Churches (WCC).

The role of the plenary commission

The Faith and Order by-laws have been revised since the last meeting to bring us in line with the new four-unit structure of the Council. Faith and Order is now one stream in Unit I: Unity and Renewal. However, the aim remains unchanged:

> to proclaim the oneness of the Church of Jesus Christ and to call the churches to the goal of visible unity in one faith and one eucharistic fellowship, expressed in worship and in common life in Christ, in order that the world may believe.[1]

Our constitution reminds us that, in carrying out this aim, both the plenary commission and the board (as we must now call the standing commission) are constitutionally responsible to the central committee through the Unit I commission. In the last years those of us who represent Faith and Order on the unit commission, both commissioners and staff, have struggled to see how Faith and Order can best contribute to the unit's work and how our work can be enriched by the work of the other streams within Unit I. The restructuring of the World Council of Churches following the Canberra assembly in 1991 meant not a little of the board's time has had to be spent on learning to understand the new structures and our place within them.

The primary tasks of this plenary commission, as set out in our by-laws, are theological study, debate and appraisal. We are here in Moshi to "initiate the programme on Faith and Order, lay down the guidelines for it and share in its communication to the churches".[2]

It is the board which is responsible for implementing the programme laid out by the plenary commission, guiding the staff, making administrative decisions and supervising ongoing work. There is a further task given to the plenary commission: the appointment of a nominations committee to prepare a list of names for a new board which will be elected by the central committee immediately following the next assembly of the WCC in 1998.[3]

Our inherited mandate, then, provides us with a clear agenda for this meeting. We are to take stock of what has been done since Budapest in 1989 and lay down general guidelines for the future, and we are to communicate this to the churches.

With these aims in mind the director and staff, in consultation with the board, formulated the agenda for Moshi. They have provided space for rendering account of work done and for formulating the next steps for Faith and Order's work. But before this twofold task begins time has been given for us to reflect on the impact Faith and Order's work is having at the local and regional levels, and in the different contexts from which we come. We shall try to identify what particular challenges to our work arise from our different contexts, both cultural and ecclesial.

Our statement to the churches on *Baptism, Eucharist and Ministry* (BEM) from Budapest urged: "listen to the other's story with compassion, share the other's experience with empathy, and bear one another's burdens with mercy". I suspect the quality of the work we do here will be in direct relation to the quality of our listening to each other in the days ahead.

With that reminder of the mandate of the plenary commission and the shape of the programme ahead, let me turn to my main theme of continuity and newness.

Continuing ecclesiology

At its last meeting in Budapest in 1989 the plenary commission voted to undertake a major study: "Ecumenical Perspectives on the Understanding of the Nature and Mission of the Church". Our then director, Günther Gassmann, told the commission that there was need for an overall ecclesiological framework for our three studies, "Baptism, Eucharist and Ministry" (BEM), "Apostolic Faith" and "Church and World", to locate and to give coherence to the separate but international parts of our work. The theme "koinonia" (communion) was to serve as the overall framework.

The call to work on ecclesiology came also from another direction. The central committee of the WCC requested Faith and Order "to consider the concepts and forms of the unity we seek, and to prepare a statement for the 1991 assembly of the WCC".

How successful have we been since our meeting in Budapest in responding to those internal and external requests? A first contribution came in the statement sent to the assembly. The assembly did not simply rubber-stamp it; it revised it in significant ways and made it its own. "The Unity of the Church as Koinonia: Gift and Calling".[4] I cannot speak for other churches but this Canberra statement has become foundational for my own church in agreements which have moved us to a new communion of Anglicans and Lutherans in Northern Europe and to a new stage on the way to unity with Moravians in England, and with Lutherans, Reformed and United churches in Europe. There has been in a very real sense a reception of the words of the Canberra statement into changed and changing relationships in our life in the Church of England. I profoundly hope that the World Council will not give up on its assembly vision but go on to deepen and mature that vision.

A second major contribution to the work on ecclesiology came in the fifth world conference itself. The theme of the conference, chosen at Budapest, "Towards Koinonia in Faith, Life and Witness", provided a framework in the notion of koinonia for ecumenical perspectives on ecclesiology. All of the contributions at Santiago de Compostela – presentations, reports, sermons – are a rich quarry waiting still to be taken into our work on ecclesiology.[5] But the world conference did more than talk about ecclesiology. In the memorable worship life, many of us recognized an experience of koinonia as we rediscovered what we already knew, that unity is not only sought in words and in common struggles for justice, but in the prayer of the faithful gathered to pray to God, in Christ through the Holy Spirit. It depends on metanoia, renewal and spiritual discipline. The message of the fifth world conference on Faith and Order transmitted to the churches affirmed the ecclesiological direction for our work which was set in Budapest when it said:

> *There is no turning back*, either from the goal of visible unity or from the single ecumenical movement that unites concerns for the unity of the Church and concern for engagement in the struggles of the world.[6]

The work on ecclesiology, on the nature and mission of the church, has been at the heart of Faith and Order's task since Budapest. The theme of koinonia has continued to be fundamental to our work. Six months after the world conference, the board prepared a conspectus of studies for its work from 1994 to 1998 in the light of reports and the message of the world conference. The board affirmed a major study programme, "The Church as Koinonia: An Ecumenical Study". It distinguished between the major study programme on ecclesiology, several other specific study projects, collaborative studies to be undertaken with other units of the WCC, and ongoing tasks of Faith and Order. Among the specific study projects the board identified work on a study guide on the apostolic faith, ministry and authority, ecumenical hermeneutics, interpreting and communicating the one faith in koinonia, unity of the church and nationalities and ethnic identity, towards koinonia in worship and spirituality, and the church as a koinonia of women and men. The board called for collaboration with Unit II both on gospel and cultures and on evangelism, religious liberty and proselytism, and with Unit III on ecclesiology and ethics, it outlined the continuing Faith and Order tasks in relation to united and uniting churches, the Week of Prayer for Christian Unity, bilateral dialogues and the Joint Working Group.

The conspectus of studies adopted at Crêt-Bérard to direct the work from 1994 to 1998 made a useful distinction between the major study on ecclesiology, specific study projects (not all of which have been taken up), collaborative studies and ongoing tasks.[7] (The text of the conspectus of studies is attached as an appendix to this report).

During this meeting we shall review the progress made in the various studies and lay down directions for the future. I do not intend in my moderator's report to repeat what those who have taken major responsibility for directing the work will say. I want instead to offer you four themes that I believe must be central to our work as we continue to develop and deepen our understanding of the unity that is God's gift and our calling. It seems to me urgent to make sound progress with these themes in the next two years.

Ecclesiology and newness

First, in our work on ecclesiology we need to place greater emphasis on the communion of the local church.[8] Ecumenists speak much about the call to visible unity: it sounds so abstract, so far from where people live and work, celebrate and suffer, where they experience what being church really is. In fact, the church is conceivable only as a structured local community.[9] We must help people to envision what the unity and communion of the church might mean in the particular place where each person lives. What sort of life together in faith and sacraments would be a foretaste and a sign in that place of the unity God desires for all? What sort of love, service and witness together would be instrumental in helping to bring about God's kingdom? Quoting the message of the WCC's first assembly in Amsterdam, Konrad Raiser insisted at the fifth world conference that: "We have to make of the church in every place a voice for those who have no voice, and a home where everyone will be at home."[10]

Our work must show why the unity of the church matters; why it matters for the sake of this world, God's world, not just in some global de-contextualized, de-localized sense, but why it matters to God's world in the very local places where individuals live and die, "wash socks and share food" and get on with the ordinary stuff of everyday living and loving, living and dying.

It makes no sense to preach a gospel of unity and reconciliation when those in the same towns and villages remain sealed off from one another, defining their identities over against one another, fostering one-sided views of the past, duplicating efforts of service and making separate plans for the future. To look for unity at the local level is not to seek to stifle diversity, or to work for the disappearance of those distinctive aspects of faith which our different traditions have sought to safeguard in their separation. It is to bring them together so that they may complement and enrich a united life. The local church must be, as Metropolitan John of Pergamon said to us in Santiago de Compostela, the place where two things are simultaneously guaranteed: unity and oneness must be safeguarded, and with unity and oneness there must be diversity. Moreover, each local church must be authentic in its own historical and geographical context, not a little replica of another place and another time.

Unless we can get into clearer focus together our understanding of the local church as the place where unity with diversity is experienced, the local church as the primary place for evangelism and service, and the local church as the sign of reconciliation, then our work on visible unity will seem irrelevant. Further, in developing the perspective of the local church we need to listen much more attentively to the experience of Christians who are already worshipping and witnessing together locally, in some places in officially recognized covenanted partnerships with the blessing of their churches, but in other places informally and even, at times, contrary to the discipline of their churches.

Second, a renewed emphasis on the local church must send us back to the question of how the local church is to be held together with all the local churches for the sake of unity and mission. How can the local churches be bound together in a way that does not stifle the richness of their diversity which arises from the particularities of a given place, a given culture and a given time? How can local churches be bound together in a way that allows for mutual sharing and support and mutual correction for the sake of authentic diversity in unity? How can local churches be bound together so that challenges in one place are faced together, burdens of one place shared by all, joys of one place celebrated by all and restraint sometimes exercised for the good of all?

Aram Keshishian, the moderator of the central committee of the WCC, called in Santiago for "inner continuity and dynamic interaction between the 'old' and the 'new'" in our Faith and Order work.[11] We have, I think, been careless in failing to continue the work of Salamanca, Bangalore and Accra on conciliarity.[12] Perhaps this is because to some conciliarity speaks of centralized, bureaucratic structure. To be fair to our predecessors, conciliarity was never understood as a merely structural dimension of the church, but rather as belonging to its very nature; an interconnectedness that springs from its relation in Christ to God through the binding of the Holy Spirit. Conciliarity concerns all that upholds an interdependent life: the bonds of faith, sacraments and ministry; all that keeps Christians mutually accountable and mutually supportive; all that promotes one heart and one mind; all that maintains Christians together in openness to the world around them.

It is conciliarity that sustains diversity: a diversity "which will match the love of God for variety which is so positively evident in the universe and in history".[13] Conciliarity enables us to stop diversity becoming a cause for division and sees that we do not draw limits too quickly or too narrowly. Conciliarity implies subsidiarity. Subsidiarity does not mean that everything has to be done locally. It does mean that there is an appropriate level for every kind of decision and activity (the very local, the regional/national, the international/worldwide).

Work on ecumenical perspectives on ecclesiology needs to go back and continue the work done in years past on conciliarity. It is the context in which we might explore what Metropolitan John of Pergamon urged on us at Santiago, a ministry of synodality and primacy, those two issues which he told us cannot be avoided as long as our approach is an ecclesiology of communion. Moreover, if our Roman Catholic sisters and brothers tell us that the communion of particular churches with the church of Rome, and of their ministers of oversight with the bishop of Rome, is in God's plan an essential requisite for full communion, then it is incumbent upon all of us to engage with that challenge, whatever our own tradition.[14] The invitation of the pope in the papal encyclical, *Ut Unum Sint*, provides an important and timely ecumenical opportunity. If our churches respond in the spirit in which the invitation is offered, this could be a major contribution to the forming of an ecumenical convergence on primacy set in the context of conciliarity and exercised in the service of the koinonia of the church.

Third, we need to explore together in a fresh way how the church today is maintained in continuity with the church through the ages. I do not think we have begun to understand the richness of ecumenical work already done, including our own Faith and Order work, on how the church lives in continuity with the faith and mission of the apostles. To describe the church as apostolic is to claim it is instrumental in God's mission. I find this following quotation from one bilateral dialogue marvellously suggestive:

> The apostolicity of the church is the mission of the self-offering (not self-preservation) for the life of the world. The church thus serves the reign of God, not the reign of sin and death. The church serves the mission of God's suffering and vulnerable love, not a mission of its own devising. The church serves the mission ground in, and shaped by, Christ's way of being in the world.[15]

This is a description of the life of the whole church. Apostolic continuity is found in the whole company of the faithful as it witnesses to the apostolic faith, proclaims and interprets afresh the gospel, celebrates the sacraments, transmits the responsibility of ministry, lives in common prayer, hope, joy and suffering, serving the sick and needy and sharing the gifts God has given to each.[16]

If we could get hold together of the fact that apostolicity belongs to the whole people of God, we just might be able to locate in a fresh way the discussion concerning a ministry of oversight in the service of the apostolicity of the whole church – a ministry exercised in, with and among the whole people of God. None of our churches is without a ministry of oversight. This might help the churches to move beyond the question which has so often been in the past, and remains, a major if not *the* major stumbling block on the way to greater unity.

Fourth, together with a fresh examination of the local church, the fellowship that holds local churches in interconnectedness and the bonds of their apostolicity, we need fresh work on the holiness of the church. The church is holy because it is claimed by, and summoned to, a life of dedicated loyalty to the triune God. Through the Spirit, it participates in the holiness of Christ and the Father, and is to live in God's world as God's ethically distinct people embodying and promoting just relations in a world of distorted and fragmented relations. We have said this in the past. Now we must develop this by bringing the freshness of insight from *Costly Unity, Costly Commitment* and *Costly Obedience* to our work, seeing concrete actions for justice and peace as a distinctive mark of koinonia and central to the holiness of the church and to faithful discipleship.

Here then are four themes which deserve exploration in our work on ecclesiology. They relate to our major study programme in an obvious way but they relate also to our study projects and our collaborative work. They are perspectives which could contribute towards a common understanding of how Christians might live in visible unity. To set down convergences in these areas (as convergences were set down on baptism, eucharist and ministry) could serve to challenge the churches. On the basis of these convergences they might be prompted to examine what needs reforming in their own lives and what closer relationships might be entered into with others on the way to visible unity. To set down convergence in these four areas would be a way in which Faith and Order carries out its mandate "to call the churches to the goal of visible unity".

Answering a need

Any clarification we in the multilateral dialogue can give to the unity which God wills for his church, will help to respond to the puzzling questions being raised by those who are already living together in local covenants and partnerships and who are beginning to ask "where do we go next?" How can we move into a visible unity which is not only experienced locally? It will also help to set in context those regional bilateral moves to fuller communion which are encouragingly taking place in South Africa, parts of Asia and the Pacific, in the USA and in Europe, and which we ought to celebrate more convincingly.

There are more signs of steps being taken than we sometimes are prepared to celebrate. The ecumenical movement is still moving, but there remains the question that Metropolitan Daniel of Moldavia put before us when we were last together in Budapest and which is becoming a more crucial question: Is the unity of the church we seek a unity of separated Christians in their different confessions? Is this the unity the creed means when it speaks of the one, holy, catholic and apostolic church?[17]

We know that we are not after an administrative merger of denominations. We are not after a loose, cosy federation. We are *not* after merely a unity in service. What, then, are we after? I have put the question sharply because that is how it is being asked in my own context. Are we, are our churches, ready to face the explosion and expansion of our narrow identities for the sake of a deeper unity and a more effective mission in the world? Are we ready to move, by steps and stages, to a richer identity than any of us possesses in our separation? Or was Konrad Raiser right when he said at the fifth world conference, "securing their own identity often takes precedence over ecumenical opening and renewal, with its unpredictable consequences".

Second, our work on ecclesiology ought to contribute to the World Council of Churches' major and important study on a "Common Understanding and Vision (CUV) of the WCC". As long ago as 1990 at the meeting of the standing commission in Dunblane, in discussion with Emilio Castro, Faith and Order said that any serious review of the Council needs to be set in the context of an understanding of:

- what the church of God is called to be within the history and drama of the whole of humanity and in the light of the coming of the kingdom;
- the primary task of the WCC to call the churches to the visible unity of the church; a communion in confession of the apostolic faith; in sacramental life; in conciliar life expressed in service and witness in the world.[18]

Any attempts to understand the nature of the WCC, its agenda and structures must flow from a developing common vision of the unity of the church, God's gift and our calling. Faith and Order can offer at least a provisional portrait of that unity. It is that unity which Faith and Order has been seeking to understand in its work and which the World Council of Churches is privileged to assist in bringing to bear. Our work on ecclesiology, even in its rudimentary and provisional form, has something to contribute to the self-searching of the WCC for its vocation and its structuring for the next millennium. It is Faith and Order's task to help the World Council of Churches face and respond to the "crisis of possibilities" before it.

Third, by developing an understanding of the reconciled life God wills for the church we shall get hold at a deeper level of the reconciliation and unity God wills for all people, for the whole creation. For, as we are never tired of proclaiming, the church is called to be a sign of the kind of life together God wills for all, and a sign and foretaste of the kingdom to come.

Conclusion

I have concentrated on our major study on ecclesiology to which all our work in its different ways relates, because it seems to me that this work is much needed both by the WCC as a whole and by our churches.

I have not mentioned the impressive progress made by those working on ecumenical hermeneutics nor the study guide for apostolic faith. One of my hopes for this meeting is that we shall use this time as an opportunity to renew the challenge to the churches to take up the apostolic faith study, for the sake of moving us out of our isolation towards a time when we can truly make a common confession. I have a feeling that neither we in Faith and Order, nor our churches, have begun to glimpse the real potential of this work on apostolic faith for drawing us into a communion in faith, a faith we are called to express in word and in the fabric of our lives. We must consider issuing a new invitation to our churches from Moshi to engage more intentionally and actively with this work.

A tribute to the staff

I cannot end my moderator's report without paying tribute to the members of the board who have carried out the mandate which the plenary commission set in Budapest, as well as being responsible for implementing the fifth world conference. There has also been the overseeing of Faith and Order's response to the restructuring of the WCC, the tedious task of the revision of by-laws, and the demanding search process for new staff. Each year the minutes of the board meetings have given a full report of the scope of the board's work in carrying out the tasks which the plenary commission outlined for it in Budapest.

Since Budapest we have said farewell to Günther Gassmann, whose work for Faith and Order was crucial in this period, not least of all his direction for the preparation for the fifth world conference. We remember him with affection and gratitude. Since Budapest we have also said farewell to Gennadios Limouris, whose work we shall honour as we promote the apostolic faith study guide; and to Silke-Petra Bergjan, now a member of the commission, and to a number of interns – most recently, Barbara Schwahn who we are delighted to have with us.

Farewells have led to new arrivals. We have welcomed our new director, Alan Falconer, who brings to our work his experience at the Irish School of Ecumenics and a commitment to reconciliation and healing. Peter Bouteneff, too, has joined us and his contribution is already there in the apostolic faith study and our work on ecclesiology. Carolyn McComish has come to us from the Ecumenical Theological Education stream as our administrative assistant to replace Monica Schreil, who has moved to work with the Youth desk in Unit IV.

Freshness is important but so too is continuity. What is true of the agenda is true with the staff. Thomas Best, Dagmar Heller and Renate Sbeghen have carried enormous workloads with distinction and patience at a time of transition. To each we extend our thanks. With the team at full strength we must move into the next phase of Faith and Order work with a care for continuity and an openness to new things that God wills to do in and through our work. This meeting – this Tanzanian experience – will be crucial for moving us into that future. May God give us strength, wisdom and delight in our work and in each other in the days ahead as we carry out that task.

NOTES

[1] Faith and Order by-laws, appendix VII, *Minutes of the Meeting of the Faith and Order Board,* January 1996, Thailand, Faith and Order paper no. 172, pp.139ff.

[2] *Ibid.,* 4.2.

[3] *Ibid.,* 4.6.

[4] In *Signs of the Spirit: Official Report of the Seventh Assembly,* M. Kinnamon, ed., Geneva, WCC, 1991, pp.172ff.

[5] *On the Way to Fuller Koinonia,* Thomas F. Best and Günther Gassmann, eds, Faith and Order paper no. 166, Geneva, WCC, 1994.

[6] *Ibid.,* p.225.

[7] Conspectus of Studies, *Minutes of the Meeting of the Faith and Order Standing Commission,* January 1994, Faith and Order paper no. 167, pp.95ff.

[8] J M Tillard, *L'Église locale,* Paris, Cerf, 1995.

[9] Metropolitan John of Pergamon, "The Church as Communion", in *On the Way to Fuller Koinonia, op. cit.,* p.106.

[10] Konrad Raiser, in *ibid.,* p.169.

[11] Aram Keshishian, in *ibid.,* p.177.

[12] Aram Keshishian, *Conciliar Fellowship: A Common Goal,* Geneva, WCC, 1992.

[13] Crêt-Bérard, *op. cit.,* p.42.

[14] *Ut Unum Sint,* papal encyclical, 1995.

[15] Report of the Anglican-Lutheran Consultation on Episkopé, *The Niagara Report,* CHP, 1987, para. 23.

[16] *Baptism, Eucharist and Ministry,* Faith and Order paper no. 111, Geneva, WCC, 1982, M.34.

[17] Daniel Cibotea, in *The Faith and Order 1985-1989 Commission Meeting at Budapest,* Thomas F. Best, ed., Faith and Order paper no. 148, Geneva, WCC, 1990, pp.254ff.

[18] Raiser, *op. cit.,* p.170.

[19] *Minutes of the Faith and Order Standing Commission,* Dunblane, 1990, Faith and Order paper, no. 152, p.81.

Beyond the Limits
of the Familiar Landscape

ALAN D. FALCONER

Throughout its history, anxious and critical questions have been raised about the future of the ecumenical movement and the search for the visible unity of the church. In recent years, the language of "fatigue", "uncertainty" and "malaise" which hitherto characterized the loss of ecumenical motivation and the decline in ecumenical impulse, has been superseded by the language of "crisis". This crisis seems to have been precipitated by a number of factors. The Strasbourg Ecumenical Institute in its report *Crisis and Challenge of the Ecumenical Movement* identifies some of these. Among the outside factors, they point to the

> growing discrepancy between North and South, general estrangement from
> global ideas and programmes of unity; the turn to smaller, distinctive regional,
> ethnic, and cultural unities and identities; the reawakening of an often militant
> national consciousness; the return to the past and its values; the strengthening
> of fundamentalist trends.[1]

All of these conflict with and impede the concerns and goals of the ecumenical movement. They make it harder to argue for unity. The motivation to search for unity is weakened. However, it is not only "outside factors" which have led to the language of "crisis". The decline in ecumenical impulse in certain places is evident within the churches and the ecumenical movement itself.

After a century of intense theological activity, the churches in most places seem no closer to unity. Despite theological consensus, the churches appear in many places to be content with co-existence. Despite theological consensus, the process for receiving the insights of theologians and the various interchurch commissions seems ever more laborious, and to make little impact on the curricula of theological colleges and seminaries. Undoubtedly, interchurch relations at international, regional and national levels have been improved in the course of the century. On the whole, however, competition between churches has disappeared;

greater tolerance between Christian communities has emerged; cooperation in a variety of fields has increased. In some places, church union
schemes have been effected. Clearly, relations between churches and
individuals have been significantly transformed at all levels – and yet the
fruits of the struggle for consensus have not materialized. Expectations
have been frustrated; hopes dashed.

In seeking to account for this crisis in the ecumenical movement, a
number of commentators have firmly placed a large measure of responsibility on the churches themselves. The Strasbourg Ecumenical Institute, for example, stresses:

> The [ecumenical] movement is not so much borne by the churches as
> increasingly controlled or "administered" by them. Church-political interests
> and "strategic considerations" intrude ever more strongly.[2]

There seems to be a growing impetus on the part of the churches to
seek to control the ecumenical agenda. There seems to be a growing tendency in the churches to wish to assert their confessional identity and to
resist change. The new language of "crisis" in respect of the ecumenical
movement and the search for visible unity is not, I believe, hyperbole.
However, it seems to me that this "ecumenical crisis" is the logical
development of the ecumenical movement itself. The crisis might be
termed "the growing pains of the movement".

Principal elements or "moments" in the growth
of the ecumenical movement

In the first stage of the ecumenical movement, as the churches sought
to move from a situation of competition with each other towards acceptance of each other's existence and co-existence, they adopted an
approach which was at root "comparative". Churches compared their
stances on doctrinal questions with each other. Thus in the early Faith
and Order conferences a comparative approach to eucharist, ministry,
intercommunion and grace, for example, was evident. Each tradition
presented papers on its confessional understanding of the subject under
discussion. The points where agreement was reached were affirmed and
the points of difference were identified for continuing discussion. This
methodology, evident in both doctrinal and ethical questions,[3] enabled
the churches to move from positions of isolation or hostility to acceptance and cooperation with each other insofar as agreement was evident.
However, it is at root not a method of dialogue, but one of monologue.
It can be characterized as "we will accept you as long as you are the
same as us, but we will reject you at the points of difference". The Scots
poet, Edwin Muir, phrases this well in his poem "The Solitary Place":

If there is none else to ask or reply
But I and not I,
And when I stretch out my hand my hand comes towards me
To pull me across to me and back to me,
If my own mind, questioning, answers me,
If all that I see
Woman and man and beast and rock and sky,
Is a flat image shut behind an eye,
And only my thoughts can meet me or pass me or follow me,
O then I am alone
I, many and many in one
A lost player upon a hill.[4]

With our own perspectives as the only acceptable positions, it was possible only to affirm the status quo – "the solitary place". The comparative method evident in doctrinal and church and society discussions in the first phase of the ecumenical movement moved interchurch relations from conflict, competition and coexistence to comparative acceptance. However, it was evident that such a method could not effect real relationship – communion. At the Lund Faith and Order world conference in 1952 a different methodology was adopted. Theological discussions now proceeded on the basis of an attempt to reach consensus.

This approach to doctrinal questions was matched also by the attempt to act as churches in a cooperative and consensual manner. The Lund world conference adopted what came to be known as the Lund principle.

> Should not our churches ask themselves whether they are showing sufficient eagerness to enter into conversation with other churches, and whether they should not act together in all matters except those in which deep differences of conviction compel them to act separately?[5]

This question addressed to the churches proposed a new relationship between them. It in fact became a methodology adopted in doctrinal and church and society discussions. The comparative methodology began to give way to a consensus methodology. In this, the churches sought to do theology together. They sought together out of the riches of their confessional traditions to affirm a common theology. A first stage was reached through the attempt to agree on how to do theology together – the discussion on scripture and Tradition, and the interpretation of scripture.[6] On the basis of this agreement it has been possible to reach consensus on baptism, eucharist and ministry, on the common confession of the apostolic faith, and on a wide variety of doctrinal questions evident in bilateral and multilateral dialogues. The consensus methodology pursued in doctrinal and church and society discussions has encouraged the churches to move beyond "the solitary place". The journey from competition and coexistence to comparative acceptance has continued on the path to cooperation and consensus and an awareness of complementarity. The awareness has emerged that no tradition can exist without the others. We need each other. The various confessional traditions enrich each other. The consensus achieved is now the subject of reception.

But how do we receive each other? How do we move beyond the recognition of consensus to living in a consensual manner? This is the contemporary crisis of the ecumenical movement. In response to this crisis, the call from a number of ecumenical theologians and dialogue groups is for the churches to move beyond the consensus methodology to a conversion. Indeed, John Hotchkin in an address to the North American Academy of Ecumenists last year identified this as the third phase of the ecumenical movement.[7]

The ecumenical journey has involved the path from conflict and competition to coexistence, thence to comparative acceptance, and from there to cooperation, consensus and complementarity. This has been effected by a comparative and then a consensual methodology. Now the journey seems to require a radical conversion.

This journey and these methods have been evident in the international multilateral ecumenical movement, but they are also evident through the bilateral dialogues conducted since the Second Vatican Council (cf. ARCIC or the Reformed-Catholic International Commission) and in regional and national discussions, though obviously the pace of the journey varies from one context to another. From comparison to consensus and now to conversion. This stage of the journey poses radical challenges to the churches and to the ecumenical movement as a whole.

The journey towards conversion

The report of the influential French discussion group the Groupe des Dombes, which was founded by the Abbé Paul Couturier, entitled *For the Conversion of the Churches*[8] is a radical call to the churches, and explores the relationship between identity and change, and the understanding of conversion as a framework for change. The call to conversion has been reiterated by the late René Girault, the one-time executive director on ecumenism for the French Roman Catholic Episcopal Commission, in his book *One Lord, One Faith, One Church*,[9] and in the 1994 report by the bilateral forum. Such a call has of course been evident throughout the history of the ecumenical movement. It is, however, the appropriate moment on the ecumenical journey to respond to it now.

But what is conversion? In what ways will conversion affect the current identities of the churches? Will the ecumenical movement and ecumenism not be charged with ever greater insistence and persistence that it leads to the betrayal of our different Christian histories? Surely "conversion" is more appropriate in evangelical rather than ecumenical circles? Can such a word, or experience, be appropriate at this stage of the journey when it normally heralds an event or experience of initiation? This call seems to threaten our identity as Christian churches; after all, identity implies both "distinctiveness" and "continuity".

Harding Meyer, the prominent Lutheran ecumenist, notes that identity "... is a sign of the intrinsic health and external capacity of a person or a group to act consistently".[10] Yet the churches, in their very distinctiveness, manifest the one apostolic faith and the one catholic church, according to the self-understanding of each tradition. But that concrete embodiment varies and changes according to time and place.

The Reformed churches, for example, have embodied different accents in theology throughout history. There has been a period of Calvin and the Reformers, a period of neo-Calvinism, a period of neo-Orthodoxy and a period associated with the "crisis" theology of Karl Barth and Emil Brunner. These periods have sought to hold the impulses of the Reformers in the different periods of Christian history, yet they exhibit different perspectives in response to changing circumstances. Similarly, while there is undoubtedly a common thread running through the teaching and ethos of the Reformed churches in different parts of the world, there are significant differences arising from the different contexts of the churches. Thus the Presbyterian Church of Cuba articulates the faith in response to the Cuban experience of socialism and has established different priorities over against the Church of Scotland or the Reformed Church in France. Each Christian tradition is subject to this differentiation according to time and place, while maintaining a continuity of identity.

The language of conversion, however, carries with it overtones not simply of continuity and change but of a radical change of identity. In many circles, "conversion" is seen as a turning round in a completely different direction. Is this an appropriate call to the churches? If this is where the ecumenical movement is leading us – if it is – surely the language of "crisis" is appropriate. Before we submit too easily to this rather negative atmosphere of crisis, it is important to examine the nature of conversion.

The nature of conversion

In her important study on aspects of conversion in the New Testament, Beverley Gaventa – one of our plenary commission members – identifies three categories of personal change.[11]

The first category is "alternation". This is a relatively limited form of change which develops naturally from an individual's previous behaviour. It is a natural progression, where the roots of later developments can be identified in earlier stages of the person's growth and development.

The second category is that of "pendulum conversion". This "type" involves a radical change in which past affiliations are rejected and replaced by a new commitment and identity. The catalyst of such change may be an event, person, group or other agent which triggers the dramatic change in the individual's perceptions and values. Past associations and convictions are rejected when new ones are formed. Past and present are disconnected. This type of conversion leads to discontinuity.

The third type of conversion identified is that of "transformation". This is an altered perception reinterpreting both the past and the present. A transformation is a radical change of perception in which some newly gained cognition brings about a changed way of understanding. Unlike a pendulum conversion, a transformation does not require a rejection or negation of the past or of previously held values. A transformation involves a new perception, a re-cognition of the past. As with conversion, however, the catalyst of change is an event, person, group or other agent. Transformation is a continuing process – a series of "moments" or "events" where the horizon is transfigured. This is a transformation into a community of mutual responsibility and commitment.

In the contemporary "crisis" of the ecumenical movement, the call to conversion is primarily a call to transformation – rather than pendulum conversion. It invites us to live in the context of a new horizon in which the other's perceptions are incorporated.

The call to transformation

The invitation to churches to move towards a new phase in the development of the ecumenical journey in which commitment to transformation predominates is a call to search for new and more inclusive expressions of the Christian faith. Such a call invites the recognition by each tradition of the diversity in time and place within the tradition itself. Such a call invites the churches of the different confessional traditions to acknowledge that they have learned from the other traditions and recognize a complementarity which has become evident through theological dialogue, and common reflection and action on issues of social justice. Such a third phase of the ecumenical movement invites the churches to commit themselves to each other, to a process of conversion by incorporating the other into themselves, and to the embodiment of realized communion. Such a call invites the churches to move, in a phrase of the

Scots poet Iain Crichton Smith, "beyond the limits of the landscape that I knew".[12]

This is a real and disturbing challenge. Throughout this century, in particular, churches have taken the risk of moving to and embodying realized communion. On the basis of the results of bilateral and multi-lateral dialogues, church unions have been effected as an attempt to give expression, albeit partial expression, to the unity which is the gift and calling of our Lord. Indeed, there is now a radically different profile of the church throughout the world as a result of such unions, and of the entering of churches into covenants with each other. In different parts of the world there are also the equivalent of "local ecumenical parishes", where at congregational level there is shared membership and ministry, even where there is not yet full communion between the churches involved. Increasingly, churches in different contexts are moving "beyond the limits of the landscape that I knew". The churches involved in such embodiments of complementarity and communion are, however, conscious that as yet they have only taken the first steps towards embodying the vision of our Lord. They invite others to take the risk of venturing towards communion.

On the whole, however, churches find themselves at different points on the tenfold journey from conflict to communion.[13] The configuration of churches in one context who have entered union or covenant fellowship find themselves in other contexts at a different stage of relationship. Churches even with the same confessional background in the same country find themselves in relationship of conflict or coexistence, a problem being addressed currently by the World Alliance of Reformed Churches. With different partners, churches find themselves at different stages on the journey from conflict to communion. For every church and confessional tradition there is continuing activity in every phase of the ecumenical journey, as Hotchkin notes.[14] As churches and confessional traditions undertake the journey towards communion, they oscillate between the various stages and methodologies of the spectrum.

What is it that holds us back on our journeying? In his encyclical letter *Ut Unum Sint*, Pope John Paul II poses the question: *Quanta est nobis via?* How much further do we need to go?[15] In answering the question, he notes that theological agreement needs to be reached on six issues, four of which are evident in the Roman Catholic Church's response to *Baptism, Eucharist, Ministry*: viz. scripture-tradition; eucharist and sacramentality; ordination; magisterium; Mary; and the role of the papacy. Other confessional traditions will no doubt have their particular list of theological topics which require resolution before it is possible to move into the third phase of the ecumenical movement, e. g.

episcopacy, justification, conciliarity. On the basis of agreement already reached, however, how far is it possible to allow of diversity of expression and divergence of view on even these issues? How far does our being "in Christ" impel us to take the risk of communion, and to work out a more comprehensive theology as a number of churches have done *after* they have entered union, e. g. the Church of South India, the Uniting Church of Australia (compare the method of the Church of North India of seeking an agreed theology on all issues *prior* to entering union)?[16]

In his paper to the third consultation of the ecclesiology and ethics programme in which Faith and Order has been involved with Unit III of the World Council of Churches, John de Gruchy drew our attention to the importance of non-doctrinal factors which impeded the attempt to embody communion in South Africa:

> As in many other places, social, personal, cultural and political forces were more prevalent. The churches could not unite because they reflected the social realities present in a highly stratified country. By the same token, they fragmented precisely because these realities often proved stronger than any convictions about the unity which Christians have in Jesus Christ, especially at moments of national crisis.[17]

Economic, social, political, personality and race factors have played a dominant role in the story of the division of the church. They are continuing church-dividing issues. As we examine the history of the failure of church union schemes, or the diminution of church union to church cooperation schemes, such factors emerge as determinative. The quality of our church fellowship continues to be hindered by nationalism and ethnicity both within and between our confessional traditions. Our ability to move as communities towards more evident expressions of fellowship is constrained by "our" community's memory of relationship with the other communities. Our communities remember the pain and suffering resulting from the activities of other communities, such actions having been given theological justification by other churches. All of these factors impede seriously the ability of churches to proceed on the spectrum from conflict to communion. Significantly such factors are no longer designated "non-theological" factors but are called appropriately non-doctrinal facts. They are profoundly theological factors which need to be addressed on the road to visible unity. And yet these factors, however understandable, have been allowed to determine the ability of churches to manifest visible unity.

The late Bishop Oliver Tomkins, former chairman of the Faith and Order working committee, ruefully reflected towards the end of a life committed to the ecumenical movement at the international, national and local level:

> Ecumenism now sees that churches have no greater courage, love and unselfishness than any other institutions to change structures, relinquish power and renounce vested interests.[18]

Tomkins had played a decisive role along with others at the meeting of the Faith and Order world conference at Lund in 1952 in crafting the Lund principle, in affirming an ecclesiology of the pilgrim people of God, and in articulating the movement from a comparative to a consensual methodology. As architect of the second phase of the ecumenical movement, towards the end of his life he perceived the reluctance of the churches to continue the movement into the third phase – the time of decision-making – as Hotchkin asserts; the time of conversion, as the Groupe des Dombes affirm; or the time of transformation or transfiguration, which seem to me to be appropriate terms for this phase.

In a famous interview with Olivier Clément, Patriarch Athenagoras stressed:

> What churchmen most lack is the spirit of Christ, humility, the dispossession of self, a disinterested welcome to others, the capacity to see the best in others. We are afraid, we want to keep things that are out-of-date because we are used to them, ... we hide a spirit of pride and power beneath conventional expressions of humility.[19]

It is this fear of change in identity which needs to be addressed if there is to be any realistic response to the call to transformation. Patriarch Athenagoras recalled us to the spirit of Christ – humility, dispossession of self, the disinterested welcome of others – a spirit encapsulated by St Paul in his letter to the Philippians where he recounts his transformation experiences in the context of his treatment of having the same mind of Christ evident in his self-emptying or kenosis.[20] Paul outlines the life of transfiguration "in Christ", a life which emphasizes the being of each Christian as interdependent through having the same mind of Christ. In this transformation, each becomes vulnerable to the other. Such vulnerability, of course, induces a sense of apprehension and fear. Yet our identity is an identity in and with each other through baptism in Jesus Christ. We have a common identity which transcends all the factors which impede the visible embodiment of communion. This attitude of Christ, this call to transformation invites us, as the Lund conference in 1952 perceived, to let go of that which is not essential in the interests of embodying communion. This attitude and call invites us "to move beyond the limits of the landscape that we knew", to embrace, as essential for the third phase of the ecumenical movement, a kenotic ecclesiology.[21]

In their report, the Groupe des Dombes highlight a number of examples from Christian history which exhibit an attitude of conversion or transformation. They demonstrate a kenotic ecclesiology at work. Their examples emphasize the fact that it is possible for churches to change. It is not solely individuals who are called to a life of kenosis. Christian communities are called to exhibit this life of transformation – this life which embodies our interdependence. By noting these stories of the transformation of the church, the Groupe des Dombes have called for a serious commitment to Christ as centre. In particular, they invite the churches to take responsibility for participating in the divisions of the church by acknowledging the interdependence of the churches and by really embracing the concerns of the others. This will involve, as they perceive, a letting go of insisting that "our" way is the only way to be church by engaging in a common discussion of how as church we can embody the gift and call of our Lord to unity, and how we can be more faithful to the gospel in our age and context so that the church may indeed be a sign and sacrament of the world as God intends it to be.

In the section I report of the fifth world conference on Faith and Order, held in Santiago de Compostela in 1993, this kenotic ecclesiology is affirmed thus:

> The dynamic process of koinonia involves the recognition of the complementarity of human beings. As individuals and communities, we are confronted by the others in their otherness, e. g., theologically, ethnically, culturally. Koinonia requires respect for the other and a willingness to listen to the other and to seek to understand them. In this process of dialogue, where each is changed in the encounter, there takes place the appropriation of the stories of action, reaction and separation whereby each has defined himself or herself in opposition to the other. The search for establishing koinonia involves appropriating the pain and hurt of the other and through a process of individual and collective repentance, forgiveness and renewal, taking responsibility for that suffering. Confrontation with the other, individually and collectively, is always a painful process, challenging as it does our own life-style, convictions, piety and way of thinking. The encounter with the other in the search to establish the koinonia, grounded in God's gift, calls for a kenosis – a self-giving and a self-emptying. Such a kenosis... invites us to be vulnerable, yet such is no more than faithfulness to the ministry of vulnerability and death of Jesus as he sought to draw human beings into communion with God and each other. He is the pattern and patron of reconciliation which leads to koinonia. As individuals and communities, we are called to establish koinonia through a ministry of kenosis.[22]

The third phase of the ecumenical movement invites the churches to embrace the way of kenosis – in respect of their relations with each other and in respect of our being in the world. The call to koinonia, the call to be sign and sacrament of transfiguration of the world as God intends it to be, is for the sake of the world and creation. Such a call to kenosis involves all the churches placing at the centre the attempt to stand in the event of the common memory and hope of Jesus of Nazareth.[23]

Ubuntu – a vision of kenotic ecclesiology

As we meet on African soil, it is particularly appropriate to receive the gift of the African vision of kenotic ecclesiology, viz. *Ubuntu*. At the end of June 1996 I had the privilege of representing Konrad Raiser and the World Council of Churches at the service of thanksgiving for the ministry of Archbishop Desmond Tutu in St George's Cathedral, Cape Town. As you can imagine, this was an exuberant, colourful, poignant and moving occasion. It also provided an opportunity to meet prominent South African churchmen and church women, as did the gracious hospitality to the participants of the ecclesiology and ethics working party extended by Brigalia Bam and the South African Council of Churches later that week. In discussions it was evident that there was a high expectation placed upon the churches by the South African government to act as agents of reconciliation in this critical period of South African history. Such expectations have been created to a large extent by the very ability of many South African people to forgive, and to engage in the constructive task of building a just and peaceful society. This is the astonishing miracle of South Africa. In seeking to find an explanation and expression for this capacity for reconciliation and communion, theologians and commentators have identified *Ubuntu*.[24]

The major elements of a theology and ecclesiology of *Ubuntu* stem from the insight that "a person is a person through others". Drawing on a theology of creation, *Ubuntu* asserts that "God has created us for interdependence as God has created us in his image – the image of a divine fellowship of the holy and blessed Trinity"[25] – an affirmation central to the Canberra statement and the Santiago report. We learn to be human through our association with other human beings. Identity and relationship go hand in hand. The environment for this interdependence is the absolute dependence of each on God and neighbour. In other words, we have the potentiality of becoming human because we are in community and only in community is justice done to individuals. Through this interdependence, there is a deep-rooted sense of community and caring, of relationship and friendship, and there is created an enormous capacity of forgiveness. Human beings become persons only by living in this environment which is conducive to the interaction of diverse personalities and cultures. This environment of interdependence depends upon an ethos of vulnerability. As Tutu notes, *Ubuntu* embraces individuals and communities:

In the African *Weltanschauung*, a person is not basically an independent solitary entity. A person is human precisely in being enveloped in the community of other human beings, in being caught up in the bundle of life. To be is to participate. The summum bonum here is not independence but sharing, interdependence. And what is true of the human person is surely true of human aggregations.[26]

To emphasize the fact that this refers to not only individuals, but communities, Archbishop Tutu goes on to point to the concept of *ujamaa* in Tanzania and *harambee* in Kenya (and *utu* in Tanzania).

Through the stories of those victimized in South Africa, both individuals and communities, glimpses of *Ubuntu* are evident. Clearly the churches in that situation are aware of their inability to manifest *Ubuntu* sufficiently. That is why I hold up the concept as a vision – one not yet manifest. Yet the vision of *Ubuntu*, on the basis of our being "in Christ", is an important expression of an ecclesiology appropriate to the third phase of the ecumenical movement.

Beyond the limits of the familiar landscape

The language of crisis is currently being used about the contemporary ecumenical movement and the search for the visible unity of the church. This crisis is a feature of the "growing pains" of the movement itself. The ecumenical pilgrimage involves the ten-stage journey from conflict to communion. That journey has basically been undertaken by methodologies of comparison and consensus. The ecumenical crisis is that, for further growth and development towards unity, a new methodology is required – in other words, that of conversion, and a new ecclesiology, in other words, kenotic ecclesiology needs to emerge. Such a transformation involves placing the familiar in the context of a new horizon – that of *Ubuntu*, for example, thus moving us all "beyond the limit of the landscape we know". By thus accepting each other, and so reordering our lives and institutions, we give a sign to the wider humanity of community through the embrace of a life-style of kenosis. Such a transformation may enable us to be the sign and the sacrament of the world as God intends it to be.

The Irish Nobel laureate Seamus Heaney has challenged the people of Ireland to move towards a reconstructed Ireland in his poem "From the Canton of Expectation":

> We lived deep in a land of optative moods,
> under high, banked clouds of resignation.
> A rustle of loss in the phrase "Not in our lifetime",
> the broken nerve when we prayed "Vouchsafe" or "Deign"
> were creditable, sufficient to the day.

Having noted the ways in which constraints of identity and experience maintained the fixity of the optative mood, he then goes on to note a new sudden change of mood brought by a new generation.

> and a grammar
> of imperatives, the new age of demands.
> They would banish the conditional for ever,
> this generation born impervious to
> the triumph in our cries of *de profundis*.
> Our faith in winning by enduring most
> they made anathema.

Yet Heaney notes the yearning to move out of both optative and imperative moods. If community is to be realized, it requires the force of the indicative mood as portrayed by the one who builds his boat, like Noah, and the bringing to birth of "the rainbow people":

> "I yearn for hammer blows on the clinkered planks
> the uncompromised report of driven thole-pins,
> to know there is one among us who never swerved
> from all his instincts told him was right action,
> who stood his ground in the indicative,
> whose boat will lift when the cloud burst happens."[27]

The third phase of the ecumenical movement invites us to move beyond the optative and imperative moods to that of the indicative through a transformative kenotic ecclesiology and way of acting and thinking so that we may indeed become the sign and sacrament of the communion that God intends the world and the whole creation to manifest.

This, I believe, is the challenge before us.

NOTES

[1] Institute for Ecumenical Research, Strasbourg, *Crisis and Challenge of the Ecumenical Movement: Integrity and Indivisibility*, Geneva, WCC, 1994, p.3.

[2] *Ibid.*, p.13. The authors of this report emphasize both the positive and the negative elements of church commitment to change, and note that the ecumenical movement is homogeneous. Nevertheless they identify an important trend.

[3] In the discussion in the Life and Work conferences surrounding the question of the relation between church and society this approach is evident.

[4] Edwin Muir, *Collected Poems*, London, Faber, 1960, p.81.

[5] Oliver Tomkins, ed., *The Third World Conference on Faith and Order*, London, SCM, 1953.

[6] The principle discussion documents were published in Ellen Flesseman-van Leer, *The Bible: Its Authority and Interpretation in the Ecumenical Movement*, Faith and Order paper no. 99, Geneva, WCC, 1980.

[7] "The Ecumenical Movement's Third Stage", in *Origins*, 25, 21, 95, pp.354-61.

[8] Groupe des Dombes, *For the Conversion of the Churches*, Geneva, WCC, 1993. For the history of the Groupe des Dombes, see Alain Blancy, "The Group of les Dombes", in *One in Christ*, 23, 3, 1987, pp.235-41; René Girault, "Fifty Years of Ecumenical Dialogue: The Groupe des

Dombes'", in *Ecumenism*, 95, 1989; and Patrick Rodger, introduction in *Ecumenical Dialogue in Europe*, London, Lutterworth, 1966.

9 René Girault, *One Lord, One Faith, One Church*, Maynooth, St Paul, 1993.

10 Harding Meyer, "Christian World Communions: Identity and Ecumenical Calling", in *The Ecumenical Review*, 46, 4, 1994, p.386. The nature of identity is also explored in the report of the Groupe des Dombes, *op. cit.*

11 Beverley Gaventa, *From Darkness to Light: Aspects of Conversion in the New Testament*, Philadelphia, Fortress, 1986. See esp. pp.148f., from which much of the following paragraphs of my text is drawn.

12 Iain Crichton Smith, *Collected Poems*, Manchester, Carcanet, 1992, p.9.

13 Conflict – competition – coexistence – comparison – cooperation – consensus – complementarity – commitment – conversion – communion.

14 *Op. cit.*, p.355.

15 *Ut Unum Sint*, Vatican, 1995, p.88.

16 Two major approaches have been evident in the agreements leading to church union – that of agreeing to unite and then to write a common confession of faith which arises out of the new context of witnessing together, e. g. Church of South India; and that of writing a common confession prior to the act of embodying visible unity, e. g. Church of North India.

17 "Church Unity and Democratic Transformation", in *The Ecumenical Review*, vol. 49, no. 3, July 1997.

18 Cited by Ronald Preston, *Confusion in Christian Social Ethics*, London, SCM, 1994.

19 Olivier Clément, *Dialogues with Patriarch Athenagoras*, cited in René Girault, *One Lord, op. cit.*

20 See Gaventa, *op. cit.*

21 Ladislas Orsy in his article "Kenosis: The Door to Christian Unity", in *Origins*, 23, 3, 1993, pp.38-41, also articulates a kenotic ecclesiology and identifies issues which the Roman Catholic Church needs to address in the attempt to manifest "kenosis".

22 Section I, para. 20, in T. Best and G. Gassmann, eds, *On the Way to Fuller Koinonia*, Faith and Order paper no. 166, Geneva, WCC, 1994, pp.232-33.

23 Memory and hope are central to the reports of the ecclesiology and ethics programme. In his work, H. Richard Niebuhr noted that the measure of our unity is the extent of our common memory (see *The Meaning of Revelation*, New York, Macmillan, 1941, p.115). For the force of "anamnesis" (memory) see my article "Healing the Violence: Christians in Community", in *Mid-Stream*, 35, 2, 1996, pp.163-76.

24 This is particularly evident in the volume of essays presented to Archbishop Tutu on the occasion of his retirement from the archbishopric of Cape Town. See Leonard Hulley, Louise Kretzschmar and Luke Lungile Pato, eds, *Archbishop Tutu: Prophetic Witness in South Africa*, Cape Town, Human & Rousseau, 1996.

25 See citation from Desmond Tutu, *ibid.*, p.96.

26 "Viability", in Hans-Jürgen Becken, ed., *Relevant Theology for Africa*, Durban, Lutheran Publ. House, 1973, p.38. Cited above p.100.

27 In Seamus Heaney, *New Selected Poems: 1966-1987*, London, Faber & Faber, 1990, pp.236f.

Plenary Discussion

A number of issues were raised in the discussion. At the fifth world conference on Faith and Order there had been difficulty for some participants in discussing the "conversion" of the churches. The language of "transformation" in the director's report therefore was seen by one commissioner to be more helpful, and he hoped that this might receive further development. Attention was drawn to the danger of a polarization between what occurs prior to a union of churches and what follows such union. Clarification was sought on the distinction between "convergence" and consensus, and with regard to conversion, it was asked how far conversion depends on human activity and how far it is a matter of grace.

A range of questions and points emerged on the moderator's discussion of "conciliarity": how far are we seeking administrative mergers and how far the development of an actual practice of common decision-making in church life which involves administration? It was stressed that the calling of the churches includes the need to bring together the means of common decision-taking. Concern was expressed at the moderator's discussion of conciliarity belonging to the nature and essence of the church which seemed to go beyond the Canberra statement's discussion of conciliarity as a form or model of full communion. It was asked whether there was a clear enough distinction between conciliarity and koinonia when it was stated that "conciliarity sustains diversity" or "koinonia provides framework for holding together diversity and unity". A further question was raised as to the plans for discussion of primacy in the context of conciliarity.

A number of questions focused on the issue of identity when the need for encouraging dialogue on the relation between doctrinal and non-doctrinal factors was emphasized as non-doctrinal factors play an important role in identity formation. The importance of taking seriously the differing identities of the various regions and sub-regions of the world was also emphasized.

Finally, it was stressed that when churches celebrate worship together, especially the sacrament of the Lord's supper, the sign of unity which gives credibility to a commitment to the proclamation of the gospel of reconciliation is evident. The world hears the churches in a different way.

The moderator responded by stressing that church unity is not merely administrative but needs to be understood in the context of the discussion of conciliarity. She felt that the appropriate point to raise the issue of primacy in this plenary commission meeting would be in the discussion of the ecclesiology draft.

The director stressed that the language of transformation needs to be situated in the context of the awareness of the work of the Holy Spirit. Many discussions on the nature of unity give the impression that the churches are in control. However, the churches are being led to a time of responding to the impulse of the Spirit. In the Canberra assembly small groups, many participants spoke of their churches being led to ecumenical activities and unity by a force from outside, and for which they found themselves affirming that they were being led by the Holy Spirit. The language of conversion and transformation, therefore, is not a language of church control, but of risk-taking and vulnerability to the work of the Spirit. But the question to the churches is the need to acknowledge that this risk-taking belongs to the very identity of what it means to be the body of Christ. With this question of identity there is a need to face the quality of interdependence as churches, particularly in the ways that identity has been crafted over and against others. The search for manifesting visible unity draws on this interdependence.

I
Major Programmes
of Faith and Order

Reception as Ecumenical Requirement

The Example of the Theological Dialogues between Christian Churches

ANDRÉ BIRMELÉ

The Roman Catholic theologian Yves Congar defined reception in the following way in a famous 1972 essay:

> By reception we mean the process by which a church tradition appropriates a truth which has not arisen out of that tradition, but which it yet recognizes and adopts as a formulation of the faith. In the process of reception, we understand something other than what the Scholastics meant by obedience. For them, this was the act whereby a subordinate regulated his will and his conduct according to the legitimate precepts of a superior, out of respect for his/her authority. Reception is not merely the expression of the relationship *secundum et supra*; it includes the active giving of assent, even the exercise of judgment, where the life of a body which draws upon its original spiritual resources is expressed.[1]

Congar pursued a double objective. He noted on one hand the obvious necessity for the Roman Catholic Church, in the wake of the Second Vatican Council, to reflect upon the reception of the texts and conciliar decisions. He also wanted to bring attention to the fundamental task incumbent upon the contemporary ecumenical movement if the churches were not to lose the benefits of their rapprochement these past few years.

Following a detailed study of the process of reception (and of non-reception) of the decisions of the councils in the history of the church, Congar established certain fundamental theological principles:

– Reception cannot be limited to a judicial act by which a local church adheres to decisions taken at a superior hierarchical level. Only the acceptance by the community, which recognizes in the points to be received the faith of the apostles, gives them their full authority. Reception refers to the process whereby either an individual, or the

---

• This paper builds on the principal themes of an article presented to Father J.M. Tillard on his 65th birthday and published in 1995. A. Birmelé, "La réception comme exigence oecuménique", in *Communion et réunion: Mélanges,* J.M Tillard, G.R. Evans and M. Gourgues, eds, Leuven, Leuven UP, 1995, pp.75-94. It has been translated from the French.

people of God as such, receive as truth, in the fullest sense of their faith, a word spoken to them.[2] Thus the faithful and the local churches are neither inert nor purely passive. They have a faculty of discernment and they cooperate in the determination of the content of their faith and the form of their spiritual life.

– Such reception implies a certain kind of ecclesiology. It depends on a theology of communion which itself requires a theology of the local church, an understanding of ecclesiastical authority, a pneumatology, a deep sense of the conciliarity of the church. Congar points out above all two convictions which carry this process forward: (1) only the church universal *(sensus fidelium)* is infallible in matters of faith, (2) the consensus of the church and its reception are the work of the Holy Spirit and a sign of his presence.

– This process of reception demands time and is never finished. That which is received must constantly be re-received.

This important work of Congar remains today the standard reference work, a mine of historical and theological information. Building on this foundation, a number of authors over the past twenty years have studied this question which was previously discussed very little in theological research; they have insisted above all on the urgency of reception in the ecumenical movement.[3]

In ecumenical theology this term is used to qualify the procedure whereby the communities and separated churches appropriate the theological consensus resulting from dialogues between churches or any other fruit of ecumenical efforts and rapprochement aimed at the re-establishment of ecclesial communion.

In the ecumenical sphere, "reception" is currently the major challenge facing the churches. It is useless to accumulate a new theological consensus or renew dialogues which will simply repeat the gains of the past years. It is imperative today that everything be done so that all the communities can appropriate these gains for themselves. This stage is a complex phenomenon which concerns every level of church life, from the decisions of the highest levels of leadership in the churches to informal acceptance of these fruits by the faithful. The issue is not simply information but the translation of theological consensus, the fruit of dialogue, into a truly ecclesial consensus and communion, the "appropriation" of ecumenical advances and experiences with the goal of responding to the primary motivation of the ecumenical movement in this century, a new quality of communion between churches claiming their allegiance to the gospel of Christ. Such reception is an absolute necessity without which the contemporary ecumenical movement could become a simple moment in the history of the church, important no doubt but ephemeral.

The term reception is so often used today in ecumenical circles that it runs the risk of becoming a simple slogan signifying everything and nothing. It is for this reason necessary to use it carefully and give a precise definition of this notion in the ecumenical context. We would like to contribute with this study to the clarification of its usage by showing in the first part that the sense of this term in ecumenical theology must be distinguished from the sense which we can call "classical", the sense which was given to the term in the general history of the church where it designates above all the appropriation of the decisions of a council. The second part will point out some of the particular difficulties which this process of reception generates in ecumenism and some of the conditions of ecumenical reception. In the third part, we will suggest some concrete examples which will enable us to gain awareness of the effective application of the process of reception. We will limit the discussion to the reception of the conclusions of theological dialogues led by the churches.

The specificity of "reception" in the ecumenical context

Only a few rare studies attempt to distinguish between "ecumenical" reception and "classical" reception.[4] The majority of other studies move from one to the other without taking any particular precautions and assimilate contemporary ecumenical requirements with the "classical" process of reception. Is the reception of the results of theological dialogues between churches comparable with the reception of conciliar decisions in history?

1. There are certainly important common points[5] that bind together "ecumenical" reception and the "classical" reception of the decisions of councils. Four of these should be mentioned:

a) Only the appropriation of the fruits of the ecumenical dialogues by all levels of church life gives these dialogues their true authority. The dialogues were not conducted for their own sake. They were not concerned simply with an exchange of opinions among theologians of different traditions. The dialogue commissions were authorized by the churches to seek consensus in the expression of the faith and thereby to contribute to the realization and visibility of the one church of Jesus Christ. From this perspective, the situation is thoroughly comparable with that of the church councils. The conciliar decisions had to be received by the local churches; only this gave them their true authority and made possible the visible expression of the one church. It is the same today. The theological dialogues have taken place; their theological conclusions have been presented to those who mandated them and the ecclesial assemblies (World Council of Churches, world confessional families) have transmitted their conclusions to their member churches. They now must be received by the local churches. This required reception corresponds not only to the intention of the dialogues; it belongs to their essence. In reception, we move beyond the dialogues and place their fruits on a different ecclesial and spiritual level. In this move beyond the dialogues, the dialogues paradoxically receive their true sense and their true authority.

Will the churches and especially the local congregations appropriate these results? The process is underway and one can already assert that some conclusions of the dialogues have in fact been received. Others have not been, and perhaps never will be. Here also, the parallel with the reception of conciliar decisions is possible. In his study, Congar shows that several conciliar decisions, for example those of the council of Florence, were never received and others required a reception process that took centuries.[6] This reception process, like the reception of the councils, never comes to an end. That which has already been received must always be received anew.

b) A second analogy between "ecumenical" reception and "classical" reception concerns the path of the dialogues. The doctrinal decisions of the councils were always both an end-point and a beginning point. The doctrine under consideration was already under discussion in the church for some time and in many cases an informal consensus had been reached prior to the council's deliberations and conclusion. So also with the dialogues. They are in themselves a decisive moment of reception. Many examples can be given: for example, Catholic-Lutheran dialogue over the understanding of salvation *sola fide*, a highly controversial theme in the 16th century. The international dialogue that led in 1972 to the Malta report could content itself with receiving the theological research of the present century. It had simply to summarize this work and state the existing consensus.[7] A second example is the Leuenberg accord, which has bound together Lutherans and Reformed in Europe since 1973. This text, which established full communion between these churches, could also content itself in the end with stating that in many countries recent theological developments had led to a clear rapprochement of the two families. The accord did not need first to work out the consensus; it stated it and offered it to the churches for ratification.

The dialogues are not in fact the beginning point of the ecumenical movement. Many formal and informal encounters between the churches precede them. It is thus false to understand the dialogues as abstract and theoretical theological discussions without relation to the reality of the churches. They are themselves the result of concrete ecclesiastical conditions. Thus they were set to work by the churches to contribute to a clarification of an already present new situation.

c) A third element also allows for a direct comparison between "ecumenical" reception and the "classical" reception of conciliar decisions: both processes of reception are not simply formal and judicial acts. These acts are certainly necessary but they can only be the conclusion of a spiritual process within the churches concerned. An institutional decision alone can never constitute reception. It must be accompanied by and even preceded by the genuine adherence of believers who recognize in the tradition to be received a true affirmation of their faith. It is not therefore merely a matter of formal adhesion but a reception in the confession of faith, piety, liturgy and more generally in ecclesial practice. This is true for the reception of a council and for the reception of the conclusion of an ecumenical dialogue. In this latter case, it is worth noting that a dialogue group is much more than simply a place for theological reflection. Liturgical practice and shared spiritual growth are a constitutive part of the dialogue group's experience. These elements are however difficult to communicate and the dialogue in fact only transmits a "skeleton" which must be fleshed out in the life of the local church. This necessary incarnation of dialogue inside a local church is an important moment in the reception process and is both the work of the community called to receive and the work of the Holy Spirit. The modern ecumenical movement, conscious of this dimension, insists on the pneumatological and eschatological dimensions in the search for unity. The unity of the church is the work of God and not simply the formal acceptance of a theological text. Every reception of a council experiences the same difficulty. Even when it concerns reception within one Christian family, the authority of the magisterium alone should not be made to stand on its own. It remains sterile as long as it is not accompanied and translated into the life and practice of the faith of the whole church and of each local church. This interaction of the *sensus fidelium* and of the institution is not something which is easy; it is the work of the Holy Spirit who builds the church in the life and practice of the faith of each one of its members and at all structural levels. This appropriation will not be any easier in the ecumenical world than it is for a particular church's reception of conciliar or synodal decisions. It cannot be done to the detriment of each parish and each local church. That which is to be received must be clarified, judged and measured in such a way that all can appropriate it for themselves and open themselves up to the necessary modifications which this reception will entail. A poorly engineered reception will only be a source of new divisions.

d) Finally, ecumenical reception is, like the "classical" reception of the conciliar decisions, a process which presupposes a total ecclesiology and an ecclesial practice. It is only conceivable if the church itself has a strong conciliar consciousness. It requires especially a readiness for conversion and for a transformation of traditional identities. The reception of the fruits of the dialogues cannot occur without a conversion of the churches; in no way will it permit the preservation of the status quo. A community that takes reception seriously and brings it about can never again exist as it was in the past. These words are not merely theoretical; one can already detect definite shifts in ecclesial practice and theology in diverse churches. Without any ranking, one can mention: a new emphasis upon the sacraments and a more frequent celebration of the eucharist in many Protestant churches; a new emphasis on the Catholic side upon soteriology and salvation in Jesus Christ alone, which is not without ecclesiological consequences; the appropriation from other traditions of new liturgical forms... In some cases, a conversion of church practices has even preceded the conclusion of the dialogue (for example, the common celebration of the eucharist). The last point shows only the extreme complexity of the process of reception, in which the sequence of events can be displaced.

2. After having first named the elements which place ecumenical reception close to the classical reception of the conciliar documents, one must now in a second moment *show that reception in the ecumenical sphere very clearly departs from the classical reception of the conciliar decisions.* Here lie the new elements which make the reception process so difficult because one does not yet know precisely how to deal with them. For this reason, reception remains lacking and one has, in fact, the impression of a lasting winter.

a) A first important difference lies in the fact that the churches today are in a situation of division. We are not in the situation of a council which seeks by means of a doctrinal decision to further develop the confession of the church or to define it more clearly in order to adjudicate a conflict within a united church. The modern ecumenical movement is in a pre-conciliar phase. The idea of conciliarity has certainly been emphasized often in the ecumenical research of recent years. The assembly of the World Council of Churches in New Delhi in 1961 had already placed special weight on this concept and requested a precise investigation of it by the Faith and Order commission.[8] After the assembly in Uppsala in 1968, such concepts as conciliar fellowship and conciliarity became absolutely central in the attempt to describe the unity we seek. The idea of calling a general council had often been played with inside the ecumenical movement. This interest in conciliarity cannot hide, however, that such a council of all churches is today still not possible and thus we must apply the idea of reception within a pre-conciliar situation.[9] Ecumenical reception serves the preparation of a general council and not the appropriation of such a council's results by the churches and the faithful. This is a new situation, without a precedent from which ecumenical theology could take instruction. One could no doubt refer back to the surprising and unique case of the council of Florence and its efforts to establish unity between the East and the West in 1439. But the decisions of this council were in fact not received and the procedure of the time was strongly influenced by the political environment, and this significantly relativizes its value as an example for the contemporary ecumenical movement.

The current pre-conciliar phase is complex; the fruits of rapprochement are such that their reception is possible and necessary, precisely in preparation for a conciliar assembly of all churches.

b) This preconciliar situation explains also the second important difference between ecumenical reception and the classical reception of conciliar decisions: *the nature of the texts to be received.* The reports of the dialogue commissions of recent years are highly diverse. This diversity concerns not only the dialogues' theological content, which is also of uneven quality, but also the forms of their results. Some are only the protocol of an encounter; other offer an inventory of agreed and still undecided questions; some demonstrate convergences, while yet others spell out a full consensus in propositions of the faith.[10] There is no one way of receiving these differing forms of dialogue. In some cases, one must be satisfied with taking notice of the results; in others, reception is much closer to the appropriation of a truth of the faith. The processes of receiving ecumenical texts thus require formal and qualitative differentiation, a differentiation that is neither simple nor obvious. A clear example is the reception of the so-called Lima document: *Baptism, Eucharist and Ministry.*[11] In its introduction, the text rightly says that it deals only with convergences. The churches are invited to ascertain to what degree the statements within the texts correspond to their own fundamental faith convictions. The text does not present itself as a new confession of faith, but only as a first stage on a long path. The text set in motion perhaps the most important reception process of the modern ecumenical movement. In reading the responses of the churches,[12] however, one sees again and again that the churches have often misunderstood the document and have simply compared it with their own confessions. This comparison inevitably shows that the Lima document is not identical with the confessions of faith and doctrinal formulations of the individual churches. One has confused a dialogue result with a confession of faith. So it is not surprising that one must then speak of a non-reception of the Lima document. This example clearly shows the difficulty of a precise determination of the text to be received: the churches approached the text and dealt with it as if it were a doctrinal formulation produced by a council. The Lima document itself only wished to show certain convergences and asked the churches to affirm its general orientation.[13]

c) This necessary differentiation at the level of the kind of theological dialogue shows the need to establish more precisely the content that is to be received. This content is the third element which distinguishes ecumenical reception from the reception of conciliar decisions. The results of dialogues are not confessions of faith and do not present themselves as such. Their goal is the development of convergences and, if possible, a consensus which can lead to an overcoming of the situation of division. On the whole, one can find in the dialogue results four different kinds of affirmations:[14] (1) a common repetition of fundamental, common formulations of the faith, (2) a further development of convictions which have marked a particular tradition without being explicitly stated or lived out, (3) suggestions for overcoming deficits in one or the other tradition; (4) the acceptance of the legitimate presence in another tradition of elements which do not stand in the way of a rapprochement with this tradition, but which are not taken up by the other partner.

Even if some dialogues often are similar to a common formulation of the faith, they have a different intention: *the goal is a consensus which expresses the common conviction without either desiring or requiring the elimination of a legitimate doctrinal diversity between the churches.* The church-dividing difference should be worked through and transformed until it loses its dividing character and so does not represent an obstacle to a true fellowship between the formerly divided churches. The international Lutheran-Catholic dialogue made this point clearly:

> Diversities – be they diversities of church traditions or diversities caused by specific historic, ethnic and cultural contexts – can be understood and lived as different forms of expressing the one and the same faith when they are related to the central message of salvation and Christian faith and do not endanger this centre, and when they are therefore sustained by one and the same gospel. It is not necessary that each church adopt the specific forms of belief, piety or ethics of the other church and make them its own. But each church must recognize them as specific and legitimate forms of the one, common Christian faith. Then it is justified to recognize a legitimate diversity in the plurality of traditions and to assess them positively.[15]

What is new in contemporary dialogues is that the desired consensus can also positively evaluate differences and accept differing understandings as long as they are not church-dividing. Thus one can often find in the dialogues formulations of the sort: "Where it is taught that... (then follows a common theological assertion), then one must ask whether in this area the existing differences have not lost their church-dividing character."[16] Some dialogues, for example the Lutheran-Reformed dialogue in Europe, have gone so far as to be able to say: "On the basis of the consensus they have reached in their understanding of the gospel, churches with different confessional positions accord each other fellowship in word and sacrament."[17] The dialogue thus does not attempt to write a new confession, but rather to build a bridge between ecclesial identities. This bridge does not seek to remove the differences as such, but only their dividing character. This goal of dialogue diverges clearly from the goal of a classical council. It thus naturally follows that the reception of such a process will be of a different sort than the reception of a "classical" conciliar decision.

d) These remarks about the content and process of the dialogues lead finally to a fourth important difference between ecumenical and classical reception. This concerns the goal of reception which may at first surprise those doing the receiving. The definition which Congar gives to reception, insisting on the appropriation of faith and which we recalled in the introduction, applies only partially to ecumenical reception. There are certainly some conclusions to dialogues which concern the faith common to all and these are the indispensable foundation for reconciliation. Each church is called upon to adopt it and this adoption will lead to a necessary ecclesial conversion and will allow for correction and openness to a greater fullness. But the conclusions of dialogue have as their primary goal reciprocal recognition, i.e. the recognition of the other church as another, but legitimate and true, expression of the one church of Jesus Christ. While reception and recognition cannot be equated, they relate together and are complementary.[18] There can be no reception without a recognition of the legitimacy and authenticity (truthfulness) of the other. This recognition leads conversely to a process of the acceptance of the particularity of the other, without the otherness of the other tradition being placed in question. The churches are thus called upon to receive the mutual recognition suggested by the dialogue, a mutual recognition which is the first step on the road to an authentic life together. Such a reception of a legitimate otherness is unusual for churches used to reception in the classical sense of the word. One need not add that such a step is not a search for compromise for its own sake but rather the first step towards true reconciliation. If mutual recognition is to have any meaning, it must lead to a truly common life, a real communion within the context of churches which are legitimately different. It is not a question of maintaining the status quo which tolerates any kind of otherness and which would only seal the divisions. Ecumenical dialogue implies – this has already been said but it is worth saying it again – "ecclesial conversion". It is a matter of reforming my own tradition, of verifying or even modifying my own convictions as well as having an appreciation of the "truth" of another tradition which "my" church no longer considers heretical but which it now understands as a legitimate expression of the church of Jesus Christ. In this striving, ecumenical reception differentiates itself from classical reception; ecumenical reception has reconciliation and a council as its goal, not as its starting point.

The special difficulties of "ecumenical" reception

In its differentiation from "classical" reception, this ecumenical reception cannot look back to precedents in church history. It is thus not surprising that this reception encounters new difficulties, unknown to classical reception. What are these problems? How can the ecumenical movement solve them?

As a first step, I would like to list the essential difficulties, without claiming that this list is complete. These difficulties are not secondary and must be taken seriously, for on them depends the future of the ecumenical movement as such.

A *first* problem arises through the unusual character of this kind of reception. This reception requires a creativity and the presence of structures and instruments which most churches did not previously possess. The call to reception which we hear in many places will be of no help if it remains a general appeal, lacking nuance and ill-adapted to the requirements of the place and the moment. It will remain a slogan carried along by good intentions but without real effectiveness if the ecumenical movement does not spell out in some detail the process it is referring to when it uses the term reception. Its task is the elaboration, in concertation with all the levels of ecclesial life, of a methodology of reception taking care to distinguish this from "classical" reception. Only a tool such as this will enable us to grasp the issues and specific difficulties and propose appropriate solutions. We might add that such a process is under way and that a number of remarkable examples and promising experiments exist.[19] This difficulty is amplified by the fact that the element of "newness" in the ecumenical movement which still fascinated and motivated the churches several years ago is today often felt as something foreign and disturbing. In many communities, and even among church leaders, a fear arises that traditional convictions will be lost in the ecumenical movement.[20] The hour certainly demands concrete decisions, ecumenical progress calls for ecclesial transformation. Ecumenical research certainly attempts to show that the fear of a loss of identity is unfounded, that a true "ecumenical" reception requires, on the contrary, a new consciousness of one's own identity so that one can open up to the otherness of others. Such arguments may be unconvincing, since church structures, like all structures, are by nature wary of all change. It is certainly encouraging that the ecumenical movement, which earlier had been a matter of individual specialists, has today touched the breadth of the churches and their institutions. The consequence follows, however, that reception is impeded and made more difficult.

A *second* difficulty arises from the feeling that local ecumenism has been left out of the work of the international dialogue commissions. This difficulty is many-sided.

Reception must now take place within the context of a generally reserved climate as far as ecumenical matters are concerned. Ecumenical motivation, which was very lively up until quite recently, is waning today. Reception presupposes churches which are ecumenically motivated. The necessity of motivation or of re-motivation remains an urgent task which goes beyond the simple context of reception while being at the same time its driving-force. From 1964, the general secretary of the WCC, Willem Visser 't Hooft, pointed out this urgency and underlined the fact that only one motive was sufficient to give strength and independence to the ecumenical movement: the realization that unity is part of the very being of the church, the church does not need unity because it is beautiful, desirable or pleasant but because full communion is constitutive of its being.[21] Reception will only take place when it is carried along by powerful motivation.

Even if ecumenical motivation exists, reception does not necessarily take place. Local congregations place a much greater weight on lived fellowship than on theological consensus which they consider is incapable of changing everyday reality. What, then, is the use of the reception of the conclusions of dialogues? The problematic of local ecumenism has been studied often in recent years,[22] its challenges and particular problems go beyond the single issue of reception. Nevertheless, the exigencies of reception run up against these particular difficulties of local ecumenism and are not able to resolve them alone.

Even in places where at the local level there is an awareness that unity limited to experience alone is very fragile and needs to be accompanied by a more solid theological foundation, the difficulties of reception do not necessarily disappear. Above all it is difficult to conceive of mutual recognition of the other community in its otherness as the basis for a new life actually shared in common. Here too the absence of precedents and models which might simply be copied is felt. In some cases it even happens that the partner with whom the dialogue has been held at the international level is not present at the grassroots level of the local congregation. What is the point of "receiving" the results of a dialogue with a partner one hardly knows?

Added to this set of problems is the well-known tension between the different levels of church life, between what is commonly described as the grassroots and the leadership. In the case of the reception of the results of dialogues, local ecumenism often has the impression that a "foreign" element is being imposed from the outside for it was not born from within its ranks.

A *third* difficulty which is specific to ecumenical reception lies *in the nature of the reception process*. The convergence texts are the fruit of dialogue and have a dialogical character. They are like the text of a play which specialists, mandated by the church, have worked out, written and lived. This group now offers its "play" to the churches as a help, so that the local congregations can for themselves duplicate and experience the dialogue. Methodologically these texts must be received in a dialogical process. This requirement of a dialogical reception, however, is seldom fulfilled by the receivers. In most cases, reception occurs monologically and mono-confessionally. This response does not correspond to the requirement of the dialogue and leads rather to a confessional hardening. The example mentioned of the Lima document and its reception here speaks for itself. One compares the dialogue text with the confession of one's own tradition and then inevitably comes to the conclusion that the two do not fully coincide. This methodological difficulty can bring the entire reception process to a halt. Also in this area the churches need to find new, creative ways.

A *fourth* difficulty, one which particularly clings to the ecumenical movement, is of a more theological nature. It concerns the *specification of the unity recommended by the dialogues*. The ecumenical debate of the last decades has always been accompanied by reflection on models of unity. What should the desired unity actually look like? What role should theological consensus play in it?[23] Despite significant movement closer together, this question still lacks a final answer and the articulation between theological consensus and the realization of unity is seen differently from one ecclesial tradition to another. For Catholic theology, for example, theological consensus is important, but this consensus has a different function in the re-establishment of unity than it does, for example, in the Reformation tradition. Since this problem of models of unity has not been adequately clarified in the theological discussions, it is not surprising that it reappears in the process of reception at the local and regional levels. The receivers will always ask how and to what degree a theological agreement will lead to true progress towards church fellowship at the local level. It cannot be excluded that the reception of a consensus will finally change almost nothing, so long as the model of unity itself, the transition from theological consensus to church fellowship, remains unclarified. It is thus not surprising that the churches often simply note the results of a dialogue, without drawing the ecumenical and ecclesial consequences which cannot be drawn by the dialogue commissions themselves.

In this same connection appears an additional, *fifth*, difficulty, the understanding of consensus. The issue here is less the place of theological consensus in the total process of the search for unity than the extent and content of this consensus. What consensus is necessary and sufficient for a mutual recognition by the churches, for the declaration and realization of ecclesial fellowship? This debate has also often been on the agenda of ecumenical research over the past years, but an adequate answer has not yet been produced.[24] The Reformation traditions maintain that the consensus in the understanding of word and sacrament is necessary and sufficient. All other areas of Christian life are areas of legitimate diversity. Catholics and Orthodox, however, emphasize the necessity of a consensus in the understanding of ministry and church structures and thus define differently the border between dividing and legitimate differences.[25] This difficulty, still unsolved within theological work, inevitably reappears within the reception process, where it constitutes a definite obstacle. The reception of a particular consensus is given a different weight in different church families; each gives to this particular consensus a particular weight in accord with its own hierarchy of truths. Thus the reception of a consensus in one tradition will have an ecumenical and ecclesial weight which will be less (or greater) than the reception of the same consensus in another tradition.[26] For example, a consensus on ordained ministry will have a different ecclesial significance in the Roman Catholic or Orthodox traditions than in a Reformed or Congregationalist tradition, where this question is church constitutive in a different way. In addition, voices will be raised in each tradition which assert that the achieved consensus is insufficient because not all convictions of one's own tradition are fully accepted. Here again the goal of a mutual recognition of the other is forgotten in favour of a simple comparison of the dialogue results with the confession of one's own tradition, a problem already mentioned in the previous section.

This long list of difficulties must finally be completed by a *sixth* one: ecumenical reception is made more difficult by *the question of which authority can address the dialogue results in a binding way*. Who is formally and ecclesiastically authorized to "receive" and who can make this reception binding for the concerned church? This question would appear not to arise in the Roman Catholic Church, for there the task is addressed to the magisterium. But even there the question comes up when, for example, a national bishops' conference undertakes steps which are not unconditionally blessed by Rome. This question arises *a fortiori* in all other churches. The World Council of Churches, the Lutheran World Federation, the Anglican Lambeth conference and all other world organizations can hardly claim to speak in a binding way for their member churches. Here again, opinions differ, and this difference of opinion places the problem in profile. All agree that the final decision lies with the local churches and their synods. But what happens when within a single church family the answers of different local or regional churches differ? This question must also be answered within the process of reception. Again, the reception problematic points beyond itself to a fundamental and difficult theological question, unsettled within the dialogues themselves: the question of authority within the churches. It is not by accident that within the theological dialogues, the decisive, still resistant obstacles are the problems that surround authority: ordained ministry, the bishop's office, teaching authority, and finally papacy. Even where the dialogues have achieved their most significant results, as between Anglicans and Catholics, Lutherans and Catholics, Orthodox and Catholics, or Lutherans and Anglicans, the question of authority remains in the end a partially unsolved problem. The relationship between theology, dogmatics, confession and synod, and the bishop's office remains controversial. It is not surprising that this problem reappears in the reception process in the form of the question: Who has the authority in the local and regional church to receive the dialogue results in a binding way and draw from them the consequences for the church?

This listing of difficulties has the goal of *making clear the special problems of ecumenical reception.* These difficulties are not unique to the problematic of ecumenical reception alone but go back to problems which have accompanied the ecumenical movement since the beginning. In the specific case of reception, the problems of motivation and the particular challenges of local ecumenism reappear as well as certain ecclesiological questions not yet sufficiently clarified in ecumenical theological thinking: models of unity, the understanding of consensus and the problems of authority in the church. It would be naive to think that they will take care of themselves in the process of reception.

It would be equally wrong to say that the theological dialogues have functioned poorly and neglected these challenges of which they are perfectly aware. In all these areas, the dialogues could propose a way forward, but such propositions must still be receivable and correspond to the requests and current possibilities of ecumenically motivated churches. We can cite for example the most recent text of the international Lutheran-Roman Catholic dialogue, *Facing Unity* (1985), which proposes a certain procedure including a model for unity, a vision of consensus and an integration of ministries. Of all the texts of this dialogue, the latter was the least well received. In this area also, the only way forward is not in the form of a monologue, a one-way process from the dialogue commissions towards the churches, but in the form of dialogue. It is incumbent upon the receiving churches that they enter into dialogue with the dialogues themselves so that the dialogue commissions can revise their work and make it more receivable in the churches. Only this kind of dialogue will permit real progress in reception.

This is a long-term enterprise. It is not that of the classical reception of conciliar decisions. It is a new procedure which cannot refer back to the antecedents of history, which knows and will yet know hesitation and failure and which will advance necessarily in stages.

Practical achievements
    1. Despite the difficulties just mentioned, the task is not impossible. A variety of Christian traditions have received the conclusions of various theological dialogues and have put in place an original ecumenical methodology. In order to harvest the theological and ecclesial fruit, different ecclesial families first of all checked the conclusions of the dialogues with their respective theological authorities. Next they elaborated a brief text, *a declaration which draws together the conclusions of the dialogues, applies them to the concrete situation of the churches concerned and determines the necessary consequences. Such a declaration is submitted to the decision-making authorities and becomes an authorized text of the churches concerned.*

    a) It is not therefore a question of having the synods or authorized bodies approve the conclusive texts of the dialogues in and for themselves. These texts are born in a particular context and are not directly transferable. They do not claim – they cannot claim – to be integrated into the corpus of reference of the different churches. It is rather a matter of receiving the dialogues and picking the fruit in terms of the declaration in question.

    b) Such a declaration is in fact a "bridge". It establishes the link between the families concerned and their respective identities. It affirms a consensus which no longer existed, lifts long-standing doctrinal condemnations, affirms mutual recognition, declares ecclesial fellowship... Its content and its impact will be different according to the families concerned and the level of development of the dialogue.

c) Such a declaration does not replace the confessions of faith of the churches concerned. It is rather an interpretative key for the affirmations of these reference texts. Its objective is to show that the differences which up to now separated the churches have now lost their divisive character and permit a new quality of fellowship. Some will be surprised not to find all the elements which characterize "their" tradition and will be tempted to want to correct it in that direction. In doing so they miss the significance of such a declaration which is a first attempt to conjugate consensus and difference.

d) This is obviously only a first step. This step is however decisive. Now is the time to continue and deepen the dialogue by setting in motion the commitments made in such a declaration, filling it out and preparing new steps which will permit us to arrive at the fully visible fellowship of the one church of Jesus Christ. Such a declaration opens the way to a long-term process.

e) It is scarcely necessary to add that such a declaration, though an important moment in reception, is only one of the aspects of the reception process. Simple synodal approval is not enough. It must be accompanied by spiritual and ecclesial reception and open up a phase of real rapprochement between the families concerned.

2. This is not simply a theological vision. Such a process of reception has been decided in various places in the course of the last few years. We will conclude by giving some concrete examples.

a) A first example is the *Lutheran-Reformed dialogue in Europe*, which led in 1973 to the Leuenberg agreement by which these churches declared themselves to be in full communion or fellowship. The theological dialogue was conducted locally in various countries and then at the continental level. The conclusions of these dialogues were considered positive and it was decided at the European level to draft an agreement. On the basis of a consensus, this agreement declares mutual recognition, fellowship in the word and in the sacraments, as well as the mutual recognition of ministries. This agreement was submitted to the synods of all the European Lutheran, Reformed and United churches and was approved by them. The clarification of particular doctrinal questions was from the beginning accompanied by agreement on the model of unity, necessary and sufficient consensus and the setting up of a common procedure, the adhesion of the synod of each church. Signing the agreement, however, was understood as only a first step: the declaration of fellowship should be followed, according to the terms of the agreement itself, by the realization of fellowship. The actors in this rapprochement understood that realization would require time and thus a series of instruments were created to accompany this reception process: the continua-

tion of theological dialogue, an ongoing exchange among the signatory
churches, and the search for a common witness and a common service in
the world. To do this, the churches set up an agreement executive committee and regular general assemblies responsible for making a progress
report every six years (Sigtuna in 1976, Driebergen in 1981, Strasbourg
in 1987, Vienna in 1994).[27] Between these assemblies the theological
dialogue has continued and has been able to arrive at a remarkable deepening of consensus (for example concerning baptism, holy communion,
the church or ministries). The local, regional or national churches have
for their part developed a web of relationships which have made concrete fellowship in the word and the sacraments and the interchange-
ability of ministers decided in 1972. One may also note the increasing
number of services and agencies common to several signatories (catechetical work, training of ministers, church aid programmes, etc.).

The process of reception is certainly far from being complete but
even those who had been the most hesitant would agree that definite
progress has been made towards fellowship which today is much more
real than it was on the day of the signing of the agreement. At present,
this agreement binds together more than 90 national or regional churches
of the European continent.

b) A second example is the dialogue between the European Lutheran
and Reformed churches (signatories of the agreement of Leuenberg) and
the Methodist churches in Europe. Here also, the dialogue was conducted in several countries and led in many places to the experience of
fellowship. To these initial results were added the positive conclusions
to the international dialogue between these families. On these foundations, a declaration of ecclesial fellowship was elaborated in 1992 which
in its aims and consequences is parallel to the agreement of Leuenberg.
This Lutheran/Reformed/Methodist declaration is at the present moment
being submitted to the synods, many of whom have responded positively. Its application is imminent and will require here also specific fol-
low-through so that this fellowship be fully visible.

c) A third example is the dialogue of the Anglicans with the
Reformed and the Lutherans. Unlike the Leuenberg model, its point of
departure was not so much the rapprochement of local churches as the
work of international dialogues. These have arrived at a broad consensus
which now has to be translated into local concrete situations.[28] Some
European countries, (the Anglicans of the British Isles and the Lutherans
or Reformed of Scandinavia, the Baltic countries and Germany) as well
as the churches of the USA, took the initiative. Initially, Anglicans,
Lutherans and Reformed invited each other to their worship services (in
the USA, where the Reformed are not involved, "temporary eucharistic

hospitality" was proposed). This phase opened up the possibility of grassroots meetings and the experience of life together as well as the deepening of theological dialogue. On the basis of this first experience which encountered the majority of the difficulties described in the previous paragraph but which was able to overcome them, the churches engaged in this process went one step further and arrived at declarations of fellowship which have been submitted to the synodal bodies. In Germany fellowship in the celebration of the word and the sacraments with the Church of England was reached, an agreement which was approved by the synods concerned but which does not yet include the full, mutual, recognition of ministries (cf. the Meissen agreement).[29] Full recognition was however possible in Scandinavia and in the Baltic countries where the Lutheran churches have drawn up with the Anglican churches of the British Isles a declaration of fully visible ecclesial fellowship (Porvoo statement 1993).[30] A similar procedure is under way in the USA. In both cases, accompanying structures are provided so that the declaration of full fellowship is not limited to the simple signing of an agreement but is translated into effective change in the life of the churches.

In Germany where a lesser degree of fellowship has been reached, and where some differences remain between Anglicans on one hand and Lutherans and Reformed on the other in the understanding of full fellowship and therefore of the model of unity, the dialogue on the mutual recognition of ministries and apostolic succession in the episcopal ministry continues. This was not however considered an obstacle preventing all progress. This example encouraged other churches from other countries to engage in a similar procedure (cf. the current dialogues between the British and French churches).

This dialogue is the perfect example of a reception in stages, a reception adapted to times and places. Its point of departure is theological consensus reached at an international level. It is translated into fact through the elaboration of a declaration of fellowship submitted to the synods, precise definition and the systematic search for intermediate objectives.

d) A fourth example is *the reception of the Lutheran-Roman Catholic consensus in the understanding of justification through faith alone*. The international dialogue stated such a consensus in 1972 (the Malta report). What consequences should be drawn from this consensus and translated into deeds? Pope John Paul II himself specified a way forward when he instituted a commission on the occasion of a visit to Germany, with the mandate of reflecting on a lifting of the doctrinal condemnations in this area. The commission was able to arrive at some propositions for the lifting of doctrinal condemnations concerning essentially justification by faith. These were submitted to the churches.[31] At the same time, the international Lutheran-Roman Catholic dialogue picked up the work begun in 1972 and came to some decisive conclusions (Church and Justification 1993). On this basis Lutherans and Catholics drafted, in 1995, a declaration on the understanding of justification by faith which was submitted to the churches for study. The reactions of the churches are encouraging and a lifting of the traditional doctrinal condemnations today appears possible. This represents an important phase in the reception of the fruits of an international dialogue and the realization of which seems possible in the near future; it is one step which will call for others. Its objective and scope are clearly defined; it can there fore take on a concrete form. Such a step would be a decisive sign of fel lowship given even if it represents only a first stage towards fully visi ble fellowship between these two traditions. The reception of all the con clusions of the dialogue will require a certain amount of time which shows the urgency of consensus in ecclesiology.

This example serves as a type of reception in stages. The intermediate stage which is about to be reached is the sign of growing fellowship between these two families.

These examples present important common characteristics which car serve as an orientation to the ecumenical reception process:

- in all these cases, a precise objective was fixed in which the current state of the question has been clearly defined;
- texts were proposed to the synods which were succinct and were such that these synods were able to discuss and approve them;
- the stage reached is not an end in itself but a first step which remains perhaps less than what some would like to see realized immediately.

But only this first step could create a new dynamic calling for a new deepening of the theological dialogue which will allow for a new phase of reception and, through that, a deepening of the fellowship already achieved.

NOTES

[1] Y. Congar, "La 'réception' comme réalité ecclésiologique", in *RSPhTh*, 56, 1972, p.370. With this definition, Congar tries to go beyond the notion of "reception" used by A. Grillmeier, which in his opinion, remains too narrow: "Konzil und Rezeption. Methodische Bemerkungen zu einem Thema der ökumenischen Diskussion", in *Theol. und Phil.*, 45, 1970, pp.321-52, where the author adopts the definition of the legal historian F. Wieacker for whom "reception" is always "exogenous" in that a group takes unto itself a law brought by another while continuing to belong to a different cultural milieu.

[2] We use here the terminology of J.M.R. Tillard who took up and added to the work of Y. Congar. Cf. J.M.R. Tillard: "Reception: A Time to Beware of False Steps", in *Ecumenical Trends*, 14, 1985, pp.145-48; "Did We Receive Vatican II?", in *One in Christ*, 4, 1985, pp.276-83; and above all *Eglise d'Eglises*, Paris, 1987, pp.58,164f.

Tillard also underlines that reception is a matter of hermeneutics. It is nothing other than the transmission of the gospel *(traditio)* which must not be merely repeated but rather restated in a fresh way and received by the believers and local churches in such a way that communion within the local churches and between them be not only preserved but strengthened. "It concerns nothing less than a moment in the unfolding of the Tradition *(paradosis)*, belonging therefore to the economy of the Spirit, by which the once and for all of the apostolic faith must invade all the ages" *(Eglise d'Eglises*, p.169).

3 Without pretending to be exhaustive, we note the most important contributions to which should be added the studies cited later in this work: as early as 1972, G. Alberigo published a special issue of *Concilium* (7, 1972) in which he writes the preface: "Wahl-Konsens-Rezeption im christlichen Kontext" (pp.477-83). Among more recent publications, we note the important studies of W. Beinert, "Die Rezeption und ihre Bedeutung für Leben und Lehre der Kirche", in *Catholica*, 44, 1990, pp.91-118 (which includes a good bibliography in the conclusion); I. Bria, "La réception des résultats des dialogues oecuméniques", in *Etudes théologiques*, 5; *Les dialogues oecuméniques hier et aujourd'hui*, Chambésy-Geneva, 1986, pp.286-93; M. Garijo, "Der Begriff Rezeption und sein Ort im Herz der katholischen Ekklesiologie", in *Theologischer Konsens und Kirchenspaltung*, P. Lengsfeld & H.G. Stobbe, eds, Stuttgart, 1981, pp.97-109; W. Hryniewicz, "Die ekklesiale Rezeption in der Sicht der orthodoxen Theologie", in *Theologie und Glaube*, 65, 1975, pp.250-66; A. Houtepen, "Rezeption, Tradition, Kommunion", and U. Kühn, "Rezeption als Erfordernis und als Chance", in *Ökumenische Perspektiven von Taufe, Eucharistie, Amt*, M. Thurian, ed., Frankfurt, 1983, pp.158-78 and 179-89; U. Kühn, "Rezeption", in *Ökumene Lexikon*, Frankfurt, 1983; W. Küppers, "Rezeption. Prolegomena zu einer systematischen Überlegung", in *Konzile und die ökumenische Bewegung*, Studien des ÖRK 5, Geneva, 1968, pp.81-104; E. Lanne, "La réception", in *Irénikon*, 55, 1982, pp.199-213; H. Meyer, "La réception ecclésiale ou le problème de la recevabilité", in *Irénikon*, 59, 1986, pp.5-19; J. Mühlsteiger, "Rezeption, Inkulturation, Selbstbestimmung", in *Zeitschrift für katholische Theologie*, 105, 1983, pp.261-89; Th. Rausch, "Reception, Past and Present", in *Theological Studies*, 47, 1986, pp.497-508; G. Routhier, *La réception d'un concile*, Paris, 1993; W.B. Rusch, *Reception: An Ecumenical Opportunity*, LWF Report 22, Philadelphia, Fortress, in collaboration with the Lutheran World Federation; L. Vischer, "Rezeption in der ökumenischen Bewegung", in *Kerygma und Dogma*, 29, 1983, pp.86-99; L. Vischer, "The Process of Reception in the Ecumenical Movement", in *Midstream*, 23, 1984, pp.221-33; *Report of the Sixth Forum of Bilateral Dialogues*, Geneva, WCC, 1994; *Directory for the Application of Principles and Norms on Ecumenism*, Vatican, 1993, paras 178-82.

4 Theologians insisting on the necessary distinction between "reception" in the broad sense of the word and "ecumenical reception" are not very numerous. We note the following: J.M.R. Tillard, *Réception, op. cit.*, p.145; G. Routhier, *Réception d'un concile, op. cit*, p.45; and above all G. Gassmann, "Rezeption im ökumenischen Kontext", in *Ökumenische Rundschau*, 25, 1977, pp.314-27, and "Die Rezeption der Dialoge. Eine lutherische Perspektive", in *Les dialogues oecuméniques hier et aujourd'hui*, Chambésy, 1985, pp.305-15. It seems to me important, however, to go beyond the distinctions made by Gassmann. We find the distinction in a study by the Orthodox theologian J. Zizioulas (Metropolitan John of Pergamon), "The Theological Problem of Reception'", in *Bulletin du Centro Pro Unione*, 26, 1984, pp.3-6. The author insists however, as an Orthodox theologian, on the identity of the two concepts. The same is true of N.A. Nissiotis, "The Meaning of Reception in Relation to the Results of Ecumenical Dialogue", in *The Greek Orthodox Review*, 29, 1985, pp.147-74.

5 Cf. the studies already mentioned in note 3 by Beinert or by Rusch as well as by Congar.

6 Y. Congar, "La réception comme réalité ecclésiologique", *op. cit.*, pp.384f.

7 For more details about the history of this dialogue cf. my book *Le salut en Jésus-Christ dans les dialogues oecuméniques*, Paris, 1986, particularly pp.29-104.

8 *Councils and the Ecumenical Movement*, WCC studies 5, Geneva, WCC, 1968.

9 This was underlined by the Faith and Order commission responsible for reflection on the subject of conciliarity; cf. the report from the Bristol meeting 1967, Geneva, WCC, 1968.

10 A rapid glance at the complete collection of the reports from 1932 to 1990 confirms this impression. The most complete collection today is the German version, *Dokumente wachsender Übereinstimmung*, H. Meyer, J. Urban and L. Vischer, eds, joined by D. Papandreou in the second volume, 2 vols, Paderborn, 1983 and 1992. The first volume only is translated into English: *Growth in Agreement*, New York, 1984. The other texts appeared in different periodicals.

11 Faith and Order paper no. 111, Geneva, WCC, 1982.

12 The answers have been assembled and published in 6 volumes by Max Thurian, *Churches Respond to BEM*, Faith and Order papers NOS 129, 132, 135, 137, 143, 144, Geneva, WCC, 1986-88.

[13] This misunderstanding of the ecumenical process of reception is found not only in the responses of the churches but also in the individual positions of the theologians. Cf. H. Fischer, "Rezeption in ihrer Bedeutung für Leben und Lehre der Kirche. Vorläufige Erwägungen zu einem undeutlichen Begriff", in *ZThK*, 87, 1990, pp.100-23, in particular pp.103ff.

[14] G. Gassmann, "Die Rezeption der Dialoge", *op. cit.*, proposes five types which we borrow in part.

[15] Quotation from the last text of the third round of this dialogue: *Facing Unity*, 1985.

[16] Cf. the Lutheran-Catholic dialogue on the Lord's supper, 1978 (paras 16,48-51) and the dialogue on the ministry (paras 32,33,39). The first place where this type of formulation was used was the Lutheran/Reformed dialogue in Europe concluded in 1973 by the Leuenberg concord.

[17] *Ibid.*, para. 26.

[18] The difference between the two terms has often been underlined; cf. an important note in the document quoted *Facing Unity*. See also the study of H. Meyer, "Anerkennung, ein ökumenischer Schlüsselbegriff", in *Dialog und Anerkennung*, Beiheft zur *Ökumenischen Rundschau*, 37, 1980, pp.25-41.

[19] Cf. the examples quoted by H. Fischer, in *Rezeption in ihrer Bedeutung für Leben und Lehre der Kirche*, *op. cit.*, pp.115f., and those mentioned by W. Rusch, *Reception: An Ecumenical Opportunity, op. cit.*, pp.45-65.

[20] Cf. the study by Harding Meyer, "Wenn Verluste drohen", in *Lutherische Monatshefte*, 29, 1990, pp.205-208.

[21] W.A. Visser 't Hooft, "Bilanz", in *Ökumenischer Aufbruch. Hauptschriften*, Bd. 2, Stuttgart, 1967, pp.210f.

[22] Cf. for example the study of the Strasbourg Institute for Ecumenical Research, *Local Ecumenism: How Church Unity is Seen and Practised by Congregations*, A. Birmelé, ed., Geneva, WCC, 1984.

[23] Among the numerous studies related to this question we note simply the official dialogues dealing with this problematic: The international Lutheran-Catholic dialogue has devoted two texts to the subject, *Ways to Community*, 1980, and *Facing Unity*, 1985. These highlight well the problems and what is at stake.

[24] For an exposé and study of this problematic, we refer to the work of A. Birmelé and H. Meyer, eds, *Grundkonsens-Grunddifferenz*, Frankfurt, 1992.

[25] For different understandings of the indispensable elements for full communion between churches cf. the study *Communio-Koinonia: A New Testament-Early Christian Concept and Its Contemporary Appropriation and Significance*, Strasbourg, 1990. Also published in *A Commentary on "Ecumenism: The Vision of the ELCA"*, W.G. Rusch, ed., Minneapolis, 1990.

[26] For the value of theological dialogue in Roman Catholic theology, consult the study of Alois Klein, "Rezeption der ökumenischen Dialoge", in *Iustus Iudex*, K. Lüdicke et al., eds, Ludgerus, 1991.

[27] Cf. the acts of these assemblies edited by M. Lienhard, *Zeugnis und Dienst reformatorischer Kirchen im Europa der Gegenwart*, Sigtuna, 1976, Frankfurt 1977; by A. Birmelé, *Konkordie und Kirchengemeinschaft reformatorischer Kirchen im Europa der Gegenwart*, Driebergen, 1981, Frankfurt, 1982; and by A. Birmelé, *Konkordie und Ökumene. Die Leuenberger Kirchengemeinschaft in der gegenwärtigen ökumenischen Situation*, Strasburg, 1987, Frankfurt, 1988.

[28] The Lutheran-Anglican dialogues: Pullach 1972, Cold Ash 1983 and Niagara 1987, and the Anglican-Reformed dialogue "God's Reign and Our Unity", 1984.

[29] The Meissen Agreement. Texts published by the Council for Christian Unity, London, 1992.

[30] *Together in Mission and Ministry: The Porvoo Common Statement*, London, 1993.

[31] *The Condemnations of the Reformation Era: Do They Still Divide?*, K. Lehmann and W. Pannenberg, eds, Minneapolis, 1990.

Reflections on Ecumenical Reception

WILLIAM HENN

Reception in general

"He came to his own, and his own people *received* him not. But to all who *received* him, who believed in his name, he gave power to become children of God" (John 1:11-12). The concept of reception is relatively new as an object of explicit theological reflection. However, it intends to convey something which is absolutely fundamental to the relationship between God and human beings as brought about in Jesus Christ. "Reception" intends to convey that acceptance of the word of God in faith and trust and that assimilation of this word into the life of individual believers and into the body of Christ as a whole, by means of participation in the sacraments and transformation of life, in such a way that individual believers and the church as a community become effective, prophetic signs of the kingdom of God which Jesus came to inaugurate.

In this broad sense, the term "reception" is a general category which, depending upon the specific theological framework one is using, may be roughly equivalent to other concepts such as "faith", "salvation", "conversion", "confession", "reign of God", "tradition", "communion", "mission", "martyrdom" and so forth. Each of these theological categories can be understood as an aspect of Christian existence in which the seed of God's initiating activity on behalf of human salvation falls upon soil which receives the seed in such way that it is able to bear fruit, thirty, sixty and even a hundred fold (cf. Matt. 13:3-9). Some authors who have written about reception in recent years are fond of pointing out the profound congeniality between the theme of reception, on the one hand, and Jesus' parable of the sower, on the other.[1]

At the same time, while we might be delighted by the apparently rich potential of the concept of reception as a theological category, nevertheless there is an aspect of reception which can be troubling, so much so that one of the most famous essays written about reception begins with the words: "Reception – a dangerous theme!"[2] The danger which Yves

Congar believed some Christians might see in the idea of reception was an aspect of it which allows it to be contrasted with simple obedience. While obedience may be understood as "following orders" or "doing what one is told without question", reception includes a much more active nuance. The analogy of eating and digesting is almost unavoidable in reflecting about reception. There is a double transformation involved in such reception: both what is received as well as the receiver are changed in the act of reception.

This, no doubt, is where Congar saw the potential danger of reception. Because it draws attention to the active nature of receiving and hence to the impact of the subject in receiving, this theme could lead in the direction of a subjective relativism. Moreover, since diverse subjects or communities can receive the same message somewhat differently, the activity of various subjects in assimilating that which is received would seem to imply some degree of pluriformity. How can such pluriformity cohere with the unity of the word of God, to which Paul alludes when he insists in Galatians that there is only one gospel, and introduces within Christianity the expression *anathema sit* in reference to those who would preach a different gospel (cf. Gal. 1:6-9)? Reception may also seem to raise difficulties regarding authority within the church. How does the authority of the word of God and the authority of the interpretation of this word by ordained ministers within the community of the church cohere with the active reception of the preached word by intelligent, free, human subjects?

These can be difficult questions to answer. But they do find an adequate answer, I believe, if we think of the church's unity in faith and life in terms of a process of living together in dialogue and communion, with all of the members and ministers cooperating to build up the body, in such a way that the whole matures into the fullness of Christ (cf. Eph. 4:11-16).

Within this general perspective, one needs to situate specific instances of reception, such as the reception of the sacraments or the reception of a teaching of an ecumenical council. Once again, in these specific cases, there is always the element of divine initiative and human acceptance and response. Reception is a moment of communion. Reception of a sacrament, such as baptism, is communion in divine life with all of its various grace-filled aspects. Reception of the doctrine of Nicea – that the word and Son who became flesh is consubstantial with the Father – is communion in faith.

Reception of ecumenical documents

The reception of ecumenical documents is marked by the very unique nature of these documents themselves. They tend to be predominantly doctrinal in nature, having as a primary intention the aim of overcoming divisions in faith. Because of this, ecumenical documents are efforts to express together, in a new way, the unfathomable riches of Christ (cf. Eph. 3:8 and Vatican II, *Unitatis Redintegratio* 11). In this regard they have something in common with the statements of the great ecumenical councils from the first millennium. At the same time, however, one has to keep in mind the rather sharp difference between ecumenical documents and conciliar teachings. Conciliar teachings are determinations of the faith, decided by the church in full communion, which are made so as to clarify the boundaries within which the community is maintained in unity of faith. Ecumenical documents, on the other hand, seek unity in faith between two or more communities which are not yet in full communion; such documents usually provide encouraging indications of the depth and extent of shared faith but also bring into relief whatever conflicting doctrines yet remain to be reconciled. This clarifies a fundamental difference between the reception of ecumenical documents and the reception of conciliar teachings. Ecumenical documents do not claim to achieve that kind of unity in faith which the councils do achieve. They seek an affirmation of unity in faith which is as complete as that made by the ancient church in council, but they do not claim to have arrived at such unanimity or consensus – such believing with one heart and soul (cf. Acts 4:32). This being so, how do the churches receive ecumenical documents which do not yet achieve full unity in faith?

According to Günther Gassman, until recently director of the Faith and Order commission, ecumenical dialogues must be seen within the context of the dynamic nature of the ecumenical movement, which strives to render visible the unity of the church of Jesus Christ.[3] This cannot happen without the reception of what is achieved in ecumenical dialogue. In this sense, dialogue is essentially incomplete without the reception of its results.

But Gassmann proposes a shift in perspective which is most helpful. The aim of dialogue is not to receive or to ratify documents but rather to realize and manifest unity. In light of this, he proceeds to what I would call a "relativization" of ecumenical documents. First of all, the very fact of entering into dialogue, even prior to the production of any agreed statement, is already an act of reception, recognizing the other community as a sister to one's own community with whom, according to the will of Christ, one should be in full communion. Jean Tillard nicely points out that reception can occur at all only on the basis of a communion that already exists.[4] Moreover, the actual text which results from dialogue should also already be seen as a mutual reception of the parties involved, as well as, in many cases, a reception of the ideas expressed in other bilateral or multilateral dialogues. Thus, elements of mutual reception precede the holding of a dialogue and are woven into the text which emerges from the dialogue process. This leads Gassmann to suggest that churches in dialogue should seek above all to "receive" the *dialogue event as a whole*; the official response by church leaders to the text and the use of the text in various ways within each community is only part of this broader reception process.

By situating the reception of ecumenical documents as only one piece within a broader ecumenical reception, Gassmann opens the road-block which would result if the whole dynamism towards Christian unity depended solely on the acceptance of dialogue results which do not yet claim to have achieved full agreement on all relevant points. This broader vision of reception as a more comprehensive process opens the path for realistic intermediate steps forward, which utilize the dialogue documents but which do not require full agreement on all relevant issues.

This comprehensive approach has recently gained acceptance in several official or semi official statements.[5] These statements agree on several points. First of all, they understand the agents of this comprehensive process as including all of the members of the church, specifying the particular roles of church leaders, of the whole body of the faithful and of theologians. This trilogy of the agents of reception has been reiterated by a number of individual authors. Cardinal Willebrands provides one of the best summaries of the various competencies of these subjects when he writes:

> Inasmuch as the entire people of God partakes in the search for and the unfolding of the truth of God's word, all the charisms and services are involved according to their station: the theologians by means of their research activities, the faithful by means of their preserving fidelity and piety, the ecclesial ministries and especially the college of bishops with its function of making binding doctrinal decisions. One can say that ministry and charism, proclamation and theology, magisterial ministry and sense of faith of the people, all act together in the reception process.[6]

Second, this plurality of agents is matched by a plurality of means, as the Lutheran-Catholic statement notes:

> ...the *integration* of dialogue results and insights into the life of the churches occurs in a large variety of ways. The churches' official acceptance and integration of dialogue results will be preceded by a general change of attitude of our churches to each other, as e. g., described in *Facing Unity* (paras 50-54), and by a growing integration of dialogue insights into liturgical life, pastoral care, preaching, theological education and spiritual formation.

There can even be occasional changes and modifications in church law and the official teaching of the churches stemming directly or indirectly from the dialogues.[7]

Third, these statements offer a valuable proposal for addressing the problem posed by the fact that most ecumenical documents contain varying degrees both of agreement and of disagreement. As the sixth forum on bilaterals states:

...where a dialogue has a positive outcome, this represents the discovery of a greater degree of real communion which it may be appropriate to express in some new forms of relationship. As the dialogue is taking place, the dialogue commission ought to give consideration to what practical steps it might recommend to the churches in order to express the agreement they are working out. As the dialogue progresses, the churches themselves should also consider what steps towards deeper communion would be appropriate if they can receive the dialogue positively.[8]

The report goes on to state that, even when the parties are not yet able to arrive at that level of communion needed for sacramental sharing, nevertheless practical steps can be taken to express the "greater degree of communion [that] is being discovered.... acting on these provisional and intermediate results of dialogue" is not only appropriate but can also help clarify the "ultimate goal of full visible unity". What is important here is that the presence of some level of disagreement should not be allowed to completely vitiate the considerable unity in faith which most ecumenical documents express. Appropriate intermediate steps offer a means to move closer on the basis of the agreement achieved, without disregarding the fact that some important doctrinal points still remain divisive.

A final comment about the specific nature of the reception of ecumenical documents, which is mentioned to some degree in these recent statements which we have been considering but which is developed more fully in the contributions of individual authors, is the spiritual climate needed for reception. Paul-Werner Scheele has argued that if, as Vatican II states, spiritual ecumenism is the "soul" of ecumenism, then without this soul the ecumenical movement will effectively be dead.[9] He goes on to suggest that the considerable mutual recognition of baptism among Christians could provide a foundation for developing a common baptismal spirituality which could help believers to more fully recognize that what unites them is much stronger than what divides them. He encourages the fostering of basic spiritual attitudes such as the effort to listen to others, to be faithful to one's tradition and ancestors, to be open and optimistic. Shared activities in the areas of repentance and conversion, confession of faith and prayer, liturgical celebration and proclamation, catechesis and theology can all help to promote a reception-favourable climate.

Conclusion

The reception of ecumenical documents moves towards its own demise. The greater the reception achieved, the less will be the need for additional ecumenical dialogues and for the reception of documents which would result from them. But, ironically, ongoing dialogue may turn out to be one of the lasting legacies of the ecumenical movement. The ecumenical movement was largely responsible for initiating and sustaining the discussion of reception. But this discussion has not only assisted divided Christian communities on the way to fuller communion. In addition, it has greatly enriched ecclesiology, for it has shown that ongoing dialogue and its reception are intrinsic to communion, to tradition and to the very being of the church. Even if the day should come when "ecumenical" dialogues have been superseded, dialogue and reception will remain, just as they always had been, though perhaps in a less explicitly acknowledged or institutionally structured way. Unity in faith is always the result of a process.[10] It involves receiving the word of God and, at the same time, receiving those companions who also welcomed the word. This reception of the word and of those others who have also received it, finds efficacious symbolization in the celebration of the sacraments, especially in the eucharist. When we at last can receive the eucharist together, not only will we receive Jesus Christ; we will also receive one another. This is that for which Jesus himself prayed, when he asked his Father "that they may all be one" (John 17:21).

NOTES

[1] For example, see P.-W. Scheele, "Die Rezeption ökumenischer Dokumente als geistliches Geschehen", in K. Aland and S. Meurer, eds, *Wissenschaft und Kirche*, Bielefeld, 1989, pp.266-67; and W. Beinert, "Die Rezeption und ihre Bedeutung für Leben und Lehre der Kirche", in W. Beinert, ed., *Glaube als Zustimmung*, Freiburg, 1991, p.24.
[2] Y. Congar, "La réception comme réalité ecclésiologique", in *RSPT*, 56, 1972, p.369.
[3] Several short works express Gassmann's approach to the reception of ecumenical documents: "Rezeption im ökumenischen Kontext", in *Ökumenische Rundschau*, 26, 1977, pp.314-27; "Die Rezeption der Dialoge", in *ibid.*, p.33, 1984, pp.357-68; and "The Official Responses to the Lima Document", in *Ecumenical Trends*, 15, 1986, pp.186-88.
[4] J.M.R. Tillard, "Fondements ecclésiologiques de la recéption oecuménique", in *Toronto Journal of Theology*, 3, 1987, pp.37-39.
[5] See Anglican-Roman Catholic Committees of South CA, "On the Process of Reception", in *Ecumenical Trends*, 15, pp.188-90; Joint Staff Group of the Pontifical Council for Promoting Christian Unity and the Lutheran World Federation, "Strategies for Reception: Perspectives on the Reception of Documents Emerging from the Lutheran-Catholic International Dialogue", in

The Pontifical Council for Promoting Christian Unity, Information Service, 89, 1992, 11, pp.42-45; "Sixth Forum on Bilateral Dialogues. I: Aspects of Reception; II: Authority within the Process of Reception; III: Opportunities and Difficulties within the Present Situation of Reception", in *Sixth Forum on Bilateral Dialogues*, Geneva, WCC, 1995, pp.5-21 (the second of these reports includes extensive quotations from the Pontifical Council for Promoting Christian Unity, *Directory for the Application of Principles and Norms on Ecumenism*, Vatican City, 1993, paras 178-82); and finally, John Paul II, *Ut Unum Sint*, 1995, paras 80-81.

6 Johannes Cardinal Willebrands, "The Ecumenical Dialogue and its Reception", in *One in Christ*, 21, 1985, p.222. See also W. Marrevee, "How Do the Churches read a Convergence Text?", in M. A. Fahey, ed., *Catholic Perspectives on Baptism, Eucharist and Ministry*, Lanham, MD, 1986, pp.45-62; T.P. Rausch, "Reception Past and Present", in *Theological Studies*, 47, 1986, p.502; and C. Andrews, "Reception: A Plain Person's Survey", in *One in Christ*, 27, 1991, pp.71-76. For the most extensive discussion of the inter-relation of ministers, community and theologians in the process of reception, see the "Ergebnisse und Perspektiven" of the Societas Oecumenica symposium on "Theological Consensus and Ecclesial Reception", in P. Lengsfeld and H.-G. Stobbe, eds, *Theologischer Konsens und Kirchenspaltung*, Stuttgart, 1981, pp.143-58. A most interesting attempt to promote the reception of ecumenical documents by the community as a whole is J.T. Ford and D.J. Swan, eds, *Twelve Tales Untold: A Study Guide for Ecumenical Reception*, Grand Rapids, MI, 1993. This book presents material from ecumenical dialogues by means of stories from everyday experience, so as to provide an instrument for discussion at the level of the local community.

7 "Strategies for Reception", *op. cit.*, para. 7.

8 *Sixth Forum on Bilateral Dialogues*, *op. cit.*, 6.

9 Scheele, *op. cit.*, p.260.

10 I have tried to demonstrate this in *One Faith: Biblical and Patristic Contributions toward Understanding Unity in Faith*, Mahwah, NJ, 1995.

Reception: A Canadian Perspective

DONNA GEERNAERT

Reception has been called "the new holy word" in ecumenism.[1] While this designation may be disputed, the centrality of the concept of reception in the current phase of the search for Christian unity cannot be denied. The ecumenical significance of the term reflects its use in earlier canonical discussions about the authority of councils or synods, the validation of legislative action in and among the churches, and the validity of baptism, eucharist and ordination within heretic communities.[2] Yet a review of biblical terminology and ecclesial history indicates that "reception" is correlated to "tradition" and "communion" and "is not first of all a canonical, but a theological category".[3] Further, it is evident that the reception of conciliar decisions is not limited to agreement on texts but includes "the unending process of interpreting these decisions in theology, proclamation and the devotional life".[4] Thus, reception is a vital spiritual process which takes place under the guidance of the Holy Spirit. "The churches can indeed be open to reception, but they must not conclude that they can orchestrate it."[5]

While acknowledging that the reception process cannot be orchestrated, ecumenical reflection over the past few years has attempted to identify some instruments or suggest a few programmes that might render the churches more receptive to the guidance of the Holy Spirit. In this context, a Joint Staff Group of the Pontifical Council for Promoting Christian Unity and the Lutheran World Federation has published a working paper on "Strategies for Reception". The text affirms that "it is appropriate to distinguish basically two, often overlapping phases" in the reception process: "the *response* of the churches to the dialogues and their results and the *integration* of these results and insights into the life of the churches, taking into account the responses of the churches".[6] Since the ultimate goal of reception is to bring separated churches into full unity, moreover, official responses from the churches will have a certain priority. But, as Emmanuel Sullivan asserts, "the practical involvement of lay members of the churches" is "essential to the reception process".[7] Thus, both pastoral leaders and lay members are involved in each of these two inter-related phases of the reception process.

For the purposes of this panel presentation, I have been asked to reflect "from my official position as a secretary for a conference of bishops" on the way in which documents are received and on the processes which help or hinder their reception. In order to make the presentation as concrete as possible, I propose to use the WCC's *Baptism, Eucharist and Ministry* document as a kind of "case study". My particular focus will be on the "baptism" section of the document and I will look at its reception both within the framework of the Canadian Conference of Catholic Bishops (CCCB) and through the activities of the Canadian Council of Churches (CCC).

Reception: CCCB process

The working paper on "Strategies for Reception" outlines procedures for reception in the Roman Catholic Church as follows:

> ... reception must reflect the bonds of communion based on shared faith and sacramental life that exist within the whole church. Local churches are presided over by bishops who are in communion with one another and with the bishop of Rome, who within the collegiality of bishops presides over the whole church. It is appropriate that the whole church participates in reception. The Pontifical Council for Promoting Christian Unity, as the office charged with promoting Christian unity on the international level, would coordinate the development of official Catholic responses to ecumenical documents, taking into account views expressed by the local churches and, when doctrine is involved, collaborating with the Congregation for the Doctrine of the Faith in order to bring a response to its final form.[8]

At the CCCB, the task of coordinating "official Catholic responses to ecumenical documents" falls within the mandate of the Episcopal Commission for Ecumenism. Documents are received from the PCPCU, a consultation is initiated, replies are synthesized, members of the commission, executive and/or permanent council are consulted and the final response is then forwarded to Rome.

In December 1982 the PCPCU forwarded the *Baptism, Eucharist and Ministry* text to the CCCB with an accompanying letter calling attention to the questions at the end of the preface and requesting a response particularly to the first and last of these: How far is the Catholic faith recognizable in the text, and what are your suggestions for the continuation of the work of Faith and Order in its long-term search for a "common expression of the apostolic faith today"? Also enclosed was a copy of a paper by Jean Tillard entitled "The Theological Axes of the Lima Convergences on the Eucharist".

On 20 January 1983, these documents were sent to the members of the Episcopal Commission for Ecumenism with the suggestion that they should be a topic for consideration at the next meeting. In March 1983, the texts were sent to the members of the Canadian Roman Catholic-United Church Dialogue for study and response. On 2 December 1983, the Commission staff person initiated a consultation with faculties of theology and major seminaries. Deans and directors of Catholic theological institutions were asked to review the BEM document from "a specific Roman Catholic point of view", to consider how far the Catholic faith is recognizable in the text and to make appropriate suggestions for the continuation of the work of Faith and Order. In February 1984, a second letter was sent to these same theological institutions requesting a "progress report" by the end of June and a final report by mid-December of 1984. From the correspondence on file, it is evident that the Commission's request was taken seriously and a number of study sessions were held in several Catholic theological institutions.

At the CCCB plenary assembly held in October 1984, there was a half-day study session for the bishops on BEM. The session included a presentation by Jean Tillard on "L'Eglise catholique interpellée par l'accord de Lima", and workshop discussion on three questions: (1) As bishop, how do I accept the positions taken in BEM? (2) In what way do these positions assist or question the present pastoral situation in my diocese? (3) Identify one or two ecumenical areas which could be of more concern to the CCCB. Workshop discussion was recorded, compiled and synthesized to assist in developing the CCCB response to the BEM document.

In spring 1985, replies from the theology faculties and seminaries were synthesized and combined with the results of the plenary workshop discussions to prepare a draft CCCB response. In April, this draft was circulated to give the bishops an opportunity to vote and/or make further comments on the proposed response. In light of the bishops' comments, the text was forwarded to the PCPCU at the beginning of July 1985.

In September 1985, the Episcopal Commission for Ecumenism forwarded a recommendation to the CCCB permanent council that

> In the context of the CCCB's becoming an associate member of the Canadian Council of Churches, bishops be encouraged to promote the study of BEM in their respective dioceses. Wherever possible, local ministerial associations could be invited to spend time on BEM. Other groups could also be invited to study the text with the help of appropriate resources.

This recommendation was unanimously endorsed by the permanent council and the Ecumenism Commission was asked to suggest concrete ways to implement it. In August 1986, at the request of the Commission for Ecumenism, a "Study Guide on BEM" was sent out to all bishops, diocesan directors of ecumenism and presidents of diocesan ecumenism commissions. This "Study Guide" offered a number of options for study of the text as well as identifying a variety of resources to assist local groups in their study and discussion.

In the fall of 1987, the PCPCU's "Catholic Response to *Baptism, Eucharist and Ministry*" was forwarded to the bishops with an accompanying letter which explained the process used in preparing the response and outlined Catholic participation in the WCC Faith and Order commission.

Reception: ecumenical process

Canada is a vast land with a northern climate. Settlement stretches along the southern border leaving large parts of the interior and the north sparsely populated. Canadian society is a multilingual, multicultural mosaic of people from diverse ethnic origins. Respecting our history, however, the country is constitutionally bilingual with English and French as the two officially recognized languages.

According to Canadian government statistics, approximately 83 percent of the population identifies itself as Christian. While there are more than thirty Christian denominations represented in Canada, five of these (Roman Catholic, United Church, Anglican, Presbyterian, Lutheran) account for 80 percent of this number. Slightly less than half of the Christian population is Roman Catholic with about 50% of these being French-speaking. A major proportion of the Francophone population lives in Quebec. Since the other churches of Canada are mainly Anglophone with their numbers residing throughout the other nine provinces, Canadian ecumenism faces a peculiar set of geographic and linguistic challenges.

Before the official reception of dialogue results can take place, according to "Strategies for Reception", there must be "a general change of attitude of our churches to each other".[9] This preliminary step in the reception process occurs when churches break out of their isolation, when "a particular church acknowledges that it is neither the sole bearer of Christian truth nor the only witness to Christian faith".[10] For members of many Canadian churches who live in remote or sparsely populated areas of the country, this has not seemed a particularly difficult step to take. Further, in light of the well developed tradition of Christian social activism in Canada, it is not surprising to find that the churches' initial cooperative ventures tended to address a variety of justice issues. While collaborative efforts on specific social concerns have led churches to increased mutual understanding and respect, participation in the Canadian Council of Churches' commission on Faith and Order has allowed for a more focused reflection on ecclesial relationships.

Canadian Council of Churches

The Faith and Order commission of the Canadian Council of Churches (CCC) was established in 1950, six years after the Council's own formation. Faith and Order was considered a more delicate matter than many of the justice issues on which the Canadian churches were beginning to collaborate and there was a tendency to proceed with caution. In the early years, meetings consisted of the members' taking turns to present papers to the group, usually in series around a selected theme.

Roman Catholic participation in the work of the commission began during the Second Vatican Council, and in 1969 the CCC triennial assembly recommended that fully official Roman Catholic representation should be sought. The proposal was sent to the Canadian Conference of Catholic Bishops where it was favourably received. By January 1971, a new by-law had been approved and in March of that year a six-member delegation was appointed.[11]

Early in 1972, the commission took up the topic of baptism with a view to providing documentation that would support mutual recognition among several churches. Within a few months, the commission was able to send a report to the churches with a two-part proposal: (1) that baptisms conferred with flowing water accompanied by the trinitarian formula be accepted as valid; (2) that a common certificate of baptism be agreed upon and adopted. In September 1975, five churches (United, Presbyterian, Lutheran, Anglican and Roman Catholic) announced that they had reached an understanding through which any one church would recognize the validity of baptisms conferred according to the established norms of the other churches. Although the commission continued to work on the question of a common baptismal certificate, agreement could not be reached and in 1980 the matter was dropped.

Following the World Council of Churches' sixth assembly in 1983, the commission decided that one of its primary tasks would be to encourage study of the *Baptism, Eucharist and Ministry* document. With this in mind, a consultation on the pastoral and practical implications of recognizing in that document an expression of "the faith of the church through the ages" was planned for November 1985. Among the consultation's recommendations for the ongoing work of the commission was the suggestion that, given the agreement already achieved on the meaning and practice of baptism, a common catechesis on baptism might be developed. In the spring of 1986, the commission began work on this new project by comparing baptismal liturgies from eight of the member churches. At the CCC triennial assembly of 1988, an outline of the project and some of the sections were reviewed in workshop groups. The text, *Initiation into Christ: Ecumenical Reflections and Common Teaching on Preparation for Baptism*, was published in 1992.

The publication of *Initiation into Christ* marks an advance in reception of the ecumenical study of baptism in Canada. In the first place, the process which produced this document was able to include a number of new participants: Coptic, Greek and Ukrainian Orthodox, as well as Mennonites, Salvation Army and Society of Friends. Second, Baptists, who had felt marginalized in the earlier discussion, were fully involved in the development of this document.[12] Finally, the text is oriented towards use as: a resource for ecumenical dialogue and study, a five-session study guide for congregations or parishes, a reflective Lenten study, a resource for pastors in pre-marriage and baptism preparation, a unit on baptism in a confirmation or catechetical curriculum, a resource for high-school religion teachers. As such, it represents a concrete attempt to promote "the *integration* of dialogue insights into liturgical life, pastoral care, preaching, theological education and spiritual formation".[13]

While there is much to celebrate in the Canadian churches' efforts to promote the ecumenical reception of BEM, the possibility of new divisions arising out of contemporary concerns illustrates the fragility of what has been achieved. In particular, the CCCB's Episcopal Commission for Ecumenism has received reports of divergent practice in the use of the Trinitarian formula among members of some of the churches who had joined the 1975 agreement on mutual recognition of baptisms. At the CCCB's request, this matter was brought to the attention of the CCC's commission on Faith and Witness in the spring of 1995.[14] The members of the Faith and Witness commission agreed to survey the position and practice in their respective churches on the use of the trinitarian formula in baptism. At the commission's fall meeting, there was an extended discussion of this question and it was agreed that a report should be forwarded to the CCC's governing board. In spring 1996, the commission reviewed its earlier discussion and approved a brief statement: "The CFW has surveyed the churches represented on the commission, and finds there is no departure of any significance to the use of the formula as stated in the CCC agreement of 1972."[15] At the governing board meeting of 15-17 May 1996, the commission's statement was discussed and some amendments were suggested. There will be ongoing discussion at the commission's fall meeting and the members of the CCCB's Episcopal Commission for Ecumenism must be informed of the CCC's action in response to their request. At this time, it is difficult to see how the legitimate concerns of all of the dialogue partners can be met.

Bilateral dialogues

From the fall of 1982 until the fall of 1984, reception of the *Baptism, Eucharist and Ministry* document was given careful consideration by two of the Canadian bilateral dialogues. In addition to formal inter-church discussions through these two dialogue groups, moreover, there are indications of an informal sharing of responses among churches in Canada. This kind of information sharing which has characterized inter-church relations in Canada for a number of years seems to highlight the de facto ecclesial recognition that has been achieved.

Beginning in October 1982, the Roman Catholic-United Church Dialogue Group devoted three meetings to the discussion of this topic. The dialogue group prepared a response, dated Pentecost 1983, which was forwarded to the two sponsoring churches with the request that they concur in its being transmitted to the Faith and Order secretariat and to the Vatican Secretariat for Christian Unity. The 25-page response was seen by the members of the dialogue group as a contribution to "the widest possible involvement of the whole people of God" in the spiritual process of receiving the text. The response was forwarded to the CCCB's Episcopal Commission for Ecumenism in October 1983. On 8 May 1985, the text was sent, as requested, to both Geneva and Rome.[16]

The Anglican-Roman Catholic Dialogue of Canada began its discussion of the *Baptism, Eucharist and Ministry* document in April 1983. After spending seven sessions on the topic, the minutes of 23 November 1984 conclude:

> While it would be good to see where BEM and ARCIC are in accord and where they correct one another, it is the churches that are required to state their reception of BEM. As a national dialogue group we are not directly involved in this process and for the time being, therefore, we will not continue with the drafting of a response.

From a review of the minutes of these meetings, it seems evident that this group's need to focus on its response to the ARCIC *Final Report* did inhibit its ability to consider the BEM text.

Reception: involvement of the whole people of God

For theological agreements to be translated into practice as envisioned by the reception process, a broad involvement of the whole people of God will be required. As churches enter ecumenism's reception phase, Karl Staalsett remarks:

Theologically qualified work remains a must... However, our dialogue must in the future be broadened... This is the time to involve the great resources of the lay people, social scientists, psychologists, pedagogues, philosophers, industrialists and workers in various fields, men and women, to address the many non-theological issues which divide our communities of faith or impede our common witness and service.[17]

Further, lay involvement means more than setting up study groups for the integration of dialogue results. According to Rusch, "ecumenical reception will force all churches to rethink the active role of the people of God".[18]

The *Directory for the Application of Principles and Norms on Ecumenism*, affirms that "the members of the people of God according to their role or charism must be involved in this critical process", and urges that appropriate ways be found to bring the results of dialogues to the attention of all members of the church.[19]

In the five-year period following the publication of BEM, there were many different approaches to presenting the document and encouraging reflection on its implications. Public lectures by Jean Tillard, staff from the Canadian Centre for Ecumenism, and other "ecumenical experts" were often well attended. Articles and interviews in the religious and some secular media attempted to popularize the document's contents. In May 1984, the *Prairie Messenger* published the text along with a series of articles and a study guide. There were a number of study sessions of varying lengths sponsored by local dialogue groups, theological colleges or ecumenical centres. In the fall of 1984, for example, the Saskatoon Centre for Ecumenism sponsored a five-week study which had some 75-90 participants and produced a written report which was forwarded to the CCCB. On a more popular level, the Canadian Christian festival of 15-17 May 1986 included a number of workshops on the BEM text.

Did these efforts assist in the reception of BEM by the whole people of God? While it is difficult to assess results, it is evident that some integration has occurred. The *Baptism, Eucharist and Ministry* document is being used as a text in some theology courses. The CCC's text on *Initiation into Christ* is being used by some pastors in confirmation classes and in baptismal preparation. Challenges to reception as outlined in "Strategies for Reception" are also evident. In the Canadian context, three of these could be highlighted: (1) the aim of visible unity is played down in favour of simple cooperation; (2) there is a lack of interest in ecumenical documents dealing with doctrinal expressions of Christian truth; (3) dialogue documents couched in technical theological terminology are difficult to communicate to those who are unfamiliar with such language.[20]

Conclusion

For this presentation, I was asked to reflect on the process of reception from the perspective of "my official position as a secretary for a conference of bishops". One point to be noted is that "my official position" includes a number of variables. In my capacity as director of ecumenical and interfaith relations, I serve as staff to the Episcopal Commission for Ecumenism and thus play a role in coordinating, drafting, and revising official CCCB responses to dialogue documents. From 1984 to 1988, my CCCB staff function also included joint staffing of the CCC's commission on Faith and Order. This implied involvement in planning a major consultation on BEM and in drafting the text of *Initiation into Christ*. Also, my staff position at the CCCB requires direct involvement in staffing and helping to set agendas for the Canadian bilateral dialogues. In all of these roles, the major focus of my work has been on promoting response and integration at an official or leadership level. While I am convinced of the importance of response and integration for lay members, the lack of direct contact has inhibited my effectiveness in this area.

From my perspective, what helps or hinders the reception process? Time is a major factor. Consultations with theological institutions or bishops require a good deal of time. Time is needed to compile and synthesize the results of a consultation. Even more importantly, time is needed to reflect on the results of a consultation before and during the drafting of a response. For a broad based consultation involving the laity, moreover, the style in which a document is written is very significant. A large part of the success with the reception of BEM can be traced to its inviting style and its attempt to use relatively simple language. Finally, the recognition that reception is a spiritual process which requires nothing less than conversion, serves as a kind of reality check. What may be most helpful in this context is prayer, patience and a sense of humour.

NOTES

[1] T. Ryan, "Unpacking the New Holy Word: Reception", in *Ecumenism*, 72, 1983, pp.27-34.
[2] A. Houtepen, "Reception, Tradition, Communion", in M. Thurian, ed., *Ecumenical Perspectives on Baptism, Eucharist and Ministry*, Faith and Order paper no. 116, Geneva, WCC, 1983, p.144. W.G. Rusch, *Reception: An Ecumenical Opportunity*, Philadelphia, Fortress, 1988, pp.29-31, compares "classical" and "ecumenical" reception.
[3] Houtepen, *op. cit.*, p.149. U. Kuhn, "Reception – An Imperative and an Opportunity," in Thurian, *op. cit.*, pp.165-66, discusses active and passive roots of the term.
[4] Kuhn, *op. cit.*, p.167.
[5] Rusch, *op. cit.*, p.63.
[6] Joint Staff Group of the Pontifical Council for Promoting Christian Unity and the Lutheran World Federation, "Strategies for Reception", in *Information Service*, 80, 1992, p.42.

[7] E. Sullivan, "Reception: Factor and Moment in Ecumenism", in *Ecumenical Trends*, 15, 1986, pp.109-10. The text continues: "What is needed is *some experience* of the unity of the church 'even now, but not yet.' Only when such experience is possessed by a notable number of the faithful in all the churches of the ecumenical movement can the reception process be validated in terms of an honest *sensus fidelium*, a real growth in faith on the part of the faithful."

[8] "Strategies for Reception", p.43. See also J. Radano, "Response and Reception in the Catholic Church", in *Mid-Stream*, 33, 1996, pp.71-103, for a more detailed review of Roman Catholic procedures.

[9] "Strategies for Reception", p.42.

[10] Rusch, *op. cit.*, pp.65-66.

[11] From 1976 to 1988, the CCCB provided joint staff support for the work of the commission. From 1990 to the present, a CCCB representative has served as commission chair.

[12] The "Report from the Canadian Faith and Order Commission to the Joint Working Group" of May 1972 included a two-page appendix in which the Baptist Federation of Canada offers an explanation for its decision to dissociate itself from the report.

[13] "Strategies for Reception", p.42.

[14] At the May 1989 meeting of the CCC general board, the commission's name was changed from Faith and Order to Faith and Witness. This represents a broadening of its mandate to include a concern for mission and participation in interfaith relations. Recent changes in CCC structures have highlighted the importance of Faith and Order questions for interchurch relations.

[15] The discrepancy in dates stems from the fact that the report was submitted to the churches in May 1972 but the agreement was announced in September 1975.

[16] It may be of interest to note that the current topic under discussion in the RC-UC dialogue is the question of trinitarian language.

[17] K. Staalsett, "Entering Ecumenism's Reception Phase", in *Origins*, 22, 1993, p.746.

[18] Rusch, *op. cit.*

[19] *Directory for the Application of Principles and Norms on Ecumenism*, Pontificium Consilium ad Christianorum Unitatem Fovendam, Vatican City, 1993, no. 179, p.83.

[20] "Strategies for Reception", p.44.

Plenary Discussion

The discussion of the theme of reception during the meeting was divided into two phases. First, participants exchanged in small groups their experience of reception of Faith and Order documents in their own contexts, after which in a plenary session the most important points discussed were brought together. Reception was seen to be fundamentally a hermeneutical process which is a complex of several stages – speaking, hearing, understanding and agreeing common action. It concerns above all how the insights of ecumenical dialogues are put into practice in local situations. The process of reception has two directions – the discussion at international level of the insights of local churches and the receiving of the international dialogues by local churches. In part, bilateral and multilateral dialogues are a reception of events on a congregational level. Therefore an important element in the understanding of reception is the nature of authority. What role have those who exercise authority in the reception process? What structures of authority are helpful? A frequent block to the reception process is mis-communication and at times dependence on the interest of individual persons. A duel problem becomes evident – the need for texts to be written in a simpler manner and, on the other hand, the need of universities for a high level of text for discussion. It was stressed that ecumenism should be a compulsory subject for the formation of theologians and pastors.

The second phase of the discussion was in the plenary dealing with the papers on the theme presented above. The following points were made: the addressees of the Faith and Order studies need to be clearly identified and the purpose clearly stated. In principle, the texts are addressed to the churches, but some are for specific groups or institutions of the churches. It was emphasized that reception concerns discernment and should aid the process of seeking to discern God's will concerning the unity of the church. In the light of this discernment, conversion or metanoia becomes possible at a final stage of reception.

The Church as Koinonia: An Ecclesiology Study

NEVILLE CALLAM

In the introduction to the first in a series of four preparatory texts, issued before the inaugural assembly in 1948 of the World Council of Churches, we read the following:

> The fundamental problem of the church is the existence of the churches. This is not an abstract theological proposition; it is our admission of a fact of life... There is no agreed Christian interpretation of the doctrine of the church.[1]

Of course, this was no new discovery. Already in the history of the church concern had been expressed repeatedly over the precise definition of the nature, unity and mission of the church. Indeed, the primary concern of Faith and Order has always been with ecclesiological issues and, as John Zizioulas once put it, "ecclesiology is a subject which is... omnipresent in ecumenical theological discussion".[2] It was important, however, that at the very inaugural assembly of the WCC the ecclesiological problem was put directly before the participants.

The landmark *Baptism, Eucharist and Ministry* (BEM) text, adopted by Faith and Order at Lima, Peru, in 1982, has become a celebrated ecumenical document. In the publication in 1990 of the *Report on the Process and Responses to BEM*, the need is admitted for a careful study of the "many different presuppositions but also convergences regarding the nature of the church".[3] A call is issued for future Faith and Order work to include "a major study" on ecclesiology.[4]

> Such an ecclesiology in an ecumenical perspective must take into account the various ideas of the church which reflect the churches' different self-understanding and their views on the nature of the church and its unity. It also requires the search for basic ecclesiological principles which could provide common perspectives for the churches' different ecclesiologies and serve as a framework for their convergence.[5]

To be sure, the meeting of the plenary commission of Faith and Order, held in Budapest, Hungary, in 1989, had already determined that the new phase of Faith and Order work should treat with "Ecumenical Perspectives on Ecclesiology". This decision to focus on ecclesiology was reaffirmed at the plenary commission which convened at the end of the fifth world conference on Faith and Order, held in Santiago de Compostela, Spain, in 1993.

Between these two meetings of the plenary commission, a significant consultation on "The Unity We Seek" and "Ecumenical Perspectives" was held in 1990 at Etchmiadzin, Armenia, in the former Soviet Union,[6] where a draft was prepared of what eventually came to be known as the Canberra statement, "The Koinonia of the Church: Gift and Calling". The consultation also produced comments on a draft outline for a future project on the "Nature and Mission of the Church: Ecumenical Perspectives on Ecclesiology". The standing commission meeting in Dunblane, Scotland, in 1990, received the report of the Etchmiadzin consultation and revised the statement on the purpose of the ecclesiology study to read as follows:

> The purpose of the study is not to develop a detailed ecclesiological treatise or even an ecumenical ecclesiology. Rather, its aim is to bring together basic ecclesiological perspectives which have emerged in ecumenical dialogues (particularly in the three main studies of Faith and Order) and which could lead to a convergent vision on the nature, unity and mission of the church.
>
> Such a study should consider how the presently separated churches and their traditions are related to the one church of Christ. Can the separate ecclesiologies be transformed in such a way that the remaining differences become complementary rather than being mutually exclusive?[7]

When the standing commission met at Crêt-Bérard in 1994, it took note of the fact that the fifth world conference on Faith and Order called for future work to be done on ecclesiology.[8] In the "Conspectus of Studies for the Future", the major study programme was identified as "The Church as Koinonia: An Ecumenical Study". The title "Ecumenical Perspectives on Ecclesiology" was changed owing to the desire to avoid the impression that Faith and Order was seeking to create "one ecumenical ecclesiology for the whole of Christendom".[9] A note of warning was sounded regarding "the prospect of putting too much into the ecclesiology study, or, conversely, of being so diffuse that the work would not hold together".[10] The linkage to the ecclesiology study of the other facets of Faith and Order work, as outlined in the conspectus, was also emphasized.

In May 1994, a consultation was held in Dublin, Ireland, where the focus was on issues already identified, especially at Dunblane[11] and at Crêt-Bérard,[12] as some areas of concern, namely: apostolicity and catholicity; forms of authority and decision-making; the place and mission of the church in God's saving purpose.

An attempt was made to bring the themes in line with the expressed centre of the study so that the material produced would form "building blocks" for the ongoing study on ecclesiology. As the Dublin report indicates, the meeting analyzed: apostolicity and catholicity as elements of life and faith of the church as koinonia; forms of authority and decision-making in the service of the church as koinonia, and the place and mission of the church as koinonia in the saving purpose of God.

At a subsequent consultation in Codrington, Barbados, in November 1994, work was done in pursuance of a provisional outline of a future convergence text on ecclesiology. The outline depended largely upon the "Perspectives and Aspects" proposed by Faith and Order staff as the content of the study at the consultation at Etchmiadzin in July 1990. The procedure also followed in part the Etchmiadzin suggestion, ratified at Dunblane, i.e. developing a draft outline after assembling and summarizing extant materials on ecclesiology.[13] A progress report of the work on ecclesiology was presented to the standing commission meeting in Aleppo, Syria, in 1995. Later that same year, the ecclesiology core group met at Annecy, France, and fitted the "building blocks" produced at Dublin and Barbados into a schema based on the framework of the Canberra statement.

In employing the framework of a statement of an assembly of the World Council of Churches, not only will the reception/critical appropriation of the Canberra statement be assisted, but also it is hoped that the churches will be encouraged by this to grow towards a greater degree of visible unity.

Earlier this year, the meeting in Bangkok, Thailand, of the Faith and Order board (formerly standing commission) affirmed the direction of the ecclesiology study and reaffirmed the importance of relating to the study insights drawn from the work on hermeneutics, koinonia in prayer and worship, and ecclesiology and ethics. Insights from studies dealing with, for example, the ministries of women, episcope-episcopacy, and the ministry of primacy should also be appropriated for the ecclesiology study.

At the Bangkok meeting, the preliminary Annecy text was discussed and many suggestions were made for its development. Work started on this process has not yielded a sufficiently mature text for presentation at this conference. What we present, therefore, is the preliminary Annecy text based on the framework of the Canberra statement. This text, representing an initial phase of the work on ecclesiology, represents an illumination of the Canberra statement. Following the discussion both at Bangkok and at this plenary commission meeting, and the various other inputs that have already been made and, during this week, will be determined as necessary contributions to the process, the text will eventually be developed into a more substantial convergence text.

The hope is that such a convergence text will be instrumental in helping the churches recognize the *church* in themselves and in others, thereby enabling progress towards the visible unity of the church.

NOTES

¹ See *Man's Disorder and God's Design*, vol. 1, New York, Harper, n.d., p.17. Although this question was not discussed directly in the assembly itself, it is important to note that it was in the minds of those helping to prepare for it.
² "Suggestions for a Plan of Study on Ecclesiology", in *Faith and Order 1985-1989: The Commission Meeting at Budapest 1989*, Thomas Best, ed., Geneva, WCC, 1990, p.209.
³ *Baptism, Eucharist and Ministry 1982-1990: Report on the Process and Responses*, Faith and Order paper no. 149, Geneva, WCC, 1990, p.147.
⁴ *Ibid.*, p.148.
⁵ *Ibid.*
⁶ See *Minutes of the Standing Commission, Dunblane, Scotland*, Faith and Order paper no. 152, Geneva, WCC/Faith and Order, 1990, pp.26-37.
⁷ *Ibid.*, p.70.
⁸ See, for example, Santiago report, section I, para. 34 and recommendation 8; section III, paras 29-31 and recommendation 2; section IV, para. 38: *On the Way to Fuller Koinonia: Official Report of the Fifth World Conference on Faith and Order*, Thomas F. Best and Günther Gassmann, eds, Faith and Order paper no. 166, Geneva, WCC, 1994.
⁹ See *Minutes of the Standing Commission, Crêt-Bérard*, Faith and Order paper no. 167, Geneva, WCC/Faith and Order, 1994, p.73.
¹⁰ *Ibid.*, p.82.
¹¹ See *Minutes*, Dunblane, *op. cit.*, pp.33-35.
¹² See *Minutes*, Crêt-Bérard, *op. cit.*, p.74.
¹³ See *Minutes*, Dunblane, *op. cit.*, pp.70-71.

Reflections on Ecclesiology

Introduction to the Study

SUSANNE HEINE

My setting is the Lutheran church in Austria and six years' experience of the Reformed church of the canton of Zurich in Switzerland. What is present-day Austria sided about 90 percent with the Reformation in the 16th century, and was forcibly re-Catholicized by the Habsburg rulers in the 17th century. Today's Protestant church (Lutheran and Reformed) is a minority church in diaspora, which owes its existence to the imperial act of toleration of 1791, and continues to have difficulties today in being culturally part of a setting marked by Catholicism. Almost 80 percent of the population is Roman Catholic, 4 percent is Protestant, and the other non-Catholic churches are minorities within that minority.

What issues relevant to ecclesiology arise out of this history for today's ecumenical situation? I would like to make ten comments on the WCC's ecclesiology documents and mention some points which could perhaps be filled out and further developed.

1. My historical background demonstrates that political factions strongly determine the self-understanding and social setting of the churches. It is often difficult to disentangle political history from faith and confession, but it could be significant to make the effort to define more closely the essential theological characteristics of the church. This would result in a greater awareness of political factors, and reflection on them, for much mutual resentment arises more out of politics than theology.

2. The perception of how others see us from outside could help us to see ourselves in the mirror others hold up to us, not only other churches but also wider secular society. At a time when institutions are in crisis

and privatization is taking place in the economic realm, the church has become in the eyes of many an institution which can be dispensed with as regards their personal faith. It is rather perceived as only one bureaucratic institution among others. This is shown, for example, by the numbers leaving the church. Every year between 30,000 and 40,000 Christians in Austria leave their church. The percentage of Christians in urban areas has already sunk to below 50 percent. The second largest "confessional group" are those with no religion, while the Muslims come third. The situation in Switzerland is similar.

Confronted with this situation, how can we credibly communicate that the church is more than an institution?

3. In my situation, we see that confessional differences meet with incomprehension and people thus lose interest in Christian ecumenism. In contrast, there is increased interest in other religions, especially Islam, and that not least for political reasons. The consequence to be drawn from this could be that study on ecclesiology should now be done in cooperation with those groups concerned with dialogue with other religions, especially Islam.

4. The situation I have described is to a certain extent due to the practical, but not yet sufficiently theoretical success of the ecumenical movement. In Austria there is thus a "horizontal schism". There is a discrepancy between what the parishes do and what the church leadership permits, especially in the Roman Catholic Church. Let me give three examples:

- intercommunion and eucharistic hospitality take place in many parishes, with the bishop turning a blind eye;
- unmarried couples and remarried divorcees participate in the eucharist in many parishes;
- the Reformed city church in Vienna has each year for many years now issued a public, unchallenged invitation to intercommunion on Thursday of holy week.

Conclusion: practice has, happily, been ecumenical for a long time, but over against that the church leaderships run the risk of losing credibility. That encourages yet further the already evident hostility towards institutions.

5. The crisis surrounding institutions creates a growing interest in those religions and religious groups which manage with a minimum of institutionalization and dogmatics, e. g. Buddhism and Hinduism. This religious pluralism leads to yet further rejection of the churches. In that connection it could be important to see what attracts people to go off into the esoteric – for them the inner way is more important than outward

order. This would suggest that for an ecclesiology in the spirit of ecumenism, we need to have a particular debate on the inner meaning of the church, including the important core theological doctrines of the Trinity, Christology, sin, etc., which hardly anyone today understands. In these ecumenical documents, I see the danger of their remaining too much at the level of theological formulations. In order for people to be able to receive them at the grassroots, much exploratory and interpretative work is today necessary; this would also wrestle with the elements of our contemporary cultures which are critical of religion. That could also lead to a revision of the tradition of the Western church, deeply marked by legal terminology which causes problems to many, a revision which would bring us nearer to the Eastern churches.

6. As I see it, we cannot ignore the fact that even among theologians there are today great difficulties in developing the inner meaning of Christian belief and in applying it to their own lives so as to be able to communicate it credibly – at least, that is the case in my own situation. Today there are even theologians who are speaking of the end of theism, of Christ as a human being "like you and me", and of sin as a concept used by power-hungry hierarchies to maintain their dominance.

Fundamentalism, I think, is a reaction to this secularization of the confession of faith within the churches, although it is very conflictual and difficult to accept. I would thus like to see an extension of ecumenical dialogue to include a more thorough conversation with history and our fathers and mothers in the faith in the ancient church.

7. The question which is raised again and again in ecumenical documents about the nature, the *esse* of the church, thus seems to me to be decisive. It brings with it ontological implications, which in my context have dropped out of modern theology. For the reception of ontology much can especially be learned from the ancient church, for example, from Gregory of Nyssa who in his 38th letter to Basil uses the following comparison to explain the Trinity. The threefold being of the one God is mutually related as in a human being: *the* human being, the *essential* human being never appears as a phenomenon in and for itself, but always and only in the multiplicity of distinct moral individuals and historical persons. And at the same time, these different individuals and persons must make the effort to conform ever more closely to the essence of a human being, of the human. So the dialectic of the one and the many also becomes evident in relation to the church. But that cannot happen without a reception of ontology.

This reception has recently again become relevant in philosophy, which could be of use to theology and be a bond between the Protestant churches and the Roman Catholic Church and especially the Orthodox churches. In my context a discussion in this direction has already begun in theological faculties.

8. In accordance with the basic belief of the ecumenical movement, the invisible essence of the church must be given appearance and become visible. This happens in the variety of the local churches. From my context I can only agree with what Mary Tanner said on this in her report.

But what form should the local church take in a highly mobile urban society? My feeling is that the parish church three streets away from one's apartment, with regular services, has lost its significance. The demand is rather for centres of spirituality, determined not by geography but by type. People are prepared to travel a long way to a quiet place of prayer and meditation, while the church around the corner remains empty. Although the essence, the nature, of the church remains unchangeable, local churches must constantly rediscover what form their concrete life could take in their particular context, although no form can perfectly correspond to that essence. The church as a human institution is charged to set forth the essence of the church, but not to identify itself with it. People in my situation are talking a lot about identification – with Jesus, with God, with the church. That abolishes the distinction between God's activity and human activity, which can be maintained if we differentiate between "representation" and "identification". I do not find this distinction in the ecumenical documents.

9. Since the crisis in institutions has also affected the family, local churches could take the place of the wider family community, which has broken down, and the New Testament concept of the *familia Dei* could take on new meaning. The welfare state has taken over many of the functions of the family, for example care of the elderly, which are at present breaking down in Europe. In face of this, the church has much to offer which would be worthy of further consideration.

10. Finally, I should like to make a brief observation on the question of the reception of ecumenical documents at the grassroots level of the local church. In universities and churches there is now a so-called "women's officer" for the particular concerns of women. Could we not in the same way have in each congregation an "ecumenical officer" who would foster conciliarity at local level? For the whole congregation they could read through the many ecumenical documents produced and use them as a springboard for action by the members of the congregation.

Ecclesiology at the Crossroads

S. MARK HEIM

Each of us has only a partial perspective on the whole church. The concerns I offer reflect the limitations of my perspective but also, I hope, enrich our wider koinonia.

I am a Baptist, from a believer's church tradition, one which emphasizes the role of personal confession of faith, active discipleship and an associational church structure.

I live in the United States, where the sharpest divisions that separate Christians do not necessarily correspond to distinct denominational groups. These divisions often run right through the middle of existing churches like my own: differences over sexuality, evangelism and the nature of other religions, gender, economics and social policy.

Christianity in the United States may be numerically strong, but denominations like my own are not growing at anything like the rate of the population and Christian witness in the society is fragmented and often contradictory. In fact, observers routinely speak of a "culture war" in the churches over social issues. At the same time, some of the most dramatic ecumenical developments are taking place outside the churches traditionally oriented to conciliar ecumenism: among Pentecostals and Evangelicals on the one hand (for instance, the recent important reconciliation between African American and white Pentecostal churches in the US) and within "new ecclesial realities" like women-church on the other.

I should like to make a brief, methodological comment and then two more extensive observations. The methodological comment relates to the use of the Canberra statement. In my view the ecclesiology study must develop a free-standing text which does not have the character of a commentary on the Canberra statement. Only in this way will the study be able to reach its necessary audience and have the needed effect.

I

In the ecclesiology study Faith and Order returns to many of the difficult, fundamental questions faced at the beginning of its life – particularly questions of authority and common decision-making.

In one sense the ecclesiology study represents a culmination of earlier stages in the search for visible unity. At earlier stages Faith and

Order dealt with comparative ecclesiology. Then it formulated a vision of Christian unity that included several dimensions: agreement on baptism, eucharist and ministry; common confession of the apostolic faith; common means of teaching and decision-making. A convergence process has made significant progress towards mutual recognition of baptism, eucharist and ministry and towards common confession of faith, though much remains to be done. Now we return to the question of the nature of the unity – the koinonia – that characterizes the one church of Christ. We are trying to envision more fully and specifically the character of the church into which these convergences are leading us.

I come from a tradition that has tended to emphasize the invisibility of the universal church and thus to see unity on the largest scale as a spiritual more than a structural reality. We have greatly emphasized the tangibility and visibility of the church's unity at the local level – a visibility manifest in the confession and witness of individual Christians and in the discipleship of the local community. Therefore the koinonia that we most readily understand is the active koinonia of "all in one place" manifest when local churches in a given area show forth in confession, worship and action their participation with and in each other as one body in Christ. However, through the inspiration of the ecumenical movement, we have been increasingly led to see the need and the legitimacy of visible expression of the one universal church. The apostolic faith study process has been an important element in this. My tradition likes to say there are many ways of belonging to the one church. What the ecumenical movement teaches us is that there must be, in sign and substance universal, common ways all Christian communities make visible their belonging to the one church.

For most of our churches, the key element of the ecclesiology study will be the subjects of conciliarity and diversity in unity (paras 9-17 and 23-30 in the current text). Our own ecclesiology provides extraordinary space for diversity – not for the sake of diversity itself but in the interests of the freedom of the Holy Spirit. Our history is a history of suspicion towards synodical and episcopal authority. We therefore are deeply concerned that the vision of our future koinonia should encompass real diversity... not as an excuse to maintain the existing differences among us, but to ensure that the unity we achieve is authentic and durable. For we can be certain that that unity will have to be capable of meeting new challenges and nurturing renewals we cannot yet even conceive. Our ecclesiology must be such that the next Reformation can take place within one church, with renewal and new vocations developed within the bonds of full communion.

A primary resource for this task is the work already done in the apostolic faith study process and reflected in the report from Santiago on

"Recognizing Apostolicity" (section II, chapter II, paras 10 and 11). In reflecting on the criteria of apostolicity summarized in BEM, we recognize that in nearly all cases each of these elements are present in our diverse churches. The real differences arise from the varying priorities and relationships through which the apostolic elements are bound into a living whole in our communions. Two local Christian communities – or even two Christian communions – may find their deepest bond of koinonia with each other in one particular element of apostolic faith and life: liturgy, for example. But when one of them turns towards a third Christian community, it may be a quite different element of apostolic life and faith that establishes the strongest foundation of trust and mutual recognition: perhaps scriptural exposition. Our current, partial ecumenical koinonia largely has this character, the character of interlocking relationships, very few if any of which are the *identical* relationship.

Our vision of unity must be one that clearly provides that the necessary elements of apostolicity may and should be unified in varying constellations, depending on the leading of the Holy Spirit in various cultures, contexts and mission needs. As trinitarians, we recognize that our oneness *requires* distinctness. Unity in Christ is discernable only in and through these differences – cultural and otherwise – which can be seen as real but are also harmonized and unified in one body.

There is both provisional diversity and integral diversity in the church. Provisional diversity is that which should be overcome (as in differences over how we view the nature of the church itself) or which *might* be overcome without any prejudice to the church's apostolicity and vitality. Integral diversity is that which *must not* be lost or the church's life would be diminished and distorted. The life of our historical denominations is largely provisional, but at least some of the diversity they represent is integral. What we should seek in the ecclesiology study is the common confession of the nature of the church which can assure us that our legitimate diversities are rooted in the same triune God.

II

But the ecclesiology study is at a crossroads in another sense. In addressing the nature of the church, we cannot succeed unless all the ecclesial realities are part of our study. To my mind this means that the ecclesiology study cannot simply be a continuation of the process Faith and Order had mapped out: it must be the occasion for us to go back and to bring into the study major elements that have been missing.

Our work so far has the great virtue of addressing thoroughly and seriously the traditional confessional differences that divide our churches. Nowhere else has this been done in the same way. But the situation has changed. The *problem* of unity has shifted significantly. Frequently ecumenical leaders point to "new ecclesial realities", to forms of unity that arise apart from the churches (as, for instance, the koinonia of Christians and non-Christians in groups struggling for justice). We have given less serious note to another aspect of our situation: the fact that divisions even more devastating than the traditional confessional ones now run right through the middle of our individual, and supposedly united communions. These divisions – over questions of sexuality, gender, mission, the nature of world religions, race, economics, social policy – are increasingly not only experienced as church-dividing but defined so, theologically, by Christians on either side. We have taken account of these to some extent in our work – usually by subsuming them under the heading of "ethics" and affirming that ethics is an integral part of ecclesiology. But rarely do we treat differences over these issues with the same patient "comparative ecclesiology" method that we treat differences over baptism or ministry. Yet in fact at *certain points* these divisions become ecclesiological issues of the most profound sort.

The ecclesiology study requires a return to the beginning in one sense, an expansion of the table. If the ecumenical movement is where Christians come together to overcome their deepest differences we – in the World Council of Churches or Faith and Order – are not yet that movement, and we cannot truly be that movement until those differences themselves are fully and proportionately represented here. This surely is one of the fundamental meanings of catholicity. We must bring together not only *all* the divisions of the whole church before we can overcome them; we must bring the full reality of our actual divisions into the ecumenical dialogue before we can become one.

In many ways, in the life of the church, these new divisions are the moral equivalents of the confessional divisions from the 4th or 16th century. There are, of course, some extreme cases, instances of matters of *status confessionis*, where the views of some must be rejected as heretical, as antithetical to the very being of the church. But in everything short of that we need the same tenacious, respectful mutual study and dialogue we have given to traditional theological differences.

We often speak of the service which Christian unity can provide to a broken world, in the sense that a united church could speak and act so much more effectively amid our social conflicts and struggles for justice. But we Christians seem resistant to one quite feasible step which we could take that would surely contribute towards peace and harmony in the wider world: the step of meeting and dialoguing earnestly with those other Christians with whom we are most at odds – not only over episcopacy and primacy and sacraments and creeds, but over economics, evangelism, social policies on gender, race and sexuality. This means that it is urgent that the ecclesiology study process draw in significant participants from churches that do not belong to the WCC or Faith and Order (notably many Pentecostals and Evangelicals), as well as participants truly representative of the full range of views in the churches that do belong. This may even mean we must enter new arenas of discussion with these Christians, arenas in which the World Council of Churches and its members are not proprietors but partners with others. Faith and Order, with the growing breadth of participation, can play an important role in this process.

It is both a challenge and an opportunity for the ecumenical movement that increasingly the issues that sharply and internally divide our churches are those that divide the societies around us. And there is nothing so lacking in our world as examples of peaceful and respectful approaches to deep conflict. This is the very least that we owe the world by way of witness! In taking up this challenge we may also find renewed interest from our churches, who see we are facing issues that truly afflict them.

If Christians can successfully engage with each other across the chasms of social differences, by virtue of their shared faith, then we will have contributed something quite extraordinary both in terms of substance and example. I hope the ecclesiology study may be the occasion for us to face this challenge in the ecumenical movement more fully than we have before – which will mean in the end nothing less than a renewed ecumenical movement, more diverse, at times even more conflictual, in order to be meaningfully one.

Thoughts on the Ecclesiology Text

MARY O'DRISCOLL

I would like to thank all concerned for the present draft text on ecclesiology. I know that much work has gone into it. As we are aware, the study on ecclesiology from an ecumenical perspective is eagerly awaited by the churches and by Christians everywhere. The responses to BEM stress repeatedly that the search for common ecumenical perspectives on ecclesiology must be pushed forward. So there is need for this study for the sake of the ecumenical goal at this time. Obviously our discussions and decisions in Moshi are an important step in the development of the study. A positive aspect of this text is that it does not allow us to become complacent about what has already been achieved in the ecumenical movement, but rather urges us forward and opens up to us to new vistas.

I would like to reflect very briefly first on the present text in general, and then on a few particular issues within it, with a view to helping the discussion.

The explanatory preface is very helpful in giving us a sense of what the present text is. It is an "exploratory text", we are told. We are therefore acknowledging that we are only at the exploratory stage of our study where often there are more questions than answers, where some issues need to be more solidified and where others are still unresolved and unreconciled. In fact, I am happier with terming it an "exploratory text" rather than regarding it, as the preface does, as an "outline" or as a text which has all its "building blocks" ready. There is more work to be done around certain issues, and many more voices, particularly regional ones, need to be heard; and some blocks are not yet firm enough, or well enough in place (and some blocks assembled at Dublin and Barbados seem to have been left behind) to start building. The preface (para. 11) acknowledges that "new perspectives and possibilities" have still to emerge. These might require a different structure for the text, and we need to remain open to this possibility. Perhaps paragraph 10 of the preface best summarizes our present position.

Use of the Canberra statement

The Canberra statement seems a good basis for the study for it adopts koinonia as the key concept to describe the unity we seek and develops the three most important dimensions of koinonia: common confession of the apostolic faith; common sacramental life rooted in one baptism, nourished by the word and celebrated in one eucharist; and common mission to all people and the whole of creation. However, we must be careful not to allow the statement to limit us in any way or to cut us off from other avenues, nor must we ever regard our study as merely an explication or commentary (as in para. 29), still less as a rephrasing (as mentioned in para. 5) of the Canberra statement. If we follow the structure of this statement, we need to keep reminding ourselves that it cannot constrain or restrain in any way the most mature and best development of this very important study on the church. If something is significant and is not in, or suggested by, the Canberra statement, it cannot be left out.

Trinitarian and pneumatological dimension

The doxology at the end of the Canberra statement (4:1) is quoted at the end of the present text; but it is left absolutely unrecognized and undeveloped. This brings up a difficulty I have with the whole document, in other words its lack of an explicit trinitarian character. It is the theology of the Trinity that provides the theological basis for koinonia ecclesiology. The doctrine of the Trinity must therefore offer a model and an example for a study of the church as communion. It is important to illustrate this throughout the text, e. g. to refer to the bond of love which unites the three persons when treating of communion as a bond of love which unites believers; to refer to the unity and diversity within the Trinity when treating of unity and diversity in the church; to refer to the relationship of equality within the Trinity when treating of collegiality, participation, equality of all members; to refer to the mission of the Son and the Spirit as the origin for the mission of the church. We do not want to forget that the church is a mystery grounded in the trinitarian mystery.

We also need to stress more the role of the Holy Spirit in an understanding of the church. The church is the temple of the Holy Spirit; the whole church (head and body) is animated by the Spirit. In the doxology of the Canberra statement the Holy Spirit is described as "the promoter of koinonia" (2 Cor. 13:13). The implications of this statement need to be expanded and emphasized. Scripture tells us that the Holy Spirit is the one who guides, enlightens, teaches, yet the Spirit is not even mentioned in the section on conciliarity even though section II of the Santiago report (p.243) emphasizes that structures for common decision-making and teaching "will have to correspond to the pneumatological dimension of the church".

Greater balance

A greater trinitarian and pneumatological emphasis would, I think, rectify another shortcoming which I see in the document: it seems to incline too much towards a one-sided sociological concept of the church. Of course, the church is human, visible, earthly, needing social structures, but it is also the church of the living God (1 Tim. 3:15), spiritual, invisible, constituted in its essentials by Christ its founder and head, informed by the Holy Spirit. It is both incarnational and pneumatological. The balance between these two realities, these two inseparable essential aspects, needs to be better kept in the text. Perhaps this is one of the greatest challenges of this study.

It is in the section dealing with "conciliar structures and ways of life and action" that the lack of balance is particularly obvious. While it is necessary to spell out the "how" of the conciliar process, it is also necessary to keep in mind that the Spirit of God is guiding the church, leading it into the fullness of truth and unity. This need for balance is emphasized in the report on the responses to BEM (p.148) which notes that many churches and traditions "welcome a Christocentric and Trinitarian perspective for the understanding of the church, which implies a corrective for an ecclesiology which is primarily concerned with the church as a historical institution".

Koinonia

I would like to make some remarks about the concept of koinonia which is central to the study. I agree that it is good and helpful to develop the study in terms of the church as koinonia, for this is, or has become, a key understanding of the church within most of our traditions, as well as in bilateral or multilateral dialogues. At this point in the ecumenical movement, therefore, communion can be regarded as the best analogy available to express the reality of the church and to offer a solution to many (although not all) of the issues that divide us.

However, it is important to stress that koinonia in its biblical sense denotes communion with God as well as with one another (1 John 1:3). The church in its members is continually being called into fullness of communion with God as well as into fullness of communion with one another. These two are inextricably linked.

It would be helpful not only to have a section on koinonia in the text, but also to allow the concept of koinonia to influence and colour whatever is being said about the church in the different sections, e. g. to reflect on the different ecclesiological issues and aspects in the light of koinonia – the ministry of oversight, conciliarity, laos, sacramental life, mission, and so on. This would contribute newness, freshness and hopefulness to the text.

In paragraph 2 of the text, four areas concerning koinonia for further exploration and investigation are listed. These are all good. However, the list could be enlarged to include (a) a consultation of other exegetical studies besides Reumann's, and (b) an in-depth theological study of koinonia in patristic writings, e. g. Irenaeus. Remembering the past, particularly the undivided past of the church, is a rich method of expanding our understanding of the church as koinonia.

In the same paragraph, a distinction is made between koinonia and various models and images of the church. And we are told, "koinonia is not another image or model". While this is true, it does not mean that models and images cannot be used. In fact, as the report on the responses to BEM shows, the concept of koinonia can be further developed with the help of different biblical key concepts and images which are emphasized by different Christian traditions so that all may be able to embrace it (p.150). There is a very real way in which supplementary images can serve koinonia by underlying different aspects of it, e. g. body of Christ, temple of the Holy Spirit, people of God. This last mentioned, for example, allows for many interpretations which bring out both the divinely instituted aspect of the church ("a chosen race, a royal priesthood, a holy nation, God's own people" [1 Pet. 2:9-10], a people with whom Christ established the new covenant in his blood [Matt. 26:28; Heb. 9:15-28]) and the organized, social reality which the church is as the pilgrim people of God still groping within the darkness of history.

Historical context
The "explanatory preface" (para. 9) refers to the historical context in which the present study is being done – a world in which "divisions of the churches are linked to divisions of humanity and where the divisions of the churches are tragically linked to the struggles and sorrows of the world". This context – which is also described and expanded in the Canberra statement (1, 1-2) – can never be forgotten in the study but rather needs to be alluded to, for it must affect what we say about the church as koinonia. The present historical, social, political, economic and cultural circumstances of our world offer a new and different context from that of past times in which to understand from an ecumenical perspective what it means to present the church as koinonia today.

Finally, there are certain ecclesiological issues that are either not mentioned in the text, or, if they are mentioned, they need more development and recognition. These include:
– authoritative teaching in the church;
– primatial ministry and a universal ministry of Christian unity (this would be particularly welcomed by Roman Catholics in conformity with the invitation in *Ut Unum Sint*);
– the communion of the local church;
– the rootedness of the church in the faith of Israel and the covenants of God (cf. report on BEM, p.148);
– the role of Tradition in conveying the faith.

Plenary Discussion

After presentations of the group discussions, the following points were raised. The need for a change in the title of the study was stressed. A number of speakers noted that while the Canberra statement provides a rich resource for ecclesiology, recognizing as it does the present state of convergence on ecclesiology, it does not easily facilitate identification and discussion of points of divergence. A number of issues were identified as requiring specific attention: conciliarity; local-universal; limits to diversity; the Petrine office; oversight and authority. It was felt that it would be helpful if there were a major focus on the four marks of the church. Attention was drawn to the need to heed more regional perspectives, and to pay attention to sociological insights on the nature of the church and of community. Emphasis on the context of the church in the world, and how the understanding of the mission of the church affects ecclesiology, was seen to be essential. While there were a number of participants who questioned the advisability of focusing on koinonia, others saw this as an essential feature of the study.

A Hermeneutics of Unity

KONRAD RAISER

I should like to pick up and develop a train of thought which I outlined briefly in my paper to the world conference on Faith and Order at Santiago de Compostela, in 1993. I spoke then of the need to channel the bilateral and multilateral dialogues into a constructive dialogue among the different Christian "cultures" – "a dialogue which aims at increased understanding of the integrity of the other, the alien, and does not stand under the pressure of having to dissolve the differences into consensus". I went on to say:

> For this we need an ecumenical intercultural hermeneutic which will enable us to comprehend unity as a fellowship of those who continue to be different and to offer criteria for this. This does not mean to take for granted the sinful separations and divisions of the church or to be indifferent to the disintegration of the church universal. But a hermeneutic of this nature would have to go beyond the much-discussed limits of diversity and consider also the limits of tolerable, acceptable unity, i.e. set criteria for "necessary and sufficient" unity. The hermeneutical discussions and studies carried out by Faith and Order in the 1960s need to be taken up again with this perspective in mind.[1]

The need for renewed hermeneutical reflection in an ecumenical perspective was picked up from different angles in the section reports of the world conference. Section I in particular, with its considerations on the relational structure of catholicity in the church, the process of dialogue and encounter with the other in koinonia and its reference to the need for self-emptying and conversion as the way to reconciliation, offered important pointers to the conditions that must be fulfilled if ecumenical communion among the churches is to come about. The section specially emphasized how important it is for the ecumenical pilgrimage that we be able to understand one another's theological language and cultural ethos, adding that "we would be assisted... in our interconfessional dialogues

---

• This paper has been translated from the German by the WCC Language Service.

by a renewed Faith and Order study on hermeneutics, and new ways of doing theology which provide more adequate tools to express community on the way to the goal of visible unity" (para. 28). This suggestion is repeated in the first recommendation at the end of the section report.

In examining the question of koinonia in confessing the faith, section II turned its attention to the apostolicity of the church as "a critical concept in reference to which the faith, life and structure of the church are to be repeatedly measured and oriented" (para. 8). It then notes: "Our divided communities have not yet succeeded in recognizing full apostolicity in one another. The question of how we *recognize* apostolicity in each other's communities is never only a question of recognizing ministries... It is a question of recognizing whether the risen Christ *we* know is present in the life of others, and whether another church has means for opening itself to the reality of this same Christ" (para. 9). This led the section to recommend "that Faith and Order undertake a study listing the criteria for discerning apostolicity which have been discussed in the bilateral dialogues, as well as a reflection upon the compatibility of these criteria" (para. 12.1). Further references from the section reports could be mentioned.

Following up these recommendations, the commission has in the last two years initiated a study on ecumenical hermeneutics, the interim results of which are given in the document "Towards a Hermeneutics for a Growing Koinonia".

The first part of the study takes up the well-known statement by the fourth world conference on Faith and Order in Montreal in 1963 on the problem of Tradition and traditions, and tries to move on beyond Montreal by clarifying the criteriological question of how to distinguish between diverse traditions or to discern the authenticity of faith in a situation of conflicting cultural perspectives or hermeneutical standards. Here the study offers an interesting interpretation of the basis of the World Council of Churches, which speaks of confessing Jesus Christ "according to the scriptures". The study then looks briefly at the problem of one gospel in many contexts, and hence takes up the issues of intercultural and cross-cultural communication, which have been developed in particular in the study process on gospel and cultures undertaken by the WCC's Unit II. Of particular interest is the third part of the study in which the church is interpreted as "a hermeneutical community". One of the marks of this community is mutual accountability among the churches as together they verify the truth of their proclamation of the gospel. It refers to the ministry of episcope and common decision-making as examples of mutual accountability within and between churches. The study is then also able to interpret the process of reception, which was at the centre of our discussions during the first few days of this meeting, as a "hermeneutical process".

The church: a hermeneutical community

The three parts of the study outline three different but related dimensions of an ecumenical hermeneutics. At the same time, the understanding of hermeneutics is opened up and broadened out from the narrow classical focus on understanding and interpreting texts. Understanding the other and "alien", especially other cultures and different, contextually conditioned incarnations of the gospel is also described as a hermeneutical process. To my mind, however, the most fruitful seems to be the interpretation of the church as a "hermeneutical community". The slightly moralistic or legalistic sounding concept of "accountability", which is open to misunderstanding, is translated into the idea of an open hermeneutical process in which the community of the church is constantly proved and purified. But the idea of the church as a hermeneutical community takes us still further and has consequences for our understanding of unity. In its statement on unity, the assembly in Canberra in 1991 introduced "koinonia" as the hermeneutical key to an understanding of unity, and gave its reasons for doing so. This idea was taken up by the fifth world conference in Santiago de Compostela with its theme "Towards Koinonia in Faith, Life and Witness". Now the study on ecumenical hermeneutics is suggesting a yet more precise focus: koinonia, and hence the unity of the church, can and should be understood as a hermeneutical community of common confession, common action in discipleship and common striving for the kingdom of God.

This echoes ideas which I first heard from Anton Houtepen.[2] Against the background of a critical analysis of the history of theological hermeneutics and the hermeneutical situation in contemporary philosophy, he comes to the conclusion: "In faith and also in ecumenical dialogue the important thing is not texts, but the event, the kingdom of God... The church of Christ is a hermeneutical narrative community in many different contexts. In this community the subjects, the bearers of tradition are more important than the instruments of tradition." Linking up with Paul Ricoeur, he understands hermeneutics as "the recollection of meaning", and the "constructing of coherence". The writings and symbols of Christian Tradition are normative "because they enable us through symbols and narratives to discover the divine coherence of meaning which is given to us". Houtepen is therefore concerned to develop criteria for an "ecumenical hermeneutics of coherence" gathering together that which is fragmented and healing that which has been split apart. Such a hermeneutics of coherence, of gathering together the

fragmented and scattered, is in my view also more appropriate for interpreting the way in which the unity of the church is talked about in the
New Testament, i.e. not in the sense of uniformity and centralization, but
in metaphors which "point to participation, community, solidarity, communication, gathering, coherence and love".

Unity as the fellowship of those who continue to be different can
then be understood in the sense of an open hermeneutical process aimed
at gathering and coherently linking the diverse concrete incarnations of
the gospel. While the hermeneutical problem has hitherto been discussed largely with reference to the diverse confessionally determined
approaches to the interpretation of scripture and confession of the faith,
the focus now is the wider process of the encounter, mutual acceptance
and recognition of the different culturally and contextually determined
forms of theology and the church. The missionary movement of the past
two centuries has carried the gospel to the ends of the earth, but at the
same time it has set the question of the church's unity in a much wider
horizon. The challenge here is highlighted by the large number of
steadily growing churches in the Southern hemisphere which cannot be
attached to one of the historical families of tradition. Mission made
diaspora a predominant characteristic of the church, thereby changing
the quality of the search for visible unity. It is this still-increasing plurality of churches, together with a heightened awareness of the fundamental unity of the church as gift and calling, which makes it imperative for us to pose the question of a hermeneutics of unity. Can the
search for church unity be understood in a way that does not contradict
the fact of church plurality but aims rather at creating coherent community?

An understanding of plurality

In the light of the foregoing considerations, the theme "Hermeneutics
of Unity" now comes to focus on this basic question: In face of the new
awareness of the unity of the church, how is the actual plurality of Christian churches to be understood? The ecumenical movement has led to the
insight that the different churches do not confront one another as sovereign and autonomous bodies, but are indissolubly related. Understanding
the nature of this inter-relatedness in plurality is the real theological task.
It concerns the hermeneutical problem of interpreting unity and diversity
within and among the churches. If unity is understood not as uniformity
but as the inter-relatedness in community of entities that remain different, then diversity and plurality are not necessarily in contradiction with
unity but are in a sense the condition for the possibility of community. I
shall develop this initial thesis in what follows.

The tension between unity and diversity is only one of various dialectical concepts which spring to mind for grasping the reality of the church. In other contexts a distinction is drawn between the church as an institution and the church as an event ultimately beyond our reach, or between the church we believe in and the church as we actually experience it, between the visible and the invisible church. All dialectical distinctions of this sort run the danger of being broken down into alternatives or reduced to one of the two poles. This invariably happens when the reality of the church is made the object of doctrinal definitions, for then the need for logical coherence leads to the elimination of contradictions. This tendency to reduce the tension or dialectic in the relationship of unity and plurality can be found in all the attempts made so far to tackle the problem.

The reduction is most obvious in the classical approach of dogmatic theology, with its clear distinction between orthodoxy and heresy. According to this, there is only the one church; all other groups are non-church, that is to say, sects. Despite all the attempted modifications that have been made to this approach in the interval, it is still very much alive today. This way of dealing with the problem of plurality in dogmatic theology was given another twist with the famous distinction which says that the true church is an invisible reality hidden beneath the visible forms of the church which are at the mercy of historical events at any given time. Neither of these distinctions offers a satisfactory solution for understanding church plurality.

Yet another approach starts from historical development. According to this, the one, holy, catholic and apostolic church existed in visible form in the beginning. With this approach, either the maintenance of unbroken continuity with the apostolic origins, notably in the form of episcopal succession, becomes the criterion for the true church; or else the history of the church is interpreted as a history of decay and the task is therefore to restore the church to its pure original form. Both these versions of the historical approach to explanation avoid of course the contradictory nature of the church's historicity. The tension between continuity and discontinuity cannot be resolved any more than that between the church of belief and the church of experience.

A third approach to interpreting church plurality, widely used in the contemporary discussion, starts from the assumption that every form of church is the result of a process of adaptation to a social and cultural context, the "socialization" or inculturation of the gospel. This statement of the problem is still relatively new and presupposes the process of secularization on the one hand, and the missionary spread of Christianity in the 19th and 20th centuries on the other. A lively discussion has recently begun on the subject of gospel and culture and this is also influencing the current ecumenical debate. In regard to the understanding and assessment of church plurality, it culminates in the accusation of syncretism, i.e. an adaptation and inculturation of the gospel which removes the necessary critical distance, and in so doing obscures the uniqueness of the gospel. This approach to interpretation reminds us that the tension of adaptation and critical distance, and likewise that of universality and particularity, have to be included in any attempt to understand the plurality of the church.

Taken in themselves, the three approaches to interpretation briefly outlined here remain unsatisfactory. None of them on its own can provide an adequate basis for understanding the problem of plurality. They are inherently related and taken together they can form an analytical grid. What is at issue in the tension between the unity and the plurality of the church is ultimately the identity of the church. Is there only the one Christian church identity, or do we always find different, confessionally, contextually or culturally determined identities, so that the church's full unity can only be understood as eschatologically hidden and a matter for faith? This question leads to difficulties so long as identity is regarded as something fixed and unchanging. The considerations I have just presented suggest or even require that we understand the identity of the church as a relational reality, which is formed in relations of tension but which can also be lost. In the course of their history the churches have responded in different ways to the task represented by these relations. The identity of the church is a complex matter. Provided the tension inherent in the fundamental relations is sustained and not resolved, diverse identities are possible in the coherence of a hermeneutical community.

Four areas of tension
I see four fundamental relational fields that can be linked with the classical marks of the church: oneness, holiness, catholicity and apostolicity. First, there is the fundamental relationship to God in Christ. Here the oneness or truth of the church is at stake in the tension between the church of belief and the church of experience. This tension can already be recognized in the development of the trinitarian and Christological creeds of the ancient church. The ancient church's fundamental soteriological concern to be able to express the communion with God *(theosis)* inaugurated through Christ, obliged it to place the oneness of Jesus Christ and God at the centre of the creed and thereafter to emphasize the union of divine and human nature in Jesus Christ. The biblical witness, on the other hand, made it necessary to maintain the distinction

between Jesus Christ and God and between the divine and human nature in Jesus Christ. The trinitarian concept and Christological categories could only be developed by breaking with the internal logic of Hellenistic thought. They represent an attempt to maintain the inner tension, or mystery, and safeguard it against reduction. Even without retracing the differing historical circumstances, the identity of the great confessional traditions can be seen as different forms of the common confession of God's self-revelation in Jesus Christ. The sacramental interpretation of this confession is common to the Roman Catholic and Orthodox traditions. Central in this is God's incarnation in Jesus Christ, the mysterious union of God and human, in which the church partakes through Jesus Christ, whose body it is. As a community of people in history the church effectively participates in God's world, indeed itself becomes the mediator of salvation, and that means not only the sign, but the instrument of the union of God and humanity. In contrast to this, the Reformation tradition represents the concern to keep the distinction between the divine and the human, and hence also the distinction between Christ and his church – for the sake of the unfathomable divinity of God and the humanity and historicity of human beings, and also of the church. The corresponding dialectical distinctions in Reformation theology, between the hidden and the revealed God, between the invisible and the visible church, between the human being as sinner and as justified will be familiar to you.

These two classical hermeneutical traditions – which of course deserve further differentiation – belong together, and only together do they express the irreducible tension in the church's fundamental confession of faith. Historically they have become the points around which different confessional identities have crystallized and defined themselves polemically in opposition to one another. My thesis is that they need one another. The different confessional traditions and the ecclesiologies deriving from them are not mutually exclusive in the sense of truth and error; rather, they are different ways of understanding the fundamental tension which is built into the confession of Christ.

The second field of tension concerns the relationship of the church to the "world". At stake here is the holiness of the church, its vocation to be in the world but not of it, and this in the tension between adaptation and critical distance. I have already mentioned the problem of adapting to other cultures, ways of thinking, understandings of reality and also forms of religious life, with the attendant danger of syncretism, that is, the loss of critical distance. But this also includes the process of conforming to social structures, above all in relation to differences of race, class and gender. In the ecumenical movement this dimension and its significance for the identity and unity of the church were recognized early on. It spoke, for instance, of the "non-theological factors" affecting the unity or separation of the church. Besides the issue of poverty, the more recent discussion has concentrated chiefly on racism and sexism. Lastly, this also includes the conformity of the church to a particular legal and state order. While the processes of cultural and social adaptation have been frequently examined, too little attention has been paid to this latter aspect of the adaptation problem. This is especially true as regards the influence of Roman legal tradition on the development of Roman Catholic identity. In all the areas mentioned, the distinction between adaptation or critical distance is not a straightforward alternative but a field of tension in which church identity is constantly re-forming and changing, but in which it is also at stake.

The third field concerns the relationship with other churches. This involves the classical marks of the church, its catholicity, in the tension between the universal and the particular, or local church. In the concept of *ekklesia*, the ancient church maintained the unity between the universal church and the church in its local form. The whole church, the universal body of Christ which encompasses the baptized in all places and at all times, can be seen wherever the faithful are gathered in one place, especially in the celebration of the eucharist. The universal church and the individual gathered community form a duality in which both poles are essential. The universal church is not the sum and the gathered community is not a part.

The duality of universal church and gathered community means that all communities, as the embodiment of the universal church in one particular place, are indissolubly linked with one another. This made it necessary to express this fundamental inter-relatedness in a structural form by developing particular churches. These structures are essential, but they serve an intermediary function and as such have a derived ecclesiological dignity. The pre-Constantinian church had no structural representation of the universal church. Catholicity in time was more important than catholicity in space. With the change that took place in the Constantinian era and the summoning of imperial councils, the church was given a structure for its universal unity, but at the cost of the subsequent separation of the churches in Armenia, Syria, Persia, Ethiopia and Egypt.

Since then the tension of universality and particularity has become a crucial factor in church identity. Wherever priority is given to universality, and hence to a uniform structure for the whole church – as in the Roman Catholic tradition – there is the danger that the particular churches will be treated as sub-divisions of the universal church, thus breaking the tension. The churches of the Reformation, on the other hand, never made any attempt to give form to the catholicity of the universal church. The revival of the congregational principle led in fact to the dominance of the particular church in the form of regional or national churches, or else, in the extreme congregationalism of the radical Reformation, to the loss of the fundamental inter-relatedness of local congregations as embodiments of the universal church. The manner in which a church understands and orders its relationships with other churches is an important factor in determining its identity. In this respect, an ecclesiastical identity which excludes the fundamental catholicity of the church is bound to be regarded as stunted.

The fourth fundamental relation concerns the church's relationship to history and hence the question of its apostolicity or, in other words, the value placed on Tradition. Every church defines its identity on the basis, among other things, of its understanding of its own history; every church has, as it were, its own history of the origins. I have already referred to the two types of symbolization of this history, in other words, the sense of unbroken continuity with the church of the apostles, or else the sense of rupture and separation. The churches belonging to the catholic tradition in the widest sense live in the certainty of unbroken continuity. All church history is the unfolding of God's plan under the guidance of the Holy Spirit and is, therefore, salvation history. The institutional form of this sense of continuity in salvation history is the unbroken chain of apostolic succession. For all the Reformation churches and for post-Reformation churches the constitutive element is the memory of their historical origin in the form of separation or rupture with the catholic tradition described above. The break is justified by reference to the critical principle of holy scripture.

The two types are a mirror image of one another and remain contradictory because they do not take the historicity of the church really seriously. That is why the clarifications made by the fourth world conference on Faith and Order on the problem of scripture and Tradition – or to put it differently, Tradition and traditions – represented an important step forward. Since then we have come to recognize still more clearly that the belief in God's presence in history forbids any sacralizing of history in the sense of an unbroken history of salvation. The continuity of God's history with God's people is a statement of faith, made despite the appearances of discontinuity, rupture and contingency. The theological postulate of the continuity of salvation history, like the idealized notion of original purity, are forms of escape from history.

If, on the other hand, we take seriously the historicity of the church in the tension of continuity and contingency of the new, then the emergence of plurality in the church can be understood as a process of differentiation taking place in the course of the transmission of the gospel and the missionary expansion of the church. When one specific part of the transmission process is declared to be normative, the openness to the unfinished eschatological fullness of the revelation is lost. The coherence, the continuity of God's action in history is not positively given, but lives in the power of remembrance, *anamnesis* and eschatological hope. Prophetic intervention, i.e. the interruption of continuity, is constantly necessary to preserve the freedom of God's action, God who creates the new and also seeks and makes possible new responses on the part of human beings. But the criterion of the apostolicity of the church in turn binds prophetic criticism to the unique origin of the church in the history of Jesus Christ and to the process of tradition from which no church can escape.

* * *

The aim of these remarks has been to reach a better understanding of the actual plurality of the church, as an entry point for a hermeneutics of unity. What has this attempt achieved?

1. First, we may note that there is often a hidden relationship between the different confessionally or contextually shaped ecclesiastical identities. A normative approach obscures the inter-relatedness, as does a purely descriptive one, and neither is therefore appropriate as a means of understanding church plurality. If the aim of hermeneutics is the "re-collection of meaning" or the "construction of coherence" (see above) then a hermeneutical effort is needed to show the underlying connections.

The decisive step lies in understanding the identity of each church as a relational entity evolving in a context of fundamental relations. The church is a relational reality, as was strongly emphasized by section I at the world conference in Santiago. The truth of the gospel, in which the church is grounded, unfolds in community. Where the recognition and confession of the truth is detached from the open (hermeneutical) process of dialogue, reciprocal questioning and endeavour to understand, confession of the faith atrophies and risks becoming sectarian.

This in turn means that the attempt to deal with the problem of church plurality through doctrinal definitions and delimitations is bound to fail. Precisely in trying to exclude or guard against doubtful or dangerous forms of church plurality, the church cuts itself off from the network of dynamic relationships which alone keep its identity alive. The purely defensive attitude that can be observed in many places towards Pentecostal forms of life and witness to the faith is a good example of this. The more a church seeks to limit or even suppress plurality, the poorer it becomes.

2. The inner connection between the different church identities lies in the fact that they are all responses to a series of fundamental relationships. Within the fields of tension staked out by these fundamental relations, an unlimited variety of "solutions" and emphases are possible, and remain linked with one another provided the tension is sustained and not broken. The hermeneutical approach aims to uncover the fundamental relationships and the tensions they involve and so to reveal their coherence and inter-relatedness.

The pluralism in principle postulated by some people today denies the possibility of meaningful relations. In the last analysis, it makes no attempt to understand plurality and in this it represents the opposite of the tentative hermeneutics of unity as coherence outlined here. It is no less dogmatic than the response discussed above, which seeks to tackle the problem of church plurality by means of clear doctrinal definitions. Some forms of Protestant denominationalism – more or less consciously – represent this type of pluralism in principle, which not only tolerates the loose coexistence of ecclesiastical identities but actually regards it as a natural consequence of growing individualization. The whole, the quest for coherence, is here replaced by competition, dignified with the name of mission, for the goal of church growth. Ecumenical efforts to formulate and gain acceptance for rules of fellowship are received as a limitation of religious freedom.

3. Bringing to light fundamental relationships is first of all an analytical procedure. The four relationships I have mentioned – with God in Christ, with the "world", with the other churches and with history – represent a heuristic grid. Its plausibility and usefulness in the task of developing a hermeneutics of unity remain to be proven. I hope I have been able to go at least some way towards furnishing that proof.

I have gone a step further and linked the four fundamental relations respectively with one of the traditional marks of the church: oneness, holiness, catholicity and apostolicity. In doing so I have suggested that these marks of full church identity are likewise to be understood as relational concepts and not as inherent qualities. One might even say that they denote a quality of essential relationships and can therefore be understood as critical concepts, as hermeneutical criteria – as indeed section II at the world conference in Santiago has already done in the case of apostolicity. Whether or not the tension implicit in each of the fundamental relationships is sustained rather than being resolved or reduced, and whether therefore the inner coherence of the diverse church identities is preserved, could then be tested against the respective qualitative yardsticks of oneness, holiness, catholicity and apostolicity. The fourth assembly of the World Council of Churches in Uppsala (1968) spoke of the catholicity of the church in this sense as a quality of church fellow-ship which makes it possible to hold universality and particularity together. This and other examples which could be given suggest that it could be fruitful to take the classical marks of the church as hermenuet-ical criteria in the framework of a hermeneutics of unity.

4. Anton Houtepen, in the essay I quoted earlier, recalls the notion of the "hermeneutical quadrilateral", familiar to us from antiquity, which was taken up by the church fathers in the doctrine of the fourfold sense of scripture. In classical hermeneutics it served to create and justify coherence (*op. cit.*, p.280). He then goes on to show how, at the latest since the European Enlightenment, this comprehensive understanding of hermeneutics was lost through concentration on literal meaning, texts and facts, and proposes a new "ecumenical quadrilateral" for an ecu-menical hermeneutics, which could lead to the rediscovery of coherence (p.293).

I follow the line he takes, without discussing the content of his pro-posal. Indeed, I believe that with the dimensions of the oneness, holi-ness, catholicity and apostolicity of the church we already have a hermeneutical quadrilateral which sets the framework for a hermeneu-tics of unity. The basic idea of the quadrilateral is that the full meaning only becomes apparent when all four interdependent and interacting cri-teria are brought to bear at once and can thus make coherence visible. Oneness and catholicity have to be both differentiated and held together; likewise holiness and apostolicity, i.e. the question of how a particular church is bound into context or traditions. The traditional ecumenical discussion, especially in the bilateral dialogues, suffers from a one-sided focus on the questions of unity and tradition/apostolicity, to the neglect of the dimensions of holiness and catholicity. This limitation in the hermeneutical process of mutual understanding and the formulation of agreements could be one reason why there has been so little reception.

5. The study document on ecumenical hermeneutics calls the church a "hermeneutical community". In an open process of examining and mutual questioning, recognition and encouragement, this community holds the plurality of ecclesiastical identities together. The oneness of this community is grounded in the confession of Jesus Christ, which all hold in common, and is verified by the hermeneutical criteria of oneness, holiness, catholicity and apostolicity. The Canberra statement on unity said that "the goal of the search for full communion is realized when all churches are able to recognize in one another the one, holy, catholic and apostolic church in its fullness" (2.1). It then expressly adds, "diversities which are rooted in theological traditions, various cultural, ethnic or his-torical contexts are integral to the nature of communion" (2.2). When, in

the midst of these diversities, mutual recognition of the presence of Christ takes place through the power of the Holy Spirit, the churches live in communion which is expressed "through conciliar forms of life and action" at all levels. These enable common recognition and action. The common confession of Jesus Christ as God and Saviour therefore sets the internal limit to diversity; but at the same time, diversity is not lack of unity, but the precondition for genuine communion. Coherence is not just a criterion for the success of the hermeneutical process. The quest for coherence must also be expressed in structures for uniting, binding communion, in which the relatedness of plural church identities can be proved and deepened. Conciliarity is the discipline which keeps the church alive as a hermeneutical community. The bilateral and multilateral dialogues and the reception of their results should therefore be transposed into a binding conciliar, or rather, preconciliar framework so that the coherence of the hermeneutical process can be seen and the four interdependent criteria can fulfil their critical function. It would then become clear that considerations of this nature on a hermeneutics of unity not only serve the need for systematic clarification, but also have direct consequences for the direction of further ecumenical theological work on the question of ecclesiology and church unity. That, however, lies outside the scope of this particular reflection.

NOTES

[1] Cf. *On the Way to Fuller Koinonia: Official Report of the Fifth World Conference on Faith and Order, Santiago de Compostela 1993*, Thomas F. Best and Günther Gassmann, eds, Faith and Order paper no. 166, Geneva, WCC, 1994, p.171.
[2] Cf. his essay "Ökumenische Hermeneutik: Auf der Suche nach Kriterien der Kohärenz im Christentum", in *Ökumenische Rundschau*, 3, 1990, pp.279ff.

Plenary Discussion

A rich discussion followed Dr Raiser's presentation, which brought out the following points. There is a need to distinguish between a qualitative and descriptive account of the four marks of the church, and to explore the relation and interdependence between the local and the universal church. While the understanding of the church as simultaneously visible and invisible is essential, there is a paradox that communion can exist between those who are not known to each other, while in one visible united church there can be division. Discussion also focused on the limits to diversity. The danger of "consensus" sometimes meaning "conformity" not "uniformity" was noted. It was suggested that the section 2 report of the fifth world conference needs to be developed. The need to continue dialogue when consensus is not possible was stressed. The distinction between councils and conciliarity was emphazised. Concern was expressed as to how to speak of the church as a hermeneutical community which did not imply "intellectual community" and how hermeneutics is a tool of, for and with intercultural dialogue. The hermeneutical community was emphasized as being a narrative community which developed rules for mutual interpretation.

Responses to the Hermeneutics Paper

Ecumenical Hermeneutics: An Asian Response

KYUNG SOOK LEE

The story about Naaman is taken from 2 Kings 5. Naaman was a general of the Syrian army, a man of great power. The Syrian king gave him strong support. But Naaman was a leper. He came to Israel to heal his leprosy. He came to Israel to Elisha, the man of God, with great expectations. He was ready to do anything Elisha wanted him to do. He had imagined that Elisha would perform a great ceremony, calling loudly on the Lord and waving his hands over the diseased place. He would certainly ask Naaman to keep many strict rules. But Elisha simply said, "Go and wash in the Jordan seven times." Naaman was very disappointed and became angry. But he followed the advice of his servants and went down to the River Jordan and dipped himself seven times in the water. His flesh became fresh and clean like that of a small child. Naaman was very happy and said to Elisha, "Now I know that there is no God in all the earth but Israel. I will offer neither burnt offering nor sacrifice unto other gods, but only unto the Lord God of Israel." However, he was a Syrian general and when he returned to Syria he would have to accompany his king into the temple of Rimmon to assist him there. He was worried – would the Lord pardon him in this matter? Elisha, the man of God, answered him very briefly, "Go in peace."

As I think about the hermeneutical process in the Asian context, I am compelled to think of Naaman. Many Asians are Christian converts; most were Buddhist or Confucianist before. They are a minority group in their society: therefore they frequently have an identity crisis, like Naaman. They have questions like "Is it permitted to keep our old traditions? Or is it not permitted for a Christian?"

I can understand the question of Naaman very well. It is therefore quite natural if many Asian Christians tend to be conservative or aggressive or even exclusive. It is because they want to have their own Christian identity. They will stress their new Christian identity and forget all their old traditions. They have accepted the whole Western missionary tradition as their standard norm and there is no compromise. As a result, there are many conflicts among families and societies.

Many say that Christians have destroyed the harmony of the multicultural and multi-religious traditions in Asia. Many Christians become angry or disappointed if someone tells them that Christianity is just for peace and harmony in life; they want more ceremonies and regulations. Similar questions were raised by Western Christians in early Christian times and in church history we find many questions on heresy also.

But what did Elisha say to Naaman? His answer was very simple: "Go in peace." With this answer, Elisha permitted Naaman to follow his duty with regard to Syrian customs as before. The fact that Naaman confesses that Yahweh, God, is the only God was the important thing. I think Christianity is a religion which is very open and inclusive. Jesus himself was the one who accepted all the outcasts, the powerless, the women and the children, the Greeks and the Jews, etc. So we too must be careful to avoid being exclusive.

What is authentic or real Christianity? What is so-called Tradition? Since Montreal our documents have described Tradition as (1) preceding events and testimonies leading to the scriptures; (2) the scriptures themselves; (3) the ecclesial preaching and teaching (see app. 2, para. 13).

According to my understanding, the second part of the first step of Tradition (testimonies leading to the scriptures) is already influenced by the traditions of witnesses. So I wonder if we can really separate clearly the Tradition and traditions, text and context, Christianity and syncretism. Our document tells us very correctly that Tradition cannot be captured by one theology. I agree fully that Tradition is a living, eschatological reality which eludes all attempts at final linguistic definition and conceptual disclosure. Therefore it is unfair if Western Christians claim that their traditions are a good part of Tradition, but Asian or African traditions cannot be included in Christian Tradition. Tradition and traditions cannot be separated. They should make one hermeneutical spiral. Tradition must give the power to reform the traditions, but traditions can also change one's view of Tradition. So Christianity can be very diverse.

We cannot import the other's theology from outside. In order to have our own theology, we must overcome our Naaman complex and see our own context.

Asia is very rich in natural resources and in the diversity of its cultures and traditions. It also has a long history of exploitation under Western imperialism and Japanese colonialism and military dictatorship. Asians have suffered very much. Now in Asia, there are two quite different worlds: that of the privileged, and that of the marginalized and exploited. Our problem now is, how all of us can be more united and find our human dignity and equality. The barriers between the rich and the poor, male and female, Christian and Buddhist, etc. are very high. In this context those who suffer most are the poor, lower-class women. They are called to constant sacrifice; usually they have a threefold burden: Western colonialism, the social system and family structures. These poor women are also the victims of the churches. They come to church to learn something to improve their situation. But what they hear in the church is that Jesus was to die for our sins and therefore we must also sacrifice ourselves until death for our family, factory, society, etc. The whole of Western theology, which speaks to them of "spiritual grace", "salvific death", "salvation in heaven", does not help them at all. They only learn why they should suffer.

Jesus' atoning death is easily misused and misunderstood. So the scripture itself or Tradition without proper interpretation/hermeneutics means nothing to them. Asian feminists are searching for a new Christology and a new ecclesiology. And they urgently need a new biblical hermeneutic, because the church has oppressed them with the authority of the scriptures. The scriptures have enough verses to allow the oppression of women.

How can we deal with these verses? Scripture as "word of God" contains too many negative concepts, holy war, exclusiveness, condemnation of others, and so on.

Jesus is a power for new life. Jesus' mission is above all to proclaim the kingdom of God. To build this kingdom of God, we must struggle with Jesus against injustice and inhumanity. Asian Christians will struggle for their dignity and freedom with their own hermeneutical methods. To do this, they must use not only scripture but also Asian scriptures, which tell of the people's movement or peasant revolts or other stories. With this diversity of resources, we should keep our liberating power of Jesus.

In conclusion, I want to recommend that Faith and Order help develop Asian resources to build up a new Christology and ecclesiology. It could be through translation of available materials or mutual exchange of resources. Furthermore, through dialogue with other religions on issues of common interest such as human rights, environmental issues and women's liberation, we can try to live in harmony and peace in a multi-religious and multi-cultural society and to encourage the other religions to solve these problems in their own way.

Ecumenical Hermeneutics: Working Principles Pondered

MELANIE MAY

My assignment is to address myself to the working principles for ecumenical hermeneutics, as stated in the text "Towards a Hermeneutics for a Growing Koinonia". More specifically, I have been asked to comment on this section in ways that might be helpful to our subsequent discussions together. In response, I will raise one point for us to ponder, a point I put forward as an invitation to us to look behind these principles to assumptions I believe are as yet inadequately examined, in order to articulate even more clearly the already sharply-stated insights offered by this study document.

I would further specify that my main point about these working principles relates in particular to their adequacy, or lack of adequacy, relative to the third part of the study in which the church is considered as "a hermeneutical community". This is my focus, at least in part, because my perspective is informed by my radical reformation formation. Here I cannot resist a parenthetical remark: the Church of the Brethren is one of at least a couple of churches of the radical reformation that has held and continues to hold in lively tension the locality and particularity of the church as koinonia and an ecumenical spirit of openness.

My point is this: despite a brief note, i.e. "Tradition is transmitted orally as well as through written texts", and accordingly a call to attend to "oral sources as well as written sources" (II.B.2,32), the working principles are predicated on the primacy of the written text. To assume the primacy of the written text is, I think, to predispose the hermeneutical task to be a task of deciphering, i.e. interpretations or meanings already inscribed and then communicating this meaning or these meanings in and for the present context.

Scholars who compare traditions that feature oral and written texts suggest that in most oral traditions, by contrast, meaning is a matter of ongoing negotiation, is struggled for and clarified in continuing dialogue. This is not to say the negotiation and the struggle characteristic of oral traditions is altogether inaudible in written texts. Consider the biblical stories of the Syro-Phoenician woman or of the woman who anointed Jesus, stories whose meaning surfaces precisely as we attend to the tension that anticipates transformed hearts and minds. Consider also the negotiation and struggle that is the heartbeat of ecumenical texts, texts that are testaments, especially to a practised eye, of face-to-face exchanges at meetings such as this one.

But I nonetheless believe that with hermeneutical working principles predicated on the primacy of the written text, we risk reading over and rendering inaudible such instances of inscribed orality. Principles predicated on the primacy of the written text put closure on the telling and re-telling of stories by particular peoples in particular places, and so closes off the common understanding that emerges only out of such lively and enlivening interaction as each other's stories are heard, are received, and, by God's grace, become our story, a story bearing witness to our reconciled life together.

Implied in the distinction I am sketching all too briefly between written and oral traditions is an assessment of the relative openness or closedness of these traditions. Accordingly, a second aspect of my main point follows. Here again, despite a section on "Openness to being challenged" (II.A.2), a section that calls for an account of "the openness of Tradition to possible further development" and convokes "the spirit of metanoia" for the ecumenical hermeneutical process, throughout the working principles there pulsates a tension between open words and a less open assumption. The less open assumption to which I refer is the unexamined notion of normativity, an assumption indicated by a statement such as: "... all agree that the whole of apostolic faith is not confined to the formulations of that faith as contained and expressed in scripture, but that normative faith is also discernable in the life of the church through the ages".

I invite us to examine this assumed notion of normativity not from a perspective that endorses an unexamined plurality. Rather, I invite us to examine the notion of normativity, together with an examination of the primacy of written texts, from the perspective of a woman who is a member of a radical reformation tradition, this is to say, from the perspective of one among many persons and traditions most often marginalized, relative to what has been taken to be the normative Christian tradition. Seeing and speaking from the margins, it is clear we have not yet wrestled well enough between the rock of normativity and the hard spot of our ever more richly visible and voiced diversity. And let us be this honest; our diversity *is* a hard spot. On the one hand, we encounter the richness as even more profoundly promising of life abundant and, on another, we experience ever more painful and destructive consequences of diversion for persons and churches.

And let us be honest yet again: despite our rhetoric about bearing one another's burdens and solidarity in suffering and so on, we walk away from and not into the pain of our woundedness. We retreat, filled with fear, we close ourselves (together with our texts and traditions) off from one another.

I suggest that attention to orality in these working principles would help us articulate and practise ways of together touching our woundedness so that we may be healed. Here, those of us from a North Atlantic setting, whose ears have lost a lot of tonality, need to stop and listen carefully to those of us coming from cultures and traditions that craft connection and continuity first and foremost by face-to-face contact. This will make us aware of the necessity for recovering intercultural aspects of our hermeneutical task.

I am arguing neither for an abandonment of written texts and traditions nor for the primacy of orality. I am suggesting that as we attend with keener awareness to oral and written traditions, in dialogue with one another, we will come to appreciate anew the ways all traditions are themselves testimonies to ongoing struggles for meaning and to the pain through which we will pass on the way to mutual, respectful understanding.

Following from this perspective on struggle and pain internal to traditions, I invite us to examine another aspect of my main point, namely the extent to which these working principles for ecumenical hermeneutics assume dialogue between and among persons and churches "out there", overlooking the urgent importance of "internal dialogization", to borrow a phrase from Bakhtin.[1] This is to say, I am convinced, as are others who have already spoken here, we are called to consider the ways in which many of the most painful and perplexing matters that challenge us to clarify all ecumenical hermeneutics in the first place have to do with matters internal to churches, are rooted in issues requiring interpretation, clearsighted and courageous communication, for the sake of mutual respectful understanding within our churches.

The working principles, therefore, need to address "internal dialogization" in order to invite us to be relentlessly honest about our own complex and multi-layered identities as churches and as persons, identities accordingly often painful and perplexing. To speak of "internal dialogization" is to invite us to be radically open: to reveal ourselves to ourselves in the hope we may so honestly be present with one another.

Finally, I want to suggest that attention to orality, particularly to the struggle for meaning and understanding both internally and with partners, in turn directs our attention to our work on ecclesiology, especially to a renewed emphasis on "the communion of the local churches" as our moderator put it, to the church gathered "in very particular places where each lives". Our hermeneutical attention is and needs to be directed to the church thus concretized because it is here, in very particular places, that orality becomes face-to-face conversation. It is here, in very particular places, that the struggle for meaning and understanding is daily dealing with the ordinary stuff of life out of which the sacrality of life abundant may, by God's grace, be created. It is here, in very particular places, that we encounter one another and ourselves, sometimes in ways that disturb us or hurt us, but always in ways that confirm our flesh-and-blood humanity.

In short, I am suggesting that the locus for living with, and so for articulating, these working principles is and needs to be more explicitly ecclesial, just as the method of our ecclesiology study, in which locality and catholicity must after all meet in the integrity, needs to be hermeneutical through and through. Making this summary statement I confirm the commitment underlying my main point about orality in relation to written text: the commitment to understanding one another, to communicating with one another and, by God's grace, to receiving one another as churches and as persons. For as Anton Houtepen has said and Konrad Raiser cited: "... the subjects, the bearers [and I would add, creators] of tradition are more important than the instruments of tradition".

NOTE

[1] M.M. Bakhtin, *The Dialogic Imagination: Four Essays*, Austin, TX, Univ. of Texas Press, 1981.

Some Reflections from a Pentecostal/Evangelical Perspective

CECIL M. ROBECK, JR

I have been invited today to reflect on "Towards a Hermeneutic for a Growing Koinonia" from the perspective of Evangelical approaches to scripture, and to raise a few questions for our consideration. First, I should like to thank those who have worked so hard on this document. I believe that there is considerable usefulness to what is being done, and I hope you will understand that my intention is to make a positive contribution.

I need to make a couple of other introductory comments about the traditions from which I speak. In one sense, I am an Evangelical. But

Evangelicalism is difficult to define. There are varieties within this large and growing movement, some of which have contributed substantively to the work of the World Council of Churches and to this commission. But there are few of us who have done so. I am a Pentecostal, and thus a member of the fastest growing part of Evangelicalism, if not the church. I do not state this triumphantly, but merely as a matter of fact. But for me to say that I am an Evangelical is to say something different from saying that I am a Pentecostal. I participate in both worlds, as well as in the larger conciliar world of the church. While these worlds do intersect at points, they are not synonymous.

Both Evangelicals and Pentecostals share a great deal theologically, though they have arrived there by different routes. Evangelicals have most frequently been informed by the Reformed tradition while Pentecostals emerged first from the Anglican tradition by way of Methodism and the Wesleyan-Holiness churches. What these two movements (Evangelicalism and Pentecostalism) share regarding scripture, however, is significant. Both of them believe themselves to embrace an historic, high view of scripture. Evangelicals, following the lead of their fundamentalist forebears, are more likely to argue that scripture is inerrant, though many do not, while Pentecostals, who embraced certain fundamentalist affinities but were formally rejected by modern fundamentalism, much prefer the language of infallibility, though there are some ardent "inerrantists" among them.

1. While historically Evangelicals and Pentecostals came to accept aspects of higher criticism, both slowly and grudgingly, most of them today are fairly comfortable using certain aspects of the historical-critical methodology. In recent years, it appears that a somewhat higher percentage of Pentecostal scholarship in scripture studies has diversified beyond the norm of Evangelical scholarship, and now includes a number of individuals who are quite comfortable using "rhetorical, narrative, structural-linguistic, semiotic, psychological, and sociological approaches" (I.18).

But these are all scripture specialists who are ultimately answerable to the *people* with whom they are in fellowship. They are performing "a service of discernment that cannot be separated from the life of the community as a whole" (I.35). The document before us speaks of the "Episcope and Mutual Accountability" (I.C.2). From an Evangelical and a Pentecostal perspective, this section may work well for churches which take seriously the magisterial offices. But how do we speak about mutual accountability when the scripture specialists and hermeneuts are ultimately responsible to the people with whom they are in fellowship? How is the service being provided, kept in fellowship with "the life of the community as a whole"? How are the bishops ultimately "subject to episcope by the whole church"? How are all members of the church guaranteed inclusion and "participation in the common task of discerning and carrying out the church's mission"? How do we set the hoped-for parameters for common decision-making? And what are they? Evangelicals and Pentecostals will need to be convinced that this process extends beyond a magisterium and functions on their behalf, even at a congregational level.

2. One of the fears which many Evangelicals and Pentecostals share when they are confronted by the ecumenical movement is a loss of identity. They fear that the quest for visible unity is something which poses a danger to what they believe is a legitimate call to the diversity they see in scripture. "Unity in diversity" is a phrase that they, like the WCC, might embrace, but what they see as the legitimate extent of unity would begin and frequently end in the spiritual realm. Visibility carries a threat of uniformity for many of them.

In this document, much is said about the dialogical character of hermeneutics and our responsibility to enter into this dialogue (I.5,6, 32; II.5-9; etc.), as well as our commitment to unity within diversity (I.6,27,43). But the document is at times highly prescriptive. Prescriptions can be made legitimately only when everyone is in the dialogue. But everyone is not yet at the table. "Why *must* one 'take into consideration issue of power as well as social, political, and other interests' in order to expose the presupposition, prejudices, and hidden agendas of any paradigm of interpretation'?" my Evangelical colleagues might ask (I.23). Why is it necessary to bring about the dialogue of interpretations before all are able to recognize the basic narrative of Jesus Christ in each of these interpretations (I.27)? Why does the process of ecumenical hermeneutics need to involve the dialogue partners in a critical examination of the way in which their interpretation affects the lives of people, particularly the marginalized (II.22)?

To be sure, there is a need for all of us to hold one another accountable when we are confronted by "selective and prejudicial readings" (I.23), but where does this principle run the risk of becoming a threat to the richness we claim to discover when diversity is held in tension (I.27)? What safeguards are built into the process of hermeneutics which will guarantee that something is not ultimately treated as "selective and prejudicial" simply because it does not concur with a popular social or political agenda now in vogue? This document attempts to describe such things as a "range of legitimate interpretations" (II.25) and declares that an interpretation "may be judged invalid if it contravenes the biblical imperative to act with justice and charity" (II.26). But

on what basis are such decisions made (II.9)? How are justice and charity to be defined?

3. I suspect that Evangelicals and Pentecostals alike would be somewhat nervous over the number of times this document refers to particular, contemporary social and cultural issues. We are told of the "pervasive patriarchal perspective within scripture" (I.2); "situations of injustice and the struggle for liberation" (I.18,30; II.28); "issues of power as
well as social, political, and other interests" (I.23); the need to be "relevant" to the immediate cultural or social setting (locally) without claiming to be "absolute" (I.30); the need to be especially attentive of those
who are "marginalized for social or economic reasons" (I.36; II.22),
especially towards the weak, oppressed, poor, voiceless, and victimized
(I.30); the need to recognize, with dignity, the unity of Christians who
are divided by "cultural or social differences" which "produce conceptual shifts in society", such as the "growing awareness of the oppressive
patriarchal traditions" (II.8); and the need to avoid "discrimination based
on gender, race, class, and culture" (II.22).

Many, perhaps even most Evangelicals and Pentecostals today share
these same concerns. For us to be reminded of specific contemporary
social concerns may be helpful if it is done once or twice, but Evangelicals and Pentecostals will be concerned by the sheer number of times
specific contemporary issues are cited here. "Is there a social agenda
which is presupposed in this ecumenical hermeneutical approach?" they
will ask.

When these issues are juxtaposed to the requirement that we must be
"relevant", and that no claim can be "absolute", do we really allow the
scripture to speak in any normative way, or has the norm in some way
shifted to the contemporary social situation as it is read by the various
communities? Evangelicals and Pentecostals will argue that the world
and the church need more certainty here, especially as we face a growing number of difficult social, moral and ethical issues in a broad range
of life's circumstances. Where do we reach some sort of convergence on
such issues? How do we set limits in concrete situations? How and
where do the contexts in which we find ourselves, or out of which we
emerge, enter into our interpretation together under the searchlight of the
sacred text? At present, we do not even have full agreement on who or
who is not Christian (I.40). While BEM has helped many, in the Evangelical and Pentecostal movements there are still many who do not recognize baptism as a legitimate basis for such a recognition.

4. Continuity with the apostolic faith and life is important to all of us,
and our text is correct to note that "continuity with the apostolic faith and
life" should not be confused with "mere repetition of the past without

any recognition of the present" (I.11). It is, therefore, right for the framers of our document to note the need for "a disposition of metanoia" within a "spirit of koinonia" when we confront our differences together (I.24; II.13). In spite of our desire to claim continuity with the apostolic life and faith of the past, whether through succession, confessions of faith, claims of the presence of the Spirit, or other means, all of us are frequently tempted by the issues of the present to re-read and reinterpret what was originally meant by the apostolic faith and apostolic life we have received.

The document before us frequently refers to such things as "the one Tradition (which) is hidden within the mystery of the person of Jesus Christ" (I.16), or "the one life-giving gospel" (I.34) as though we all shared a common understanding of these things. But do we? Or does each of our communities hold to a different understanding here? Where is the centre, for instance, in the tension which exists in the "one life-giving gospel" and the presupposition surrounding the need for an ecumenical hermeneutic which embraces the "unity of all humankind" in such a way as to expect us to interpret, communicate and receive non-Christian texts, symbols and practices in exactly the same way as we do (II.3)?

Surely, a strong theological case can be made for the unity of humankind. After all, we were human before we were Christian. And we frequently share the same hopes, dreams and aspirations and are subject to the same fears, disappointments and injustices as everyone else. But Evangelicals and Pentecostals understand scripture to reveal a gospel centred in the person of Jesus Christ, and they will fear the call to receive non-Christian texts, symbols and practices as an open invitation to recognize multiple, efficacious paths to God.

The recognition of the desire to stand in continuity with "apostolic life" as well as the call to a disposition of metanoia when exploring our differences lead ultimately to issues of sanctification. Other than in our common exploration of our difference, though, where are metanoia, ongoing conversion, sanctification, and the "fruit of the Spirit" encouraged to stand over against the "works of the flesh" (Gal. 5:16-6:5) in such an ecumenical hermeneutic? Is it possible that they have been buried under the category of justification rather than being allowed to find their own appropriate place within the larger contexts?

The task presented by the draft before us is a formidable one, but it is also an important one as we seek to understand our koinonia together. We would be greatly helped by bringing to our discussions many of the questions which are taught in any basic journalism class: Who? What? Where? When? Why? How? As we listen to one another in light of such questions, may we move closer yet to the ecumenical hermeneutic for which we are searching.

Plenary Discussion

After the plenary commission members had discussed the draft text in groups, the main points were presented in a plenary discussion. There was general agreement that the structure and title of the study needed to be changed by dividing the text into two parts, for example. The language needed to be accessible, and it was suggested that biblical, patristic and contextual references be given throughout the text. Discussion also focused on the need to bring into tension scripture, Tradition and experience, and that connections be made to the studies on ecclesiology and gospel and culture. The social agenda of the text was criticized and the need for the Orthodox to find themselves in the text, perhaps through an emphasis on doxology, was raised. The issue of fundamentalism and an exploration of the meaning of "symbols" was seen to be an extension of work to be undertaken in the hermeneutics study's further development. Finally, it was emphasized that it is important to stress that the relation between text and context is to be understood dynamically rather than statically.

The development and main points of the draft text were introduced by Turid Karlsen Seim and Emmanuel Clapsis (co-moderators of the drafting group), after which Kyung Sook Lee, Melanie May and Cecil M. Robeck, Jr, gave their reflections on the text.

The Role of Worship
in the Search for Christian Unity

JANET CRAWFORD

In this plenary session we look to the members for guidance as to how the concern for worship and spirituality might be developed in the work of Faith and Order. This concern may seem new to some members but in fact the by-laws of the commission call Faith and Order to study such questions of faith, order and *worship* as bear on visible unity. Also, of course, as churches move closer to realizing visible unity, whether on a local scale or more widely, there are clearly implications for their worship life.

Indeed, it seems to me that it is impossible to separate questions of faith and worship – although we may attempt to do so – for ultimately our worship depends on our faith and our faith is both formed by and expressed by our worship. For the majority of Christians their experience of worship expresses and forms their faith far more than theological study does. Only a few people study theology, but all Christians worship.

However, although worship is an integral part of Faith and Order's mandate and although Faith and Order did a great deal of work on worship in the 1950s and 1960s, there followed quite a long period of neglect when the emphasis was all on the theological study of baptism, eucharist and ministry with very little attention paid to worship aspects.

I think that perhaps the great unplanned, unexpected success of the Lima liturgy told us something about how people want to find theological convergences expressed in some kind of liturgical manner. The fifth Faith and Order world conference in Santiago seemed to renew interest in worship and there have been many comments made here in the plenary sessions indicating that people are interested in and want to make some connections between theology and its expression in worship. So it seems timely for Faith and Order to take up this concern again. Following the world conference the board approved a study on the theme "Towards Koinonia in Worship and Spirituality", to explore both the role of worship and spirituality in the search for visible unity and how this concern might be integrated into all the programmatic work of Faith and Order. I have to say that so far our focus has been on worship rather than on worship and spirituality. Worship is part of spirituality but they are also two rather separate subjects and so far we have only begun to look at the question of worship. This has been a modest beginning, undertaken with enthusiasm but limited resources.

The one major step that has been taken so far was the consultation held at Ditchingham in 1994 in cooperation with the Worship and Spirituality stream of Unit I. All members of the plenary commission should have received the Ditchingham report, *So We Believe, So We Pray*. To summarize the results of the consultation: it looked at the significance of an *ordo* or pattern of Christian worship shared by many churches; it explored criteria for inculturation, seeing it as a force for unity in local situations; it looked at examples of ways in which worship is contributing to the search for unity. The members of the consultation emphasized the importance of worship for Faith and Order's work and made a number of suggestions. I am happy to say that *So We Believe, So We Pray* has received considerable interest from liturgists and worship specialists as well as theologians.

In January 1996 in Bangkok the board agreed that the next stage of this process would be a small consultation on baptism, to be held in January 1997; it will look particularly at the baptism section of *Baptism, Eucharist and Ministry* and at the consequences the churches have drawn, or might still draw, from that text for the actual practice of baptism.

There are at this point no plans for further work after that consultation and so I hope that the plenary commission will give us some guidance as to how the study of the relationship between worship and unity might be developed in Faith and Order's work. I believe two particular aspects should be considered: the question of a more general study of the relationship between faith and worship, and the inclusion of worship as one of the components in the other studies. In the papers we have received there are already some indications as to how that might be done.

The relationship between Christian worship and Christian unity is complex. Clearly worship may foster unity but at times it may make the realization of unity more difficult because worship may be one of the things that in fact divides us. And so we are very happy that three commissioners have agreed to share experiences from their own particular contexts of the relationship between worship and visible unity of the church.

Responses

KWAME J.A. LABI

I have been asked to reflect, as an African and an Orthodox, on the importance of worship to our quest for unity. I must say that I lay no claim to being an Orthodox theologian, either in the academic sense of the word or in its fully patristic sense; but I will speak for myself as an African and an Orthodox Christian. My reflection will focus on a couple of issues raised by the report of the Ditchingham consultation on worship and koinonia (of which I was a participant).

I should like to begin with a story. In 1974 at the plenary commission of Faith and Order in Accra, two young men appeared. They were looking for Orthodox participants in the commission; they found the late John Meyendorff, Thomas Hopko, Nicholas Lossky and announced to them that they too were Orthodox but did not know what that meant. One of these two young men is this now not-so-young theologian addressing you at this Faith and Order plenary commission in Moshi. That meeting on 4 August 1974 was the miraculous reward for a three-year personal search, and the sure beginning of a journey into Orthodoxy and the Orthodox church for me and for a whole community that was eventually received into the patriarchate of Alexandria in 1982. Unfortunately there is no time to go into all the detail that makes this story really interesting.

I tell this story not only because I like to show that mission is the work of God in which we participate, but also because it touches on something that I cannot say enough. I said that that meeting on 4 August was a miraculous reward for a personal search. I was born into a church that called itself Orthodox, but the only thing Orthodox about it was its name. Perhaps because I was the son of a priest in this church I could not leave it and go elsewhere. I was virtually born at the altar and I do not think I could ever have turned my back on Christianity, but I hope you will forgive me when I say that the kind of Christianity that had been brought into my part of the world (or at least the way I perceived it) did not sit well with me. I did not know then what it was that I could not accept, but I was never really at home anywhere. However, even as a lay person who had never even seen an Orthodox church, let alone attended a service, when I first read Bishop Kallistos's book *The Orthodox Church*, long before that August 1974 meeting, things began to make sense. Most of the questions I was having problems answering for myself began to have acceptable answers. The pieces of the puzzle began to fit together, and I knew that I was on sure ground. I think I can say for sure that Orthodoxy helped being an African Christian to make sense. And I believe that being African really helped my understanding of and grounding in Christianity and Orthodoxy.

It is in this light that I think African theologians of all confessions have a significant contribution to make to the discussions on the ongoing search for unity and meaning to life. The new and fresh insights that our language (note that I did not say languages), our thought patterns and symbolisms, our world-view and mentality could bring to these discussions could have significant impact on their outcome and contribute towards achieving the koinonia that we seek and, in Africa, long for. Unfortunately, I do not believe that we have even begun this task. We have all too often been satisfied with speaking the foreign languages in which we have been trained, most of which have little relation to our own.

To try and touch on all the areas in which I think African theologians could make an impact – in fact, to deal with worship alone and how it could help build our koinonia – would require much more time than is available. I would like to refer only to three.

Incorporation

I do not think I need to say that African life, its ethos, the African world-view is intensely religious. However, what I should probably emphasize, because I do not believe this is understood too well, is that this religiosity is also intensely spiritual – not only spiritist but also spiritual. There is a spiritual dimension to every reality and every action. I do not believe that the word "secular" could exist in African traditional life. Even economics is intensely spiritual. But what I must also emphasize, because most people may not know this at all, is that it is in the ritual of life, that could be equated with worship, that this spirituality is most manifest. In African traditional religion(s), Africans celebrate all of life in joyful thanksgiving and supplication to God, the gods, the ancestors and the spirits of all of creation. However, this is done in community, a community that is not only not abstract but also has a very real spiritual dimension. A community in Africa, even today, is not only a collection of persons bound by blood ties alone or certain geographical realities – although these may provide outward forms. A community is first and foremost a spiritual, almost sacred reality. That is why, for example, people from different tribes and towns living in the same house in Accra, for instance, bond together to the extent that, should one of them refuse to participate in certain common events of the community, he or she would be frowned upon and ostracized.

However, there are different levels of this communal existence and reality. Some are more intense and more sacred than others. Communities such as the family, the town, the tribe, the nation (in the old sense), communities such as faith communities, people bound together by common allegiance to a particular deity, will fall under this category of a more sacred spiritual reality.

The point I want to make, however, is that many of our cultures have a process of incorporation into the community, such as through the naming ceremony and other rites of passage. This is what makes one a member of that community. Incorporation, however, has a number of implications: the following are only a few.

In the first place incorporation to a large extent means losing oneself and finding oneself anew in the koinonia of the community. When Komfo Anokye united the Asanti tribes of present-day Ghana into the great Asante nation, he bonded them together by a process of incorporation into a new Asante whose spirit was symbolized by the Golden Stool which he is said to have commanded from the heavens. All the tribal chiefs gave up their sovereignty to the new Asante king, Osei Tutu, to become a new nation united by one spirit.

In addition to this, and on the more personal level, incorporation means a personal commitment to the ideas, practices, beliefs, observances, taboos and celebrations of the community. In the case of "faith" communities or communities bound by allegiance to a deity, this is even more serious. People do not just join, they become "at one" with the community and the deity; they are grafted. The word used in my language to signify becoming a member is "eat". One eats one's faith. This signifies a total "becomingness" in a rather deep spiritual sense, a oneness that is not easily broken without causing harm to the person or the community.

Incorporation also means acquiring new symbols of the community one joins; their totem, for instance, or adapting old symbols to serve the purpose of the new reality. I believe this is why the Western missionaries had such success in destroying our culture. Our people felt that in order to be a faithful part of this new community they actually had to let go of the old, especially if the custodians, the spokespersons, of the new said so.

Unfortunately, it is becoming increasingly clear to many Africans that Christians do not take and do not have to take the implications of their incorporation too seriously, and in our context I believe this accounts in large measure for the lack of interest in issues of faith and theology, as well as for the problem we have with ethics and morality and even tribal and ethnic conflicts. I believe that in any discussions of ecclesiology, koinonia or ethics, African theologians could make a significant contribution to the debate, bringing their insights from their cultures to bear, and they perhaps make a difference.

Inculturation

This brings me to the issue of inculturation. First, let me say I feel strongly that what I have said earlier about the contribution African theologians could make to the ongoing debate is an important aspect of incorporation, cutting across all areas of Christian life. Our attempt to catch the spirit of the "big T" Tradition with the spirit of our "small t" traditions is what inculturation should be about. We cannot stop this attempt.

I would like to make my second point with another story. In January 1996 I was one of a privileged group of Orthodox to go to Ethiopia for a consultation. I believe it was timed to coincide with one of the greatest celebrations of the Ethiopian church, the feast of theophany. I have no words to describe my experience there. Let me only say, with due respect to my Eastern Orthodox sisters and brothers, that in Ethiopia I found real direction for the future of the African church, at least in terms of what inculturation means. But the point of my story is this: as we watched the replicas of the arks of covenant in procession, as we watched the clergy and faithful do the dance of David before the arks, as we watched the veneration of these replicas and learnt about the all-night vigil with the replicas in an open field in the cold January night of Addis Ababa and other towns and cities, some of us could not help but wonder what these people were doing. Why couldn't they leave these Old Testament symbols and practices behind? For us good Eastern Orthodox, epiphany meant the great blessing of water in commemoration of the baptism and manifestation of Christ in the Jordan. And many of us, in fact, remarked that what they were doing was taking things a bit too far. However, as I thought about it, it began to make sense. Is it not true that most of the Old Testament readings on the feast in the Eastern Orthodox tradition centre around the Jordan and the mighty acts of the Lord? Is it

not the case that, both for us as for them, this prefigures the epiphany at
the Jordan? Is it not a fact that the ark was a symbol of the Lord's presence among his people? I believe that for these people the ark had taken
on a new meaning. It was the Lord – Jesus Christ – among his people,
leading them across the threshold of a new Jordan into a new land of
promise. The presence of the Lord, the God of the Trinity, had been
revealed, in the Jordan, in and through Jesus Christ. That is why they
take the ark, which incidentally is their version of our antimension, and
carry it in procession, just as we in the Eastern tradition carry the wind-
ing sheet on holy Friday.

Inculturation is when we are able to use our own symbols to express
the true meaning and reality of what we celebrate in worship. For symbol in the Orthodox understanding is the coming together of two reali
ties – an earthly and a heavenly – to become one, to express one reality.
Our inculturation cannot be limited to incorporating a few African songs
and dances here and there, as we are often made to believe. It is not even
replacing all the old German tunes with new African choruses. It means
much more. It is when our language speaks the language of the liturgy,
when our symbols express the true meaning of the liturgy and what it is
that we celebrate in it. But this requires a metamorphosis – a transfiguration. It requires a purification from inside that only the light from
Tabor could effect; so that our words and symbols are now filled with a
new meaning, a new content, making them appropriate to the liturgy,
appropriate to God.

This brings me to the last point I want to make on inculturation. And
I will simply put it as a question. Are there transcendent symbols, symbols that transcend all cultures? In other words, when do local symbols
become universal and what does it take? In fact, can they become universal? Let me try to illustrate my question by one hypothetical example. Could I say, for instance, that because in my culture death by crucifixion is unheard of – there are much more cruel, more humiliating forms
of death – to make the point stronger, for the cross I could substitute
something else more meaningful, more relevant to my people? I know I
am touching on a very sensitive issue, as Ditchingham rightly put it, but
I raise this in the light of some of the discussions around the elements of
the eucharist. I do not believe that all the dimensions and all the important implications have been properly considered and studied. We could
do more work here.

Spirituality of worship

Finally I want to say something about worship that I probably should
have said at the beginning. I believe that at the heart of the life of the

church is its worship. We can all say that in its outward form, at least, what distinguishes the church, any church, from any other social organization or institution is worship. It is the first mark by which a church is identified. The church, I believe, speaks more through its worship than through any other activity. I believe that in the search for unity, we should pay more attention to the role of worship than we have done so far. In the discussions during this meeting, the occasional reference has been made to worship but I believe that much more needs to be said and done.

One area in which African theologians could make an impact is in our understanding of worship or liturgy. All too often when people think of African worship or Africans in worship, they think of dancing and drums. But I do not believe this is the essence of African worship. They are important, of course. But the spiritual dimension of African worship is in much more than the drumming and the dancing. These only help to express our belonging together and our total dependence on each other. The joys of the community are shared by all as are the sorrows and concerns in worship. Liturgy and all forms of ritual are not only corporate, they bind, making us all one. In this sense, worship is not what makes *me* feel good. It is what the community requires and needs. The festivals before the eating of new yam, the various festivals of purification and dedication, the periods of embargo on all drumming and noise-making are not something that make the people feel good. They are important because they are the requirements of the community as perceived by the community. They bind the community together and even if they sometimes inconvenience me I am part of a whole. This is the spiritual ethos of liturgy and ritual in African religiosity. I believe that a closer look at the spirit behind this religiosity could also enhance our koinonia and unity.

J.W. GLADSTONE

The Church of South India is a union of the Anglican, Presbyterian, Congregational and British Methodist traditions. When the church was formed and inaugurated in 1947 there was no common form of worship. However, a consensus form of worship was adopted for the consecration of bishops, mainly following the Anglican liturgy. The church members, who had belonged to different traditions, felt that as a sign of unity there should be a new form of worship, and in 1950 the synod decided to fashion new worship services, beginning with the eucharist. The synod approved the suggestion of the liturgy committee concerning the main elements. The convenor of the liturgy committee, L.W. Brown, then principal of the Kerala United Theological Seminary, took a keen interest in its formation. A draft liturgy was drawn up, incorporating prayers from the different traditions of CSI and some elements from the St James liturgy which had been used by Malabar Syrian churches in Kerala. It was experimented in the theological colleges – mainly in the Kerala United Theological Seminary and the United Theological College, whose students come from different traditions. It was then translated into four regional languages and used in different regions. In 1954 the synod approved it and it was given out for the use of the churches.

The following points were taken into consideration:

1. The unity of the church would have visible expression in following a common form of worship (in fact, in spite of linguistic and other diversities within the CSI the worship shows that this is a united church).

2. True worship is in spirit and in truth. Therefore congregations would not be forced to adopt the liturgy immediately; they would have sufficient time to experiment with the worship service, to study it and make it their own. The exciting experience of the CSI was that no congregation rejected the new form. Instead, gradually they all owned it as their form of worship and as a visible expression of their unity. For some churches and traditions it took many years, but with time they saw the need for unity and this led to the acceptance of the worship form.

3. Meanwhile the theological students, who would in the future be pastors, were made aware of different aspects of the question, namely: the need for a common form of worship; the richness of the new form of worship; practice in the new form of worship. As a result, when they went back to their parishes they were the instruments of change.

4. The new form of worship ensured the participation of presbyters, deacons and laity. This partly helped the congregations to make the liturgy their own. Moreover, the liturgy included almost all the main elements of worship which they practised.

After this successful experiment with the eucharistic worship, other forms of worship – marriage, funerals, etc. – were introduced, and were accepted without any difficulty. From the experience of the CSI, we can affirm that one of the visible expressions of the unity of different churches is unity in worship. This clearly demands common forms of worship, which should be implemented gradually; nothing can be introduced suddenly. There have been experiments in forms of worship with elements from local culture, but these attempts have not yet received the approval of the people for various reasons.

Since the formation of the Church of North India, we in India have entered into a new phase of ecumenism with the formation of the joint council between CSI, CNI and the Mar Thoma churches. As a result, table fellowship has been established and communion is accepted mutually. This has had tremendous impact on the life of the church, mainly in the freedom for mutual relationships, including marriage.

Every year we observe one Sunday as "unity Sunday", when CSI-CNI pastors will celebrate holy communion in the Mar Thoma church and the Mar Thoma holy communion will be celebrated in the CSI churches by the Mar Thoma priests. Though the people are not very enthusiastic about this type of exchange, there is no real objection to it. This enables people of both churches to see and appreciate different forms of worship.

The Mar Thomas liturgy as far as I can see is a liturgy with richness and tradition. The only thing which can be imagined at present is this freedom and encouragement to use these liturgies in both the churches. The theological seminaries are places where orientation, training and encouragement to use the other form of worship may be given. No such effort has been made so far, but there is no keen need as ecumenical relationships are yet to take definite shape. At present, the need is to recognize each other's forms of worship.

However, in some places outside Kerala CSI-CNI-Mar Thoma people worship jointly. When a CSI presbyter is available there will be a CSI worship, and when a Mar Thoma priest is available worship of that tradition. Personally I have experimented with a combination of both Mar Thoma and CSI liturgies for a few CSI-Mar Thoma parishes in Germany. But such experiments have no ecclesiastical authority, and people accepted them because there was nothing else. Worship has an important role in the unity process.

Prayer on the Way towards Christian Unity

Our Experience in Argentina

JORGE A. SCAMPINI

It will be useful to begin this paper by explaining the situation in Argentina within the wider context of Latin America, as well as the situation within the churches. This will illustrate the path we have travelled and its weaknesses.

The situation in Argentina does not reflect the whole Latin American reality, nor even that of the southern cone. I would emphasize, therefore, that this is a testimony from Argentina, and only from Argentina. Before the Spanish conquest the present territory of Argentina was not as heavily populated as other regions of the continent, nor did it have such an obvious cultural identity. During the colonial period, perhaps because it lacked riches that could be quickly and easily extracted, it was not heavily settled by the Spanish, unlike the present territories of Mexico, Colombia and Peru. All this meant that, in the period of consolidation immediately after independence, one of the priorities was a policy of immigration under the slogan "to civilize is to populate". As a result of this immigration policy, some 90 percent of the present population of Argentina is of European origin, with a much smaller percentage coming from the Middle East. This is one of the peculiarities of Argentina compared to the rest of Latin America.

As to the church situation, there is a marked numerical difference in membership between the Roman Catholic Church and the other churches; this is because of the Spanish colonization, and the fact that later the Roman Catholic faith was incorporated in the country's constitution as the official state religion. The picture became more diversified with the arrival of more immigrants: to immigration we owe the presence of the Orthodox church of the patriarchates of Constantinople, Antioch and Moscow, the Armenian Apostolic Church, and the Anglican, Lutheran, Reformed and Presbyterian churches. At the end of the last century missionary Protestantism brought the Methodist church, the Baptist church and the Disciples of Christ. In recent decades the Pentecostal churches have also appeared.

All the churches are not present to the same extent in the different parts of the country, so that experiences vary. I shall speak only of what I have had occasion to see for myself in my work as secretary of the Episcopal Commission on Ecumenism of the Argentinian Bishops' Conference, in which members of the Roman Catholic Church have been involved. There will be many other experiences, especially at the popular level and, above all, in the popular reading of God's word or in work led by members of other churches.

The Week of Prayer for Christian Unity

Celebration of the Week of Prayer began after the end of the Second Vatican Council. Thirty years on, the situation differs greatly from place to place, often depending on whether or not there is any real possibility of sharing in the life of brothers and sisters of other churches. Let me mention four examples.

Buenos Aires, the capital city, has a population of almost 12 million, and the whole variety of Christian churches is present. Until five years ago the Week of Prayer was celebrated with daily gatherings, each in the church of a different confession. Because this met with little response it was decided to concentrate on a single gathering. This is held in a different church each year, involving in turn the Orthodox, Roman Catholic and Protestant traditions. The vitality of the service depends on the vitality of the host community. The hierarchies of the different churches always attend, but the practice has not been widely taken up by ordinary church members.

In Mendoza, a city of half a million in the west of Argentina, the Week of Prayer is lively and meaningful. A service is held each day in a different church and I have seen for myself how dynamic they all are.

Azul, a small town in the centre of Buenos Aires province, some 300 kilometres from the capital, has two Trappist monastic communities, one for men and one for women. The latter is an Italian foundation, the same community to which the blessed M. Gabriela Sagheddu belonged, named by John Paul II as the patron of ecumenism in the Roman Catholic Church. These two communities consider prayer for unity as their special mission, and they have become the centre of the diocese. During the Week of Prayer they devote an entire day to prayer, meditation, study and fasting, in which members of all the churches in the area take part, including, interestingly enough, the oldest Pentecostal churches.

There have been new initiatives. A major concern has been how to instil the desire for Christian unity in the minds of young people and how to introduce them to the way of prayer.

We have made two efforts in this direction. In Buenos Aires city we have held a vigil of prayer for unity, organized by and for young people. The response has been positive. In the Roman Catholic Church it is our custom to hold a vigil on the night of Pentecost, starting shortly before midnight and ending at dawn. In the vigil organized for those involved in university chaplaincy work we have sought to make prayer for unity an important element in the celebration. It should be noted, however, that for the moment this is a gathering of Catholics praying for unity; it is not yet an ecumenical celebration.

Perhaps the most interesting experience is in the city of Córdoba, where the churches hold moments of common prayer at other times, where possible, and not only during the Week of Prayer: on Good Friday, a common celebration of our Lord's Passion; on Easter morning, when they meet before the services in each church for a moment of common prayer; at Christmas; and on an annual family day of prayer.

Problems not yet solved

The path to unity has shown that there are situations which have to be resolved ecumenically.

One is the translation of the Lord's prayer. Six years ago the Roman Catholic Church harmonized the vernacular version of the missal in all Spanish-speaking countries, including the translation of the Lord's prayer. The translation was modified without consulting the other churches and at ecumenical gatherings we now find ourselves with two versions.

Another problem concerns the celebration of the Te Deum on national occasions, in the Catholic cathedral. This could be seen as a lack of sensitivity, since it fails to recognize that today the people of Argentina are not all Roman Catholic.

Prayer for unity and sharing in common prayer are the soul of the ecumenical movement. In a context such as Argentina, where theological dialogues do not carry definitive weight, prayer and common service may be the only possibility many Christians have for moving towards visible unity.

Plenary Discussion

Twenty people took part in the discussion. One insisted that Faith and Order must look at worship in its wholeness; it is in worship, after all, that all dimensions of human existence come together. Some addressed the question of the nature of worship itself, emphasizing the need to move beyond easy "polarities" (reason and emotion, the heart and the head). Nor can we shrink from considering the dimensions of power and enthusiasm in worship (as seen in the Pentecostal experience of worship). Another pointed to the importance of the *place* of worship, as a reminder that worship has many and diverse dimensions.

The commission was reminded of its own statement at Louvain in 1971 that all Faith and Order studies must include the dimension of worship: we must recover this earlier awareness of the fundamental importance of worship in all aspects of the search for unity. For example, one speaker noted the important role of worship in fostering the "reception" of theological agreements in the churches: worship is a key channel for reception, for prayers and hymns serve also as mediums of teaching among the people of God. How could the theme of worship be included in Faith and Order work on reception? Another noted the crucial link between worship and the former Faith and Order study on the apostolic faith: one of the memorable events at the fifth world conference on Faith and Order had been Bishop John Zizioulas's remark that the creed was not primarily for theologians to study, but for the worshipping congregation to *sing*. How could insights from our work on worship impact our understanding of the apostolic faith? It is, said one commissioner, not only a matter of worshipping together: it is also essential to pray for unity regularly *within* each church, for then all Christians would be made aware of the importance of the search for unity and the commitment of their own church to that search.

Looking ahead to the planned consultation on baptism in relation to Christian unity (January 1997), one commissioner welcomed the intention to develop the work on *ordo* (the common pattern or structure of worship) which had begun at the Ditchingham consultation in 1994. Could this lead to a common order and set of elements for the baptismal service, as a contribution to the churches' search for unity? One speaker urged that questions of the *content* of worship not be overlooked. Another expressed concern that the focus on common patterns might lead to uniformity in worship; this would be unfortunate, since a proper diversity in worship corresponded to certain human needs.

Several persons referred to issues of inculturation. The churches must be encouraged to develop forms of worship appropriate to their own context, forms which should include some aspects of indigenous culture. Others noted that this point raised sensitive and difficult questions. Inculturation involves the appropriation of cultural means to convey the one gospel; but who finally "draws the line" between such appropriation and syncretism? Can Faith and Order help to develop criteria for discernment in this area? Another speaker noted how in some churches worship was "frozen" in the earlier, and foreign, forms brought by the missionaries who had founded them – forms which sometimes continue locally long after they had been abandoned in the "parent" church. Legitimate inculturation is hampered by the need some newer churches feel for external "endorsement" of their efforts; how can Faith and Order promote reflection in this area?

Another speaker referred to the ethical dimensions of worship, encouraging Faith and Order reflection on the ethical implications of, for example, baptism. Yet another speaker took a different approach, emphasizing our accountability for the way in which we worship and for the "message" this sends about the nature of our faith and our community. In certain situations, for example, some Christians are effectively excluded from the church's worship on economic or cultural grounds; surely this is a challenge to the church in that place.

Several speakers addressed issues of continuity and change in worship. One noted that for the Reformation, worship was not static and fixed but should be sensitive to the changing situation of the church in each place. But this, not to mention the widespread efforts at "experimental" worship, raised profound questions: how to balance fidelity to Christian tradition with new aspects and expressions of Christian experience? Could Faith and Order help reflect on the dynamics of such developments in worship – for example, under what conditions does worship foster unity, and when does it actually promote division?

Some encouraged Faith and Order to help produce common worship materials, asking, for example, if it would be possible to bring out an ecumenical lectionary which would be simple and straightforward to use. Another speaker noted that great sensitivity would be necessary in using such material, which would inevitably include texts unfamiliar to some traditions. Another speaker urged that churches find common ground in such events as harvest festivals (which strike some echo also in secular cultures) for the celebration of *creation*. This could combine the common concern for the state of the earth with a spirituality of and for the creation. One asked how Christians could approach the issue of worship with other faith traditions, a sensitive matter which would only become more significant in future years.

One commissioner sounded a note of warning: lay persons around the world, having experienced worship in ecumenical situations, were becoming more and more impatient with the slowness of the churches in finding their way to visible unity. The people, it was said, "are practising an 'ecumenical' faith which they hope the churches will finally catch up with". Visible unity is a matter of *urgency*: something for our generation, not for our grandchildren. Commissioners also referred to the importance of studying spirituality and its role in the search for Christian unity. One emphasized the need to combine academic study with actual experience (using case studies from a variety of specific situations) of spirituality. Another commissioner explained how spirituality combined two dimensions, the action of the human spirit and the guidance of the Holy Spirit; it was the resulting dialogue which enabled worshippers to enter into the presence of God. This was analogous to the fact that the most complete "common worship" would be among churches which were in full communion with one another. For another speaker, spirituality was significant in leading to missionary proclamation; would our study of spirituality maintain sufficiently the notion of the uniqueness of Christ?

Study moderator Janet Crawford thanked the plenary commission for its thoughtful discussion of these issues, and for the helpful practical suggestions which had been made. She pointed out that Faith and Order, in faithfulness to its mandate, must focus on worship in relation to the visible unity of the church; as Faith and Order is not an ecclesial body, its role is to foster discussion and common action among the churches in this as in other areas. She suggested that a concern for uniformity in worship was unfounded; even if it wanted to, the ecumenical movement could hardly create uniformity when there is so much variety already within each church!

* * *

The discussion focused in the next plenary session on worship on proposed recommendations for future work. Janet Crawford responded to the points made, indicating that as far as possible they would be incorporated into the recommendations. She emphasized the intention to work in collaboration with other studies in Unit I and within Faith and Order itself (though the small group discussions had produced few concrete suggestions for this, the point would be kept in mind in future planning). In addition she noted a specific issue raised by one group: the question of common worship services requested by civil authorities for civic and national events. These, she agreed, raised issues which needed to be considered by the ecumenical community.

Week of Prayer
for Christian Unity

The commission held a plenary session to consider possibilities for even more widespread and effective observance of the Week of Prayer for Christian Unity around the world. (The material for the week is produced each year, on the basis of an initial draft by a local ecumenical group, by Faith and Order in cooperation with the Pontifical Council for Promoting Christian Unity of the Roman Catholic Church. It is then sent to the churches and councils of churches for local adaptation.)

The session was introduced by Neville Callam, who surveyed the development of the Week of Prayer observance and its potential for encouraging local work for unity. He was followed by Herman Shastri, who noted the relationship between the Week of Prayer and other popular prayer observances; Sr Margaret Jenkins, who noted also some practical difficulties facing local Week of Prayer observances; and Matthias Sens, who urged that more information from the local initial drafting group be brought into the text each year.

Eight persons participated in the ensuing discussion. Several affirmed that the Week of Prayer was still the most widely celebrated ecumenical event in their local and national contexts. Other speakers, while affirming this, stressed that it was difficult for persons to "go on" praying when they did not see sufficient *concrete results* from ecumenical efforts; perhaps the inspiration of the year 2000 would offer the incentive for decisive progress towards unity.

One speaker noted how – since Christ himself prayed that we may be one (John 17:21) – taking prayer seriously led *inevitably* to prayer with others for the cause of unity. Another referred to the work from 1932 to 1944 of the Mirfield community, and Abbé Paul Couturier. Recalling the phrase "in prayer we meet Christ with no barriers between us...", the speaker urged Faith and Order to use the Week of Prayer to stimulate awareness of the central role of prayer in the Christian life in general, and in the search for Christian unity in particular.

Several persons emphasized that more opportunity for common prayer and prayer for unity was needed, insisting on the importance of praying for unity not just once a year but on special occasions throughout the year (as the Week of Prayer materials themselves suggest). Others stressed the need for local adaptation of the materials; while this is urged in the Week of Prayer materials sent from Faith and Order and the Pontifical Council, it is not always done, whether at the local or the national level.

One speaker explained the Orthodox perspective on prayer for unity, stressing that prayer for Christian unity is an integral part of each Orthodox liturgy. Another recalled how it was a letter from the Orthodox community which had been decisive for Abbé Couturier's "conversion" from an "ecumenism of return" to the broader understanding of the Week of Prayer which prevails today. Another drew attention to the very successful situation in the city of Rome, where several English-speaking churches of various traditions work together in observing the Week of Prayer.

One person noted that, in their situation, the sales of Week of Prayer materials had declined and called for study of why this might be so. The World Day of Prayer observance seemed to be more popular in their situation; was this because it is a lay movement, locally based? In any case, what could Faith and Order learn from this situation?

Another speaker emphasized the importance of interesting *local pastors* in the Week of Prayer; the materials are available, and the challenge is to take them into our leadership and teaching in local congregations. The *Ecumenical Prayer Cycle*, it was noted, also offered the chance to bring an awareness of the wider church into the life of local congregations.

This discussion had not been intended to produce resolutions and specific plans for action; but the commission clearly felt that the Week of Prayer programme should continue and be strengthened, especially in its relation to local congregations. These results, it was noted, would be communicated to the Joint Working Group of the World Council of Churches and the Roman Catholic Church, and to the Week of Prayer international preparatory group.

Ecclesiology and Ethics

A Panel Discussion

KEITH CLEMENTS

I begin with a story to illustrate how profoundly different theological and ecclesiastical approaches can nevertheless lead to a strikingly unanimous ethical conclusion. It comes from the wild west days of North America. A certain frontier town had become so wicked that even the clergy had taken to gambling. Eventually a new, very strict sheriff was appointed to clean the place up. One day in the saloon bar the Presbyterian pastor, the Catholic priest and the Episcopalian priest were busy at their poker table when they saw the sheriff about to come in through the swing doors. Immediately they swept the table clear of their cards and money and adopted an air of pious contemplation. The sheriff, highly suspicious, came up to them and asked each in turn if he had been gambling. "Pastor," he asked the Presbyterian, "were you playing poker?" Being a good Calvinist, the pastor realized that since he was already predestined either to salvation or damnation it made no difference what answer he gave, so he said, "No, I wasn't playing poker." The sheriff turned to the Catholic priest: "Father, were you playing poker?" The priest recalled his seminary training which taught him, that whatever else, you do not bring the church into disrepute, and replied, "No, of course not." Finally he questioned the Episcopalian. Faithful to his Anglican tradition which gives such a high role to the use of reason, the priest looked the sheriff in the eye and said, "Sheriff, when did you ever see a man playing poker by himself?"

You may think I'm cheating with this story because a Baptist doesn't feature in it. But what else could the sheriff have been but a Baptist?

In the study on ecclesiology and ethics I hope we are concerned with sounder grounds than those, for ethical agreements! I would like to express great appreciation for the results of this study so far. The documents *Costly Unity* and *Costly Commitment* and the paper by Lewis Mudge for the Johannesburg consultation have begun to expound in creative ways the notion of the church as a moral and morally formative community. In contrast to much abstract ecclesiology, as a whole they call us to a vision, both more imaginative and more true to real life, on what we mean by the community of the church, and on the diverse forms of interaction between that community, its individual members and the life of society in which it is set. For me, the relation between ecclesiology and ethics is crystallized in Philippians 2: the mind of the Christian community formed by the mind of Christ, the self-emptying servant of God. This mind is of the *esse* of the church as church – and cannot be left at the church door when we go into the world. My first comment is that one helpful consequence of this new approach is in enabling us to see that "what the church teaches" and "what is the ethical consequence of being in this church" are not necessarily the same thing. I do not mean by this the truism that Christian living often falls below the standards set by Christian preaching and official teaching. Rather, it is the fact that ecclesial patterns are capable of generating positive, social ethical influences, far beyond the conscious intentions of their founders. In England, for example, the free church tradition began with the concept of the "gathered church" separate from the world and independent of the state. But while the Anglican state church claimed to be the guardian of national life and order, by the last century no religious influence proved more powerful in *actually shaping* English social attitudes than the free churches. Their emphasis upon individual freedom, equality before God and participatory forms of government learnt in church were crucial in the movement towards a democratic society. However, it cannot be assumed that all social behaviour engendered in church life is good. Churches need to examine themselves to see whether, consciously or not, they are complicit in the social order and merely accommodating themselves to it.

My second point is one which I would like to develop more fully. Surfacing in this study is a recognition that "what the church teaches" implies something else: "what the church is learning". This, like other basic and naive facts of life, can seem so obvious that we tend to ignore it. But it has been borne in on me in the last few years, as one who occupies a desk which is supposed to help the churches in the British Isles respond to international issues. Repeatedly, I am beset by demands to know what the churches are saying, or ought to be saying, about any number of issues, from international debt to intervention in the former Yugoslavia. The typical assumption is that the churches can and should have some instantly available answer to each and every problem set by the world. Do you remember that phrase so much in vogue in the 1960s, "Let the world write the agenda"? I basically still agree with it, but not with the implication that we have a box-file bursting with ready-made solutions.

I also agree that there are times when the churches can and must speak without hesitation, notably in the face of patent injustice and brutality. "Open your mouth for the dumb," as Dietrich Bonhoeffer urged his church in face of the persecution of the Jews in Nazi Germany. Ironically, one of my own greatest frustrations was caused recently by the hesitation of some church leaders in Britain to express solidarity with Palestinian Christians on the grounds that this might upset some people connected with the state of Israel.

But there are issues on which we cannot give an instant answer, because we genuinely do not know it. The temptation is then either to run away from the issues altogether or to try and keep the news-hungry media happy with some banal platitude. Both are denials of our calling. I have tried to address this challenge in a recent book entitled *Learning to Speak: The Churches' Voice in Public Affairs*. In doing so, I found myself wrestling again with the biblical notion of "prophecy". In our time, prophecy has become a kind of catch-phrase for anyone, from garrulous clergy to angry professors, saying anything critical about anything in a loud voice. Prophecy in the Bible is much deeper: it is speaking which arises out of prior engagement with the God who is at work with an alternative history in and for the world. The listening, the envisioning, the learning are as important as the eventual speaking and are its essential ground. "The Lord God has given me the tongue of those who are taught, that I may know how to sustain with a word him that is weary. Morning by morning he wakens, he wakens my ear, to hear as those who are taught" (Isa. 50:4).

In view of this, the element in the texts on ecclesiology and ethics which I would especially wish to highlight is that which speaks of *discernment* in the church as a moral and morally formative community. I quote from *Costly Commitment*, paragraphs 25 and 26 in the Tantur report, and if I had a single wish it would be that we could focus entirely on these words, and what they mean in concrete terms:

> 25. A process of discernment is proper to the Christian community as koinonia...
> 26. Thus as disciples we are called together in a constant process of discernment how best to participate, in the light of our faith, in the moral struggles, complexities and challenges facing humankind. The discerning of the signs of the times is a constant responsibility for Christians and the church (Matt. 16:1-4). It is only to the faithful and the humble that it is given to dis-

cover the signs of the coming of God's reign in the midst of the confusions of the world's history, and to adjust their behaviour to this discernment of God's purpose and call...

I am sorry that the paper we have just been presented with, *Costly Obedience*, does not develop this insight very far, except by implication as for example in paragraph 79. My anxiety is that we as churches are always too impatient for discernment to be a *process*, a *constant* process. Surrounded by a chattering culture, we succumb to the temptation to join in its chatter rather than find words which judge and redeem. We find the silence out of which the genuine word of the Lord speaks too much to bear. We do not like to admit our uncertainties, our ignorance, our blindness. We like to imagine ourselves as teachers and managers of the world who do not need the humbling, educative process, the dark night which the true prophets knew. To quote T.S. Eliot:

> In order to arrive there,
> To arrive where you are, to get from where you are not,
> You must go by a way wherein there is no ecstasy.
> In order to arrive at what you do not know
> You must go by a way which is the way of ignorance.
> In order to possess what you do not possess
> You must go by the way of dispossession.
> In order to arrive at what you are not
> You must go through the way in which you are not.

To emphasize the church as a koinonia of learning is not, as someone has put it, to replace the church militant by the church studious. It is a matter of spirituality, of metanoia, conversion of mind, as much as information-gathering and analysis. Though, if we are to pursue the military metaphor, we may note that military operations mostly founder because of inadequate intelligence. And what kind of koinonia is it which will engender discernment? Therefore, I would like attention to be given to what it will mean, practically, in the koinonia of our churches and our ecumenical fellowship, for time and space to be given to this process of prophetic discernment, for the sake of truly prophetic witness.

NESTOR MÍGUEZ

In the discussion on ecclesiology and ethics there seems to be a growing consensus about the intrinsic nature of the ethical being of the church. There is no place in the ecumenical dialogue for an extreme position that reduces the church to a moral entity or one unconcerned by ethical decisions concerning both its own constituency and the whole of creation. But, given this, this whole area still needs serious consideration.

The usual way this is done, through dialogues, meetings and documents, may led us to agree at certain levels on the nature and scope of this relationship and to word it in a way which most of us can accept without relinquishing our particular theological understanding, tradition and context. But this will not mean that we have furthered our consensus on the fundamental ethical issues and concerns that are ecclesiologically relevant. Other methodological contributions are necessary. Some theological and biblical hermeneutics have developed a different pattern, starting with an analysis of the situation or with life stories. As the purpose of my intervention is to raise questions that might help the discussion move forward, I will propose a different approach to the issue.

It is not simply the content of the theological definitions that has to be revised and enriched by drawing on the new experiences of faith emerging from ecumenical dialogue and witness in the world but, if I understand rightly the nature of the problem, it is also the way in which we reach definitions and the value we give them that have been challenged. So if dialogue about the ethical dimension of the being of the church is to continue and advance, it must be centred not only in the nature of the affirmation of this relationship and its significance for Christian doctrine, but should also take into consideration some basic ethical questions and "test" their projection into classical ecclesiology. In other words, considering the unity and integrity of theological thinking, the way we orient our ethical reflection will affect our ecclesiology and, conversely, the way we elaborate the marks of the church will affect our ethical options. So it is also possible to enter the ecclesiological debate and the quest for greater doctrinal agreement through the ecclesiological dimensions of ethical questions. I hope this will not be understood as a diversion from the specific end, scope and concern of Faith and Order or as a new attempt to throw it into the "socio-ethical" question, but as a different approach to the same goal, through a different channel and methodology. I do not propose to work through the ethical questions themselves but consider how some ethical issues affect the questions Faith and Order has to face.

As an example, let me take an issue which is urgent in our Latin American situation. Recent information from the United Nations confirms what we have experienced in recent years: in the last three decades, the world's gross product has grown to triple the average income per inhabitant. But the "trickle-down" theory has proved incorrect: most of the so-called developing countries have had no share of that growth; the 20 percent richest sector of the population (mostly to be found in the north Atlantic countries) has increased its share in the world economy from 70 to 85 percent, while the poorest 20 percent has decreased its share from 2 to 1.4 percent. The fortune of the 358 top multi-millionaires is equivalent to the total income of the 45 percent less favoured peoples of the world. That is to say, 358 fortunes concentrate more wealth than 23 billion people together. What does this increasing asymmetrical relationship[1] and exclusion[2] of the majority in world economy mean for the life, mission and unity of the church? This question is also a way to approach the relationship between ethics and ecclesiology. There are at least four ecclesiological questions which concern the unity of the church.

1. The first is related to the prophetic and kerygmatic dimensions of the church. The word to be proclaimed is the relevant, active, incarnate Word of God. It is the Word that created the world, so unjustly abused by this economic system, and the incarnate Word that assumes the whole of humankind and thus suffers in the exclusion of the poor. The relationship Word-world is affected by the shape the world is taking because of the exclusion of the poor from the considerations of care for humankind exercised by the powers of the "world market". That dimension of the second person of the Trinity that assumes the anguish, oppression and suffering of the excluded, is excluded also in the totality of the human condition. We are moving from inequality to inhumanity. It is not new that the world resists the Word. But there are moments when the church must consider that some human practices endanger God's will for God's creatures in such a way that it becomes a matter of faith, as in the case of racism or slavery. This economic reality is not a "law of nature" but the consequence of human decisions and practices that generate, sustain and deepen these asymmetries and exclusions. Surely the time has come to consider the development of this economic mechanism not only as an "ethical" issue, but as a challenge to the unity of the church, to its vocation for the inclusion of the integrity of humanity in humankind.

2. Exclusion is not the same everywhere. Those who are excluded are found mostly in certain parts of the world and the powerful in others, reinforcing the already existing asymmetries. The responsibilities of those who live in one or the other part are not the same, in practical terms, and our witness cannot assume the same forms. But the oikoumene demands some kind of interaction that can overcome the imbalance generated by this economic qualification. The unity of the church must be expressed in ways that stimulate mutual recognition and support

of those who are taking concrete ethical options in different contexts. These differences in witness must tally with a common understanding of the kind of struggle we face as a body. On the other hand, some of the divisions we face as churches tend to reinforce the divisions we find in the world.[3] So a second question would be, how does our witness, our living out the trinitarian *typos* in the church catholic and in creation, generate signs and symbols that could reverse the practice of exclusion and asymmetry?

3. This economic practice (which is in fact more than just economic) renders more visible and painful the existing asymmetries and exclusions among and within the churches. Intra- and inter-ecclesial relations carry the same overtones that are often a mark of economic and social relations. The practices and needs of the poor and the excluded are many times judged "from the top", from power centres. Ethical criteria do not always take into account the reality from the perspective of the powerless (which is central to a theology of the cross and resurrection). Dominant theological canons are constructed from power centres (usually located in rich countries). The theological systems that address the "problems" of the powerless (with more or less empathy with them) seldom consider that their own power structures and standards are part of the mechanism of victimization. Ecclesiastical structures built on centralized schemes normally reinforce asymmetries. Those that work without considering the distribution of power (which is more than mere representative quotas) tend to perpetuate inequality as an organizational principle, even involuntarily. The processes that have led to asymmetries and exclusions have also been fed by theological arguments and ecclesial developments. An alternative ethos will also require a different theological ethic and ecclesiological practices.

4. Finally, it is this reality that truly calls into question the possibility of a koinonia ecclesiology. The sacramental practice that conceals or ignores its commitment to the poor, the marginalized or the hungry denies the body of Christ and is not a proclamation of God's reign but judgment upon itself (1 Cor 11:29). There is no spiritual koinonia if the asymmetry of power is not challenged. There can be no koinonia if diversity is not accepted, but neither can there be koinonia if diversity is such that it affects the life and dignity of the other by exclusion. In preparation for the fifth world conference on Faith and Order in Santiago de Compostela, the Latin American regional consultation already affirmed: "When, in situations of power or in non-theological matters, there is an attempt to establish inequality in a relationship, this cannot be considered as koinonia. It works against the fulfilment of both partners in the relationship, building a 'customer relationship' ["patron-client

relationship", in Spanish] that obscures the full meaning of koinonia. The strength of the communion language needs to be evident in ecclesial practices which involve true reciprocity and common submission to the word of God. Thus the witness of the church in everyday life can confront the dehumanizing asymmetry of our society."

If the trinitarian relationship is the *typos* of the church, then the growing exclusion of vast sectors of people from the fullness of life challenges the word the church should be proclaiming and enacting in its trinitarian vision and mission. The church as "moral community", for example, will be judged not only in this way, but also for its ability to be ethical vis-à-vis the sins that affect our world and the way the church is built. Issues such as sacramental practices, the prophetic proclamation of the word, reconciliation, the ministry of episcopé, can also be considered – even though it is difficult – from the point of view of the ethical options implied in each theological definition and ecclesial model, or the theological and ecclesial consequences of ethical decisions that witness to God's presence and action in our world.

NOTES

1 By asymmetry I understand here a relationship based on the lack of the ability or possibility of reciprocity. It is characterized by an imbalance in the capacity of those involved, so that the weaker party is denied its right to act in the same way as the stronger.
2 Exclusion in this context means that the decisions of the social sector in power consider the needs and existence of other sectors to be incompatible with their own.
3 Already in the 1950s Faith and Order considered this theme in a study on "Non Theological Factors" (cf. a letter by C.H. Dodd).

OLGA GANABA

In the context from which I come, we are experiencing a time of growth – practically every day new members join the church, new parishes come into being, church buildings destroyed under the communist regime are reopened and renovated. People who, for various reasons, were outside the church up to now are discovering the church anew, enjoy the freedom to attend openly, to confess their faith openly, to speak openly about the church and work for it.

Therefore ecclesiology is becoming one of the questions most discussed in Russian society today, where the new-found reality of the

• This paper has been translated from the German by Renate Sbeghen and Thomas Best.

church as an institution enjoys considerable authority. This raises questions, e. g. what is the nature of the church, what is the basis of its authority, what is its place in society.

We also need to take into account the present-day missionary situation in Russia. Preachers and missionaries of various kinds have flooded into the country, and groups have emerged, unrelated to the church, which declare that in order to be loyal to Christ and his gospel the church in its present form is not necessary; it is enough to keep the ten commandments, read the gospel and do charitable works. There are also voices which criticize the church as institution, saying it is outdated and in need of "modernization" along "Western" lines!

Questions of ethics are no less important in contemporary Russian society. At a time of searching for new directions in politics and in public life, and restructuring the economy, moral values often get lost. Ethnic conflicts, increasing criminality, terrorism, corruption and nationalism are all part of the reality experienced today by the people of Russia and the former Soviet Union.

In these circumstances society demands from the church a clear answer to the questions of ethics and the meaning of life, and guidelines for daily life. It is the duty and nature of the church to give that answer.

These questions are also central for the study before us. What is the church, and to which ethical requirements of the time does it need to do justice? It is not possible to answer without considering the principal vocation of the church. The apostle Paul speaks about this in his letter to the Ephesians (Eph. 4:12-16):

> ... to equip the saints for the work of the ministry, for building up the body of Christ, until we all attain to the unity of the faith and of the knowledge of the Son of God, to mature manhood, to the measure of the stature of the fulness of Christ; so that we may no longer be children, tossed to and fro and carried about with every wind of doctrine, by the cunning of men, by their craftiness in deceitful wiles. Rather, speaking the truth in love, we are to grow up in every way into him who is the head, into Christ, from whom the whole body, joined and knit together by every joint with which it is supplied, when each part is working properly, makes bodily growth and upbuilds itself in love.

From the standpoint of Orthodox theology it is impossible to speak about Christian ethics without taking into account aspects of trinitarian dogma and the teaching about salvation.

If we consider the church in the light of Ephesians 4:16, we have to emphasize that the truth and grace of God are not given to each believer individually but to the community of the faithful in the church. This represents a body created by the spirit of God who brings the members of the body into a unity of love so that they may live this unity; they will die spiritually if they fall away from it.

Thus the church is the new being, the new beginning, and the only way through which human beings can enter into community with God. People are also brought into a new community in which all differences, separations and hostilities will be overcome through love and grace. This new unitive being – the church – is not modelled on any earthly institution but on the unity of the Holy Trinity, that reality where life is integrally one.

What is most important in this new being are the relationships between the individual members, between the church and the human beings who form this body, human beings whose relationships are based on love.

Just as the original God-given unity of the human being, the Old Adam, was not abstract but a real and living power, so the church is not simply the sum of many individuals or a mere juridical institution, but a new holy and gracious reality, one that will be indestructible on earth until the second coming of Christ. Thus the unitive nature of the church is the basis of the unity of human existence, of that human nature, distorted by sin, which has been re-established by Christ.

The reality of the church is manifest in the belief of the faithful, in spiritual joy, repentance, purity and love, and also in grace. All these are not acquired by a person's own efforts and powers, but are rather the characteristics of a new nature, a new humanity, which is "put on" in baptism. Thus it is the task of each person, of his or her own free will, to safeguard and increase this new life as well as to deny the opposing nature of the old Adam. Each person, according to the apostle's word, must carry the cross – that is, crucify the nature of the old Adam.

The gospel and the epistles of the apostle speak of two ways in which human beings appropriate grace: the rebirth of human nature through the word of truth, or the purification of our nature through the gospel; and in Christ's parables about human beings, the invisible growth of the seed of the new nature, and the reality of the kingdom of God in the soul of all.

Thus the church is not only the guardian of Christian doctrine, the mediator of the merciful divine energy (that is, healing power, holiness as a quality of the church). The grace which dwells in the church demands of human beings a conscious appropriation of these gifts and passing them on to others, to members of the church but also to those who stand outside the church (Eph. 4:16). So the principal tasks of the church are (1) preserving the new, grace-filled life; (2) passing on the content of this life to others; (3) guiding the faithful to the full appropriation of this new life.

Just as the life of the Divine Persons is the unitive life of the whole being of God, so the power of Christ's grace-filled life which is effective on earth proceeds from the pleroma of the church. Thus only the one, holy, catholic and apostolic church is holy and infallible, not separate offshoots of the church or local "authorities".

In Orthodox theology the church is identified as a church which must fight a constant battle in this world. This struggle has two aspects: (1) it is the battle which each church member conducts against the old Adam, or against his own nature, weighed down as it is with sin; (2) it is the battle waged by the whole church in order to bring the whole creation into community with God, that is, to redemption. This is the struggle for the reconciliation of the world with God in his love and justice, a struggle which takes place (1) invisibly, like the leaven Jesus speaks of in one of the parables, and (2) visibly, through the conscious actions of the churches' members in each place and in every situation in their lives.

Thus the church militant has as its tasks here on earth: (1) infallibly to safeguard the source of the divine life, that is, the Lord's teaching and the gracious energy of the new life, that is, holiness, and (2) to bring this teaching and holiness through prayer, the sacraments and instruction both to the members of the church for the sake of their perfection in life within the church, and to those who do not know Christ in order that they too can enter into the new being, the body of Christ.

If someone in today's society seeks an answer to ethical questions, they turn to Christian teaching or seek to formulate something helpful on the basis of the gospel. Here we come to matters which are obscure and require explanation. On the other hand, we may seek answers in the ethical teaching of the fathers from the early undivided church, as well as in the writings of modern spiritual teachers or in the ethical systems found in the world today.

When the study on "Ecclesiology and Ethics" speaks of the church as a moral community, it does not take into consideration sufficiently the institution of the church, which is built on the basis of the doctrine of the Trinity and the relationships of the Holy Trinity as the body of Christ. When it speaks of ethics, it forgets that Christian ethics is different from secular ethics, and does not have as its goal the abstract "common good". The task of the church in the world is to work, through its witness and in collaboration with public institutions, for the moral transformation of the world.

Regarding the question whether the WCC can be the "sign" of the ecumenical moral community, I would like to say the following. First, the term "ecclesio-moral community" is incorrect because it raises false expectations. The WCC has "ecclesial significance" only in the sense that it provides a framework in which the member churches can work together. It does not have an independent ecclesial significance. However, it could become a "moral community"; for Christians and for the whole world it is important that Christians can address moral problems with a single voice, such as injustice, peace, racism, discrimination, etc. But there are many matters the WCC avoids dealing with, for example homosexuality or euthanasia or abortion. These are profound ethical-moral issues, which become the touchstone for the identity of the World Council. On these questions the WCC becomes a prisoner of the moral systems of the world and thereby its moral-ethical witness is weakened.

Plenary Discussion

The commission reviewed the cooperative work on ecclesiology and ethics done, under the mandate of the WCC central committee, by Faith and Order and Unit III. The commission had before it a paper summarizing the origin and process of this work, a provisional listing of "common perspectives" on ecclesiology and ethics, and *Costly Obedience*, the report from the recent third and final consultation in the study programme.

The collaborative work was introduced by Paul A. Crow, Jr, moderator of Faith and Order's involvement in the study process. Dr Crow first noted Faith and Order's long history of work on the relation between the unity of church and issues challenging the human community (most recently in the study "The Unity of the Church and the Renewal of Human Community", culminating in the book *Church and World*), and then traced the origins of the ecclesiology and ethics study from its origins in 1992 through the three consultations held in the study process (in Rønde, Denmark, in 1993, in Tantur, Israel, in 1994, and in Johannesburg, South Africa, in 1996). He noted that the WCC central committee, and the WCC as a whole, had been keenly interested in the study as an example of inter-unit cooperation, and the texts already produced, *Costly Unity* and *Costly Commitment*, had generated considerable ecumenical interest and debate.

The purpose of this study had not been to address specific ethical issues – on some of which the churches still disagreed – but to explore new perspectives and language for *linking* the themes of ecclesiology and ethics, which were too often treated separately in the churches and the ecumenical movement. *Costly Obedience* was to be read as the report from one consultation in the ecclesiology and ethics process; it was not intended as a summary or "culmination" of the process as a whole.

Paul Crow indicated that now that the ecclesiology and ethics study had ended, further work was being proposed on the topic of "Ethnicity and Nationalism in Relation to the Unity of the Church"; this would be done in collaboration with Unit III, with the initiative lying with Faith and Order. Faith and Order would also contribute theological perspectives to the Programme to Overcome Violence, a major programme of Unit III.

* * *

Following the panel discussion and the group sessions, the commission came together in plenary. Some 22 participants spoke, both reporting on the course of the discussion in their group and speaking more from their own personal perspective.

The discussion focused on the report from the third consultation, *Costly Obedience*. One speaker appreciated the attempt to link fields of theological work which were too often separated; this effort, however difficult, was a crucial part of the ecumenical quest and could no longer be neglected. Another lauded the text's effort to think afresh about these issues. Yet another noted how the text raised fundamental questions urgently needing ecumenical clarification: what is the *ecclesiological* significance of the churches' involvement in common ethical reflection and action? How can the search for church union, and the churches' mutual engagment in ethical reflection and action, strengthen one another? Should not the fruits of our ethical reflection be Christian witness and service in the world; was it not essential, for example, for churches to be able to offer a critique of power as exercised by the state?

Several speakers offered diverse evaluations of the *nature* of the text *Costly Obedience*. One located it in the liberal debates of the 1970s, another saw it as an attempt at an academic, post-modern ecumenical ethics. For still another it was not sufficiently detailed or sophisticated in its treatment of particular confessional approaches to moral questions. Others found the text too oriented to official texts and statements at the expense of "lives lived"; surely it was the latter rather than the former which should be the starting point for our ethical reflection. For another the text raised a fundamental question of method: how could Faith and Order work be made relevant and accessible to areas which did not address theological issues or ethical questions by debating documents at all but through other methods of discernment?

For some the study ran the danger of trying to encompass too many ethical concerns. One suggested as a focal point the following question: what difference does it make for the ecumenical community to do moral formation and ethical reflection together, rather than for the churches pursuing these matters separately? Or what does the ecumenical community have distinctively to offer to the notion of "moral community"? Such starting points would clarify the *ecumenical* dimension of the study which, it was said, has been one of its main contributions (cf. *Costly Commitment*, para. 17).

The concern for formation, and especially the term "moral formation", generated considerable critical interest. For one speaker the text did not sufficiently explain the crucial role of human culture in the formation of human beings. One noted that the term, though not familiar to his own tradition, had analogies with the more familiar language of "conscience" (which however was not used at all in the text). Another found the language of *mal*formation unfortunate; the text should develop the themes of sin and metanoia rather in relation to holiness, and the eschatological notion of "becoming what we are already". Some speakers picked up the related concept of *discernment*, one saying that this was what bound together the "spiritual" realm and actual, lived experience.

One speaker expressed appreciation for the image of the "household of life", which has already been used in other ecumenical contexts, as a helpful perspective for addressing the present global crisis. But another was "surprised" to find the word *oikos* (household) in the text and "amazed" at the lack of reflection on this model, which was closely related to the patriarchal household of the Greco-Roman world and thus to a whole history of oppression. These difficulties, it was noted, had already been pointed out in the Faith and Order board's discussion of the Tantur report, *Costly Commitment*.

Many speakers addressed the language of the text. One had found this "inaccessible"; others found particular terms, such as "engagement", difficult, or noted how certain phrases – for example the reference to "purifying the liturgy" (para. 58) – would be problematic for certain traditions. Conversely, others complained about the absence of certain concepts, such as "theosis", which would be understood by some traditions as essential in a discussion of Christian ethics.

Several speakers felt the absence of a discussion on sin, insisting that this could not be replaced by the concern for "moral formation". Also lacking, according to some, were treatments of the psychological dimension of human life, the biblical concept of anthropology, and the category of *eschatology*, which needed to be dealt with not only theologically but in the local church life. For others the category of "sin" led to reflection on the suffering and injustice of the world; one speaker, moved by our meeting in the African context, suggested that the commission write a letter to the church and people of Burundi, expressing solidarity with them at this time of turmoil and violence in their country. Still another noted that no one could live entirely "outside" this world, and insisted that we needed to speak with penitence of our complicity with its structures.

Other speakers pointed to other topics which they found lacking in the text. For some it failed to emphasize the role of the Bible in Christian ethical reflection and formation. Others wanted more specific reference to traditional sources of authority such as the teachings of Jesus. Another emphasized the value of "ethics arising from scripture", particularly from the teaching and life of Jesus: we need, said another, to start with image of God, especially as seen in Christ. An explicitly "Christic basis" for our reflection, suggested another, would lead us necessarily to the search for *justice*; for another, taking the life and teachings of Jesus as our point of departure meant a radical choice: to take the side of the victim.

One speaker asked whether the text had rightly understood the relation of the congregation to the life of the church as a "moral community": in particular, what is the precise role of worship in the process of moral formation? Another speaker missed a clear articulation of the global, regional and local dimensions of ethical engagement: each has its distinct but inter-related dynamic, and the churches and the ecumenical community have a responsibility for ethical reflection and engagement in each dimension. Another focused on the ethical implications of modern media, calling for concerted ecumenical work in this area. Another speaker noted that ethical reflection and engagement is also going on in other faith communities; the churches and the ecumenical movement must learn to relate to these efforts in a more deliberate and constructive way.

Looking to a wider context, some speakers noted issues in relation to the WCC and the wider work of Faith and Order. One noted that the text raised fundamental questions about inter-programmatic work: what was the commission's relationship to such cooperative work with other WCC programme units? What principles should guide the planning and carrying out of such cooperative work? How could Faith and Order, while respecting the special dynamics of such work and the integrity of our working partners, exercise appropriate oversight for its part in such projects? How could Faith and Order best fulfill its obligations to the fellowship of churches within the WCC, while being accountable to the churches through the Faith and Order commission? In addition, one speaker asked about the intention of the concluding section of *Costly Unity* (paras 98-116), which was addressed to the WCC itself: what was its relation to the WCC's current "Common Understanding and Vision" process?

One speaker noted more generally that ethical judgments are increasingly a source of *dis*agreement, within both churches and the ecumenical movement. In this connection it was noted that the text on ethical issues as sources of common witness or of division, which had been sponsored by the Joint Working Group between the WCC and the Roman Catholic Church, touched helpfully on issues raised in the reports from the three consultations in the study process.

During the discussion various positions were expressed on the advisability, or the proper way, of publishing the text *Costly Unity*. It was felt that if the text were published it should be clearly identified as the product of a particular consultation rather than as a text emerging from the commission itself.

By general agreement the brief provisional text offering "common perspectives on ecclesiology and ethics" was judged not ready for transmission to a wider audience. While offering for one speaker an entry point into the discussion, it was criticized by others on several grounds: there was insufficient consensus on the points made; the language of section 2 was problematic; the references to the eucharist and baptism in sections 3 and 4 respectively did not reflect the diversity of Christian belief and practise.

* * *

Responding to the discussion, Paul Crow thanked the plenary for the points which had been expressed. He reminded the commission that the purpose of the study had not been to examine specific ethical issues, but to explore the inter-relation between the fields of ecclesiology and ethics. The critical comments, however, had pinpointed important issues in this field, and in relation to cooperative work in general, which would be considered carefully in planning future Faith and Order work in this and other areas. Noting once again that the text *Costly Obedience* claimed no authority from the Faith and Order commission, he indicated that a full account of the present discussion, and the minutes of the group discussions, would be shared with WCC Unit III.

Discussion on President Mkapa's address

In view of the keen interest aroused, a special plenary session was organized to explore the issues which the president had raised, and to consider their implications for the future work of Faith and Order. The discussion was initiated by reflections by three commissioners. Bert Hoedemaker pointed out the link between the president's address and Faith and Order's earlier focus on the unity not only of the church but of humankind, while Evelyn Parker emphasized the implications for Faith and Order's work on ecclesiology and ethics. Sebastian Bakare suggested that the commission had not sufficiently taken up the president's speech, and the situation in Tanzania, as a creative challenge to its work, noting in particular the country's success in creating national unity within a multi-party state, and the difficulties it faced due to global economic developments and the crushing burden of external debt.

Some 16 speakers took part in the ensuing discussion. One commissioner suggested that, had this plenary come earlier in our meeting, it would have enabled a far more balanced and fruitful discussion of the work on ecclesiology and ethics. For another, it suggested the need to recover the Faith and Order work on unity and renewal which had culminated in *Church and World*, particularly the notion of the church as "prophetic sign" and "effective instrument" of the renewal of humanity and of creation. Additionally it showed the importance in ethical discussion of striking a proper balance between individual interests and community needs, and in gospel proclamation of addressing all the people of God, poor and rich alike.

The address, it was noted, could help set our work within a truly global context. Faith and Order should address issues of justice not because "the world" sets the church's agenda, but because the church is of Christ, who became incarnate in the world. Thus a "unity" achieved without any awareness of the problems of the world would be an empty, even sinful, form of unity. Similarly, it is not enough simply to confess the Christ of history; we must be able to discern the *presence* of Christ in the world today. One commissioner noted that work for the renewal of the human community would require dialogue with persons of other faith communities: was Faith and Order ready to undertake this?

Several persons urged Faith and Order to explore the issue of international debt which President Mkapa had highlighted in his address. One commissioner identified the two key problems to be the growing disparity between developed and developing nations, and the increasing ability of the rich to set the terms even for the discussion of the issue. A theological critique was called for of economic systems which destroy impulses towards generosity and leave no room for grace; we need to recover the perspective of the prophets, for whom God's demand for justice was the expression of God's love for the whole of humanity. One speaker, recalling the phrase "forgive us our debts as we forgive our debtors", called for a study of the Lord's prayer as an entry-point for Faith and Order's grappling with issues of economics. Another noted that using the *Ecumenical Prayer Cycle* offered the opportunity to raise concerns of justice and human well-being, and urged that Faith and Order's work on worship should be alert to such issues. Another asked what *hermeneutic* was needed to address the fact that 15 percent of the world has at its disposal 85 percent of the world's resources? Still another urged Faith and Order to cooperate with other WCC programmes addressing this issue, perhaps in light of initiatives planned for the year 2000. One commissioner brought examples from his own country of projects addressing the current global debt crisis.

Another speaker called on ecumenical bodies to work with local and national media to correct false stereotypes and images of Africa, and to emphasize the *moral* realities of African society which we had discovered during our time in Tanzania: a firm commitment to help refugees, to strengthen the community, to build a just society. Another noted parallels between koinonia and the African concept of *ujama*, which links family, community, tribe and nation in a search for the well-being of individuals and the community as a whole. Such social visions, it was said, stand as a challenge to the values of this world; indeed "the world" may try to prevent such hopes from succeeding. Too often the churches themselves contributed to division (for example by having parallel aid programmes and publishing houses) while they should be modelling common commitment and engagement. After so much ecumenical advance are there really – in the words of Faith and Order's third world conference at Lund in 1952 – "deep differences of conviction" which prevent the churches from working together more comprehensively and effectively?

Towards Sharing the One Faith

A Study Guide for Discussion Groups

YEMBA KEKUMBA

"Towards the Common Expression of the Apostolic Faith Today" is one of the main projects initiated by Faith and Order in the history of the ecumenical movement of these last years. The process started early in the 1980s. The apostolic faith study produced a book, *Confessing the One Faith*, which explains in an ecumenical way the one apostolic faith Christians share. At its annual meeting in Dunblane, Scotland, 1990, the standing commission (now board) decided to prepare a short guide that could act either as a companion "workbook" or as resource material that stands on its own. The study guide you have in your hands today is a result of this preparation. Two consultations were held in 1994, in Venice, Italy, and in Bucharest, Romania. After discussion in groups and in plenary the standing commission, at its meeting held in Aleppo, Syria, in January 1995, recommended revising the draft produced by the two consultations. A small group, including the moderator and director of Faith and Order, met in London in July that year. The revision took into consideration remarks and comments from commission members made at Aleppo and received in writing later. After a week of intense work the group produced a revised and improved text with the title *Towards Sharing the One Faith: A Study Guide for Discussion Groups*. Before the annual meeting of the board in Bangkok in January 1996, the text was tested in various groups and settings in Africa, Asia, Europe, North America and Latin America. In general, reactions we received from these groups and settings were very positive.

In the light of a progress report on the revision of the text the Faith and Order board in Bangkok approved the publication of the apostolic faith study guide. Three drafters met in London in March 1996 to do the final editorial work.

The purpose of the study guide

The purpose of this guide is to stimulate and accompany involvement of ecumenical groups, congregations and institutions of theological education in the study of the apostolic faith project. For that reason the guide is not a summary of *Confessing the One Faith*. Its main purpose is stated as follows on the back cover of the booklet:

> This study guide is an initiative on the way towards the recovery of unity in faith among Christians in the world today. It is intended to help ecumenical and denominational groups enter into the process of exploring the faith of the church, and of recognizing this faith in their own lives and the lives of other Christian communities. The hope is to move us towards common witness to the faith in liturgy and life and towards growth together in visible unity.

The Faith and Order board suggested in its annual meeting in 1996 that

> continuing work on confessing the faith, both in respect of the study guide and the original study, needed to be undertaken. It was affirmed that a number of board members would keep those issues before Faith and Order, in the light of responses in both documents.

The study guide is now ready to be used in ecumenical groups, congregations and theological institutions. It will be used as a model, but it can be adapted to different situations and needs. We invite those who are going to use the text to continue the process of the apostolic faith study and not to consider *Towards Sharing the One Faith* as the end of the process. We therefore submit this study guide to you and ask for your comments and suggestions, especially on how to make the best use of this instrument concerning, for instance, its translation and distribution, and also on the future of this important study.

When *Confessing the One Faith* was sent to the churches, an accompanying letter was prepared to explain what Faith and Order was expecting of them. Should a similar letter accompany this guide when it is sent to ecumenical constituencies?

A word of appreciation and thanks

As explained, the final text you have in your hands today has been patiently prepared through a process of consultations by various groups of representatives from around the world of Anglican, Baptist, Lutheran, Methodist, Moravian, Orthodox, Reformed and Roman Catholic churches. Many participants in these consultations are present at this meeting. Each group has brought its specific contribution to the preparation of this final product. Peter Donald and Peter Bouteneff undertook the editing. On behalf of the Faith and Order board I would like to take this opportunity to express our appreciation and gratitude to all those who participated in the preparation of the apostolic faith study guide for their personal and collective contribution.

Plenary Discussion

Towards Sharing the One Faith, the study guide of Faith and Order's apostolic faith study process, had only recently been published. The secretariat requested suggestions from commissioners on the most useful channels of distribution, which led to a list of over 150 names and addresses.

The text was affirmed more or less unanimously by participants from a wide variety of Christian traditions, both those which do and do not feature the regular use of creeds. The character of the discussion was influenced by the fact that this text had reached something of a completion point; therefore there were only a few suggestions and comments made on particular paragraphs, and these were noted for future revised editions. Most interventions concerned questions and suggestions around the translation and distribution of the booklet.

Regarding translation, there was consensus that, because each region needed to adapt the text for local use, and because of the shortage of funds allocated to the study, the responsibility might well be placed on local churches and councils of churches. Translation into Asian languages should not be neglected, and translation into Russian was recommended, possibly with slight emendations.

The discussion on translation overlapped with the concern that the guide be sent out and received on the explicit understanding that the form, e. g. for discussion groups, should be considered as adaptable and not fixed in stone.

It was also agreed not to limit distribution efforts to those churches and persons who take a particular interest in the creeds or in the history of the early church: the point of the text is not the Nicene Creed itself but engagement with the basic issues of the Christian apostolic faith. As people come to recognize the apostolic faith in themselves and their own tradition, the hope is that they begin also to recognize that same faith where it exists in other traditions, despite God-given variety in forms of expression.

II
Ongoing Tasks

From BEM to Koinonia

J.-M.R. TILLARD

Of all the tasks undertaken under the influence of the ecumenical movement, the Lima text is beyond any doubt the one which has produced the most remarkable reaction. Several churches have seen in it major pointers to a serious commitment for the re-establishment of visible *communion*. Others have more or less rejected it, because they found in it viewpoints which could not be reconciled with their own confessional tradition. The six volumes containing the official responses and the major summary report published by Faith and Order in 1990 effectively make up the picture of what I called at Lima "this vast ecclesiological worksite, which we dare not open up because we are terrified of what it will cost our confessions". For everything is at stake here.

In this brief presentation I intend to describe what seems to me to be the necessary pre-condition for the "reception" of BEM. For one obstacle stands in the way of acceptance of what can and must draw together the enduringly real fabric holding us together which the Spirit maintains between us. On the foundation of the highly complex "reception" of the Lima text, what can be done:

a) to give full expression to the enduring imperfect *communion* between the confessions; and

b) to move this *imperfect communion* on towards *full communion*?

That is my concern in this all too brief paper.

Co-existence of the confessions

The first observation, which we must take as our starting point, while weighing all its consequences, is this: despite the very serious schisms and divisions tearing us apart, in all the communities of the baptized, in the West and the East, there is to be seen a surprising vitality. The Second Vatican Council took note of this and on that basis made the impor-

---

• This paper has been translated from the French by Tony Coates.

tant distinction (intuitively Augustinian) between the institutional or canonical boundaries of the (Roman) Catholic community and the Spirit's boundless field of action. From that it deduced that "the communities beyond the bounds" are not without the means of salvation, which sometimes flourish more among them than in Catholic communities.

Based on the convergences in BEM on baptism and its link with the word of God, it is now necessary, using the same approach, to perform a critical theological evaluation of the co-existence of "the confessions". It is a matter of perceiving the ecclesiological significance of their ministering of grace, building on the certainty of "the one baptism". For wherever true baptism is administered there is a universally recognized life of grace. But it is lived in a situation in which confessions co-exist, which are sometimes at odds on essential points. What conclusions should we draw concerning baptism from statements like Galatians 3:27-28, "Baptized into union with Christ, you have all put on Christ as a garment. There is no such thing as Jew and Greek, slave and free person, male and female; for you are all one person in Christ Jesus"? What is the nature of our unity *en Christo* which, now that baptism is seen as a true (valid, *bebaion*) baptism everywhere, coincides with confessions sometimes behaving in a polemical or even hostile way? First Corinthians 12:13 enables us to put the question sharply: for, if "it is in one Spirit *(en heni pneumati)* that we have all been baptized into one body", what is the relation between this Spirit of unity which we can be sure is effective, and the division between the confessions which, however, does not cause the wellspring of grace to dry up.

After BEM we can no longer be content here with questionable or diplomatic explanations, still less with a retreat behind canonical or apologetical excuses. The issue must be squarely faced. What is the meaning of our baptismal unity? What is being said to us by the obvious vitality of the confessions in a divided Christianity?

Imperfect but real communion

This leads to another question, on which we have not yet pronounced unanimously, despite some strong statements in BEM. This relates to the close link between faith and baptism. It concerns the imperfect underlying ("subsisting") communion, which is a *reality* despite our confessional difference. One of the great contributions of Faith and Order in the ecumenical movement is to have helped us to understand concretely that, despite all, our divided confessions are truly in *communion*, and that at an infinitely deeper level than that of joint action. The Spirit has inspired us to say "yes" and thus we belong to the same Christ, and that unites us, despite the divergences between our confessions which do, however, affect our faith.

The time has come for us, together, to pinpoint clearly the nature and concrete impact of these *faith convictions*, which transcend our differences and which unite us despite our confessional divisions. For – and I have been defending this position for a long time, but with very little response – these *shared faith convictions* are without a shadow of doubt what underlies by the grace of the Spirit our imperfect but none the less real koinonia. It is not in any way a question of all or nothing. There *really* is communion, albeit an imperfect communion. This communion is, moreover, *truly* based on baptism, even though it is an underlying reality beneath the chequer-board of our confessions. It is thus *truly* a communion of *faith*, even though our statements of faith often conflict.

What then is this bundle of *common faith convictions*? Why does the Spirit give it this real, albeit imperfect, unifying effect? I would guess that what we have here is a different viewpoint from that contained in the basis of the World Council of Churches. How is it that this bundle sufficiently expresses the "faith which justifies" and incorporates us into Christ?

Similarly, what is the status of those tenets of *faith* which divide us even despite this *communion*? It is no longer here a matter of the "hierarchy of truths". We must urgently clarify this point. All the more so because in each of our confessions, confessional unanimity is more and more breaking down. The "reception" of BEM thus drives us back to the issue of faith and therefore of the word, which our hermeneutics study is approaching from a different but complementary angle. We can no longer get along without a consensus on this subject. We must lance the confessional abcess! *What* is justifying faith? *How* is that faith justified? Some of the bilateral dialogues have notably opened up this area of work, particularly the dialogues with the Lutherans and the discussions between Catholics and the Disciples of Christ. The fruit of their labours must now be taken up into our study work in Faith and Order.

I have had to be brief and I hope I am making my point clear. We are no longer dealing with the tension between the one faith and doctrinal diversity in the framework of what we call "necessary and acceptable diversity". What confronts us is the tension within our imperfect but real *communion*, between a "bundle of truths" accepted by all (which is closely linked with the reality of reconciliation) and the other points which, by our accepting or rejecting them, divide us on the very basis of this justifying faith. What are we to make of the obvious discrepancy between the real *koinonia in baptism* affirmed in BEM and our *non-communion* in matters of faith considered by some to be essential and rejected by others on confessional grounds?

The scant reaction to the apostolic faith study and the oblivion into which our serious study of the Nicene-Constantinopolitan creed quickly fell are a challenge to us. They did, in fact, give us an opportunity to examine *id quod requeritur et sufficit* that "bundle of truths" which each community must make its own so as to be able, while maintaining its distinctiveness, to give adequate expression to its baptismal faith.

We all accept unanimously that if the *communion* between us is real, that is because it comes from the Spirit of God, and God is faithful. We also accept that, if this *communion* is imperfect, this arises from our resistance to God's faithfulness. Now hitherto we have failed to analyze the reasons for that "distinctiveness".

I know I will surprise no one when I say that in most cases this resistance arises from a strong desire to be faithful to the gospel. There is a conflict between the desire to be in full accord with the word of God (as we understand it) and the call to be conformed to what is proposed as a means of bringing about the *ut unum sint*, which is acknowledged to be one of the essential demands of the same gospel.

Of course, I am aware of those cases where we can see a failure of nerve before the gospel demand, which seems too costly in comparison with short-term gains which seem more promising. I am also aware of cases in which understanding of the faith is so low that it will not cross a particular threshold. Nevertheless, it seems obvious to me that the desire to be completely faithful to Christ is to be found in very nearly all Christian communities of all confessions. A disconcerting conclusion follows: it is the anxious desire to be faithful to the gospel which keeps us divided, while at the same time the Spirit keeps us united at an unsuspected depth. We should thus not speak of wilful disobedience, if the communities refuse to budge from their confessional ridge. It is a totally different level of discourse. We must see that clearly at all costs.

Conclusions

The onward thrust of BEM thus drives us to our conclusions, which must be taken seriously if we are not to continue going round in circles.

1. It is necessary to bring "confessionality" out into the open – and that not only out of ecumenical politeness or diplomacy, but because of the situation I have just described. Otherwise there can be no further progress. That is confirmed by the shaky "reception" given to BEM, if we stand back to examine it. But this reflection must be done theologically, taking serious account of the positive role played by the "confessions".

I am not suggesting that Faith and Order should copy the "comparative ecumenism" which the bilateral dialogues have engaged in with some measure of success. What I am suggesting is that we need to understand the relation between the specificity of the confessions and visible *koinonia*, in the light of what is already being contributed by the study on hermeneutics undertaken by the commission. In other words, we must *urgently* promote a hermeneutics of "confessionality" for each confessional *grouping*. Apart from that, no serious "reception" of BEM will be possible because it will continue to be rejected on "confessional" grounds.

We should note a phenomenon that has grown over the last few decades particularly in the world of the Reformation churches, which encourages us in this direction: the walls dividing the confessions are very porous. People easily change their confessional allegiance, often for purely social reasons, and do not regard themselves as being a convert to their new confession. Does that not reveal the ambiguity of "confessionality" and how it is evolving?

2. On the foundation of the imperfect but real koinonia existing beneath our dividedness, we must together prepare full visible koinonia by strengthening, tightening, explaining and developing the bonds which the Spirit maintains between us on the basis of our own baptism. We must take as our starting point the strong agreement of our confessions – beneath differences which often run very deep – on the person of Christ, his saving work and his message, all of them inseparable from the Spirit and the Father. *Communion* has not disappeared. It is there. It has not been extinguished; the embers must be fanned into flame. The confessions have kept the embers glowing by the Spirit – we should realize this. But it was in diaspora.

In this world being destroyed by divisions and hatred, the time has come to bring the scattered embers together, so that as the Spirit blows mightily on them, there becomes visible the effect of the obedience of all to Christ's *ut unum sint*. The confessions (and I include in that generic term all that the Lima text calls churches) would be being unfaithful to their history and their mission if they held back. It is a matter of all or nothing at a time when many of their foundations are crumbling away.

A turning point for ecumenism, fleshing out the Canberra statement? I do so believe.

Plenary Discussion

As Fr Tillard was prevented from attending the plenary commission meeting because of illness, his presentation was read by Fr Emmanuel Lanne, OSB. In the discussion following the presentation, many participants stressed that *Baptism, Eucharist and Ministry* (BEM) is still stimulating the churches and regional councils of churches. It was clear that the identification of the hermeneutics of confessionality was felt to be important by the members of the commission, as well as a further exploration of the idea. The plenary stressed that the churches should be self-critical, and warned of the danger of a renewed confessionalism. There was need now for Faith and Order to focus on a new issue, and not simply to build upon expectations that it is possible to repeat BEM.

Spirituality and Reception

THOMAS FITZGERALD

The woman at the well

I would like to begin our reflections with a story. It is a story of reconciliation and renewal, a story of St Photini. Who is St Photini, some of you will ask. Well, you may know her better as the Samaritan woman – the woman at Jacob's well. The story is found in the gospel of St John 4:7-42.

As I said, this story is a powerful one of reconciliation and renewal. God takes the initiative in Christ. He encounters the woman at the well. Yes, it is a woman, a Samaritan woman, a woman who appears to be living in violation of the Mosaic laws. A woman whose life appears to be out of control!

Jesus initiates the dialogue: "Give me some water," he says. Clearly, in his overture to the Samaritan woman, Jesus is going beyond the letter of the Mosaic law. He is reaching out to a person who was viewed by many as being impure and immoral. It was expected that a rabbi would not have any direct contact with such a person, especially a Samaritan and a woman.

The Samaritan woman knew this all too well. She was most probably a person who had experienced abuse and discrimination from those who claimed to be justified by the scriptures. How easy it was to use the scriptures as a justification to degrade and abuse a person! And so the Samaritan woman responds to the Lord's request first with a question. Perhaps with some measure of sarcasm, she responds: "How is it that you, a Jew, ask a drink of me, a woman of Samaria?"

The discussion between Jesus and the Samaritan woman continues. It gradually becomes more personal. Slowly the woman reveals the condition of her life. And Jesus enters into a dialogue of healing and reconciliation with her. Jesus does not shame the woman or condemn her. He recognizes her inherent value as a daughter of God. Yet at the same time, he also wants the woman to see herself and her situation more clearly.

He knows that reconciliation and healing requires an honest assessment of one's self.

Slowly and gradually, the healing and reconciliation mysteriously take place. Despite her marital situation, the woman humbly and faithfully confesses that she waits for the Messiah. She acknowledges the deep spiritual longing in her heart. She says with profound conviction: "I know that the Messiah is coming. When he comes, he will proclaim all things to us."

And Jesus honours her desire. He affirms her faith. He declares that he is the Messiah. It is truly a moment of "theophany". He says to Photini: "I am he, the one who is speaking to you." He is one who gives living water.

Jesus reveals in this encounter the love and mercy of God. And Photini – the Samaritan woman – responds to the presence of Christ. In spite of her past and the abuse she has experienced, she comes to see herself as a beloved daughter of God.

But even more than this, she becomes a disciple. Her encounter with Christ was a life-changing experience. Following her meeting with the Lord, she goes back to her village and begins to tell others about Christ. The person who has known abuse and rejection has become a person who experienced God's healing and reconciliation. And this gives her the wisdom and the courage to share the good news with others. Photini, the Samaritan woman, becomes an instrument of reconciliation. Yes, Photini, a woman, a Samaritan woman, a woman whose life was out of control, becomes the "the enlightened one", the messenger of Christ and his light.

But there is a part of the story that we should not forget. It is the reaction of the other disciples. You will remember that the disciples had gone to buy food just prior to the beginning of the encounter between Jesus and the woman. It appears that they were not present for most of the dramatic encounter between them. When the disciples did return, they were astonished that Jesus was speaking to the woman.

Why were they "astonished"? The action of the Lord challenged their religious sensibilities. The action of the Lord did not fit their expectations of how Jesus "should" behave; it challenged their understanding of scripture and of their religious tradition.

Perhaps the disciples also learned a lesson that day: that the reception of the gospel message called them to go beyond that to which they were accustomed. Perhaps they learned that the reception of the gospel message called them to go beyond their way of thinking, to a true metanoia – a true change of heart, which was open to the mighty actions of God and to the surprises of God in the present.

The ministry of the theologian

Many of us would consider ourselves to be theologians. Some of us use this title when we are asked to identify our occupation, some may use it because of our academic degrees. Some of us may have formally received this title from our church.

But what makes us theologians? Are we theologians simply because we have survived the pitfalls and snares of the academic jungle? Are we theologians simply because we teach a course in theology or because we are church administrators or because we attend theological meetings? Are we theologians because we know the right people and have made the right connections? Or are we theologians because we have been gifted with the charisma of teaching the faith? Are we theologians because we have a mysterious vocation from God, to speak about God, in the presence of God, and for the sake of God's people?

There are two observations about theologians which always come into my mind when I reflect upon our vocation. The first is from Evagrios of Pontos. In the often-cited remark, Evagrios says simply: "A theologian is a person who prays and the person who truly prays is a theologian."[1]

Immediately, Evagrios presents us with a perspective on the theologian which is different from the one to which we may be accustomed. Evagrios seems to remind us that the theologian is first and foremost a person of prayer, a person who is in relationship with God. According to this perspective, being a theologian is not first of all related to academic accomplishments, scholarly activity or teaching ability. While not denying the relative value of scholarship, Evagrios is pointing to something more fundamental: one's relationship with God. This relationship is one which is nurtured and sustained by prayer. Prayer is the key to this fundamental relationship.

There is another adage about theologians which deserves our attention. It comes from St Gregory the Theologian who was a teacher of Evagrios. At the very beginning of his *Theological Orations*, Gregory provides us with a warning and a challenge: "Not to everyone, my friends, does it belong to philosophize about God – because it is permitted only to those who have been scrutinized and are past masters of contemplation and who have been purified in soul and body... or at least are being purified."[2]

Gregory causes us to think twice about the vocation of a theologian. According to his Christian perspective, it is not a calling for everyone. Those who dare to speak about God must meet certain requirements. Firstly, the theologian needs to be examined by members of the faith community. This reminds us that the theologian is intimately related to the church. Second, the theologian needs to be a person of contemplation. This means that the theologian must be in a dynamic relationship with God. And third, the theologian needs to be a moral person who is growing in holiness. This means that the theologian cannot relate with God without living in communion with others. The characteristics about which Gregory speaks are fundamental features of what we might call today Christian spirituality.

Neither Evagrios nor Gregory would deny the value of learning, of scholarship and of intellectual honesty. They are not representatives of that narrow-minded tradition which rejected at face value the importance of learning. Indeed, we should remember that both Evagrios and Gregory were persons who had benefited from a rich and comprehensive educational tradition. We know that Gregory especially received the best "secular" education of his day. He was a person not only nurtured in theology but also schooled in the classical tradition. His rich understanding of history, his knowledge of languages and his skill in rhetoric are reflected in the vast body of writings which have come down to us.

No, we cannot say that Evagrios and Gregory are opponents of learning. Rather, they are saying that there is something more important than the skill and discipline of the scholar, something deeper which is of greater value. There is something more foundational in the identity of a Christian theologian.

This something is one's relationship with the living God. A theologian is first and foremost a person who is engaged in a loving relationship with God and his people in the midst of creation. It is precisely this relationship which provides the context and the foundation for theologizing. Authentic theology is nurtured by this relationship and is the fruit of it.[3]

A Christian theologian, according to the tradition expressed by Evagrios and Gregory, is not simply the dispenser of religious facts, one who is knowledgeable about the scriptures and various theological traditions. A Christian theologian is one who knows God, and who speaks about God not as a distant object but as an intimate friend. We simply cannot speak with integrity about God without living in communion with the living God. We cannot be teachers of God's people without living in communion with our brothers and sisters. The various disciplines of Christian life such as prayer and fasting, participation in the eucharist, and expressions of charity are important means through which these relationships are expressed and deepened.

Here I would remind you again of the story of the Samaritan woman. Her experience of Christ was a life-changing event. Through her encounter with the Lord, Photini truly came to know the living God not as an abstract concept but as a loving friend. This was not simply intellectual knowledge. Rather, it was an experience which profoundly affected both her mind and her heart, both the way she lived and the way she thought. Her experience of Christ affected her entire being. And this experience became the basis for her new relationship with God and with others. It became the dynamic foundation for new relationships as well as for her teaching and for her missionary activity.

Are we willing to take seriously our relationship with God and how it affects our identity as theologians and our theological reflection?

A number of us recently attended a consultation on theological education and ministerial formation in Oslo, Norway. It was a very fruitful meeting which brought together over 150 theologians and theological educators from all over the world. It was also a meeting which raised very serious questions about theological education and the vocation of the theologian.

Many of the participants recognized that theological education places much emphasis upon factual knowledge and scientific methodology. But at the same time it pays little attention to the relationship between theology and the spiritual life. The fear was expressed repeatedly that theologians and ministers may grasp the technical language of theology, but they may have little personal appreciation of the living God.

One of our colleagues here, Mary O'Driscoll, reminded the participants in the Oslo consultation that theological education and formation must be concerned with our relationship with God. She said that our vocation "presupposes that all involved in ministry in the church have a personal ongoing relationship with God. Their theological education and ministerial formation must, therefore, be concerned with nurturing this relationship. Without it, ministers would be inauthentic and shallow in putting before others the ultimate ecumenical vision. People who listen to us are easily able to distinguish between the minister who genuinely enjoys a relationship with God and the minister who does not. When ministers speak with conviction, their words carry weight; they are not the result simply of intellectual comprehension but also of sincere personal experience of the divine. Theological education and ministerial formation are ultimately about knowing God – developing a passion for God – penetrating experientially as well as intellectually, as much as is possible for each person, into the mystery of God's love."[4]

We cannot easily escape the consequence of these observations. Simply stated, we must admit that the quality of the theologian's relationship with God and with God's people is bound to be reflected in the activity of the theologian. Our ability to assess and to address the critical issues which affect the church and society today and most especially the challenges involved in Christian reconciliation are related not simply to our scholarly abilities, important though they may be. Rather, our ability to serve the church and the process of reconciliation is directly related in the first instance to our relationships with the living God and his people and creation. Only when we take seriously those relationships will we be able to be nurtured by the Spirit and to use our scholarly abilities properly.

It seems to me that the ecumenical movement and the WCC need persons who take very seriously their vocation as theologians. This vocation can certainly make use of scholarly abilities. It certainly demands both humility and academic honesty. Indeed, our understanding of the great issues of Christian divisions has been enriched by the thoughtful studies by theologians whose appreciations of biblical languages and historical events have enabled us to see our theological, ethical and liturgical differences in a new light, and to come to common understandings and consensus.

Yet the vocation of a theologian is not simply a matter of being an expert in church history or dogmatic theology or biblical studies. It is a vocation which requires us to be open to the workings of the Spirit in our lives and to deepen our union with Christ who leads us to the Father. It is a vocation which requires us to take seriously the values of the gospel. Even as we struggle with our divisions and misunderstandings, we must be rooted in the reality of God and open to the working of the Spirit who guides us in all truth today.

Fr Laurence, the abbot of the monastic communities of New Skete, speaks directly to this when he says: "No matter how professional and necessary our involvement in theological studies, it is the life in Christ in each of us that must be deepened at all times. Therefore, whether we speak on the sacraments or translation, on liturgical life or stewardship, or whether we consider the inner life itself from an academic point of view, we must recall that this is simply part of the whole of that mystery we call life in the church. Practically, this means that my personal inner life cannot be ignored because of academic theological considerations, for the final step in that process will be a kind of spiritual materialism, every bit as destructive of life as secular materialism."[5]

The importance of theological reflection

During his recent visit to the World Council of Churches, Ecumenical Patriarch Bartholomew of Constantinople spoke about the importance of theology for our churches and for the ecumenical movement. Reflecting on the rich patristic tradition, Patriarch Bartholomew began by saying: "When centred upon the mystery of Christ and his gospel, authentic theology always gives life or serves life. Just as the Lord is the 'Giver of Life' and his words are 'words of life', our words about God must always reflect his teachings and his ministry. This means that our theology must be done with profound humility, with prayer, in the midst of the believing community, and for the sake of the salvation of the entire world. Like the apostle Peter, we too must say: 'To whom can we go, Lord, You have the words of eternal life' (John 6:68)."6

With these words, the Patriarch reminds us that theology seeks to nurture us in true life – which is the life in Christ. Theology guides us in our relationship with God, with one another, and with the world in which we live. Viewed from this perspective, theology is profoundly pastoral. Its ultimate concern is with healing, reconciliation and union with God.

Having made some observations on the vocation of the theologian, I want to echo the words of the patriarch and to affirm in the strongest way the importance of theological reflection both for our churches and for the ecumenical movement. From its beginning, the Faith and Order movement has made a monumental contribution to theological reflection, especially on those issues related to church division and the process of reconciliation and renewal. The various bilateral dialogues and the recent agreements between the churches have been nurtured by the work of Faith and Order. Our appreciation of so many aspects of church history, the scriptures and the liturgy has been enriched by the insights of those who have been active in Faith and Order.

Central to its work has been the fact that the Faith and Order movement consistently holds before the churches and the WCC the "goal of visible unity in one faith and one eucharistic fellowship, expressed in worship and in common life in Christ, in order that the world may believe". Faith and Order reminds the churches and the WCC that the issues of Christian division must be clearly recognized and studied. Those involved in Faith and Order struggle with their churches in seeking to find consensus, in seeking to heal division so that the world may believe and God will be glorified!

Perhaps in these days we have realized again how difficult this process can be. Indeed, the task before us can easily appear to be impossible, unless we really believe that we are participating in a special way in the reconciling ministry of Christ. St Paul is reminding us of the divine actions when he says: "All this is from God, who reconciled us to himself through Christ, and has given us the ministry of reconciliation; that is, in Christ, God was reconciling the world to himself, not counting their trespasses against us them, and entrusting the message of reconciliation to us. So we are ambassadors for Christ..." (2 Cor. 5:18-20). Our theological activity is ultimately not our own. Rather, it must constantly be related to the actions of God. We are ultimately the servants of the One who gives to all believers the "ministry of reconciliation".

This "ministry of reconciliation" requires that we theologians engage together in serious and thoughtful theological reflection. But this engagement must always be one which takes place in the presence of God, for the sake of all God's people, and for the glory of God. This reflection must always be done with a humility which is open to the Spirit's actions and to the Spirit's surprises. In the end, we must humbly affirm the perspective words of St Irenaeus who says: "Not only in this present age but also in the age to come, God will always have something more to teach the human person and the human person will always have something more to learn from God."[7]

If we believe this, then we also must be ready honestly to examine the quality – the character – the spirit – of our theological reflection. As we have already said, it is of absolute importance for the Christian theologian to be engaged in a dynamic relationship with God and his people. It is equally important that we are sensitive to the quality of our theological reflection: it must be such that God is glorified through our words, that our words are sensitive to the reality of God's people, that our words lead to healing and reconciliation, that our words are open to the prompting of the Holy Spirit today.

This does not mean that we easily can ignore the historical points of differences between our churches. On the contrary, I believe that we have an obligation to resolve in the present those issues coming from the past which continue to divide us. We cannot pretend that theological perspectives and, in some cases, doctrinal differences do not divide us. But let us remember that we do not live in the past. Our approach to the disputed points must reflect the fact that we are at a different stage in history from our ecclesiastical ancestors. If we so choose, we are able to look at the issues of division in a different perspective and to look at them together precisely because of the Spirit's prompting and guidance. If we so choose!

It seems to me that our churches and the ecumenical movement can truly be enriched by this type of theological reflection. Many of you have learned about the financial crisis which afflicts the World Council of Churches. It is a serious matter. And I pray that the churches will respond to the Council with renewed support. But I also believe that there is a spiritual and theological crisis at the World Council of Churches, which manifests itself in a lack of clarity in the Council's fundamental vocation as well as a lack of internal coherence and an imbalance in the Council's programmatic concerns.

With this in mind, I maintain that Faith and Order has a special role to play in affirming the critical importance of theological reflection on issues related to the restoration of visible unity and the fundamental meaning of the ecumenical movement. But this can be done only if the theologians engaged in this critical work see themselves as servants of the Lord and his people.

Faith and Order can serve the Council by engaging in theological reflection which is not only rich in content but also rich in tone and texture:

- We long for a theology which is doxological, which is rich in the praise of God and mindful of God's mighty acts of salvation.
- We long for a theology which is salutary, which nurtures us in our growth in holiness, and which opens our hearts to God and to his people.
- We long for a theology which is rooted in the community of faith, which is attentive to the concerns and needs of all God's people.
- We long for a theology which integrates the personal and corporate, which integrates body and spirit, the material and the spiritual.
- We long for a theology which celebrates the creation as God's gift and inspires us to be good stewards of our blessings.
- We long for a theology which proclaims that we are God's daughters and sons, which reminds us that we are called to serve others in the name of the Lord.[8]

The context of reception

Not long ago, I had the special opportunity to participate in the 200th anniversary celebration of the African Methodist Episcopal Zion Church in the United States. During the course of the week-long observance, one entire evening was devoted to issues of Christian unity. Over two thousand delegates and friends gathered to pray, to sing hymns and to hear the witness of those especially active in the quest for Christian reconciliation and unity. We were together for about four hours. I had never experienced anything like this event before.

As I reflected upon it in the days following, I realized that I had experienced the process of reception. Within the context of worship, God's people were affirming the importance of reconciliation and unity. It was a process rooted in prayer, nurtured by the scriptures, which celebrated God's mighty actions in the present, which took seriously the dignity of all the people of God. I left that special gathering with a feeling that the quest for reconciliation and unity truly had been advanced.

Because of our academic training, we theologians frequently place a great deal of emphasis upon finding the "right words". Because of this, we often think that the divisions among the churches will be healed simply when we are able to find the "right words". So many of us have had the experience of spending hour upon hour in ecumenical groups trying to fashion a document which contain the "right words". Indeed, the process of reception is frequently viewed, either consciously or unconsciously, as one which seeks only to find the "right words" and then to present them to the churches for their acceptance.

Now the words with which we communicate and seek to express consensus are important. I do not wish to underestimate the importance of using the appropriate words in our theological reflections. Indeed, part of our progress in the ecumenical movement has been made because we have struggled to recapture a common theological language which enables us not only to speak together but also to move beyond the "words" which have been misunderstood or misinterpreted in the past. Words are important. And there is a sense in which we must find the appropriate words to express our unity today.

Undoubtedly, this was a major concern of those at the councils of Nicea in 325 and Constantinople in 381. In producing a statement of faith, the bishops certainly did not wish to give the impression that they were trying to capture in words the essence of Christian belief about the Trinity. But they did struggle to finds "God-worthy" words which described God's mighty actions, which celebrated their faith and which could contribute to the unity of the church. Their words were important. But also important was the context in which the words were fashioned and received.

What we sometimes overlook today is the fact that words do not exist in a vacuum. There is always a context to our words; they are always spoken by someone or by a group of persons within a context. The words are always heard or not heard by someone or a group of persons within a context. This means, quite simply, that the "right words" may not be received if the context is not supportive of their positive reception.

Most of us would be quick to recognize that the divisions which afflict Christians are the result of theological misunderstanding and doctrinal differences. But the more closely we look at the historical situations in which divisions first developed, we have to admit that the context for dialogue had become contaminated. Groups of Christians came to see one another as adversaries. There was a breakdown in mutual respect and understanding. There was a separation for worship and prayer. There was a loss of a sense of common history and mission. Ultimately, there was a loss of a common mind which prevented the development of consensus or agreement. It was not simply a matter of finding the "right words". The very context for discussion had been destroyed.

When many of the early fathers and Christian teachers spoke about Christian divisions, they clearly recognized that it was not simply a matter of "words". Certainly, the early fathers do not deny importance of theological formulations. But they recognize that it was also a matter of those who spoke the words and created the context. Divisions, they would tell us, are ultimately the result of a "hardness of heart" which manifests itself in pride, arrogance, self-righteousness. It is for this reason that St Maximos the Confessor could say very simply: "My children – nothing causes schism and heresies in the church than the fact that we do not love God and do not love our neighbour."[9]

Today, we must be sensitive both to the process of fashioning the words of theological consensus and the process of restoring the context which contributes to reconciliation. This means that the restoration of full communion between the churches will not be accomplished simply through formal doctrinal agreements formulated by theologians, not simply by finding the "right words". These theological agreements are of immense importance; but they must be fashioned and received in a context of faith, hope and love where the whole people of God see themselves both as the "guardians of the faith" and as the "ministers of reconciliation".

The context of reconciliation certainly must include the following. We need common prayer and liturgical celebrations which express our desire to be more fully united in accordance to the will of Christ. We need joint pilgrimages which remind us of the sacred places in our common history and which honour the saints from all our churches who are united in the bond of holiness. We need public acts of forgiveness which recognize the tragic excesses of the past and foster the healing of memories in the present. We need acts of common service to the needy and common witness in the society. We need to examine together our understanding of the scriptures, our patterns of worship, our style of theological education and our expressions of ordained ministry with an eye towards renewing our parish life. And we need to celebrate together every year the great feast of Easter, the festival of our reconciliation in Christ.

When we examine our common history, we see that there have been significant times when divisions have been overcome and reconciliation was received. A restoration of unity followed the Arian crisis and was expressed by the council of Constantinople in 381. The historic Nicene-Constantinopolitan Creed bears witness to this reconciliation. A restoration of unity between the church of Alexandria and the church of Antioch in 433 is expressed in a letter of Patriarch Cyrill and Patriarch John. A restoration of unity between the church of Rome and the church of Constantinople also is expressed in a statement of the council of 879.[10]

When I examine these documents of reconciliation, I am struck especially by two factors which are common to all three. First, the statements are very brief. When one remembers the heated discussions which preceded the reconciliation, the utter simplicity of the statements appears surprising. Second, each statement is not very analytical either in content or in tone. Rather, each has a strong doxological and kerygmatic character.[11]

Although these documents were composed centuries ago, I believe that their content and their tone tell us that something else happened. The reconciliations which were achieved with God's grace were not simply the result of finding the "right words". While the words are certainly important, they point to an even more basic reality. The documents do not create unity; rather, they bear witness to a deeper reality of reconciliation which words cannot fully capture. While the words are important, what appears to be even more important is the attitude of the hearts of those who fashioned the words and those who received them. Simply stated, a context had been created in which persons were open to the prodding of the Holy Spirit not simply with their minds but with their hearts as well.[12]

The restoration of Christian unity in our own time will be accomplished gradually and in a very fundamental way when our statements of reconciliation are fashioned and received by persons who are open to the activity of the Holy Spirit who guides us in all truth and who reveals the presence of Christ in our midst. Our concern for reconciliation cannot be separated from our identity as persons who are striving to live in communion with God and with others through Christ. Our concern for the reception of consensus statements cannot be separated from our willingness to engage in theological reflection which reflects these relationships.

The centrality of Christ and his gospel

Finally, we need to affirm together that the reality of Christ and his gospel is at the very heart and centre of our quest for reconciliation and the restoration of visible unity. This may seem obvious to you. But I feel that there are tendencies to find another basis and justification for the one ecumenical movement. Yes, it is true that we do share a common human nature. Yes, it is true that we do share in the same creation. Yes, it is true that we all have an inherent orientation towards God. These affirmations are true and valuable. But the Christian believer has something more to say.

For us who call Jesus Christ our Lord, God and Saviour there can be no other basis for our quest for reconciliation and visible unity. Christ is the one who reveals the Father's love and sends the Spirit to bind us together. Christ is the one who reveals that our life is most fully human when we live in communion with God, in communion with one another and in communion with the creation. It is this Christo-centricity which opens us up to the richness of the triune God and the profound dignity of human life. Like St Photini, the Samaritan women, we too must recognize that Christ is the one who the source of living water.

So, let me conclude by these words from St Ambrose which remind us of the centrality of Christ.

> In Christ we have everything.
> If you want to heal your wounds, He is the doctor.
> If you are burning with fever, He is the fountain.
> If you are in need of help, He is the strength.
> If you are in dread of death, He is life.
> If you are fleeing darkness, He is light.
> If you are hungry, He is food.
> O taste and see that the Lord is good.
> Happy are those who take refuge in him.
>
> Christ is in our midst!
>
> To him be glory and honour now and forever and unto ages of all ages. Amen.[13]

NOTES

[1] Evagrios of Pontos, *On Prayer*, 61.
[2] St Gregory the Theologian, *First Theological Orations*, I.
[3] Metropolitan John Zizioulas, *Being as Communion*, Crestwood, NY, St Vladimir's Seminary, 1985, pp.67-122. See also his "The Church as Communion: A Presentation on the World Conference Theme", in Thomas F. Best and Günther Gassman, eds, *On the Way to Fuller Koinonia*, Faith and Order paper no. 166, Geneva, WCC, 1994, pp.103-11.
[4] Mary O'Driscoll, "Response" to the presentation on "The Importance of the Ecumenical Vision for Theological Education and Ministerial Formation", in John Pobee, ed., *Towards Viable Theological Education: Ecumenical Imperative, Catalyst of Renewal*, Geneva, WCC, 1997, p.64.
[5] Hieromonk Laurence, "Orthodox Monasticism Today", *The Greek Orthodox Theological Review*, 32, 3, 1987, p.238.
[6] Ecumenical Patriarch Bartholomew of Constantinople, address at the Ecumenical Institute, Bossey, Geneva, 12 December 1995.
[7] Cited in Kallistos Ware, *The Orthodox Way*, Crestwood, NY, St Vladimir's Seminary, 1979, p.185.
[8] Nicholas Apostola, "Theology as Doxology", *Ministerial Formation*, 67, 4, 1994, pp.35-45.
[9] St Maximos the Confessor, *PG* 87, 2985.
[10] Thomas FitzGerald, "Unity and Prayer", in Thomas F. Best and Dagmar Heller, eds, *So We Believe, So We Pray*, Faith and Order paper no. 171, Geneva, WCC, 1995, p.53.
[11] *Ibid.*, p.54.
[12] Kyriaki FitzGerald, "Walls of the Heart", *Ecumenical Trends*, 22, 4, 1993, pp.13-16.
[13] St Ambrose of Milan, *On Virginity*, 16.99.

Plenary Discussion

Several speakers expressed their gratitude that Fr FitzGerald had recovered for the plenary commission the spiritual dimension of reception and, beyond that, of reconciliation. One noted that the commission's work cannot be simply theoretical, it must issue in practice. What is fundamental is to find a new quality of relationship between our churches, and what is needed for this is a new, corporate practice of prayer and spirituality.

Another commissioner exclaimed "Amen!" to the paper, saying strikingly that the plenary commission acts like a group of semi-Pelagians, persons who believe that everything is within the power of their own minds. We have today, it was said, lost the power of seeing not just with the mind but with the spirit, with God's power, and the paper is a valuable call to recognize our limitations in order to open ourselves to new possibilities. Yet another speaker praised the paper for offering reconciliation as an impulse and goal, and for giving instances of mutual forgiveness.

Another speaker, likening the presentation to the work of commissioner Roberta Bondi, noted how it had spoken directly to the concerns and struggles of the plenary commission, particularly its need to move beyond the academic training shared by most of its members to a renewed practice of spirituality (another commissioner, however, reaffirmed the importance of academic endeavour, pointing to the problems caused by anti-academic tendencies within the church). The question was posed as to *how* the dimension of spirituality might influence our practice of theology. In this connection, the speaker suggested that the Faith and Order text *Church and World* (resulting from the study programme on "The Unity of the Church and the Renewal of Human Community") was worthy of serious study.

Other speakers related the presentation to wider contexts in church and world. One commissioner affirmed that the paper "made sense" of WCC's Unit I, by showing the spiritual centre and focus at the heart of the work of all its streams (Faith and Order, Worship and Spirituality, Ecumenical Theological Education, and Lay Participation towards Inclusive Community). Could there be more clarity about the relation of the work on lay participation to spirituality? This should be especially instructive because the laity inhabit mainly the "secular" world, which is conventionally thought to be most removed from the spiritual. Another commissioner noted that the paper was relevant to the current financial and spiritual crisis within the WCC and the ecumenical movement as a whole.

It was pointed out that the "academic context" of Faith and Order is itself a complex, problematic notion. The discipline of theology is being exercised increasingly in a secular academic context, among colleagues who do not confess the Christian faith but nevertheless expect theology to contribute to the broad societal discussion of values and meaning today. Theology indeed needs to be in dialogue with secular thought – not only in order that theology may "interrogate" the world, but so that it may be interrogated *by* that world.

Another commissioner referred to the "world" as the context for the discussion of spirituality today, pointing out that "spirituality" has become a highly ambiguous term. We live in a "post-modern" world which approaches even spirituality with a consumerist attitude, and this poses enormous problems for the true understanding of spirituality.

In responding to these comments Fr FitzGerald affirmed the need for theological competence on the part of ministers: academic excellence is a gift of God, to be used for the benefit of the people of God as a whole. He emphasized the notion of a *discipline* of forgiveness, calling us not so much to perfect ourselves as to break down the barriers between ourselves and others. Regarding the present situation of the WCC, he pointed to the "Towards a Common Understanding and Vision" process as one which should bring the WCC closer to the churches, even as the WCC sought to define a new self-understanding and direction. In all things the essential point was to begin from an *orientation towards God*; this was the necessary and sound basis for our future.

Faith and Order Work
with United and Uniting Churches

The work on united and uniting churches is undertaken in fulfilment of Faith and Order's mandate "to provide opportunities for consultation among those whose churches are engaged in union negotiations or other specific efforts towards unity" (by-laws, 2.g). For its deliberations the commission had before it the "Letter from the Sixth International Consultation of United and Uniting Churches to the Director of Faith and Order".

Martin Cressey made the following points. Through "direct speaking" to the plenary commission he emphasized the "main characteristic" of church unions, namely a level of mutual commitment, community and accountability among the constituent churches so strong that it cannot be expressed through plans for "partnership" or mutual recognition, but must take the form of full structural union. Diversity is "recognized" to the radical extent that it is integrated within a single ecclesial body, with all that that implies theologically and institutionally. Thus, "to *unite* is to accept responsibility for one another in the fullest sense".

The family of united and uniting churches is very diverse, including the German unions of the 19th century involving Reformed and Lutherans; two groups of unions, one in former British commonwealth countries and the USA, and the other in the two-thirds world (both groups including Presbyterians, Congregationalists, Disciples of Christ, Churches of Christ and Methodists in various constellations, with the churches in the two-thirds world more culturally diverse); and the unions in the Indian sub-continent involving both episcopally ordered and non-episcopally ordered churches. In all their diversity, the union *experience* of united churches is valuable and must be shared with the wider church and with the ecumenical movement.

The united and uniting churches have come together over the past thirty years in a series of six international consultations. These might be grouped by twos, characterized by the terms "ready", "steady", and "go!" respectively. Thus the meetings at Bossey (1967) and Limuru (1970) were marked by the confident expectation for many further unions; those at Toronto (1975) and Colombo (1981) by growing self-understanding and confidence, but also increasing questions about their relation to the ecumenical movement as a whole, and to world; and the most recent, in Potsdam (1987) and Jamaica (1995), by a new readiness to engage with the wider ecumenical movement, and a renewed commitment to mission and service as inherent in their identity as *united* churches – but with continuing questions about how and where best to do this.

Referring to the letter from the sixth international consultation of united and uniting churches, and to the recommendations passed by the consultation, Martin Cressey drew attention to the call for Faith and Order work on issues of oversight (episcope), and to the desire of the united and uniting churches, while continuing their special relationship to Faith and Order, to relate also to a wider range of programmes within the WCC.

Martin Cressey illustrated the hunger for unity and reconciliation reflected in the union movement by reference to the Unity chapel in Coventry cathedral. He concluded by noting that fully one-third of the churches represented in Faith and Order are united or uniting churches, in a stricter or broader sense. Yet the united churches agenda is far more central to Faith and Order than even that suggests. For *all* its member churches are in a sense "united and uniting", for there is no church which does not live with diversity, and all churches bear a responsibility to seek for the fullest unity possible. If there should be a motto for churches in respect of union, it might well be: "Now then, do it!"

In the ensuing discussion it was suggested that Faith and Order should commission an historical study showing the development and various stages in the lives of united churches. Another commissioner called for further explanation of the distinctive character and "genius" of this church family. Martin Cressey replied that for the united churches the act of uniting was a first step in a process of continuing growth. Their development took place in the context of, and in a sense in dialogue with, other churches in the same nation which had retained their previous denominational identity. One distinctive element is perhaps their exploration of how different ecclesial forms, each bearing its full theological seriousness and weight of tradition, can be brought together within the same ecclesial body.

Another question touched upon the relation of united and uniting churches to other expressions of fuller koinonia among churches, such as the recent Porvoo agreement. Martin Cressey noted that at the most recent united and uniting churches consultation a very wide range of plans for union and for expressing fuller koinonia had been present, including Porvoo. He noted the involvement of united churches (including his own, the United Reformed Church in the UK) where possible in agreements such as Porvoo and Meissen, and of course in the Leuenberg agreement. Such plans were especially helpful for united and uniting churches in their efforts to relate to other church bodies in their nation or region.

A further question dealt with the notion of ecumenical imbalance: what happens when churches unite in one place, but churches of the same confession do not unite in other places? This is a serious theological and not least pastoral problem. The united and uniting churches know they must relate what is happening ecumenically in one place to what is happening in all places. This is one reason they seek a continuing role for Faith and Order as a "clearing house" through which they can interact with the worldwide ecumenical community.

The Bilateral Forum and the Joint Working Group

JOHN A. RADANO

The continuing work of the commission on Faith and Order is carried out in its own proper setting such as in this meeting of the plenary commission and various other meetings and consultations organized by the commission itself. But the mission of Faith and Order, and its influence, has been felt in the larger ecumenical movement in other settings. Two of these other settings are the forum on bilateral conversations and the Joint Working Group between the Roman Catholic Church and the World Council of Churches. In both contexts Faith and Order has made a significant contribution. And in both settings the work of Faith and Order had been supported.

Forum on bilateral conversations

The forum on bilateral conversations is "an ad-hoc non-institutional instrument of information, exchange, reflection and orientation. It was inaugurated and is sponsored by the conference of secretaries of Christian World Communions: this conference requests the Faith and Order Secretariat of the WCC to organize the meeting of the forum".[1] Actually, the suggestion for a forum on bilateral conversations was first made in 1973 by the commission on Faith and Order, and welcomed by the CWCs.[2]

The conference of secretaries of CWCs is itself an informal, annual meeting of the general secretaries (or their equivalent, or other leaders) of a broad range of Christian World Communions. The World Council of Churches has been represented at these meetings, as well as Faith and Order in the person of its director. The meetings are informal and publish no press report. The organization of the forum can be helpful in keeping these various Christian families, whatever their involvement in ecumenism, up to date concerning certain issues in the ecumenical movement.

The mandate of the forum from the beginning stressed that it was an ad-hoc instrument and not permanent. It was originally intended to facilitate the exchange of information among the bilaterals, to review recent developments in bilateral conversations, to continue discussion on themes of common interest, to promote interaction between bilateral and multilateral discussion, to study the implications of bilateral findings for the ecumenical movement as a whole, and to examine issues of method relevant to all bilateral conversations.[3] These concerns are still important today.

The forum has met six times between 1978 and 1994. A seventh forum is planned for 1997. The forum has dealt with themes of deep concern to Faith and Order and to the whole ecumenical movement. These have included: concepts of unity (1978), the meaning of consensus (1979), reception (1980), "current developments in bilateral dialogues and their relation to the Faith and Order convergence statement on Baptism, Eucharist and Ministry (BEM)" (1985). In 1990 the theme of the fifth forum was "The Understanding of the Church Emerging in the Bilateral Dialogues – Coherence or Divergence". In 1994, the sixth forum was concerned again with reception.

A central purpose of the forum is especially to keep the multilateral dialogue (of Faith and Order) and the bilateral dialogues in touch with one another. Thus, an underlying presupposition of the forum is that there is only *one ecumenical movement*.[4] The forum does not coordinate the bilateral or multilateral dialogues; each are independent entities. But the forum is a setting in which the results of bilateral and multilateral dialogues can be compared. For example, the fourth compared the findings of BEM with the findings of the bilaterals on issues of baptism, eucharist and ministry.[5] The forum is a setting where key dialogue issues can be explored. Thus the theme of the fifth was "The Understanding of the Church Emerging in the Bilateral Dialogues – Coherence or Divergence".[6] And the forum has been used to help us get insights into the way dialogue results are received by the church and therefore to give clues to future developments. And so the theme of the third and the sixth meetings in 1980 and 1994 respectively was reception.[7]

Reports of the forum have helped us to see important developments in the ecumenical movement. Thus the fourth forum indicated the positive inter-relationship between the multilateral and bilateral dialogues. "BEM", it said, "has profited from the work and insights of bilaterals (cf. Preface to BEM), and a number of recent reports from bilaterals refer explicitly (and in a positive way) to BEM. Inter-relation is happening and it is important that this shall continue during the years to come."[8] That report spoke furthermore of convergence on baptism, eucharist and ministry and the inter-relationship of processes:

As the documents have passed through various stages of development, influence has passed to and fro – through papers and personnel – among the bilateral texts and with BEM. Both BEM (deliberately) and the bilaterals (sometimes unwittingly) have worked under the aegis of the Montreal report on "Scripture, Tradition and Traditions" (1963) and its development in the Venice report of 1978 (Faith and Order Paper no. 100, *Towards a Confession of the Common Faith*).[9]

The forum has also touched on issues of specific importance to this meeting of our plenary commission. We mention two here: ecclesiology and reception. In regard to *ecclesiology* it has consistently pointed to the urgency of taking up the theme in dialogue. The evaluation made of the first three forums found that "a most important theological issue which emerges from the work of the forums is that of ecclesiology. Behind many of the doctrinal disputes dealt with in the dialogues lie fundamental questions of the sacramental nature of the church and the ecclesial self-understanding of Christian World Communions. Yet this has seldom been explicitly treated in the bilaterals to date."[10] And the fourth forum outlined convergence between bilaterals and the multilateral dialogue as well as problems not yet resolved in regard to baptism, eucharist and ministry.[11] These convergences, it stated, testify to an ever-increasing extent the importance of exploring the nature of the church. Many are asking whether there is an implicit ecclesiology lying behind the Lima text or whether it is possible for the churches to receive the convergences of the text out of different understandings of the nature of the church.[12] Faith and Order's own analysis of the responses of the churches to BEM, its *Report on the Process and Responses*, published in 1990,[13] would confirm that the responses reveal "various understandings of the church...; in the light of the Lima document, to which Christian churches throughout the world are responding, new momentum is given to the search for common perspectives on ecclesiology".[14]

The fifth forum in 1990 focused precisely on the church.[15] It found, and this is an encouragement to our present work in Faith and Order, that "almost all the bilateral dialogues in the last ten years have moved towards work on ecclesiology. What is remarkable is the degree of convergence in the way they speak about both the nature and the purpose of the church."[16] It noted also that "the notion of koinonia is central in the understanding of the nature of the church in almost all dialogues".[17] In fact, it is the "fundamental understanding of the church emerging from the bilateral dialogues".[18] And in this regard, the fifth forum repeated again an insight stated before, and lifted up again at Santiago de Compostela, namely that "the exploration of the church as koinonia has led to an awareness that those who are baptized and who thus, through the power of the Holy Spirit, are joined to Christ, already experience a 'certain but imperfect communion'".[19] That forum concluded on a positive note useful to state here:

> We have been encouraged by the convergence on the understanding of the nature and the purpose of the church. Most particularly we affirm the understanding of koinonia emerging from the bilateral dialogues. We believe that it is within this perspective of koinonia that the outstanding differences are most likely to be resolved.[20]

The forum has given significant attention also to *reception*.[21] The discussion in the third forum (1980) lifted up important issues with which we still struggle. One example: the methods used in formulating agreed statements have an impact on reception. One method according to the report is "to avoid the technical language of the past or the present, in order to avoid the difficulties which are inevitably caused by the emotionally-charged connotations inherent in that language".[22] We try instead "to use a new language in order to express a doctrinal deepening that enables the parties to overcome misunderstandings, disagreements and the partiality of those confessional positions which existed in an earlier polemical context". This will "demand an effort of profound comprehension that goes beyond the first formulation and a new perception that tries to embrace all the aspects of the question". To this theological insight the report added a pastoral concern which is a key to reception. "Such documents", it said,

> also require a pastoral explanation since most of the faithful will be surprised and disconcerted at the loss of the venerable expressions with which they were accustomed to articulate their faith. For reception to succeed, we must show the continuity between these beloved traditional expressions and the surprising new language. We must help the faithful understand that this new language is used in order to overcome the misunderstanding of the past, to overcome the partial character of earlier confessional formulations which pointed to the fullness of the mystery (a mystery which the dialogues help point to more fully).

The sixth forum, in 1994, suggested that in the fourteen years since the third, efforts to receive ecumenical texts had been a significant experience for the churches. Participants from seven different traditions were asked to describe at length the forms and structures of reception in their world communions including the reception of BEM.[23] These included Anglican, Disciples of Christ, Orthodox, Lutheran, Methodist, Roman Catholic and Reformed. Its report included brief outlines given by these and four others (eleven world communions altogether) about reception processes in their churches.[24] The report therefore documents in a certain sense what we might call a first generation of reception processes, coinciding with the age of BEM. Reception was, of course, broader than simply reception of the BEM text. But did not the Lima text have a special impact on reception? Is not BEM and its reception and its aftermath an historical event, both in continuity with what went before, and at the same time a new stepping stone into the ecumenical future? The report in fact recommends that "the Faith and Order commission should continue the BEM process beyond the compilation of the series of six published volumes of responses and the preliminary report responding to those responses".[25] We might add: In many ways the BEM process continues now in Faith and Order's ecclesiology process.

The report also outlined weaknesses and problems in reception. An interesting factor in reception concerns the questions to enable reception. The preface to BEM had four questions around which the responses were drawn up. The first was "the extent to which your church can recognize in this text the faith of the church through the ages"[26]. It has been said that this question was interpreted in different ways by different churches. The sixth forum therefore suggested an alternative which might be helpful in the reception of future texts. Namely, "is the report consonant with the faith which is grounded in holy scripture, confessed in the creeds and the tradition of the church and born witness to in the liturgy – a faith which is to be expressed afresh today by us all?"[27]

As Faith and Order develops its convergence text on ecclesiology, it might also struggle with the proper questions which will enable the churches to receive it.

Joint Working Group

Another ongoing task of Faith and Order is its cooperation with the Joint Working Group (JWG) between the Roman Catholic Church and the World Council of Churches. This has been the case since the establishment of the JWG in 1965.[28] The Joint Working Group is an important instrument of partnership between these two bodies. It oversees the various, significant areas of cooperation between the two, helping to bind them together in mutual ecumenical commitment. The director of Faith and Order is a member.

This cooperation of Faith and Order in the JWG is based especially on two factors: the official representation of the Roman Catholic Church on the Faith and Order commission and the reflections in the JWG on the visible unity of the church.[29] In the most recent report of the JWG, the sixth, one of the priorities of the period 1983-90 is listed as "Unity of the Church – the Goal and the Way".[30] Faith and Order has made contributions within the JWG, especially in the context of this priority, through participation in studies the latter has sponsored. The sixth report of the JWG included two studies attached as appendices, entitled "The Church: Local and Universal"[31] and "The Notion of Hierarchy of Truths – An Ecumenical Interpretation".[32] The first of these, especially, may provide useful insights for Faith and Order's current study on ecclesiology, as it has already had some impact on the bilaterals.[33]

The current Joint Working Group, appointed after the Canberra assembly, has produced four study documents. Two have involved Faith and Order very specifically.

The first was a JWG contribution to the fifth world conference on Faith and Order. The JWG requested a study document entitled "The Unity of the Church as Koinonia: Ecumenical Perspectives on the 1991 Canberra Statement on Unity".[34] Published in 1993, this text was included among the background materials made available to all participants at Santiago de Compostela. It included essays, bringing Anglican, Lutheran, Orthodox, Roman Catholic and United-Reformed perspectives on the Canberra statement, which was an important aspect of the world conference's deliberation, as it is today an important consideration in Faith and Order's ecclesiology study. One important aspect of this text was that, as a JWG project, it helped bring deeper Roman Catholic interest to the world conference and its themes. The second study text was published in 1996: "The Challenge of Proselytism and the Calling to Common Witness".[35]

Conclusion

These two aspects of the "ongoing work" of Faith and Order, the forum for bilateral conversations and participation in the Joint Working Group, help the commission on Faith and Order to live out its own mandate of promoting the visible unity of Christians. In doing so, they contribute in significant ways to the whole ecumenical movement. Issues raised consistently in these two settings, especially in the forum, suggest support for the choice made by Faith and Order especially at Budapest and again at the fifth world conference, to focus on ecclesiology as a central concern of its present work.

NOTES

[1] *Fifth Forum on Bilateral Conversation Report*, Faith and Order paper no. 156, Geneva, WCC, 1991, p.1.
[2] *The Three Reports of the Forum on Bilateral Conversations*, Faith and Order paper no. 107, Geneva, WCC, 1981, p.1.
[3] *Ibid.*, 2.
[4] Faith and Order made the reports of the first three forums available in 1981 precisely in the hope of contributing to the growing theological agreement within the one ecumenical movement. *Ibid.*

212   Faith and Order in Moshi

5 *Fourth Forum on Bilateral Conversation Report*, Faith and Order paper no. 125, Geneva, WCC, 1985.

6 *Fifth Forum, op. cit.*

7 For the latter see *Sixth Forum on Bilateral Dialogues*, Faith and Order paper no. 168, Geneva, WCC, 1995. For the former see *The Three Reports*.

8 *Fourth Forum*, 1985, p.6.

9 *Ibid.*, p.7.

10 *The Three Reports*, p.47.

11 *Fourth Forum*, pp.7-13.

12 *Ibid.*, p.13.

13 *Baptism, Eucharist and Ministry 1982-1990: Report on the Process and Responses*, Faith and Order paper no. 149, Geneva, WCC, 1990.

14 *Ibid.*, p.147.

15 "The Understanding of the Church Emerging in the Bilateral Dialogues – Coherence or Divergence", *Fifth Forum, op. cit.*

16 *Ibid.*, p.45.

17 *Ibid.*

18 *Ibid.*, p.46.

19 *Ibid.*, p.48. See *On the Way to Fuller Koinonia. Official Report of the Fifth World Conference on Faith and Order*, Thomas F. Best and Günther Gassmann, eds, Faith and Order paper no. 166, Geneva, WCC, 1994.

20 *Fifth Forum*, p.49.

21 Already the Second Forum (1979) gave some consideration to reception. See *The Three Reports*, p.21.

22 *The Three Reports*, p.40.

23 *Sixth Forum*, preface, p.1.

24 *Ibid.*, pp.9-13.

25 *Ibid.*, p.21.

26 *Baptism, Eucharist and Ministry*, Faith and Order paper no. 111, Geneva, WCC, 1982, preface, p.x.

27 *Sixth Forum*, p.15.

28 *Documentary History of Faith and Order 1963-1993*, Günther Gassmann, ed., Faith and Order paper no. 159, Geneva, WCC, 1993, p.342.

29 *Ibid.*

30 "The Sixth Report of the Joint Working Group", in *Information Service* (=IS) (PCPCU), no. 74, 1990, III, pp.61-74, here 62-65.

31 *Ibid.*, pp.75-84.

32 *Ibid.*, pp.85-90.

33 *Report of the Third Phase of Lutheran/Roman Catholic International Dialogue*, "Church and Justification: Understanding the Church in the Light of the Doctrine of Justification", no. 103, *IS*, 86, 1994, II-III, p.148.

34 *The Unity of the Church as Koinonia: Ecumenical Perspectives on the 1991 Canberra Statement of Unity*, Günther Gassmann and John A. Radano, eds, Faith and Order paper no. 163, Geneva, WCC, 1993.

35 "The Challenge of Proselytism and the Calling to Common Witness", *IS*, 91, 1996, I-II, pp.77-83.

III
Resolutions
and Recommendations

Statement from Younger Theologians

As younger theologians, we extend to the Faith and Order plenary commission and secretariat our deep thanks. We are grateful not only because we were included in the plenary commission meeting in Moshi, Tanzania, but also because we have been so strongly encouraged to participate fully in the ongoing work of Faith and Order. We believe we have made significant contributions to our common work these past days as rapporteurs, panellists, participants in group and regional discussions and on the floor of the plenary itself.

We encourage Faith and Order to continue its commitment to include younger theologians as full participants in its meeting – our meetings. We have benefited greatly as well from the interaction between local and visiting younger theologians; thus we hope that in future meetings local participation is as strongly supported as it has been here.

As we prepare to return to our churches, schools, families and jobs, we take with us a genuine eagerness to continue our involvement in Faith and Order work. Of course, we do not expect to come to all future meetings. We do expect, however, to be given the opportunity to contribute to current and future projects. We sincerely hope that Faith and Order will consider us – and other younger theologians from Faith and Order member churches – to be a valuable resource. We will help implement study groups and consultations in our respective regions and areas of expertise. We trust that Faith and Order will take full advantage of our fields of study and research as together we engage future work in addition to carrying out the present programme.

We have taken the initiative to build a network among ourselves, identifying our fields of study, interests and backgrounds. This network will be available as a resource both to us and to Faith and Order in planning and preparing for the next generation at work. We intend to develop, maintain, update and use a database of younger theologians who are interested in Faith and Order work. We strongly encourage the plenary commissioners to send to the secretariat the names and curricula vitae of younger theologians from their churches who would like to become part of this growing network. By means of this resource, we are committed to provide input, such as individual responses and recommendations to Faith and Order studies in progress. We have also considered the possibility of reinstituting the document service, *Study Encounter*, with the purpose of circulating drafts-in-progress among ourselves for dialogical critique and communication to Faith and Order and the wider ecumenical movement.

Again, we thank Faith and Order for inviting us as full participants in the plenary commission meeting in Moshi. We have listened, and we believe our voices have been heard. More importantly, we have begun the process of making Faith and Order work our own.

Closing Actions

Nominations Committee

In the first half of the plenary commission meeting, the moderator, on behalf of the board of Faith and Order, presented a list of names for membership of the nominations committee whose task it was to prepare the names of the future board for presentation to the central committee at its first meeting following the Harare assembly. After a short discussion, the steering commission moved to a vote and the six names put before the board were accepted.

Following the vote, Livingstone Thompson raised the issue of representation on the group. He believed that the group that had been appointed was not representative enough and for him there was a weakness in the fact that all members of the nominations committee were members of the board and not of the plenary commission. Martin Cressey then suggested that as no members were in fact stipulated in the constitution it was open to the commission to add to the number of those elected. The moderator promised to take the matter back to the board.

Following a closed session of the board, the commission returned to the question of nomination. The board considered Livingstone Thompson's concern which was primarily about the relation between the board to the plenary commission rather than about regional representation. He felt that the balance on the nominations committee should be between members of the board and members of the plenary commission.

The moderator reminded the meeting of the constitution, which simply directs that the plenary commission before each assembly shall appoint a nominations committee to prepare a list of names for the election of the new board by the central committee at its first meeting after the assembly. The members will hold office until the next assembly. The constitution makes no stipulation about numbers or whether the person should be from the board or from the plenary commission.

The practice in the past has been to elect people from the standing commission to form the nominations committee in order that they may work within the context of a meeting of the standing commission using the wider and more representative body of the plenary commission as a frame of reference.

The nominations process is as follows:

1. The director writes to the churches inviting them to nominate names for consideration. In this way the churches have the decision over what names are put forward.
2. Secondly, the slate of names is passed to the nominations committee. This committee work with guidelines for regional and confessional balance which are laid down by the central committee for its own members with adjustments made for those churches like the Roman Catholic Church which is not a member of the central committee.

The task of the nominations committee is not an easy one and is often painful when choices inevitably have to be made. The board considered Livingstone Thompson's request and in view of that continued to believe that the most workable option was to present a slate of names taken from the members of the board so that the nominations committee could meet within the context of a board meeting. Nevertheless, on reflection the board wished to add one name to the list which had been accepted by the plenary commission on the previous occasion. The name added was that of Yeow Choo Lak. The nominations committee appointed: Araceli Ezzatti de Rochietti, John Onaiyekan, Emmanuel Clapsis, Dorothea Wendebourg, Kyung Sook Lee, Paul Crow, Yeow Choo Lak.

Introduction to the Session on the Presentation of the Recommendations

The moderator felt it was most helpful that the presentation of the recommendations followed immediately the responses to President Mkapa's speech. At the beginning of the meeting, the president had reminded us of the inexplicable relation between the unity of the church and the unity of the world. As we lay plans for the future of our work, we do so within that context of church and world. Perhaps Faith and Order's work in the last few years has been less effective in setting the vision of the unity of the church within the unity of God's kingdom and

God's gift of communion to the whole of humanity. This is the right context in which to set consideration of work for the future.

The moderator reminded the commission of its major task; she believed that in this meeting the commission had attempted to honour its constitution, which reads:

> The plenary commission shall have as its primary task theological study, debate and appraisal. It will initiate the programme of Faith and Order, lay down general guidelines and share in its communication to the churches.

She noted that the plenary commission members at Moshi had heard an account of the work of the commission since the last plenary meeting in Budapest; on ecclesiology, hermeneutics, apostolic faith, worship, ecclesiology and ethics. All of this was called for by the Budapest meeting and further endorsed at the world conference in Santiago de Compostela in 1993.

The work on both ecclesiology and hermeneutics presented in Moshi was in at a very preliminary stage. Ecclesiology was little more than programme notes for the study, an outline dynamic accompanied by some disjointed building blocks. The hermeneutics paper was also at a preliminary stage.

In planning the plenary meeting, it was the board's view that the entire commission should review the total programme, rather than divide into five groups, each working on a single theme. The rationale was that the studies are still in formative stage and that the crucial task was to get overall direction from the plenary commission. It was important for everyone to look at the total programme and to note the integration between the different parts of Faith and Order's work. The demands this decision made on the meeting in Moshi were considerable as minds were stretched from hermeneutics to apostolic faith, from worship to ecclesiology and ethics. This meeting had (1) been presented with the studies, (2) heard preparatory responses, (3) discussed the material in groups, (4) reported back the work of the groups, and (5) reacted as a plenary commission to group reports.

The moderators of the studies and the staff persons responsible attempted to distil what had been said into draft recommendations to the board from the plenary commission about the future direction of work.

The process was to test whether the draft recommendations did in fact reflect the advice and mind of the commission. There had been much talk about becoming a community of discernment; it was now necessary to articulate a common mind about future work.

The moderator ended her introductory remarks by outlining the process that would be followed. Each section of the recommendations would be read aloud and then the floor would be open for comments. After the session the moderators and staff persons for each study would redraft in the light of the comments received. A final version of the recommendations would be brought back to the plenary commission for further comments and acceptance.

* * *

Successive drafts of the recommendations were brought to plenary for discussion and revision before they were adopted.

Recommendations to the Board

Concerning the ecclesiology study

The plenary commission reviewed the work done on the study on the nature and purpose of the church. A variety of helpful views were enunciated concerning the work done so far. The plenary commission recommends to the board that:

1) the aim of the study and its methodology be clarified in the life of discussion at Moshi;

2) a variety of ways in which insights from different contexts can help shape the study be integrated into it;

3) in relation to (1) and (2) above, the following should be considered and find an appropriate place in the study:
   - biblical foundations and conceptions of the church;
   - materials provided, for example, in the Santiago report, the Dublin, Codrington (Barbados) and Annecy texts, bilateral dialogues, the responses to BEM, the Community of Women and Men in the Church study, Church and World, and regional work;
   - conciliarity, primacy and the ministry of unity, oversight, authority, laity, reconciliation of memories, the four marks of the church, the visible and invisible nature of the church, the trinity as source and model of koinonia, conversion (metanoia), ministries of women in the church;
   - the insights and challenges of the studies on hermeneutics, ecclesiology and ethics, apostolic faith and worship;

4) it be considered how best to make a contribution on the subject of the nature, purpose and goal of the church in the context of the Harare assembly.

Concerning the study process on apostolic faith

The study process on apostolic faith produced in 1990 the book *Confessing the One Faith*. This describes the threefold process of explication, recognition and common confession. Faith and Order has now published the study booklet *Towards Sharing the One Faith*, which was warmly received by the plenary commission. Affirming the importance of the apostolic faith study and the book *Confessing the One Faith*, the commission recommends to the board that:

1) the study guide be sent to the churches in order to stimulate the process of response to *Confessing the One Faith* begun in 1990;
2) a small group be set up to encourage the process of engagement with the apostolic faith study and to recall the churches to the request for a response around the text *Confessing the One Faith* first sent out in 1990;
3) the responses be collated and reflected upon so as to move towards a text which indicates the degree of agreement in faith that exists, in order to help the churches recognize in one another their common faith;
4) the study guide be sent not only to "the churches" but to NCCs, other ecumenical bodies and specific persons who might best steer the guide into use in study groups;
5) as many translations as possible be made of the study guide and that members of the plenary commission in collaboration with the Faith and Order secretariat find ways of securing the translation of the guide in their own language, for their own context; the study guide offers a flexible resource for use as locally appropriate.

Concerning the study on hermeneutics

The plenary commission recommends to the board that:

1) the study be continued;
2) the studies on ecumenical hermeneutics and on ecclesiology interact more effectively and concretely, and joint consultations take place;
3) the study continue to take into account the ongoing study on intercultural hermeneutics by Unit II;
4) the present text be revised and developed so that:
    - the aims of the study are clarified; the language is simplified and become less prescriptive; examples and case studies are introduced; the structure is improved and a new title found;
    - the background and process of the study are made more explicit;
    - the approach to hermeneutics is sharpened and clarified;
    - the distinction from Montreal between scripture, Tradition and traditions is explained and its continuing adequacy be critically tested;

- the pneumatological dimension is emphasized;
- the relation between a social agenda and the quest for visible unity, a hermeneutics of suspicion and a hermeneutics of coherence are clarified and balanced;
5) further work focus on:
  - the issues posed by fundamentalists; the issues posed by Pentecostalists and evangelicals;
  - the hermeneutical significance of oral tradition as well as nonverbal expressions of the Christian faith such as symbols and practices;
  - the location and exercise of authority;
  - the hermeneutics of confessionality;
6) the working principles remain short but be developed towards:
  - greater preciseness and concrete practicality;
  - making explicit implications and applicability also for internal processes in the churches.

Concerning the study on worship
The plenary commission recommends to the board that:
1) Faith and Order work on worship in the search for unity be continued in close relationship with the ecclesiology and hermeneutics studies and any future Faith and Order work on ecclesiology and ethics, so that each study may inform the other;
2) taking into consideration work previously done, a study of the question of unity and diversity in worship and its relationship to the search for visible unity in the church, be undertaken;
3) Faith and Order continue to encourage prayer for unity not only through the Week of Prayer for Christian Unity and as special ecumenical services but also as an integral part of regular Christian worship life;
4) the consultation on baptism planned for January 1997 take up the question of baptismal *ordo*, of inculturation of baptism and the question of the ethical and ecclesiological implications of baptism;
5) suggestions for work on the following issues be communicated to other units and streams of the WCC or other ecumenical bodies as appropriate:
  - inculturation of worship (in relation to Unit II);
  - ecumenical and interfaith services at civic and national events;
  - spiritual dimensions of the ecumenical experience and the implications of Christian worship for Christian life (Worship and Spirituality stream, Unit I);
  - common ecumenical lectionaries, worship resources including

iconography, hymnody and music (ELLC, Worship and Spirituality).

Concerning the study on ecclesiology and ethics

The plenary commission reviewed the most recent work done by Faith and Order and Unit III in the collaborative study on Ecclesiology and Ethics as mandated by the WCC central committee. It considered the report *Costly Obedience* from the Johannesburg June 1996 consultation. (This was the third and last consultation in the study process, following earlier meetings at Rønde [*Costly Unity*] in 1993 and Tantur [*Costly Commitment*] in 1994.) It also considered the provisional, draft text "Common Perspectives on Ecclesiology and Ethics".

The commission:

1) notes that the WCC central committee (September 1996) will hear an account of this collaborative study process;

2) judges that the text on "Common Perspectives" is not ready for consideration by central committee, and recommends further work towards a statement of common principles on ecclesiology and ethics emerging from the study process as a whole;

3) notes that the report of the first consultation (*Costly Unity*) provided important material for discussions at Santiago do Compostela and that the report of the second consultation (*Costly Commitment*) was received with critical appreciation by the board meeting in Bangkok;

4) offers an extensive and serious critique of the report of the most recent consultation (*Costly Obedience*) and asks that the points made, in the form of a detailed account of the plenary and group presentations and discussion, be shared with colleagues in Unit III as part of an evaluation of the collaborative study process; and asks that in any further distribution of this material, its origin and status be clearly indicated;

5) asks for clarification by Faith and Order of (a) the hermeneutical task inherent in collaborative work, as differing methodologies and vocabularies are brought together, and (b) questions of accountability raised by collaborative work; these results to be shared within the WCC.

The plenary commission:

1) affirms the importance of further work reflecting the relation between ecclesiology and ethics, interacting with the ethical struggles of the wider human community and proceeding from the biblical basis and distinctive identity and witness of the Christian church;

2) recommends that further study in this area be done in continuity with

previous Faith and Order work, particularly that on the Unity of the Church and the Renewal of Human Community (*Church and World*); and infused by new insights raised in the plenary session on President Mkapa's address;

3) recommends as a starting point the proposals for work on the unity of the church in relation to ethnic identity and nationalism, as recommended at the conclusion of the Unity and Renewal study; this should be coordinated with the Faith and Order studies on Ecclesiology, Hermeneutics and on Worship; detailed proposals for further study should be considered by the board in January 1997:

4) notes that in this process the initiative would lie with Faith and Order/Unit I, with appropriate interaction with Unit III;

5) notes also that Faith and Order will respond to the request of Unit III to provide theological input to the Programme to Overcome Violence.

A Tribute to Max Thurian

MARY TANNER

At the weekend we received the news from Geneva of the death of our beloved friend Max Thurian on 15 August, a day before his 76th birthday. Max Thurian, a Reformed pastor, was one of the first people to join Frère Roger Schutz at the ecumenical community in Taizé, becoming its theologian, liturgist and spiritual director. With Frère Roger, Frère Max was invited by Pope John XXIII to be an observer at the Second Vatican Council.

From 1970 onwards Frère Max worked tirelessly within Faith and Order for the preparation of *Baptism, Eucharist and Ministry*. I once heard him introduced at a meeting as "Mr BEM". It became in a way his life and passion as he worked with a small drafting group producing revision after revision from Accra in 1974 to Lima in 1982. It was Frère Max who later edited the six volumes of official responses from the churches to BEM. Those of us who worked closely with him in those years remember that particular combination of gentleness, openness to others, clarity of mind and encouragement of new members of the commission. In Naples, in 1987, Frère Max was ordained as a Roman Catholic priest. He was an ecumenist who belonged to all of us.

Frère Max wrote a number of important books, including one on Mary. It is fitting that he died on the feast of the assumption. He would have been happy that we celebrated the feast of the Dormition with our Orthodox brothers and sisters.

The last time I saw Frère Max was in Geneva last December, walking in the grounds at Le Cénacle. He looked frail but serene. He embraced me and with tears in his eyes said, "Whatever happens, I am so thankful that I have seen that work on BEM and the Papal Encyclical *Ut Unum Sint*."

It is with thanksgiving that we remember Max Thurian and his unshakable faith in a God who called him to work for Christian unity and to be a great ecumenical leader.

Heavenly Father, we give thanks for the life and ministry of our dear brother Max, for his untiring work for the unity of your church. Into your hands we commend his Spirit knowing that death for him is the gateway to life and to eternal fellowship with you, through Jesus Christ, Our Lord. Amen.

Concluding Remarks

MARY TANNER

It was a huge undertaking to hold a plenary meeting of Faith and Order in Moshi, Tanzania, many miles from Geneva, with limitations of travel and a three-site venue. But the board took the decision to come to Tanzania at its meeting in Aleppo in January 1995 and upheld it in Bangkok in January 1996 when the financial crisis threatened us. Renate Sbeghen and Dagmar Heller were sent out like the spies of the book of Joshua to investigate and report back: they told of a land of dazzling beauty, of a mysterious mountain that revealed itself only momentarily, and of hospitality beyond imagining. "Fear not: God is in control." Yes, but Renate Sbeghen was close behind and so too was our beloved vice-moderator, Veronica Swai. One of the members of the commission said to me that if he were the president of Tanzania he would immediately make Veronica Swai minister of state for tourism.

Moshi, in the shadow of Mount Kilimanjaro, has proved to be a marvellous and memorable site for our meeting – a garden-of-Eden setting for our work. The friendship extended to us and the care for our needs has been overwhelming and humbling. I have asked myself again and again "who would want to care for me this much?" as gift after gift of kindness and thoughtfulness has been showered upon me. I know it is only those who are committed to Christ and to one another in Christ. We thank God for the example of kindness and hospitality of Christians in this place. His Excellency, President Benjamin William Mkapa, said in his keynote address to us: "We pride ourselves on having a beautiful and peaceful country. We also try to be very friendly and hospitable. I hope you will not find us wanting."

Indeed, we have not found Tanzania wanting. We have been overwhelmed by gifts of kindness and consideration, of friendship, of music and laughter. We have had a time of disclosure of what *koinonia* means and might mean.

Our work has been enfolded in prayer. We have prayed for our work, our churches and God's world and we have remembered those who have gone before us. We have celebrated together a common service of preparation and penitence for eucharists shared, and not yet shared. We have sensed each other's joy and borne each other's grieving. And we have worshipped with local congregations, knowing that while oceans and continents will divide us when we leave this place, our life hidden with God in Christ even now unites us.

And what about our work? It is too early for me at least to make a considered assessment. The kaleidoscope of bright and jagged pieces will need shaking and reshaking and settling once more before I make sense of it all.

Together as a plenary commission we have reviewed the total work of Faith and Order which has been done since our world conference in Santiago de Compostela in 1993. We have together laid down general guidelines to direct the board when it meets in January 1997 in France. I believe we have drawn a wider community into the work of Faith and Order in these days in Moshi. I have been encouraged by the expression of interest and the desire to get involved in our work by our younger theologians and by so many of those with us from this country.

We have given direction to our future work:

– We have laid down guidelines for the continuation of our main study project on ecclesiology, on the nature and the purpose of the church. We have shown that questions need to be asked both about the content and the method of this study. But there has been no doubt that this is a crucial study for the whole of the ecumenical movement and for the World Council of Churches, as the Council considers its common understanding and vision for the next millennium.

– We have given another impetus to the important study on the confession of the apostolic faith. That was a hope I expressed in my report on the first day here. I am sure that if we could get hold of our common faith at a deeper level, that would be a powerful impulse to encourage us to work for the visible unity of the church.

– We have given important directives to the work on hermeneutics, worship, and ecclesiology and ethics. Throughout this meeting there have been strong expressions of commitment to seek and to work for the visible unity of the church. We have echoed the message of Santiago de Compostela: "There is no turning back from the goal of visible unity or from the single ecumenical movement that unites concerns for the unity of the church with the concern for engagement in the struggles of the world." Indeed, the president's opening speech to us, and the responses to that speech, have reminded us sharply and

powerfully that talk of unity has to be infused with concerns for overcoming the divisions of human community.

We have not only talked about the content of our work and laid down
guidelines for the future, there have also been sharp challenges to us
about how we do our work: the relation of the board to the plenary commission, the way the studies are carried out and who is around any particular study table. These challenges reveal a commitment to the work on
the part of many of you and a desire to participate more fully. The board
has pledged itself to reviewing the ways in which Faith and Order works
when it comes together in January 1997.

But it is not merely the change of structures of work that we have
called for but a much more profound change of hearts and minds of ourselves and our communities, a constant repentance and constant turning
to Christ and conversion. This was the subject of our new director's
report to us at the beginning of our conference. The vision of visible
unity is proclaimed not only in the words we speak but in lives that are
themselves being changed. Only such conversion will respond to that
spiritual crisis in the ecumenical movement of which Tom Fitzgerald, the
moderator of our unit, spoke so movingly.

Yes, God has been in control. The work which we have done here,
with all its imperfections, we offer to the One who calls us for the good
of his church and the coming of his kingdom. We know that the One who
calls us to this task is faithful, he and not we will perform it.

At the end of this meeting we have so many people to thank; so many
have invested time and energy and have given of themselves to make
this meeting possible. I have asked others to join me in expressing our
thanks. My particular task is to thank the director and the members of the
staff team for their untiring work both before the meeting and during our
time here. The director, Alan Falconer, has only been with us such a
short time but already we can see the great contribution he is making to
the work of Faith and Order, and indeed to the work of the World Council of Churches. He is a much valued staff member within the World
Council and his advice and wisdom are sought by many of his colleagues. During this meeting Alan has been a gentle and strong presence;
we can go into the future confident that the direction of our work is safe
in his hands. Thomas Best, Dagmar Heller and Peter Bouteneff have
given secure support and help to the studies for which they have carried
major responsibility. In addition they have undertaken many responsibilities during this meeting, for preparing worship, for seeing that papers
have been ready for our sessions and by supporting us in so many ways.
That leaves two other members of staff to thank. First of all, Carolyn
McComish, with us for the first time; Carolyn has given invaluable sup-

port in working late into the night and in helping us in many other ways. Finally, to Renate Sbeghen, who with her usual skill and abundant energy managed to get us all here safely, and to foresee our needs even before we expressed them ourselves, and will no doubt have made just the right preparations for our return journeys. To the staff team we express our thanks and assure them of our prayers as they work for Faith and Order in the months ahead.

Resolution of Thanks to the Churches in Tanzania

Over the period 10-24 August 1996, the plenary commission on Faith and Order of the World Council of Churches met at Moshi, Tanzania, in the shadow of Mount Kilimanjaro.

We gathered in Moshi, at the gracious invitation of the churches in the United Republic of Tanzania, where we were warmly received and hospitably served. Our work has been facilitated and encouraged.

Choirs from several schools and churches enriched our worship life, in which Tanzanian church leaders participated. Thirty congregations gladly received us in their worship on Sunday, 18 August. The jubilant worship of these rapidly growing churches inspired us, as did their confident and courageous forward march in the struggle for development.

In the future, Faith and Order will continue to focus on the major goal of the visible unity of the church. Our work will be nourished by our experience of the sense of community evidenced in Tanzania and characterized so well by its president, His Excellency Benjamin William Mkapa, as he welcomed us to his country, as a unity which encompasses the diversity of tribes, cultures, races, religions and denominations.

Faith and Order members will not retreat from our mandate. Nor will we ever forget the correspondence between the search for the unity of the church and the unity of humankind in a world ravaged by poverty, injustice and inequality.

The commission expresses sincere thanks to the churches in Tanzania for their salutary contribution to the determined pursuit of faithfulness to its calling.

Appendices

APPENDIX 1

The Work on Ecclesiology

EXPLANATORY PREFACE FOR THE PLENARY COMMISSION ON FAITH AND ORDER, MOSHI

1. The decision that Faith and Order work on *Ecumenical Perspectives of Ecclesiology* was taken by the plenary commission at its meeting in Budapest in the summer of 1989. This was the meeting at which the commission also agreed on the title and overall framework for the fifth world conference on Faith and Order – "Towards Koinonia in Faith, Life and Witness". This title was itself a statement about the way in which the commission viewed the unity of the church.

2. Between the Budapest meeting in 1989 and the WCC Canberra assembly in 1991 the Faith and Order commission, at the request of the general secretary of the WCC, produced a statement on the nature and purpose of the church which, after revision by the Canberra assembly, was adopted by the assembly as the Canberra statement, "The Koinonia of the Church: Gift and Calling".

3. Encouraged by the one-day meeting of the plenary commission immediately following the fifth world conference, the standing commission meeting in Crêt-Bérard in January 1994 formulated its major study programme for the next years as *The Church as Koinonia: An Ecumenical Study*.

4. In the *Conspectus of Studies* prepared at Crêt-Bérard, the standing commission showed how a number of different elements might feed into the overall main study:

– a study on hermeneutics;
– work on koinonia in prayer and worship (done in collaboration with Unit I);
– work on ecclesiology and ethics (done in collaboration with Unit III);
– new work on the ministries of women, episcope-episcopacy and the ministry of primacy;
– regional reflections.

All of these studies, both inter- and intra-unit, were to enrich a developing common understanding of the church as koinonia.

5. The meetings at Dublin in May 1994 and Bridgetown, Barbados, in November 1994 had the task of "mapping out" the new study on ecclesiology

and to consider what place the Canberra statement might play within the study. Overall themes were to be the question of how the church lives and copes with diversity, and what structures of discernment and reception would hold Christians in a communion of dialogue. In all of this, the theme of koinonia was central. The result of these meetings was a set of "building blocks" and an outline for what would become a convergence text on ecclesiology.

6. The meeting of the ecclesiology core group at Annecy in September 1995 produced the exploratory text before you. The decision was taken by the board (former standing commission) in Bangkok, January 1996, to proceed with the study, linked as it is to the Canberra statement (itself a text with the authority of the assembly), and which follows the statement's threefold structure. The board felt that as work continued, the intention was not simply to repeat the Canberra statement, and certainly not to rewrite it. Rather, the new text would be designed to help the churches to appropriate at a deeper level in their lives the insights expressed in the Canberra statement. Those insights would themselves be based on Faith and Order's past work, including *Confessing the One Faith; Baptism, Eucharist and Ministry* and its responses; and *Church and World.*

7. The current text is therefore an initial exploration which takes the threefold structure of the Canberra statement:
a) the church in the purpose of God;
b) the dimensions;
c) challenges to the churches.
Before each section the Canberra statement is quoted in full.

8. The scope of this text, as it continues to develop, will go beyond helping the churches to appropriate what has already been achieved. It will try to work from the Canberra statement in the light of what has happened since Canberra, particularly in relation to the insights of the fifth world conference on Faith and Order, in such a way as to open up new vistas for the future.

9. The text will seek to link the search for visible unity with the situation of humanity today, particularly where divisions of the churches are linked to divisions of humanity and where the divisions of the churches are tragically linked to the struggles and sorrows of the world. The reconciliation and unity of the churches are integrally related to the reconciliation and unity of all that God has created.

10. This text will focus in particular on areas where we believe we can now explore and state things together in a fresh way such as the intrinsic relation between the apostolic faith, baptism and eucharist and the implication of this for visible unity; the ministry of oversight in the service of the koinonia of the church; the ministries of women; the nature of conciliarity and the ministry of primacy; the process of mutual recognition and reconciliation; ecclesiology and ethics; unity in diversity – diversity in unity. It will take many years to treat these subjects adequately to integrate them into a text on ecclesiology. The text you have before you intends to map out the areas indicating some directions for the future and calling for further work.

11. In beginning on this important task we have already glimpsed new perspectives and possibilities for greater convergence.

12. We look forward to the reaction of the plenary commission to this pre-liminary work which the board has carried out at the plenary commission's suggestion. Our intention and hope is that this text will be developed further in the light of the plenary commission's comments in Moshi so that when it meets for the first time after the Harare assembly it will have a more mature text. At that point it would need to be considered whether the text should be sent to the churches for their reaction (as the *Accra text* was sent to the churches in 1974) and then developed further in the light of their responses.

13. We emphasize that this text is preliminary. In places it points to work already done that needs bringing into the text. In other places it calls for new work to be done. Already plans have been made to continue work:
– on koinonia (December 1996);
– on the ministry of oversight in the service of the koinonia of the church (April 1997);
– on the ministries of women (March 1998) and throughout the study to give insight from regional reflections.

* * *

THE CHURCH AS KOINONIA – AN ECUMENICAL STUDY

Introduction
1. The consultative group meeting in Annecy (September 1995) deter-mined to take the Canberra statement, "The Unity of the Church: Gift and Calling", as the framework for its work on ecclesiology. What follows is a first preliminary draft exploration and explication of the Canberra statement. The exploration follows the three sections of Canberra statement:
a) Koinonia (paras 1.1-1.3);
b) the dimensions of visible unity (paras 2.1-2.2);
c) challenges to the churches (paras 3.1-3.2).
Before each section the text of the Canberra statement is quoted in full.

A. Koinonia (paras 1.1-1.3)

1.1. The purpose of God according to holy scripture is to gather the whole of creation under the lordship of Jesus Christ in whom, by the power of the Holy Spirit, all are brought into communion with God (Eph. 1). The church is the foretaste of this communion with God and with one another. The grace of our Lord Jesus Christ, the love of God and the com-munion of the Holy Spirit enable the one church to live as sign of the reign of God and servant of the reconciliation with God, promised and provided for the whole creation. The purpose of the church is to unite people with Christ in the power of the Spirit, to manifest communion in prayer and action and thus to point to the fullness of communion with God, human-ity and the whole creation in the glory of the kingdom.

1.2. The calling of the church is to proclaim reconciliation and provide healing, to overcome divisions based on race, gender, age, culture, colour and to bring all people into communion with God. Because of sin and the misunderstanding of the diverse gifts of the Spirit, the churches are painfully divided within themselves and among each other. The scandalous divisions damage the credibility of their witness to the world in worship and service. Moreover, they contradict not only the church's witness but also its very nature.

1.3. We acknowledge with gratitude to God that in the ecumenical movement the churches walk together in mutual understanding, theological convergence, common suffering and common prayer, shared witness and service, as they draw close to one another. This has allowed them to recognize a certain degree of communion already existing between them. This is indeed the fruit of the active presence of the Holy Spirit in the midst of all who believe in Christ Jesus and who struggle for visible unity now. Nevertheless, churches have failed to draw the consequences for their life from the degree of communion they have already experienced and the agreements already achieved. They have remained satisfied to co-exist in division.

2. A distinction needs to be made between koinonia and the various models of the church and images of the church. Koinonia is not another model or image. Koinonia is the underlying reality of the church. It provides a framework which holds together unity in diversity and diversity in unity. More work needs to be done in this area:
–   an exegetical study based upon the paper given by John Reumann in Santiago de Compostela;
–   an examination of the way in which koinonia is used in different traditions (koinonia-communion, Strasbourg 1995);
–   an examination of the use of koinonia in the bilateral dialogues;
–   an integration of material from section I of the Santiago report.
Koinonia is more and more central in the ecumenical discussion of the visible unity of the church. We therefore cannot abandon it. However, we are aware of a danger in using the term koinonia as an all embracing term so that it comes to mean everything or nothing (cf. criticism of Reumann).

B. The dimensions of visible unity (paras 2.1-2.2)

2.1. The unity of the church to which we are called is a koinonia given and expressed in the common confession of apostolic faith; a common sacramental life entered by the one baptism and celebrated together in one eucharistic fellowship; a common life in which members and ministries are mutually recognized and reconciled; and a common mission witnessing to the gospel of God's grace to all people and serving the whole of creation. The goal of the search for full communion is realized when all the churches are able to recognize in one another the one, holy, catholic and apostolic church in its fullness. This full communion will be expressed on the local and the universal levels through conciliar forms of life and action. In such communion churches are bound in all aspects of their life together at all levels in confessing the one faith and engaging in worship and witness, deliberation and action.

2.2. Diversities which are rooted in theological traditions, various cultural, ethnic or historical contexts are integral to the nature of communion; yet there are limits to diversity. Diversity is illegitimate when, for instance, it makes impossible the common confession of Jesus Christ as God and Saviour the same yesterday, today and forever (Heb. 13:8); salvation and the final destiny of humanity as proclaimed in holy scripture and preached by the apostolic community. In communion diversities are brought together in harmony as gifts of the Holy Spirit, contributing to the richness and fullness of the church of God.

3. As we explored the dimensions of koinonia in the Canberra statement, we were convinced of the inter-relation of the items listed in the statement. They are not separable items but interlocking. An indispensable characteristic of these several points is their inter-relatedness. Living in a communion of faith, sacramental life, ministry, overcoming denominational divisions, would bring Christians together to confront together racism, sexism and those things which threaten the unity of human community and the preservation of creation. The communion of life would provide a more credible witness and service in the world.

(i) The common confession of the apostolic faith
4. We should seek to set out together an account of the central content of the faith, a faith grounded in the holy scripture – the story of our faith conveyed in the scripture. In an accompanying commentary we need to point to the fact that that faith is grounded in the scriptures in the proclamation of the word, is set forth in the catholic creeds, borne witness to in the various confessions of the churches and proclaimed in the life of the churches, in the various restatements of the faith through the ages. These statements interpret the faith, answering particular contemporary questions. The real question is not who uses or does not use creeds but rather our unity and communion in the one faith grounded in the holy scriptures. However, we all recognize the need for common criteria. There is a difference between imposing the recitation of the creed on the one hand and acknowledging it as pointing to the faith we have in common on the other (cf. *Confessing the One Faith*, F&O paper 153; "Towards Sharing the One Faith", F&O paper 173; and the Faith and Order study on hermeneutics).

(ii) A common sacramental life entered by the one baptism and celebrated together in one eucharistic fellowship
5. The group agreed that this second element in the Canberra statement needs rephrasing to incorporate within it an explicit reference to the proclamation of the word. We suggest that this dimension should read:

A common life in Christ entered by the one baptism, nourished by the preaching of the word and celebrated together in one eucharistic fellowship.

This life in Christ is a sacramental life, grounded in the word of God (cf. Barbados 3). The responses of the churches to BEM have indicated that there remain areas where further convergence and consensus is needed for a life of visible unity, e. g. baptism-re-baptism; sacrament-sacramentality; etc. (cf. *Churches Respond to BEM*, vols I-VI, and *Report on the Process and Responses*, F&O paper 149; *Ut Unum Sint* and bilateral dialogues).

(iii) A common life in which members and ministries are mutually recognized and reconciled

6. We agreed that many of the responses to BEM were right in suggesting that there was too great a separation of the ordered ministry from the life of the whole people of God. Much more needs to be said about the ministry of the whole people of God in, with and among whom the ordered ministry belongs. Membership of the church, and all ministries, are grounded in our common baptism. The Holy Spirit works in the whole people giving to each person his or her particular charism, enabling all to contribute to the fidelity of the church, to its apostolic calling and mission. Apostolicity belongs to the whole church. The whole people of God are the laos amongst whom there are different tasks and different ministries (cf. Barbados 1).

7. The use of the terms "recognized" and "reconciled" need further explication as they are not understood in the same way by all churches. For some the two words are synonymous, for others reconciliation of ministries is a stage lying beyond recognition. For these churches the reconciliation of ministries cannot be divided from the reconciliation of the communities of the church. In other words, the reconciliation of ministries belongs within the reconciliation of the total visible life of the church as koinonia. These differing views of reconciliation can affect the model of unity which any particular church espouses.

8. A ministry of oversight, episcope, is one of the gifts for the safeguarding of the unity and continuity of the church. In all churches episcope is exercised in personal and communal (corporate) forms. The forms of oversight link the local church to the wider church. A question remains as to whether it is necessary to have episcope at all levels of the church's life. In addition here too we must seek common criteria which would enable each church to recognize the common apostolic ministry in the other.

9. We believe that the paragraph in the Canberra statement which reads

> for communion will be expressed on the local and universal levels through conciliar forms of life and action

properly belongs together with an understanding of the ministry – the ministry of the whole people of God. Conciliar forms of life and action belong within the inter-related ministry of the whole people of God and the ordered ministry of the church. Synods or councils need to embody the reflection of the whole people of God, including the ordered ministry of oversight. The responses to BEM point to areas requiring further work towards convergence for without further agreement the potential to continue or even deepen divisions between

churches remains, e. g. apostolicity-succession; the personal exercise of episcope; the ordination of women; the primatial ministry, etc.

10. The Canberra statement uses the term "local" and "universal" levels.
More clarity needs to be given to the meaning of the terms. What is meant by
the local church? Is it the congregation, the diocese, the country? Is universal
used here in the sense of worldwide or does it refer to the church reaching
across space and through time?

11. Even though we agree that a conciliar model of life is an attractive one
and many would affirm that conciliarity is integral to ecclesial life, it appears
that no one church today has a wholly convincing model of conciliar life (cf.
How Does the Church Teach Authoritatively Today, F&O paper 91, and *Signs
of the Spirit*, report of the Canberra assembly).

12. Councils, at whatever level, must be inclusive if the church is to discover the mind of Christ for it. Moreover, conciliarity only works if there is
mutual trust: trust of those chosen to represent and accountability by those
chosen by the people they represent. To act in synod is a service of discernment for the good of the whole church and not an authoritarian exercise.

13. Although we all in some way afford a place to the early councils of the
church, the model of these councils is not one that could simply be taken over
today. Moreover, there is amongst many churches a degree of suspicion about
the conciliar process based on negative experience of the past. Any strengthening of a conciliar life for the sake of unity – in particular at a world level –
would need a healing of memories and a clarification of the particular task of
councils in the overall processes of discernment and reception. In any conciliar process in the future, the degree of representation and pluralism would
need to be considerably greater than that experienced in the past.

14. Not all of us were agreed on the fact that a worldwide conciliar body
should be an ongoing and permanent form of the church's life. Nevertheless
we recognize that in a life of communion there may be times when the very
bond of communion – communion in faith, sacraments, ministry, and ethical
living – are so challenged that the life of communion is itself threatened. In
this case a world conciliar body would be needed to affirm the mind of Christ
for the people of God. In forming a common mind, boundaries would necessarily be drawn and limits set. The corollary might be the exclusion of some.
In this process not only will unity be discerned but at the same time disunity
might occur.

15. We need an ecumenical exploration of the notion of conciliarity and
what conciliar structures would best serve the unity of the church. The exploration of structures needs to be held together with the exploration of the
processes, the ongoing processes of discernment of the mind of Christ for the
church. For councils play their part within a much wider process of discernment, proclamation and reception. What is decided by a council, after taking
account of the mind of the faithful, has then to be received by the faithful. By
reception we do not mean automatic acceptance. Sometimes conciliar statements will not be affirmed. Ecumenical councils were only recognized as ecumenical because their decisions were received by the faithful. There is no
guarantee that a council would teach without error.

16. In exploring conciliarity the principle of subsidiarity needs to be recognized: namely that all the decisions are taken at an appropriate level and never at a "higher level" than is strictly necessary.

17. Today the divided churches already share in councils of churches at local, regional and world levels. These are understood by us as a pre-conciliar form of church life. The experience together even now has ecclesial significance. However we do not recognize these councils as having the same ecclesial reality as would belong to councils within a visibly united church (cf. Faith and Order response to the Common Understanding and Vision of the WCC).

(iv) A common mission, witnessing to all people to the gospel of God's grace and serving the whole creation

18. The group explored the understanding of mission lying behind the Canberra statement. What is clear is that any witness to the gospel continues to be subverted by Christian divisions. The world deserves unity in mission. The mission of the church is carried out both by what the church is, the quality of its internal life and its capacity to live the life of dying and rising with Christ, and by what the church does (cf. discussion document, *Towards Koinonia in Faith, Life and Witness*, F&O paper 161, section II.2, and Dublin report, group 3).

19. Mission involves service (diakonia) extended to all people and the task of the care of creation. Christians are called to serve and to join all people of good will in the struggle for the respect of human dignity, for peace, and for the care of creation, whether there is shared faith or not.

20. One part of mission is evangelism/evangelization where the name of Christ is expressedly named and the good news of the gospel clearly proclaimed with the explicit intention of leading others to conversion and baptism. We recognize that the terms "mission", "evangelism", "evangelization" and "dialogue" are often used in different ways (cf. *Mission and Evangelism: An Ecumenical Affirmation*).

21. Another part of the church's mission involves dialogue with people of other faiths or of none: dialogue which involves getting to know the other, undertaking common tasks for the good of humanity. Witness of faith in Christ as well as listening to the witness of other faith communities is a part of dialogue and provides space in which the Spirit of Christ, and not our own spirit, can act in leading others to Christ.

22. Christians are called to common mission, common evangelism and dialogue in order to witness credibly to God's action of grace and to serve humanity and creation. Attention needs to be given to the relationship between common mission and the other dimensions of koinonia.

(v) Diversity in unity

23. The Canberra statement points to the bonds or dimensions that belong to a life of communion. It goes on to affirm the fact that diversity and unity belong together within a life of koinonia. In communion there will be, for example, legitimate diversities in the expression of faith, in liturgical forms,

in theological positions, and in action. There are, and always will be, times when the communion in faith or sacraments or ministry or action is threatened and the limits to tolerable diversity are broken. This is why a conciliar life is necessary in order to face together threats to the bonds of unity.

24. The place of cultural diversity is one essential form of diversity as the gospel is lived out in the languages, symbols and images of a particular time and place. Culture can be both a carrier and a definition of the gospel. Nevertheless, there has necessarily to be ways of recognizing that the same gospel has been celebrated. The incarnation itself belongs to a particular time and to a particular place. There is in a sense a scandal of particularity bound up with an incarnational religion. The unity of the church depends on being able to recognize that the same gospel story is passed on within the different cultures. The gospel must be allowed both to judge and to affirm a culture. There is a problem, however, when one culture seeks to capture the gospel and claims to be the one and only authentic way of celebrating the gospel story and seeks therefore to impose its way on others. Equally, there is a problem when one culture finds it impossible to discern the gospel, as it itself proclaims it, in another cultural expression. There have been, and still are, times when the gospel has been so identified with a particular cultural, national and ethnic identity that conflicts between peoples have been exacerbated by the particular combination of religion with these aspects of identity (e. g. Ireland, former Yugoslavia, cf. work on ethnicity and nationalism).

25. The communion of the church demands the constant interplay of cultural expressions of the gospel if the riches of the gospel are to be appreciated for the whole people of God. Much more work needs to be done on the diversity of cultures (cf. the work of Unit II on gospel and culture, and Faith and Order work on hermeneutics). How, across cultures, can we recognize the "nerve centre" of that which makes us authentic and apostolic? In a world in which each place is fast becoming multicultural, the question of the admixture of cultural expressions of the one gospel in a single place can provide for a rich experience of unity held in diversity. However, different models of responding to the different expressions of cultural diversity in one place are still emerging: e. g. the melting pot model, the multicultural model, etc.

26. The group was divided on whether and how far denominational differences have a part to play in the understanding of the visible unity we seek. For some the preservation of denominational identity, at least in the foreseeable future, and even within a life of koinonia, is necessary for the safeguarding of particular theological emphases in the proclamation of the one gospel. Lutherans, for example, see as one of their gifts that of bearing witness to the centrality and critical function of the doctrine of justification by faith through grace, and of keeping the whole people of God centred around this faith. Members of other denominations in the group, however, tended to understand the visible unity of the church beyond their own identity – a unity in which the riches of their tradition would be given up into the witness and experience of the common faith and life. For some, therefore, the model of reconciled diversity remains a compelling one. There is fear of a model of merger in which distinctiveness is lost. However, all agreed that we may need to distin-

guish between a penultimate vision of the unity of the church in which denominational identities remain and a further stage of unity. What is clear is that each church is called to take now the appropriate steps that it can take on path towards fuller visible unity.

27. For some the model of unity was best expressed as a single life holding together that which is truly catholic, truly evangelical and truly reformed. To those who want to affirm denominational differences it has to be asked whether they take seriously enough the vocation to be the "all in one place", the local church, to be witnessing in that place. To those who want to go beyond denominational differences they need to ask whether they take seriously the significance of the particular witness of the denominational traditions.

28. It is impossible to map out now the precise shape that visible unity will take. It may be that for the future different models will be followed in different localities even by some world communions. An exploration of the different models of unity needs to continue. It may be that this pattern of the different orders held within the Roman Catholic Church, each with its own distinctive ethos and witness, may provide significant insights for understanding the unity we seek.

29. What the Canberra statement does is to set out in the central section a list of those things which belong to the communion of the church. There is, however, an ambiguity running through these paragraphs about whether the visible unity (or the full communion as it is sometimes called – in the Canberra statement the two terms appear to be used interchangeably) is understood as reached when local churches are bonded together by a single faith, sacramental life, ministry and mission or, on the other hand, when churches (in the sense of denominations) are brought into communion. The statement, as it stands, is capable of the two interpretations and has been used in both ways.

30. The problem any attempt of portraying visible unity encounters is the discrepancy between describing the "ideal" and the "actual". A further difficulty is whether a statement of visible unity is intended to be a penultimate statement and therefore provisional, or whether there is something lying beyond it. Full communion is in one sense an eschatological reality for the destination of our journey. Sin prevents, and will always prevent, the reaching of full communion in this life. Communion is however also the gift that God gives us out of the future coming to us in the present. The eschatological reality already in our midst. To talk of full communion as the unity we seek is therefore difficult for some. The goal is more easily spoken of for them as the realization step by step of full visible unity. Gradually, churches as they ask for repentance and conversion, experience the gift of richer and more complete expression of unity.

(vi) The goal of the search for full communion is realized when all the churches are able to recognize in one another the one, catholic, holy and apostolic church in its fullness.

31. The sentence in the Canberra statement

> The goal of the search for full communion is realized when all the churches are able to recognize in one another the one, holy, catholic and apostolic church in its fullness.

would better stand at the end of section B. It needs fuller comment in relation to the holiness, catholicity and apostolicity of the church.

C. Challenges to the churches: where are we, where are we going? (paras 3.1-3.2)

3.1. Many things have been done and many remain to be done on the way towards the realization of full communion. Churches have reached agreements in bilateral and multilateral dialogues which are already bearing fruit, renewing their liturgical and spiritual life and their theology. In taking specific steps together the churches express and encourage the enrichment and renewal of Christian life, as they learn from one another, work together for justice and peace and care together for God's creation.

3.2. The challenge at this moment in the ecumenical movement as a reconciling and renewing moment towards full visible unity is for the seventh assembly of the WCC to call all churches:

- to recognize each other's baptism on the basis of the BEM document;
- to move towards the recognition of the apostolic faith as expressed through the Nicene-Constantinopolitan Creed in the life and witness of one another;
- on the basis of convergence in faith in baptism, eucharist and ministry to consider, wherever appropriate, forms of eucharistic hospitality; we gladly acknowledge that some who do not observe these rites share in the spiritual experience of life in Christ;
- to move towards a mutual recognition of ministries;
- to endeavour in word and deed to give common witness to the gospel as a whole;
- to recommit themselves to work for justice, peace and the integrity of creation, linking more closely the search for sacramental communion of the church with the struggles for justice and peace;
- to help parishes and communities express in appropriate ways locally the degree of communion that already exists.

32. The Canberra statement sets out a number of challenges to the churches, urging them to take specific steps on the basis of the fruits of bilateral and multilateral theological agreements. The implication of the Canberra statement is that for some churches it is already possible to take further steps together. Since Canberra we have noticed the following movements in closer relations:

- the process towards visible unity and mutual recognition of the Eastern and Oriental Orthodox churches;
- the increasing number of cooperating parishes in New Zealand, local ecumenical partnerships in England and shared ministries in Canada;
- the coming into being of the United Church in Jamaica and the United Reformed Church in South Africa;

- the increasing number of signatory churches to the Leuenberg agreement;
- the Meissen agreement between the Evangelical Church of Germany (Reformed, Lutheran and United churches) and the Church of England;
- the proposed concordat between the Evangelical Lutheran Church of America and the Episcopal Church of the United States of America;
- the Porvoo agreement between the British and Irish Anglican churches and the Nordic and Baltic Lutheran churches;
- the proposal for lifting the condemnations between the Lutheran Church and the Roman Catholic Church;
- the broadening membership of some national councils of churches to include Roman Catholic and Pentecostal churches, e. g. Australia, Britain and Ireland;
- the proposal in the United States of America of the Council on Church Unity (COCU);
- the Church Unity Commission's work in South Africa;
- the examples of where churches act together or speak together in the name of justice and peace, e. g. public statements made together through the agency of the WCC, the CEC assembly at Graz in 1997 bringing together the Protestant, Lutheran, Orthodox, Anglican and Roman Catholic churches in Europe.

33. All of these are examples of churches drawing closer to one another. This has enabled them to recognize and experience a growing degree of visible koinonia. "This is indeed the fruit of the active presence of the Holy Spirit in the midst of all who believe in Christ Jesus and who struggle for unity now" (Canberra statement, 1.3).

34. The challenges set out in 1991 still remain. Every church needs to ask what steps it should take now to keep the momentum going around the list of issues in the Canberra statement. For example:

- the recognition of each other's baptism on the basis of the theological convergences of BEM;
- the move towards the recognition of the apostolic faith as expressed through the Nicene-Constantinopolitan Creed in the life and witness of one another (cf. Apostolic Faith study guide);
- on the basis of convergence in faith, baptism, eucharist, and ministry to consider, wherever appropriate, forms of eucharistic hospitality: we gladly acknowledge that some who do not observe these rites share in the spiritual experience of the life in Christ. In some traditions it is already possible to move beyond eucharistic hospitality;
- to move towards a mutual recognition of ministries;
- to endeavour in word and deed to give common witness to the gospel as a whole. The celebration of the millennium will provide the churches at local, regional and world level to witness to their common faith in the birth of Jesus Christ;
- to renew the commitment to work for justice, peace and the integrity of creation, linking more closely the search for sacramental communion of the church with the struggles for justice and peace, e. g. conferences on ecology called by the Jamaican Council of Churches;

    – to help parishes and communities express in appropriate ways locally the degree of communion that already exists.

    35. This final challenge is particularly important for it reminds us that koinonia is to be expressed in the local congregations, parishes and communities (communities in a geographical region as well as communities brought together around a common task or commitment, e. g. Iona and Corymeela or one of the religious orders). Such communities, however, will necessarily be constrained in developing a life of communion by their particular relation with the confessional world body. Experience of growth together in the local place may lead to challenges to church law.

    36. The following list is offered as an encouragement to local Christians to shared action and witness. The list is intended to be rather illustrative than descriptive:

    – Churches might become communities of intercession, identifying with each other's situation, including the possibility of praying with other churches in the same local place or with churches in twinning and other arrangements.

    – At congregational level opportunities might be found to provide an appreciation of the other traditions – sharing the treasures to which each tradition witnesses (e. g. short courses on ecumenism, Living Room Dialogues USA).

    – Congregations in one community might respond together to situations and places of human need: in relation to the locality (e. g. homelessness) or in relation to world tragedy (e. g. flood damage).

    – Representatives of churches might attend the feasts of other traditions (e. g. baptisms, confirmations, ordinations).

    – Occasional attendance at the worship of other traditions provides an occasion for discovering the hymnody and the liturgy of other traditions. This attendance at each other's feasts would be strengthened if invitations were also extended to attend each other's decision-making bodies.

    – Exchanges should be encouraged in the field of theological education, e. g. programme staff, faculty staff, theological students. Wherever possible theological education should be undertaken jointly.

    – Encouragement should be given to the arrangement of twinning arrangements with churches of different traditions who might share resources both human and humanitarian.

    – The sharing of each other's memories by the inclusion in worship and prayer life the remembrance of men and women who have played a significant part in the life and witness of other traditions. In our different traditions we use a variety of language to celebrate the work and witness of these men and women.

    – Encouragement should be given to celebrate the faith together in a locality by drawing together in the arts and drama. Such a shared initiative would be a way of inviting others to celebrate the faith with us.

    – The churches might provide together resources for social and ethical discussions in the community as and when important social and ethical issues arise.

    – Common strategies could be developed in relating together to the media.

37. A further important challenge to all our churches might be to ask whether, or how far, each church could affirm the portrait of visible unity set out in section B of the above, in order to see what concrete steps might be taken now on the way towards visible unity.

D. Doxology (para. 4.1)

4.1. The Holy Spirit as the promoter of koinonia (2 Cor. 13:13) gives to those who are still divided the thirst and hunger for full communion. We remain restless until we grow together according to the wish and prayer of Christ that those who believe in him may be one (John 17:21). In the process of praying, working and struggling for unity, the Holy Spirit comforts us in pain, disturbs us when we are satisfied to remain in our division, leads us to repentance and grants us joy when our communion flourishes.

PROVISIONAL DRAFTS
THE CHURCH AS KOINONIA – AN ECUMENICAL STUDY

Preface

The major study programme under the above title (cf. Crêt-Bérard minutes 1994, pp.73-76,95-96) was initiated in 1994 with two consultations, 2-8 May in Dublin, Ireland, and 22-28 November in Barbados. The Dublin meeting produced provisional drafts on specific aspects of ecclesiology, to be used in the further process of the ecclesiology study. They form the second part of this text. The Barbados meeting of a small drafting group produced an annotated draft outline for a future convergence document and a reflection on remaining problems in the perspective of overcoming them on the way to fuller koinonia.

It is obvious that these texts are preliminary. They have to be revised, expanded, complemented and perhaps also reordered in the work before us.

GÜNTHER GASSMANN

PART I: THE BARBADOS MATERIAL

I. Provisional outline of a future convergence text

A. GOD'S PURPOSE

1. According to holy scripture God's purpose in the act of creating is to bring about a koinonia between God and all creation. Thus, creation has its integrity in koinonia with God.

2. God's purpose in creation has been counteracted/thwarted/distorted by human sin, failure and disobedience to God's will. This resulted in the breaking up of koinonia. God's loving response to human rebellion is God's reconciling and redeeming action in his Son Jesus Christ and the transforming activity of God's Holy Spirit. This dynamic history of God's restoring and

enriching koinonia with creation reaches its culmination and fulfilment in the perfect koinonia of a new heaven and a new earth.

3. As a specific expression of this koinonia, i.e. the communion between God and humanity and communion within humanity, God established and maintained, despite human disobedience, his covenant with the people of Israel. This covenant foreshadowed that new covenant which God established in Christ with his church.

4. In these creating, redeeming and sanctifying activities God reveals to us his trinitarian character: Father, Son and Holy Spirit, an eternal koinonia of three in one.

5. The restoration of koinonia between God and humanity is the mystery of salvation in Christ revealed to the world (Eph. 3; Rom. 16).

6. Thus, God's calling and mission of the church is to be an instrument of his saving and transforming purpose for creation in which humanity occupies a special place (cf. e. g. *Lumen Gentium*; Decree on Mission; Canberra; etc.).

For this part A. cf. also Dublin, group III, 1-4.

B. ORIGIN AND CONTINUANCE OF THE CHURCH

1. The origin of the church is in the Christ event – his life, ministry, death on the cross, and resurrection from the dead – and in the Pentecostal gift of the Holy Spirit.

2. Christ is the foundation and abiding head of the church; the Holy Spirit anoints, enlivens and empowers the church.

3. Thus the church becomes the first fruits of the kingdom as a koinonia with God.

4. In fulfilling its mission, the church is called to stand in continuity with the apostolic community through its apostolic faith, proclamation of the gospel, sacraments, ministry, worship, diakonia, martyria and leitourgia (cf. *BEM*, M34).

C. CHURCH OF THE TRIUNE GOD

Introduction

1. To speak of communion (koinonia) is to speak of the way human beings come to know God as God's purpose for humanity is revealed. God in Christ, through the Holy Spirit, calls human beings to share in the fellowship within the divine life, a call to which they respond in faith. Thus, communion refers first to the fellowship with God and subsequently to sharing with one another. Indeed, it is only by virtue of God's gift of grace, through Jesus Christ, that deep, lasting communion is made possible; by baptism and faith, persons participate in the mystery of Christ's death, burial and resurrection and are incorporated into the one body of Christ, the church (cf. Disciples-Roman Catholic dialogue). Because the koinonia is also a participation in Christ crucified, it is also part of the nature of the church and the mission of the church to share in the sufferings and struggles of humankind, in a world alienated from God and divided within itself by our disobedience to his will (cf. *Church as Communion* – Anglican-Roman Catholic dialogue).

2. By the work of the Holy Spirit the church lives in communion with Christ Jesus, in whom all in heaven and earth are joined in the communion of God the Holy One: this is the communion of saints. The communion of saints on earth is nourished by the holy gifts of word and sacrament: the holy gifts for the holy people. The final destiny of the church is to be caught up in the intimate relation of Father, Son and Holy Spirit. In the working out of salvation, the three divine, mutually indwelling persons always work together.

For part C cf. also Dublin, group III, 5-6.

1. Church as people of church
3. Since the calling of Abraham God was preparing for himself a holy people: "I will be their God and they shall be my people". Through the word of God *(dabhar)* and the Spirit of God *(ru'ah)*, God chose one from among the nations to bring salvation to all: "all the nations of the earth shall be blessed in you". The election of Israel was the beginning of the economy of salvation leading towards the cross, resurrection, sending of the Holy Spirit in which the church is manifested, gift of God for the whole world.

4. The people of Israel was a pilgrim people walking towards the fulfilment of the promises to Abraham, that in him all the nations of the earth shall be blessed. In Christ, through the economy of salvation, the dividing walls between Jew and Gentile, between believers and those without God in the world, are broken down. From Pentecost the church of God continues the way of pilgrimage to the consummation of the kingdom. Thus, the pilgrimage of Israel is a foreshadowing and a prophetic sign of what was to happen in the church through Christ.

2. Church: body of Christ
5. Through the blood of Christ, God's purpose was to reconcile the two parts of broken humanity (Eph. 2:11-22) in the one body through the cross: this body is the body of Christ, the church (Eph. 1:23). Christ is the abiding head of the body and at the same time the one who, by his spirit, gives life to the body. In this way Christ is one with his body and at the same time head over his body, leading it and judging it.

6. Partaking of the life of Christ, the members of the body share in the unique priesthood of Christ in so far as they are faithful members of the body: "You are the holy priesthood" (1 Pet. 2). As Christ has offered himself, Christians offer their whole being "as a living sacrifice". This priesthood is given to every member. No member exercises that priesthood in isolation from the other members of the royal priesthood. Some have been given a specific responsibility by Christ through the church for a priestly ministry (cf. *BEM*, M17).

7. All members are given gifts for the building up of the body. Some of them have a specific responsibility for preaching the word of God, presiding at the sacraments, presiding over the forming of the mind of the church. Others have different, but inter-related responsibilities. Through this diversity of gifts the church is built up for its own life and its vocation as servant, for the furthering of God's kingdom in the world.

8. Because these gifts are gifts of the Spirit, the church is inseparably in Christ and in the Spirit. It cannot be in Christ unless it is in the Spirit of God the Father.

9. The reality expressed by the body of Christ is also expressed as the vine and its branches; the temple and its stones; the household and its members; the bride and her groom.

3. Church: community of the Holy Spirit

10. The church is the company of those anointed by the Holy Spirit and who, by the power of the Holy Spirit, believe in Christ and are enabled to confess Jesus Christ as Lord.

11. In the church of God, the different functions of the members of the body are the outworking of the gifts of the Holy Spirit. It is through the common origin and destination of these diverse gifts that the church as koinonia is both one and diverse.

12. Because of the common origin, and the common purpose of the building up the kingdom, of these diverse gifts, the church as koinonia is at the same time one and diverse through the activity of the Holy Spirit.

13. In communion diversities are brought together in harmony as gifts of the Holy Spirit, contributing to the richness and fullness of the church of God.

14. This koinonia built up by the Holy Spirit is the holy body of Christ in which what God desires to offer to the whole of humanity is already at work in the spreading of the good news; in the liturgy of the body of Christ where the eschaton is already experienced; in the diakonia of the body of Christ in which the kingdom is prepared; and in the life of its members in which the holiness of the heavenly Jerusalem is shown forth.

D. THE NATURE AND THE MISSION OF THE CHURCH

1. "Prophetic sign"

1. The church, by participating in the divine koinonia, is called to share in Christ's mission to all people. As a "prophetic sign" the church, moved by the Holy Spirit, points not to itself but beyond itself to the reign of God. The church is called to be "prophetic sign" of the purpose God has for humankind and all creatures. The church is a "prophetic sign" in so far as it lives by the renewing power of God's grace. As prophetic sign it both points to the renewal of human community and the life of the world to come. The church, set in this eschatological framework, points human communities, political systems and ideologies towards the kingdom reminding them of their provisional character. All are judged by the values of the kingdom, including the life of Christian communities themselves. Whenever these communities acknowledge failures and repent of them, they stand as a sign of the divine grace and hope for a broken world (cf. *Church and World*).

2. Servant/instrument

2. Knowing that God wills the good of all human beings, Christians commit themselves to the proclamation of the gospel in word and in life. When-

ever they can, they work together with all people of good will in the struggle for justice, peace and the preservation of the integrity of creation. The church is in that way not only a sign of the new humanity God wants, but also the servant of God to extend grace to all human situations and needs until Christ comes in glory (Matt. 25). Because the servanthood of Christ entails suffering on the cross, it is evident, as expressed in the New Testament writings, that the martyria of the church will entail, for individuals and for the community, the martyria of the Word and the way of the cross (Cf. also *Baptism, Eucharist, Ministry 1982-1990: Report on the Process and Responses*, para. 13, p.151).

3. Creature of the word and the Spirit

3. The koinonia of the church is centred and grounded in the word of God testified in the scriptures, incarnated in Jesus Christ and visible among us through the living voice of the gospel in preaching, in sacraments and in service. All church institutions, forms of ministry, liturgical expressions and methods of mission should be submitted to the word of God and tested by it. The *pleroma* of God's creative word is never exhausted in the churches' institutions (report on *BEM*, p.150, para. 12).

4. Conceived on the cross of Christ and born the day of Pentecost, through the descent of the Holy Spirit, the church is also the creation of God's Holy Spirit. Being the anointing of Christ and of Christians, the Spirit of God forms Christ in all believers, incorporates them into the body of Christ through baptism and faith and nourishes and sustains them in new life in Christ through the eucharist.

5. The Spirit unites all Christians to be the one body of Christ and his one temple. Through the distribution of gifts, the Paraclete also diversifies the members of the body of Christ.

6. The "pledge of future blessings", applying salvation in Christ to all the baptized, the Holy Spirit leads to perfection, fulfilment, and transfigured life in God's holy kingdom.

4. Sacrament

7. To speak of the church as sacrament is to affirm that in and through the communion of all those who confess Jesus Christ and live according to their confession, God realizes his plan of salvation for the whole world. This is not to say that God's saving work is limited to those who confess Christ explicitly. By God's gift of the same Spirit who was at work in the earthly ministry of Christ Jesus the church plays its part in bringing his work to its fulfilment (cf. also report on BEM, p.151).

5. Mystery

8. The church as koinonia is the church of the living God (1 Tim. 3:15), not a human association only. It lives in permanent communion with God the Father through Jesus Christ in the Holy Spirit and is not merely the historical product of Jesus' ministry. Because of its intimate relation with Christ himself as the head of the body, the church is to be confessed according to the apos-

tolic faith as one, holy, catholic and apostolic. Therefore the visible organizational structures of the church must always be seen in the light of God's gifts of salvation in Christ. The word and the sacraments of Jesus Christ are forms of God's real and saving presence for the world. As such they express the church's participation in the mystery of Christ and are inseparable from it (report on BEM, p.151, para. 13).

6. Eucharistic community

9. Being a worshipping community, with the eucharist as the centre of its life and worship, the church is also known as the eucharistic community. Traditionally, the life and mission of the church is the extension of the eucharistic celebration.

7. The unity of the church

10. There seems to be a growing ecumenical agreement on the basic conditions and forms of expression of Christian unity as koinonia. This was confirmed by the acceptance of the statement on "The Unity of the Church as Koinonia: Gift and Calling" by the 1991 WCC assembly at Canberra. The central section of this statement reads:

> 2.1. The unity of the church to which we are called is a koinonia given and expressed in the common confession of the apostolic faith; a common sacramental life entered by the one baptism and celebrated together in one eucharistic fellowship; a common life in which members and ministries are mutually recognized and reconciled; and a common mission witnessing to all people to the gospel of God's grace and serving the whole of creation. The goal of the search for full communion is realized when all the churches are able to recognize in one another the one, holy, catholic and apostolic church in its fullness. This full communion will be expressed on the local and the universal levels through conciliar forms of life and action. In such communion churches are bound in all aspects of their life together at all levels in confessing the one faith and engaging in worship and witness, deliberation and action.

For part D cf. also Dublin, group III, 8-10,12-15.

E. WORD, SACRAMENT, MINISTRY: MEANS AND EXPRESSIONS OF KOINONIA

1. Through the proclamation of the word of God and the sacraments served by the ministry, the church pursues its mission as the pillar and bulwark of truth (Eph.) and the koinonia of forgiven sinners. Through baptism and faith we become children of God and members of his koinonia. The central expression of this koinonia with the triune God through word and sacrament is the eucharist (cf. also Dublin, group III, 11).

2. The church preserves and expresses its koinonia through certain structures and forms of authority in which all members of the church participate in different ways. In these ways the church strives to be faithful to the truth given to it by God in Christ and the Spirit. Traditionally the church has been structured in personal, collegial, presbyteral, episcopal and synodal ways to discern

the meaning of the word of God and give voice to the consensus of the faithful, to lead, to take decisions and to teach with authority.

3. The authority of the church is an authority received by the faithful people of God as a royal priesthood, a koinonia of saints (cf. Dublin, Group II).

4. For apostolicity and catholicity cf. Dublin draft, whereby the qualitative character of "catholicity" should come first.

F. LOCAL CHURCH AND THE COMMUNION OF LOCAL CHURCHES

1. The catholic and apostolic nature of the church is expressed in the koinonia between local churches. Each local church is fully the catholic and apostolic church, but is not the entire church.

2. The local church is an assembly of faithful people gathered around word and sacrament presided over by an authorized minister in a specific place.

3. Bonds of communion between local churches are the affirmation of the common apostolic faith; the common word of God; one baptism; one eucharist; ministry in apostolic continuity; solidarity among churches; taking counsel together and supporting each other; mutual interdependence. Traditionally bishops in their communion with each other express the communion of the local churches through collegiality, concelebration, exchange of visits and letters and mutual counsel and decision-making.

G. CHURCH AND HISTORY

1. The church does not exist outside of time, but participates in the created state of being in time, which means participating in movement and change. This allows for both positive development and growth as well as for the negative possibility of decline and distortion.

2. In the course of the church's history there has been sin, individual as well as communal, which has disfigured its witness and run counter to its true nature and vocation. Therefore in the church there has been again and again the call for repentance and reform.

3. The Christ-event took place in the setting of a particular culture. Since then the church has always borne in its language and its life the cultural marks of its origin, and at the same time it has borrowed, challenged and transformed elements from every culture in which it has been planted. While always acknowledging its debt to the surrounding culture, the church must bring to bear the critical potential of the gospel over against all human cultures as well as offer its redemptive power to them. Thus the church combines the "treasures of the nations" in a koinonia, that is at the same time richly diverse and shaped by the one identical gospel.

4. In the midst of the different historical situations and cultural as well as social environments there develop characteristic forms of church life suited to their time and place, though they remain subject to the permanent content of the gospel and the fundamental shape of churchly existence.

5. The church in its worldwide dimension is woven into the fabric of world history, participating in the complexities of this history and being at the same time the messenger of God's will addressed to it.

6. God has promised there will always be a church sustained by his gospel in which the true faith will be confessed. This promise holds good throughout the vicissitudes of history until there will be no history any more.

H. CHURCH AND KINGDOM

1. In the event of Christ's life and ministry, death and resurrection and with the descent of the Holy Spirit the kingdom of God has been inaugurated. As the first fruits of God's kingdom the church enjoys already the life of this kingdom in an anticipated way. Having thus tasted the powers of the age to come, the church pursues its pilgrim way towards the final consummation in the heavenly city.

I. DOXOLOGY

1. When Christians live together in true koinonia according to Christ Jesus, they are able to glorify the God and Father of our Lord Jesus Christ (Rom. 15:3,4) with one heart, and one voice, in the one Holy Spirit.

II. From converging understandings towards mutual recognition

1. The foregoing is proposed as a statement of what the churches, after seven decades of work in Faith and Order, can all affirm concerning the nature and mission of the church. That they should thus have been able to find and develop a common language in which to describe the church, is a mark of the great progress that has been made in the modern ecumenical movement. The progress has shown itself concretely in the ways by which, to varying degrees and according to various theological rationales, the churches have advanced towards mutual recognition, or at least towards the recognition of Christian faith and life beyond their own respective institutional boundaries. Yet painful and scandalous divisions still remain. As the Canberra statement declared, "the goal of the search for full communion is realized when all the churches are able to recognize in one another the one, holy, catholic and apostolic church in its fullness".

2. In order for the churches to move further towards complete mutual recognition and full communion, it may be helpful to furnish a frank description of the ways in which various churches typically understand and claim their own ecclesial identity and the accounts they typically give of the ecclesial status of other churches and other Christians. Where do the respective churches locate the church described in the first part of this document? And do they suppose or allow different manners or degrees of belonging to it?

3. One typical ecclesiology identifies the church, after the manner of St Cyprian, exclusively with one's own community, dismissing other communities or persons which claim churchly or Christian status into an ecclesiological and soteriological void. In its strongest form, this ecclesiology has almost disappeared as a result of the modern ecumenical movement. Official Roman Catholic ecclesiology today recognizes at least "traces of the church" beyond the boundaries of the Roman Catholic Church; these signs of Christian faith and life belong properly (by right) to the (Roman Catholic) church and bring those who enjoy them into "a certain, though imperfect, communion" with it. Some

Orthodox ecclesiologists are seeking to give a pneumatological account of the existence of Christian faith and life outside the bounds of canonical Orthodoxy.

4. Another type of ecclesiology, while claiming for its own community a full place in the church catholic, allows equal status to some other communities, even though the degree and mode of communion actually existing between it and them may vary. One variant of this is the so-called "branch theory" by which some Anglicans describe(d) the situation among "the Western", "the Eastern", and their own churches. Another variant is the so-called "denominationalist" theory which usually allows for a quite broad spectrum of churches to co-exist in organizational independence while constituting in aggregate "the church universal".

5. Each of these various ecclesiologics, which exist in multiple nuances, struggles to give an account of the anomalous situation of a divided Christianity. From different starting points, it is perhaps becoming possible for the divided churches so to understand their affirmation concerning the church as to allow them to recognize and embrace other Christian communities which make the same affirmation in the kind of common language used in the first part of this document.

6. Another way of stating both the problem and the possibilities may perhaps be found in a re-examination of the relations between what Montreal 1963 called the Tradition and the traditions. The great *Tradition* is the eternal gospel of Jesus Christ, the faith once delivered to the saints, which lives in the Spirit-filled church against which the gates of hell shall not prevail. Christian history manifests various traditions which each claim to bear, and be borne by, the great Tradition. Each has its own estimation of its fidelity and the fidelity of the others, its own relative success and failings and those of the others. The first part of the present document is an attempt to state the great Tradition concerning, in particular, the nature and mission of the church. It is an attempt made by members of various churches which have their differing historical, theological and existential starting point but have already experienced some degree of convergence through their participation in the ecumenical movement and are now able to register that convergence. The hope is that the acknowledgment of such convergence in the understanding and affirmation of the nature and mission of the church will help the respective churches to recognize others more widely and more completely as contained like themselves within the great Tradition and as its carriers along with themselves.

7. The passage from affirmations in a common language concerning the church, through an increasingly agreed understanding of those affirmations, to an ever greater recognition of ecclesial reality in other communities than one's own, and finally to the need and possibility of establishing full communion, still requires the overcoming of certain obstacles. Certain issues crop up recurrently, which are symptoms or instances of the broader problems concerning ecclesial identity and the discernment of it in other communities as well as one's own.

Appendix

List of still controversial issues which were not further discussed at Barbados:

1) the apostolic continuity of the church and the sign of episcopal succession;
2) *who* discerns the mind of Christ/the gospel of the church over against other churches and *how* is this done;
3) church in its local and catholic expression, including the issues of primarcy and conciliarity;
4) baptism – faith – church: their inter-relation;
5) human freedom – sin – salvation;
6) presidency at the eucharist;
7) "sacraments outside the church";
8) different concepts of the church and the manifestation of its unity.

PART II: THE DUBLIN MATERIAL

Group I: Apostolicity and catholicity as elements of the life and faith of the church as koinonia

1. Ecclesial koinonia properly bears the qualities of apostolicity and catholicity ("We believe in one holy *catholic* and *apostolic* church"). For the sake of clarity, it may be said that, at a first level, apostolicity has to do with extension in time, and catholicity with extension in space. In a more qualitative sense, apostolicity has to do with authenticity, and catholicity with plenitude.

2. Apostolicity may refer in the first place to koinonia in its temporal aspect: the identity of the historical church with the church of the apostles ("communion in time"). Tertullian explains that "there is but one primitive church of the apostles", from which "all others are derived" by reason of apostolic foundation of the further spread of the apostles' faith and doctrine (*De Praescriptione Haereticorum*, 20, 4-7). The event of the Risen Christ sending the apostles and the Holy Spirit of Pentecost is always present in the life of the church through the centuries until the second coming of Christ.

3. Catholicity may refer in the first place to koinonia in its spatial aspect. In the words of St Cyril of Jerusalem: "The church is called catholic because it extends over the whole world, from end to end of the earth" (*Catechesis*, 18, 23; cf. Irenaeus, *Against the Heresies*, I, 10, 1-2: "... dispersed throughout the whole world, even to the ends of the earth"). Each local church manifests the one church of God in communion with all the local churches throughout the world ("communion in space").

4. Nevertheless, apostolicity has also a spatial dimension, as will be seen: the church is sent by God to spread throughout the world the invitation to all people to share in the communion of life with the Father through the Son in the Holy Spirit. And catholicity has also a temporal dimension: the church embraces in its living communion the faithful from every period of history.

5. The qualitative apostolicity and catholicity of the church rests upon the fact that "the apostles... deposited with her most copiously everything which pertains to the truth" (Irenaeus, *Against the Heresies*, III, 4, 1).

I. Apostolicity
  6. Apostolicity is a complex notion and reality. Its several components are recognized by all our churches; but our churches differ over the exact constitution and form of each component, over the relative emphasis placed on each component, and over the proper relationships among them. So the churches need to move from their different configurations of apostolicity towards a more common perception and practice of this quality of the church. The following four elements must find a place:
  7. a. The content of the apostolic *message* (the one *gospel*, than which there is no other, Gal. 1:6-9; the *faith* once delivered to the saints, Jude 3). "The apostolicity of the church expresses its obligation and commitment to the norm of the apostolic gospel of God's action in the cross and resurrection of Jesus Christ" (*Confessing the One Faith*, para. 220). The content of the gospel is our introduction into the divine koinonia of Father, Son and Holy Spirit.
  8. b. The *means* of transmitting the apostolic message, including confessing, the liturgical assembly, preaching, teaching, catechesis and interpretation. The entire community of the baptized has the privilege and responsibility of carrying forward the Tradition. Some receive a special charge for this service: "The church ordains certain of its members for the ministry in the name of Christ by the invocation of the Spirit and laying on of hands (1 Tim. 4:14; 2 Tim. 1:6); in so doing it seeks to continue the mission of the apostles and to remain faithful to their teaching".
  9. c. The *manifestation* of the Holy Spirit who descended on the apostles at Pentecost and inhabited the apostolic church. The pneumatic presence may be active in signs and wonders ("tongues"; miracles). The pneumatic presence and activity is sacramental (e. g. Titus 3:5-7; 1 Cor. 12:13) (*BEM*, B5,7,14,19; E14-18). It will bear fruit in the lives of believers (Gal. 5:22-23) and will bring varied gifts to the entire community (1 Cor. 12:4-13). The gift of discernment is needed, and promised (1 Cor. 12:10; 1 John 4:1-3,13-16).
  10. d. The apostolic *mission* to witness to Christ "to the ends of the earth" (Acts 1:8). "Called by God out of the world, the church is placed in the world's service; it is destined to be God's sign for the world by proclaiming the gospel and living a life of loving service to humanity" (*Church and World*, chap. III, para. 25, English text, p.28). In this common witness, the geographic dimension of koinonia becomes evident.
  11. The treatment of these four elements will need to explore the questions implied in paragraph 11 of the report from Santiago, section II, chapter II ("Recognizing Apostolicity"): "We must reflect further on the fact that our different traditions give differing levels of *priority* to various criteria; but if we can arrive at recognition of the same ensemble of criteria, even if they are being *used* in different ways, we shall have taken a step forward. We may expect the criteria and practice of another tradition at times to judge and convert us, and to send us back to the heart of our own tradition and discover it afresh. We must reflect further on the way in which we are all *called to call* each other to Christ who is always on the road ahead of us. We need to explore further the holistic model of apostolicity we have tried to outline, and what

this implies for the recognition in each other's churches of diverse ways of applying similar or related criteria of faithfulness." The phrase "criteria of faithfulness" points to the *qualitative authenticity* that is implied in apostolicity.

12. In the "temporal" dimension of apostolicity, a difference in emphasis will need to be borne in mind. Some churches stress particularly the importance of *continuity and succession from the apostles*. At moments of renewal within those same churches, and certainly among newly planted, "first-generation" churches, there is a strong sense of *repristinating (re-living) the experience of the church of the apostles*. The relation between these two accents and realities will need to be explored.

II. Catholicity

13. The church's "catholicity means that it is the gift of God for all people, whatever their particular country, race, social condition or language" (*Confessing the One Faith*, para. 220). The catholicity of ecclesial koinonia thus comprehends both the fullness of God's generosity and the rich variety of human creaturehood. The understanding and practice of catholicity must include, therefore, at least the following five aspects:

14. a. *Mutual recognition by local churches* in their divine origin, each as "wholly church" and all together as "the whole church" (using the phraseology of J.-J. von Allmen, cited in Joint Working Group, *The Church: Local and Universal*, Geneva, 1990, para. 36; the whole of this paragraph is valuable). A "conciliar fellowship of local churches truly united" (Salamanca 1973, Nairobi 1975) will find appropriate expression in eucharistic celebration and communion (see *BEM*, E19,33); it will also need pastoral and deliberative structures to maintain a common life and faith; it will need to develop and keep up a network of mutual support and service (see report of group II, para. 4). The attainment and preservation of mutual recognition among local churches raises two inter-related issues: first, *what* must be present in each place for recognition to occur *(quod sufficit et requiritur)*? And second, *who* authenticates the recognition? Do particular local churches play a special role (as now with Rome or Canterbury in their different ways), or is the recognition less centralized, more diffuse, more reciprocal (as among the Orthodox or with the Lutheran World Federation as it conceives itself as a "communion")? Can regional work on this question help to avoid a sense of "neo-colonialism" among two-thirds-world churches?

15. b. *Inclusiveness of membership and participation*. According to apostolic teaching and practice, there can be no distinction in the redeemed status of the baptized on account of race, class or gender (Gal. 3:28) (see the studies on the *Community of Women and Men*; and on *Church and World*). The question of age needs investigation: what respective accounts are given of infants and children by those churches which baptize at a young age the offspring of believers and those churches which await a personal profession of faith?

16. c. *Cultural variety*. No Faith and Order study appears to have treated this in a major way. "The church is local when the saving event of Christ takes root in a particular local situation with all its natural, social, cultural and other

characteristics which make up the life and thought of the people living in that place" (Zizioulas in *In Each Place: Towards a Fellowship of Local Churches Truly United*, 1977, p.56, quoted in *Church and World*, p.32). Features of a local culture may need variously to be affirmed, challenged, healed, transformed by the church (cf. Vatican II, *Ad Gentes*, 22). The principles of legitimate inculturation need to be examined in such matters as worship, church order, etc. What features must be constant for a "catholic" recognition of each other by churches in their cultural variety to be possible? Here links should be established with the "ecumenical hermeneutics" project.

17. d. *Diversity of spiritual/liturgical/theological traditions and expressions.* Here we have in mind the notion of ecclesial *typoi* introduced by Emmanuel Lanne ("Pluralism and Unity: The Possibility of a Variety of Typologies within the Same Ecclesial Allegiance", in *One in Christ*, 6, 1970, pp.258-79) and Cardinal Willebrands ("Moving towards a Typology of Churches", in *Catholic Mind*, April 1970, pp.35-42). All of the *typoi* may need internal reform; some may need to be reconciled among themselves. Their variety has the potential to enrich the koinonia of the church rather than divide it (so the implications of several bilateral dialogues.)

18. e. *A qualitative wholeness (kath'olon).* Components of ecclesial koinonia should find their place in a comprehensive totality of the Christian faith, life, and eschatological communion with the Trinity. According to St Cyril of Jerusalem, the church is catholic also "because it teaches universally and infallibly each and every doctrine which must come to the knowledge of people, concerning things visible and invisible, heavenly and earthly; and because it brings every race of humankind into subjection to godliness, both governors and governed, both learned and unlearned; and because it universally treats and heals every class of sins, those committed with the soul and those with the body; and it possesses within itself every conceivable form of virtue, in deeds and in words and in the spiritual gifts of every description" (*Catechesis*, 18,23). In this qualitative wholeness, the temporal dimension of catholicity also becomes evident, for the "church catholic" includes the saints and all departed believers of every generation, a living *koinonia ton hagion* (see *Confessing the One Faith*, paras 231ff.). Here, too, the catholicity of the church comes closest to its holiness and unity.

19. Catholicity includes both *unity* and *diversity*. Here tensions may sometimes appear, but a variety of spiritual gifts, human conditions, ecclesial traditions and cultural expressions may properly serve the common good. The principle of apostolic authenticity must be maintained, and the function of authoritative discernment exercised.

Nota bene: The new study needs to draw on the work of the Joint Working Group on "Catholicity and Apostolicity". An entire issue of *One in Christ* is devoted to papers from that study (vol. 6, 1970, no. 3).

Group II: Forms of authority and decision-making in the service of the church as koinonia

1. Authority within the church is always to be understood within the context of the authority of the Triune God, Father, Son and Holy Spirit, whose

unity in love is the primary exemplar of koinonia (cf. fifth world conference on Faith and Order, Santiago de Compostela, 1993, *Message*, 4). Jesus Christ, who was commended by God through powerful signs and wonders (Acts 2:22) and who inaugurated the kingdom by casting out demons, healing the sick and teaching "with authority" (Mark 1:21-34), took leave of his disciples with the words: "All authority *(exousia)* in heaven and on earth has been given to me. Go, therefore, make disciples of all nations, baptize them in the name of the Father and of the Son and of the Holy Spirit, and teach them to observe all the commands I gave you. And know that I am with you always; yes, to the end of time" (Matt. 28:18-20). For Christians, the supreme authority is Jesus himself, who teaches only what He hears from the Father (John 7:16; 12:49-50) and who does not leave his disciples as orphans (John 14:18), but sends the Holy Spirit to lead them "into all truth" (John 16:13; cf. John 14:17-26).

2. The distinctive authority of the church can be understood correctly only in light of the authority of the one who was crucified, who "emptied himself" and "obediently accepted even death, death on the cross" (Phil. 2:7-8). Paul preached Christ crucified, a stumbling block and foolishness to some, but the power and wisdom of God to those who are being saved (cf. 1 Cor. 1:23-24). When the disciples sought to exercise power over one another, Jesus corrected them, saying that he came not to be served but to serve, and to offer his life for others (Mark 10:41-45; Luke 22:24-27). It will be important to further explore the relationship between authority and power. The church cannot avoid the exercise of power, but unfortunately we are tempted and often have succumbed to the temptation to exercise it as do "the rulers of the world" (cf. Mark 10:42; Luke 22:25). Rather, authority must be understood as humble service, nourishing and building up the koinonia of the church in faith, life and witness (cf. Eph. 4:11-16).

Following the incarnational economy realized in Christ, the Word made flesh (John 1:14), the spiritual communion which is Christ's body, the church (1 Cor. 12-14), must find expression in visible forms and concrete relationships. Though the word "hierarchy" has been used to describe structures of domination and subordination, which are hardly reconcilable with the gospel view of authority as service, its original meaning of "sacred order" can convey the more fundamental meaning of authority in the church. Such authority is spiritual, in the sense that it functions under the guidance of the Holy Spirit so as to promote in a tangible way the growth of the community in unity and love. Thus the Lord's will "that all be one" (John 17:21) already begins to "be done on earth as it is in heaven" (Matt. 6:10). Today in many parts of the world there seems to be a crisis of authority. Persons in positions of authority are not accepted simply on the basis of office or status but rather for their competence, credibility and collegial spirit. At the same time, personal leadership, casting a sharper profile than leadership by a committee or a board, appeals to many. The exercise of authority in the church will have to take into account the contemporary situation.

3. Historically, this visible pattern of relationships first appeared most clearly in the life and mission of the local churches, as the pastoral letters of the New Testament begin to show (cf. Santiago, report of section II, 25-26)

and as the letters of Ignatius of Antioch, at a very early point, already testify in rather striking detail. The ministry of oversight (episkope) emerges in, among and with the communities as a pastoral service characterized by mutual giving and receiving, and not as an imposition on the local community. Among the gifts bestowed upon the church, "a ministry of episkope is necessary to express and safeguard the unity of the body. Every church needs this ministry in some form in order to be the church of God, the one body of Christ, a sign of the unity of all in the kingdom" (*BEM*, M23).

Traditionally, both the catholicity of the church and its apostolicity in sharing the same faith were witnessed to by the participation of leaders from other local churches at the ordination of any new leader to the ministry of oversight. Within each local church the ministry of oversight is complemented by other ministries and roles of service. Christ's gift of the Spirit is to the whole community and to each of the faithful. The particular role of the ordained minister is carried out within the context of the full exercise of the charisms given to all. One of the most credible and influential forms of authority is that of those who live the gospel in an exemplary way – the saints of yesterday and today. The specific authority of the ministry of oversight is exercised in virtue of its particular duty to nourish and foster the church's koinonia, always in collaboration and communion with the community as a whole.

4. In virtue of their catholicity local churches are directed beyond themselves. Under the guidance of the Holy Spirit and served by their pastors and leaders, they maintain and foster bonds of communion with all other local churches. A variety of means, deeply rooted in the tradition, have served this process: mutual support and encouragement, the sharing of resources, the exchange of letters, prayer for one another in the liturgy and collaboration in relating to the world outside the visible confines of the church. The celebration of regional and ecumenical councils was a particular and effective means for maintaining koinonia in faith. This "conciliarity" is a quality of the life of the church as a whole and not simply a matter of convoking councils. An important fruit of ecumenical dialogue in recent decades is the wide recognition of the church's conciliarity, pervading all levels of the church's life. This fruit suggests concrete steps which the various Christian communities currently divided from one another may take to enhance the prospects for arriving at full communion.

5. Our present state of division places us in a situation that might be called preconciliar. (This adjective is not considered appropriate by some.) In this preconciliar state, it is vitally important that, whenever possible, those traditional means for fostering communion be practised among and between our communities: prayer, mutual support and encouragement, common witness and so forth. In a particular way, communion-building actions within the area of authority and decision-making are to be recommended. Whenever possible, churches can make reference, in their own teaching and witness, to that faith which they already share in common with other Christians. Moreover, some occasions may present themselves as appropriate for the churches to teach or witness together. Such steps, taken already in this preconciliar phase of the ecumenical movement, can only further the prospects for full reconciliation and communion.

6. The church's conciliarity naturally invites reflection upon the presidency of the council of all local churches, particularly regarding whether an ecclesiology of communion includes primacy at the local, regional and universal levels. "For it is through a 'head', some kind of 'primus', that the 'many', be it individual Christians or local churches, can speak with one voice. But a 'primus' must be part of a community; not a self-defined, but a truly relational ministry. Such a ministry can only act together with the heads of the rest of the local churches whose consensus it would express. A primacy of this kind is both desirable and harmless in an ecclesiology of communion" (J. Zizioulas, *On the Way to Fuller Koinonia,* Santiago report, p. 108).

The delegates at Santiago added: "Today, ecumenical dialogues should take up once again the topic of a service to the universal unity of the church on the basis of the truth of the gospel. Such service should be carried out in a pastoral way – that is, as presiding in love'" (report of section II, 28). Some bilateral dialogues have already made important contributions to ecumenical reflection upon this theme (see ARCIC I, "Authority in the Church I and II", and Lutheran-Roman Catholic Dialogue, USA, V), witnessing not only to the need to take up this theme but also providing material which could be utilized in a further discussion within Faith and Order. At this point, one should acknowledge that each local church, particularly in the person of the one who exercises the ministry of oversight, is entrusted with the responsibility of promoting communion with all other local churches. Having said that, however, some local churches have been recognized as exercising a unique role in fostering unity at wider levels. Thus, a certain primacy is accorded to the head of the bishops of each region in canon 34 of the "Canons of the Apostles" and several early councils recognized a role of special importance to churches such as those at Rome, Constantinople, Alexandria, Antioch and Jerusalem.

7. Various qualities characterize the exercise of authority and decision-making in the church:

a) It occurs within a dynamic process of discernment, listening and contributing by all members of the church under the guidance of the Holy Spirit. Decision-making entails mutual accountability and dialogue between all within the church.

b) Various decisions are appropriately made at various levels. What can be handled adequately at a local or regional level should not be decided at wider levels. Those at each level must take the responsibility to exercise their proper role.

c) The pilgrim people of God humbly acknowledges that decisions are not always free from ambiguities. These can only be tested in a process of discernment over a period of time. This process is one of active reception.

d) The conscience of the individual believer obliges him or her to seek and acknowledge the truth. Authoritative teaching decisions ideally will assist in the formation and following of conscience. Nevertheless, tensions between the believer and the teaching decision of the community are not impossible and sometimes are even necessary for the process of discernment. Those in authority need to remain open to challenge just as they themselves have the duty to challenge the community to fidelity to the Lord.

e) Authority and decision-making within the church need to be carried out within a concept of attentiveness to people of other faiths and to the culture within which the church lives. Styles of decision-making may differ from culture to culture. Decisions concerning the concrete application of gospel values in the daily life of the church need to take into account the local religious and cultural situation (see the pre-Santiago consultation in Asia).

f) Confidence in the church's ability to faithfully proclaim the gospel in virtue of the promised assistance of the Holy Spirit will affect the way in which one views teaching authority and decision-making in the church. Several bilateral dialogues (ARCIC I; Old Catholic-Orthodox Dialogue, "Ecclesiology, 1981"; and Lutheran-Roman Catholic Dialogue USA, VI) have addressed this topic under such terms as "indefectibility" or "infallibility" and provide material which could enter into a Faith and Order discussion of this theme.

Group III: The place and mission of the church as koinonia in the saving purpose of God

Note: We have noted a number of elements and aspects of the above theme which need to be revised with the help of the already available texts on the church as koinonia.

1. "Koinonia" is not another and exclusive concept for designating the church. Rather, it has emerged in recent ecumenical dialogues as a major interpretative and integrating concept related to the traditional images and understandings of the church.

2. An ecumenical interpretation of the church as koinonia should begin with the place and mission of the church in the framework and service of God's design/purpose/history of salvation/economy for humanity and creation (cf. here *BEM*, M1-5).

3. God's saving purpose and the church as koinonia are inseparably linked together

a) because it is exactly the refusal of koinonia with God which has led to a sinful, broken humanity;

b) because the church as koinonia has been called and sent by the Word made flesh to heal and strengthen the communion between God and humanity and to serve as God's instrument of reconciliation among broken humanity.

4. As koinonia the church is thus called by God to be the sign and instrument of his saving purpose by proclaiming and living the love of God for all people and by glorifying God as the source of new life and hope. Glorifying God and at the same time serving humanity are inseparably connected and related with each other. In some Christian traditions this being and calling of the church in the world is termed as "sacramental".

5. The church as the *people of God* is the koinonia which has her origin and final destiny in the will of the Father. The church as the *body of Christ* is the koinonia which has her life-centre in the saving presence of the incarnate, crucified and risen Lord. The church as the *Temple of the Holy Spirit* is the

koinonia which is sustained for her mission and service by the Holy Spirit. In her trinitarian nature and mission the church as koinonia thus lives by and reflects the trinitarian koinonia.

6. As koinonia the church is a holy people, the company of all those who by the power of the Holy Spirit have been introduced into the family of God. This family, the church of God, finds its realization in each local church/community assembled around word and sacrament which necessarily includes that it is in communion/koinonia with other local churches.

7. The church lives in eschatological time and is therefore already an anticipation of the kingdom. At the same time it belongs to historical time and is thereby exposed to persecution, suffering and marginalization, following thus in the path of the cross of her Lord, in whom she puts her trust and hope. In time and history the church as a human koinonia is also vulnerable in that it is affected by human sin and the predicament and ambiguity of all human history. It is, therefore, constantly called to renewal and a renewed obedience.

8. The divisions among the churches and the refusal of its members to live in true koinonia with each other affect and hinder the mission of the church. But mission, which has as its ultimate goal the koinonia of all with God, belongs to the essence of the church's being a koinonia. This makes the restoration of unity between the churches and the renewal of their lives an urgent task.

9. The church is called to live as a celebrating *(leitourgia)*, witnessing *(martyria)* and serving *(diakonia)* communion.

10. Koinonia holds together both the divine life-giving source of the church and the visible, historical gathering of people. The invisible grace, its life centre, is normally communicated by visible means.

11. Similarly, in order to be truly a community of persons, visible structures which give continuity and identity to the koinonia are an integral part of the church as koinonia. The basic structure is given in the sacraments and ministry:

a) baptism as incorporation into the koinonia;
b) eucharist as sustaining the koinonia;
c) ordained and other ministries as serving and building up the life of the koinonia in personal, collegial and communal ways.

Structures of mutual support and of spiritual and material sharing are an essential part of the structured life of the koinonia as are gifts and callings of the Holy Spirit such as religious communities, members of the councils of the churches, etc.

12. Koinonia is made up of persons-in-community, not of independent individuals joined together. All are contributing to the life of the koinonia through the gifts of the Spirit they have received. Through such gifts they are related to the inner life of the Trinity.

13. Koinonia – despite all its imperfections – points towards a humanity God wills: a humanity of those reconciled with God and with one another; a humanity which is no longer distorted by destructive divisions of race, nation, ethnicity, gender, poverty and wealth, powerful and oppressed; a humanity in which people of different faiths work together for the common good.

14. Koinonia is the gift which we receive from God, but which we fail to fully grasp and express within our ecclesial communities and between them. However, this gift of koinonia as a dynamic reality provides us at the same time, through the grace of God, with the possibility of moving on towards its fullness:

a)   when humanity will be restored into the likeness of God;
b)   when the divisions within Christianity are being healed.

15. Ecumenical dialogue and commitment in recent decades has led to the recognition that, even though we are still related to each other in an "imperfect" communion, our churches are growing together towards a broader knowledge and implementation of the koinonia which is God's gift and calling.

APPENDIX 2

Towards a Hermeneutics
for a Growing Koinonia

PART I

INTRODUCTION

1. Hermeneutics is disciplined reflection on the act of interpreting and communicating texts, symbols and practices. Not limited to rules and principles for interpreting scripture, its aim includes the major task of making explicit the assumptions and perspectives of the interpreting subjects. Because the hermeneutical process always takes place both within specific communities and across different cultures and contexts, there can be no completely neutral interpretations. A responsible hermeneutics will recognize that interpretations often occur within institutional environments and may be thus complicit with the often ambiguous interests of power and control.

2. The Christian faith relies on the gracious gift of the gospel of God's self-communicating love to all humanity through Jesus Christ. This gift has been transmitted to us through the Old and New Testaments and through the life of the church. We believe that this transmission is a Spirit-guided, dynamic and eschatological process. At the same time it is an historical process, in which human rules of communication and interpretation are at work: we have this "treasure in earthen vessels" (2 Cor. 4:7). Examples of human fragility of this process may be seen in the condoning of slavery and ethnic divisions and, as we are increasingly aware today, the presence of a pervasive patriarchal perspective within scripture. Reflection upon hermeneutical considerations which clarify the human means of the transmission of apostolic faith is therefore necessary for a theology that hopes accurately to discern that faith. Rather than detracting from the revealing power of the Holy Spirit, or from the conviction that a "charism of truth" has been entrusted to the people of God 'and its apostolic ministry, hermeneutics serves this charism by bringing into clearer focus the Spirit's message.

3. The following considerations will explore three areas which, according to recent ecumenical dialogue, could benefit from a deeper reflection upon hermeneutics. These are (a) the healing of divisions between Christian communities, (b) the expression of the gospel across social and cultural boundaries, and (c) the ecclesial process of discernment at work in each of these two tasks.

4. Regarding the first of these areas, it is clear that during the history of Christianity diverse hermeneutical criteria have been developed in the different churches and denominations. In recent times especially, there is a growing

awareness that these criteria have played an important role in the traditional positions of the various confessions. Regarding the second area, hermeneutical factors are also present in the diverse contexts in which we live. In different cultures and societies, different modes of hermeneutics are applied by which new ways of doing theology are developed.

5. These two areas should not be thought of as completely separated from one another. In fact, contextual differences have entered into the establishment and shaping of confessional divisions. At the same time, not all differences between the churches can be classified as cultural divisions. The situation becomes even more complicated when one recalls that, on the one hand, cultural differences exist within most confessions and, on the other, even when various churches live within the same culture, inherited confessional differences remain. Finally, the issues which are important for ecumenism at the local level are not always the same as those which call for attention at a more global level. The distinctness and, at the same time, inter-relation between confessional and contextual diversity shows why reflection about an ecumenical hermeneutics which seeks to address these two areas inevitably entails a degree of complexity. Effort is required to remain attentive to all of the relevant dimensions of this discussion. But the fact that this complex subject requires much effort does not relieve us of the responsibility of addressing these important issues in our search for unity.

6. The third area to be considered concerns the ecclesial process involved in maintaining unity within diversity. Given the transcendence of the Christian mystery, which can never be completely expressed in human formulations and institutions, and given the God-created wealth of human, cultural and linguistic differences, one can rejoice in the presence of much of the diversity in the expression of apostolic faith and practice. While appreciating this multiform richness of the many local manifestations of the one faith, the struggle for visible unity in a world constantly tempted by divisive fragmentation represents a challenge to develop an ecumenical hermeneutics, exploring the common criteria which indicate the faithfulness and legitimacy of any interpretation. This hermeneutical task is especially necessary for divided Christian communities as they struggle to make manifest the unity which Christ wills for the church.

7. The hermeneutical question arises with fresh urgency when we look at the many texts which have been produced during more than eighty years of the ecumenical movement and which have come to play their own role in the life of the churches. The official responses to BEM, for example, show that different hermeneutics have been at work during the process of producing the BEM document, on the one hand, and during the study and interpretation of BEM in the different churches, on the other. The fact that the questions with which BEM was sent to the churches implied a certain hermeneutics and the fact that these were understood in different ways by the churches who responded to them illustrates how essential reflection upon hermeneutics is. Ecumenical texts require an ecumenical hermeneutics which helps the churches to keep their identity, but at the same time to transcend their confessional ways of interpretation and to think ecumenically.

8. After more than three decades of bilateral and multilateral dialogues on the common understanding of the gospel, the church, its creeds, sacraments and ministry, the fifth world conference on Faith and Order in Santiago de Compostela 1993 could speak of a "growing, real though still imperfect koinonia". At the same time the Santiago conference pointed to three different, yet related tasks:

– the need to overcome and to reconcile the criteriological differences with regard to a faithful interpretation of the one gospel, recognizing the multiform richness and diversity of the canon of the scriptures, as it is read, explicated and applied in the life of the churches, but at the same time strengthening the awareness of the one Tradition within the many traditions; (= below section A; cf. *On the Way to Fuller Koinonia*, report of Santiago de Compostela 1994, section II, para. 18);

– the need to express and communicate the one gospel in and across various, sometimes even conflicting contexts, cultures and locations; (= below section B; cf. report of Santiago de Compostela 1994, section I, paras 15-16);

– the need to work towards mutual accountability, discernment and authoritative teaching and towards credibility in common witness before the world, and finally towards the eschatological fullness of the truth in the power of the Holy Spirit; (= below section C; cf. report of Santiago de Compostela 1994, section III, para. 31 and section IV, para. 3).

A. THE COMMON UNDERSTANDING OF THE ONE TRADITION

1. Tradition and traditions

9. How can Christians and churches share in the gift of the one "paradosis of the gospel"? How do they confess and live "according to the scriptures"? How do they read their own traditions in the light of the one Tradition, given through the Holy Spirit of God? About these fundamental hermeneutical questions the fourth world conference on Faith and Order at Montreal (1963) was able to say:

> Our starting point is that we as Christians are all living in a Tradition which goes back to our Lord and has its roots in the Old Testament and are all indebted to that Tradition inasmuch as we have received the revealed truth, the gospel, through its being transmitted from one generation to the other. Thus we can say that we exist as Christians by the Tradition of the gospel, testified in scripture, transmitted in and by the church, through the power of the Holy Spirit (section II, para. 45).

> The traditions in Christian history are distinct from, and yet connected with, the Tradition. They are the expressions and manifestations in diverse historical terms of the one truth and reality which is Christ (section II, para. 47).

10. We recognize that the fourth world conference addressed the issue of hermeneutics in an ecumenical perspective: opening up the many traditions to

the recognition of the one Tradition as a gift from God. The hermeneutical process of interpretation, reception and transmission is not simply a process carried out by the human mind, whether individual or communal, but an ecclesial dynamic, led by the Spirit, embedded in worship and in the life of the church. The Holy Spirit inspires and leads the churches to rethink and reinterpret their traditions in conversation with each other aiming to make visible the unity of God's church. They have begun to develop a common understanding through which their particularities do not exclude those who understand and live the gospel differently, provided, of course, that these differences in expression and understanding do not contradict the essentials of the apostolic faith.

11. It is widely recognized that continuity with the apostolic faith and life is an important sign that Christian churches should preserve at all times and places. This continuity, however, should not be confused with a mere repetition of the past without any recognition of the present. It rather implies that the churches must interpret their present situation and understanding of the Christian faith by taking into consideration the whole of the life and tradition of the church. The churches of God as living communities constituted by faith in Jesus Christ and empowered by the Holy Spirit, must always re-receive the gospel on the basis of their present experience of life. It is this process in which the mind of the Christian community is enlightened by the Holy Spirit in order to discern truth from falsehood in concrete decisions about matters of faith. But according to the different geographical, historical and social circumstances the apostolic faith finds different expressions and interpretations in different times and in different contexts. While no ecclesial community can claim to possess, to interpret and pass on the absolute and full comprehensive truth, each of them can pray for the Holy Spirit who discerns the spirits of truth and falsehood, even by speaking to one church through the insights of another.

12. The churches have recognized that by being in conversation with each other and by sharing and appreciating each other's gifts they can enrich and correct their understanding of what God expects them to be and to do in this world. This opening up to a new understanding of the traditions of other churches, their history, their liturgies, their martyrs and saints, and even their sacraments and ministries, has changed the hermeneutical climate since Montreal. The exchange of biblical exegesis, systematic theological approaches, common historiography, and practical-theological projects has been one of its magnificent results. Exegetical research is done on the basis of open and critical interconfessional debate and also is fostered by ecumenical dialogue. Bible translations and commentaries were issued on an ecumenical basis; liturgical calendars, lectionaries, hymn- and prayerbooks borrowed ideas from one another in a process of gradual osmosis. This has created a new situation, in which a hermeneutical community is growing across confessional boundaries, without giving up the richness of the confessional traditions.

13. However, Montreal did not fully explain what it means that this one Tradition is embodied in concrete traditions. It did not deal with the criteriological question of how to distinguish between diverse traditions, nor how to discern the authenticity of faith in a situation of conflicting cultural perspec-

tives, frameworks or hermeneutical canons. It could go no further than the WCC's Toronto statement (1950), which deliberately did not provide any criterion beyond the Basis of the WCC for the authenticity or fidelity of the traditions of its member churches, to say nothing of other human traditions. It merely juxtaposed the various hermeneutical standards of the main Christian traditions. It could only point to the three main factors in the transmission process: the preceding events and testimonies leading to the scriptures, the scriptures themselves, and the ecclesial preaching and teaching.

14. After Montreal Faith and Order undertook important studies on the hermeneutical significance of the councils of the early church ("The Importance of the Conciliar Process in the Ancient Church for the Ecumenical Movement", in *New Directions in Faith and Order, Bristol 1967*, F&O paper 50, 1968, pp.49-59; *Councils, Conciliarity and a Genuinely Universal Council*, F&O paper 70; *Study Encounter*, 10, no. 2, 1974), especially on Chalcedon ("The Council of Chalcedon and its Significance for the Ecumenical Movement", in *Faith and Order Louvain 1971: Study Reports and Documents*, F&O paper 59, 1971, pp.23-34). At Louvain several reports on the authority of the Bible contributed to the hermeneutical discussions of that period. After Accra (1974) Faith and Order started to collect from all parts of the world newer expressions of faith and hope, summarized at Bangalore (1978) in *A Common Account of Hope*. This process made us aware of the many contextual aspects of our confessions of faith. The Odessa consultation on "How Does the Church Teach Authoritatively Today?" discussed aspects of the hermeneutical problem, especially the question of continuity and change in the doctrinal tradition of the church.

15. But Montreal, Louvain and Odessa did not adequately formulate means to deal with potential conflicts between the traditions themselves, between the inherited traditions and newer contexts or between various contextual approaches within each church, or within the koinonia of churches. This was why Santiago felt the need to refer once again to this problem (cf. para. 8 above).

16. Ultimately, the one Tradition is hidden within the mystery of the person of Jesus Christ. As such, it is not something which can be fully captured and controlled by human discourse. Instead, it is a living, eschatological reality which eludes all attempts at final linguistic definition and conceptual disclosure. The "one Tradition", therefore, signifies the redeeming presence of the resurrected Christ, while the "many traditions" are particular modes and manifestations of that presence. However, inasmuch as the one Tradition is experienced only through such particular modes of relation and presence, the temptation may exist to identify exclusively any one tradition with *the* Tradition as such. Given the double sense of paradosis as "tradition" and "betrayal", such identifications would misrepresent and thereby "betray" the truth rather than "convey" it.

2. "According to the scriptures"

17. The text of the scriptures is given to us and offers itself in its revelatory character after a handing on through oral transmission. The written text

subsequently has been interpreted by means of diverse exegetical and scholarly methods. Wrestling with the principles and practice of interpretation, Faith and Order affirmed (Bristol 1968) that the tools of modern exegetical scholarship are important if the biblical message is to speak with power and meaning today. These tools have contributed in a vital way to the present ecumenical convergence and growth in koinonia. The exegetical exploration of the process of tradition within the Bible itself and the recognition of the multiple interpretations of the fundamental divine narrative within the unity of the early apostolic church shows how the word of God always needs to be expressed in human language and by human witnesses in the diverse situations of human life as historically, culturally and socially conceived. "The very nature of biblical texts means that interpreting them will require continued use of the historical-critical method,... [since] the Bible does not present itself as a direct revelation of timeless truths, but as the written testimony to a series of interventions in which God reveals himself in human history" ("The Interpretation of the Bible in the Church", Pontifical Biblical Commission, 1993).

18. But the historical-critical method in no way exhausts the meaning of the text. A plurality of tools and methods, including rhetorical, narrative, structural-linguistic, semiotic, psychological, and sociological approaches, facilitates new insights into the rich and dynamic potential of meaning in the scriptures. However, hermeneutics cannot be reduced to exegetical tools isolated from the comprehensive experience of the interpretative community. This is especially true in view of experiential readings of the Bible in communities where situations of injustice and the struggle for liberation are the context within which the biblical story is read.

19. A variety of factors are woven into the comprehensive experience of the community which together make up the hermeneutical locus within which scripture is interpreted. These factors include oral tradition, narratives, memories and liturgies, as well as the life, teachings and ethical decisions of the believing community. Thus many dimensions of the life of the community provide a context for interpreting the scriptural texts. At the same time, the scriptures themselves are not only literary texts. They emerge from episodes of life, a calendar of feasts, a scheme of history, and the witnessing account of the living people of God. In addition, they become alive once again as they embrace the life, feasts, history, and witness of communities today. In this perspective the praxis of the Christian communities and people in different particular cultural and social contexts is itself a reading and an interpretation of the text and not simply a position from which to approach the text. Such praxis is the way in which the text comes alive.

20. Because the biblical texts originated in concrete historical situations, they witness to the salvific presence of the triune God in those particular circumstances. However, they transcend this particularity and become also part of the world of the reader, that is, of the witnessing community through the ages into the present. Although embedded in the life and times in which it took its written form, as the inspired testimony of the transcendent word of God, the scriptures provide a measure for the truth and meaning of our stories today.

21. The tension between past and present which occurs when the biblical text is applied to our stories today is also reflected in the eschatological dimension of scripture. The interpreting activity of the church is an anticipatory projection of the reality of the reign of God which is already present and yet to come. To that end, the praxis of the believing community has to be considered also in its celebratory character. Reading "the signs of the times" in the context of the announcement of "the new things to come" is part of the reality of the church as an hermeneutical community. The struggle for peace, justice, and the integrity of creation, symbolized and lived in the proclamation of the word and the sacraments, is also part of the constant interpretative task of the church. In this engagement, and particularly in the liturgy, the church proclaims and celebrates the promise of God's reign and its in-breaking in the praxis of faith.

3. Interpreting the interpreters

22. We acknowledge that the text is something given as part of the paradosis of the gospel. It has to be respected as something that comes from outside to the interpreter and with which the interpreter is involved in dialogue. In the process of interpretation, which takes its starting point at the particular experiences of the reader (cf. para. 19 above), the authority of the scriptures should be regarded as the primary norm and criterion. Particular traditions need to refer continuously to this norm in which they find their validity. This adherence takes shape in a communal and ecclesial way in worship and in the anamnesis of the lives of the biblical witnesses and those who live the biblical message, inspired by the Holy Spirit.

23. But as we deal with the text in our quest to understand God's will for the world and for the people called to be witnesses of God's love, we need to interpret the text always anew. In this hermeneutical task we have to remain conscious that interpretations are a result of special historical circumstances and that new issues may come out of different contexts. In considering these, hermeneutics seeks to expose the presuppositions, prejudices, and hidden agendas of any paradigm of interpretation. One must take into consideration issues of power as well as social, political and other interests. From which location is the text being interpreted? Why is this specific text chosen? How are power structures at work? The way in which the Bible was used to justify apartheid serves as an example of a selective reading which could be and was challenged hermeneutically. A clearer understanding of ideological interpretation, the wider testimony of scripture, and the experience of those oppressed all entered into this challenge. Nor is the sophisticated realm of academic and scholarly interpretation entirely immune from selective and prejudicial readings.

24. Furthermore, ecumenical hermeneutics also must take into account the possibility of complementarity. This means that those who interpret the Christian tradition differently should attempt to understand each other on the presumption that each has a "right intention of faith" (cf. *BEM*, M52). Since diversity can be an expression of the rich gifts of the Holy Spirit, the churches should become aware of the values inherent in the "otherness" of one another

and even of the right to be different from each other, when such differences do not amount to separation. In this way, differences can be an invitation and a starting point for the common search for the truth, in a spirit of koinonia that entails a disposition to metanoia, under the guidance of the Spirit of God.

25. Reconciliation which occurs between those whose common past was marked by injustice or violence can be a painful experience. Interpreting a history of this kind requires the hermeneutical awareness needed to renounce the stereotypes which such histories can generate. It also may call for repentance and forgiveness. In this way, such reconciliation requires a healing of memories, which is not the same as forgetfulness of the past. One must pray for the miracle of resurrection to new life, even if the marks of the crucifixion remain.

B. ONE GOSPEL IN MANY CONTEXTS

1. The gospel in a multicultural world

26. Our different interpretations of scripture increasingly remind us of our different contexts (cf. para. 23). Because of the many forces which today tend to shrink our planet, we can no longer pretend ignorance of one another and yet this new situation carries with it heightened potential for domination. The gospel is not given to one particular group as its private property. Rather we share a responsibility to proclaim it to the world (missionary dimension of the word). Therefore despite our different interpretations in our various contexts and cultures, we have to find ways of communicating with one another and of communicating the gospel together to the world.

27. This hermeneutical awareness is in itself a contribution to the handling or solving of conflicts. From the beginning, the church has lived in and with conflicts. In order to overcome this, unity and uniformity were sometimes imposed on conflicting parties. More than in the past, our time seems to oppose uniformity while asking for diverse expressions of faith, order and life to be acknowledged. In the past, theology could rely on a more or less common dogmatic framework. Today, out of our different contexts, more and more diverse ways of doing theology emerge which cannot be moulded into one uniform way of doing theology. The tension within this diversity can be enriching. Yet a hermeneutics which brings these different approaches into dialogue is necessary so that, while they remain different, all can recognize the basic narrative of Jesus Christ in each of these interpretations. Disintegration and fragmentation of the Christian faith may be prevented by a continuous effort to ensure that all of these interpretations are expressions of the living apostolic tradition, a tradition which is embedded in structures of worship (cf. report of the consultation "Towards Koinonia in Worship: Consultation on the Role of Worship within the Search for Unity", Ditchingham, August 1994), conciliar teaching, theological education, ministerial authority, and episcope. These structures, for all of their differences, share a fundamental similarity. Churches should seek to ascertain whether the hermeneutical keys of the other communions may be equivalent to their own.

28. Within the study process on Gospel and Culture of Unit II, insights on intercultural and cross-cultural communication are developed that are of vital hermeneutical significance. Intercultural hermeneutics is a still largely uncharted territory. But attempts have been made to locate the place where meaning resides in the interaction between speaker and receiver as they come together in an interstitial zone which is not identical with either's culture and thereby constitutes a liminal experience. Such encounters are by their very nature fragile and brief and have to be followed by "reverberations" as the experience of the encounter is carried back into each culture to gain effectiveness and appropriateness. In order to succeed, intercultural communication requires intensive and ongoing dialogue, a non-dominative exchange and motivation, knowledge and certain skills of the participants.

2. Contextuality and catholicity in ecumenical hermeneutics

29. The interpretations developed in a particular situation are not restricted to that situation alone but have much to contribute on the wider, intercultural level. Thus, the local and the global are not mutually exclusive. Moreover, while we are influenced by the immediate context in which we interpret the scriptures, this influence does not completely determine us. Even within one given context there remains a variety of interpretative and practical options. The inter-relation between local and more general interpretations reflects that dimension of the church which is conveyed by the word catholicity. Catholicity suggests the fullness of the koinonia, the inclusiveness and wholeness of the community. The local church is "catholic" by being part of this whole, to which it contributes and from which it receives.

30. From the point of view of the local situation, the hermeneutical work of the believing community has to be relevant to the immediate cultural or social setting in order to maintain its prophetic dimension, but it cannot claim to be absolute. We all must be aware of the limitations of our own positions. In a particular way, contextualization involves recognizing our responsibility to those who are weak or oppressed. The preferential option for the poor, the voiceless and the victimized is a special mark of Christian koinonia, having hermeneutical consequences for our reading of the scriptures in the tradition of the church and contributing an important perspective to the broader cultural and ecclesial community.

31. Therefore, from the perspective of catholicity, contextual hermeneutics should not be considered irrelevant. Every contextual interpretation can contribute to the general understanding of truth and represent an approach which speaks to the whole. When a given interpretation of the Bible, coming from a particular location, points to injustice or liberation, it is not simply a contextual claim but can provide a general insight, which may be tested and modified by alternative perspectives. Moreover, such a local claim may challenge and modify the conventional wisdom, which may at times uncritically be assumed as the appropriate Christian interpretation. In this way, the reconciliation of conflicting, cross-cultural views is one of the liberating effects of contextual hermeneutics.

32. Intensive dialogue in an atmosphere of mutual respect, accountability and acceptance is necessary in the struggle for discerning and being faithful to the truth of the gospel.

C. THE CHURCH AS A HERMENEUTICAL COMMUNITY

1. Ecclesial discernment and the truth of the gospel

33. In its journey through history progressing towards the eschaton, the church always stands under the word of God, as normatively witnessed to in scripture. In this state, the church is always a "hermeneutical community" which must discern that ever-present word, amid the shift of the times and under the guidance of the Spirit. This hermeneutical dimension is a condition for the apostolic mission of the church, but it is also the point of reference that allows the church to maintain its identity. In its dialogue with the biblical text, the community of believers is free to understand in new ways the truth in every new situation, to communicate it through the symbols and narratives of different cultures, and to challenge the structures and powers of any given system, within as well as outside the church, thereby enacting the prophetic dimension of the biblical message.

34. At the same time, the church must be responsible and accountable. Toward this end, interpretations based on a narrowly selective range of citations must be informed by a wider understanding of scriptural witnesses and by other interpretations of those witnesses. But the church's accountability remains incomplete if it satisfies only the bare letter of scientific exegesis. Interpretation must be attentive to the cries of victims and to the demands of social justice. The church's reading of scripture must produce the "bread" of life and liberation and not the indigestible "stones" of exploitation and oppression. In so doing, the church is called to distinguish between those interpretations which are manifestations of the one life-giving gospel and those which, on the other hand, go beyond the boundaries of unity and cause division by distortion of the gospel. An interpretation is deficient when it distorts the fundamental divine narrative or fails to connect with the life of the church and the wider human community, or lends itself to the destruction of God's creation.

2. Episcope and mutual accountability

35. In this sense, the church as a hermeneutical community is responsible for the faithful transmission of the inherited gospel throughout different times and places. This responsibility requires a service of discernment that cannot be separated from the life of the community as a whole. To that end, the different Christian communities have recognized, among other ministries, a ministry of episcope, described and exercised in a variety of ways. The forms of this episcope and its methods of communicating those interpretations of faith considered authentic and legitimate have developed in different patterns in the course of the centuries within the various traditions, and are still open to new insights, as part of the permanent hermeneutical quest of the church in the fulfillment of its mission.

36. Episcope is to be exercised collegially. "In the life of the church, bishops, presbyters, those who hold ministries in the congregation and the congregations as a whole work together for building up the body of Christ for its witness in the world. If any one of those elements is isolated, the church suffers distortion in theory as well as in practice. Bishops, too, are subject to episcope by the whole church" (*Episcope and Episcopate in Ecumenical Perspective*, F&O paper 102, 1980, p.11, no. 2). No member therefore should be excluded from participation in the common task of discerning and carrying out the church's mission. The Christian community needs to be especially attentive that the voices of those who may be marginalized for social or economic reasons are heard.

37. It is not only within the various ecclesial communities but also between them that mutual accountability must be practised for the sake of discernment and credibility. As part of a "hermeneutical community" all churches need each other's contributions and corrections in their practice and understanding of the faith. They are encouraged to increase their consultation with other churches regarding important questions which touch upon faith or discipline. Hopefully parameters for common decision-making can be developed, even though there may be issues about which a church must decide without or even against the opinion of others. Ultimately apart from Christ they have no credibility and it is to Christ that they are finally accountable.

3. Reception as a hermeneutical process

38. Active participation and dialogue between communities and within each community is a consequence of the church's nature as a communion of persons in relation. The divine being of the Triune God is the example and source of communion. The Holy Spirit is sent to create communion, bestowing the gift of faith upon each believer and empowering each one to understand more fully the revealed word of God and to apply it more fruitfully to the concrete situations of daily life (*sensus fidelium*). As a "royal priesthood" (1 Pet. 2:9), the community of the baptized engages in the active "reception" of the gospel. Reception employs the various hermeneutical factors discussed throughout this paper. Historically, the reception of ecumenical councils proved to be a process which extended through a considerable period of time, employed a wide variety of means, such as the liturgy, catechesis, theology, the teaching of pastors and popular piety and called upon the participation of all church members, according to the charisms and ministries of each.

39. In recent times, a new and different form of reception has made its appearance with the production of ecumenical documents which have the distinct purpose of helping to reunite divided Christian communities. The process by which so many communities responded to BEM shed light on this form of reception, especially by making clearer the diverse criteria by which churches read and evaluate ecumenical documents. The responses to BEM also show that reception is more than just a church's official response to a document. It is a process which extends over a considerable period of time and involves many factors. The forums on bilateral dialogues have contributed much to a more adequate understanding of these factors (see, especially, the

Sixth Forum on Bilateral Dialogues, F&O Paper 168, 1995). Ecumenical hermeneutics should facilitate this process, helping communities to read documents within the dialogical spirit in which they were written and with that self-scrutiny to which God may be calling them for the sake of the unity of the church.

40. In yet another way, the unity of Christians who are divided by cultural or social differences requires an attentive process of reception of each other in the context of the dignity of all as human beings and, within the Christian community, as sisters and brothers in Christ. This mutual reception by Christians over cultural and social differences is what St Paul is talking about when he writes: "Therefore receive one another, as Christ also has received us to the glory of God" (Rom. 15:7).

41. A collegial and ecumenical exercise of teaching authority is already in some respects beginning to develop. We may hope and pray that these developments will in time enable the churches to make together decisive judgments in matters of faith which, after due reception, would become part of their common witness according to the scriptures.

CONCLUSION

42. The vision of the church as a hermeneutical community means that ekklesia is constituted within history as a diverse martyria of the gospel. Through the power of the Spirit, ecclesial communities are called to engage the "word of life" with the "flesh" of history, so that it may be "seen by our eyes, resound in our hearing and embrace in love our bodies and souls" (cf. 1 John 1:1-2). This creative, hermeneutical engagement is at the heart of the church's apostolic mission. At the same time, the truth of the gospel must be carefully discerned by the whole people of God in and through the diversity of its historical and cultural correlations. To be distributed, the "bread of life" must be "broken", yet not divided (cf. Luke 24:35; 1 Cor. 11:24).

43. Similarly, if the limitless diversity is a sign of our times, it cannot be the sign of Christian unity. The church must discern the "signs of the times" by looking to the one who is both in and beyond time. Although the word enters history, this does not issue in a closed or static system, but in a dynamic progression dependent on the Spirit (Rom. 12:3; Eph. 4:7). The gospel cannot be confined in human bounds, nor does its truth correspond only to human thought and language: the gospel is thus not reducible to the forms of human culture and traditions. It would be an abdication of our common vocation to replace the struggle for unity with "ecumenical complacency".

44. Between the ossification of the Living Word within a closed propositional system and the silencing of that Word through an endless postponement of meaning, the churches may hope to find the path toward fuller unity.

PART II:
WORKING PRINCIPLES
FOR ECUMENICAL HERMENEUTICS

INTRODUCTION

1. Ecumenical hermeneutics shares with other forms of hermeneutics the goal of facilitating accurate interpretation, communication, and reception of the texts, symbols and practices which give shape and meaning to particular communities. Ecumenical hermeneutics, however, focuses on the way in which the texts, symbols and practices of the various Christian churches may be interpreted, communicated, and received accurately by each other as they engage in dialogue.

2. The specific goal of ecumenical hermeneutics, as linked with the goal of ecumenism itself, is to facilitate an ever-increasing degree of Christian unity, culminating in the visible unity for which Christ prayed (John 17).

3. Because Christian unity cannot ultimately be separated from the unity of all humankind, ecumenical hermeneutics should not be restricted to interpretation, communication, and reception of exclusively Christian texts, symbols and practices but must also deal with texts, symbols and practices beyond those which are contained in the Bible and in the formulations of the apostolic faith through the ages. The interplay of specifically Christian unity issues and issues relating to various social, cultural and religious discriminations affecting the unity of all humankind, dictates that ecumenical hermeneutics is, of necessity, engaged in dealing with material which relates to both. Indeed, through the process and results of ecumenical hermeneutics the churches are empowered to work together on issues other than those which separate them from each other.

4. Christian churches, despite their historic divisions, share a common biblical heritage and a common apostolic faith. This makes the task of ecumenical hermeneutics potentially both achievable and difficult. It is achievable because of the common source material belonging to the dialogue partners. It is difficult because there is often a long-standing history of significantly different interpretations of this material. Shared texts, symbols and practices which have been interpreted and understood differently in the past have the potential of facilitating reconciliation and unity, but only when ecumenical dialogue is approached in a spirit of openness. At the same time, interpreting scripture and Tradition must be conducted on the basis of common criteria.

A. CONDITIONS FOR ECUMENICAL HERMENEUTICS

1. Dialogical perspective

5. Ecumenical hermeneutics takes as its starting point that conversations leading to greater unity are conducted by representatives from the various churches whose contributions to the dialogue is mediated through their particular cultural, social, geographical, and historical backgrounds. These repre-

sentatives see each other as equal partners in dialogue. They speak to each other from the perspective of their traditional interpretations of the apostolic faith as articulated in their confessional documents, their liturgies, and their experiences, but with a willingness to view their own interpretations from the vantage point of those with whom they are in dialogue.

6. Ecumenical hermeneutics is based on the understanding that the churches are not only in dialogue, but that they themselves are the subject-matter of the dialogue. This involves being attentive to the insights provided by the dialogue partner in respect of the possible limitedness and prejudices inherent in the interpretation and understanding of one's own tradition.

7. A dialogical perspective also requires that the dialogue partners examine the social, cultural, and theological interests which affect ecumenical hermeneutics and which are inevitably brought to bear on interpretations. Texts, symbols and practices are interpreted, communicated, and received not only from the perspective of a particular church's tradition but also in relationship to specific emphases or concerns which may (and often do) affect our reading. These interests, which may even be in unresolved competition with each other, need to be acknowledged and addressed.

8. The partners in dialogue need to take into account new situations and experiences which produce conceptual shifts in society. Such conceptual shifts, evidenced for example in the growing awareness of the oppressive effects of patriarchal traditions, offer new perspectives on current issues of faith and practice, and may offer fresh ways of approaching old questions. New situations and experiences also bring to light new issues which have been hidden behind generally accepted assumptions in our society. In such cases, the churches encountering these issues jointly may contribute not only to Christian unity, but also to the unity of all humankind.

9. A dialogical perspective, in addition, means that churches are called upon to be accountable to each other in their decision-making and in the development and communication of their interpretations. Interpretations ought not to be made or articulated in isolation, nor ought specific understandings to be absolutized even if these are not in direct contradiction to the faithfully held views of the dialogue partner.

2. Openness to being challenged

10. For ecumenical dialogue to be a genuine encounter, the churches as dialogue partners must be open to the possibility of being challenged to see and to incorporate into their own understanding fuller expressions of the gospel as they learn from each other in the awareness that it is the Holy Spirit who creates unity.

11. Ecumenical hermeneutics while dealing with the texts, symbols and practices which have shaped the various Christian traditions needs to take into account the openness of tradition to possible further development.

12. New insights into the meaning of the gospel in respect of Christian life are not always received by the various churches at the same point in history. Ecumenical hermeneutics provides the opportunity for churches to gain, from each other's interpretations and understandings, the means by which their own

traditions may be enriched and made even more faithful to the Christian gospel as it is lived out in contemporary contexts.

13. It is also possible that the process of engaging in ecumenical hermeneutics may lead a particular church in the spirit of metanoia to review and revise its own previously-held interpretations and understandings.

3. Acceptance of common criteria

14. Although the dialogue partners will inevitably use a variety of hermeneutical tools, ecumenical hermeneutics can only be effective if those engaged in the process are committed to working within a range of shared criteria.

B. PROCESS AND CRITERIA

1. Process

15. The process of ecumenical hermeneutics involves not only accurate understanding and interpretation of texts, symbols and practices but also analysis of the relative weight given to those texts, symbols and practices by the various churches in respect of the authoritative nature of the sources themselves and the interpretations derived from them. Clarity about authority is a crucial element in that dimension of hermeneutics which concentrates on the faithful communication and reception of the meaning of texts, symbols and practices. Consequently, the relationship between scripture, Tradition and traditions, and Christian experience arising from liturgical and other practices needs to be dealt with in the hermeneutical process.

16. All Christians agree that, in some way, the scriptures hold a unique place in the shaping of Christian faith and practice. Similarly, all agree that the whole of apostolic faith is not confined to the formulations of that faith as contained and expressed in scripture, but that normative faith is also discernable in the life of the church throughout the ages. At the fourth world conference of Faith and Order in Montreal (1963), a significant advance was made with regard to the distinction between "Tradition" and "traditions". Ecumenical hermeneutics needs to operate in light of this understanding.

17. The process of interpreting, communicating and receiving normative faith as revealed in the sources and in the experience of Christians involves, in most instances, the utilization of generally-applicable hermeneutical tools and principles. In some instances, however, hermeneutical tools and principles specific to disciplines such as biblical studies, patristics, historical theology, liturgy, sociology and linguistics will also need to be applied. Consequently, criteria for ecumenical hermeneutics may be divided into two categories: general and specific.

2. Criteria

(i) General

18. The process of ecumenical hermeneutics must allow, at least in the first instance, the dialogue partners to analyze and explain their modes of interpreting and communicating the faith in their own categories and concepts. However, the process needs also to recognize and accept that there is a

range of well-established hermeneutical methodologies from the general field of hermeneutics that can (and should) be applied appropriately to the texts, symbols and practices which comprise the source material of ecumenical dialogue, even if such methodologies have not previously been utilized by one or more of the dialogue partners.

19. Ecumenical hermeneutics must engage in attentive listening, with a conscious awareness that distortions in interpretation may (and do) arise as a result of the listeners' presuppositions or ideological commitments. One way of guarding against distorting the dialogue partners' self-understanding is to engage the views communicated in the same categories in which they were presented. In order to do this it is crucial to avoid transposing these categories into ones with which the listeners may be more familiar. Attentive listening entails a concerted effort at understanding what is being communicated in the way it was intended. An important aspect of ecumenical hermeneutics, therefore, is ensuring that it is possible for dialogue partners to interact with the perspective of the other.

20. Change of perspective not only facilitates accurate understanding and communication but also provides the opportunity for interpretive reflection upon each other's position. Ecumenical hermeneutics includes the willingness to hear the analysis of one's own modes of interpretation as viewed by the ecumenical dialogue partners. In this way, categories and concepts shared in common, as well as divergences and challenges, are identified.

21. Ecumenical hermeneutics needs also to identify and clarify the use of language. The nature of language is integrally related to the manner in which it is employed for a specific purpose. Moreover one must take into consideration that much of religious language, for example as it relates to the divine, is symbolic. Hermeneutics must make clear whether a particular word, phrase, or concept is intended to be understood literally or symbolically.

22. Further, the process of ecumenical hermeneutics needs to involve the dialogue partners in a critical examination of the way in which their interpretations affect the lives of people, particularly the marginalized, by fostering forms of discrimination based on gender, race, class and culture.

(ii) Specific

a) Scripture

23. Ecumenical hermeneutics must allow the dialogue partners to demonstrate in their own categories and concepts the way in which they view scripture and how the interpretations they derive from scripture are based on particular biblical texts. This might be accomplished in a number of different ways within the range of methodologies offered by traditional and contemporary biblical exegesis. Methodologies inherent in traditional biblical interpretation include patristic, liturgical, homiletic, dogmatic and allegorical approaches to the text. Contemporary methodologies include: those that focus on the socio-historical origins of the texts (e. g., historical-critical and sociological methods); those that focus on the internal relationships within a text and between texts (e. g., literary, semiotic and canonical methods); and those

that focus on the potential of the text for new readings that are generated by the encounter of the text with the human reality (e. g., reader-response method). 24. In ecumenical hermeneutics a scriptural text may be considered as authoritative for a particular matter of faith or practice, even if this text is interpreted differently by the dialogue partners – as long as the interpretations are able to be shown as deriving legitimately from the range of methodologies inherent in traditional and contemporary biblical exegesis.

25. Similarly, in ecumenical hermeneutics, the applicability of a text is not to be ruled out even if a specific interpretation is deemed by one of the dialogue partners to be irrelevant to a particular matter of faith or practice. As long as the range of legitimate interpretations includes those which are applicable to the matter under consideration, the text can be included in an ecumenical discussion of that issue.

26. Not all interpretations of scripture, of course, can be deemed to be valid. Ecumenical hermeneutics must delineate the range of acceptable interpretations of particular texts as they relate to specific issues. An interpretation, for example, may be judged invalid if it contravenes the biblical imperative to act with justice and charity.

27. Interpretations of scriptural texts must take into consideration the biblical context in which they were first written and the contemporary context in which they are received.

b) Tradition and traditions

28. As in the case of the understanding and interpretation of scripture, ecumenical hermeneutics, when dealing with extra-biblical sources, must draw on established methodologies in interpreting the texts which are the sources of the apostolic faith. These methodologies include those inherent in disciplines such as patristics, church history, historical theology, canon law and liturgics, as well as those methodologies which help to reconstruct neglected dimensions of the past from the perspective of marginalized groups. Examples of the latter are feminist or liberationist reconstructions of systems of power and patronage in early Christianity.

29. The process of ecumenical hermeneutics needs to challenge the dialogue partners to declare the perspective from which they view history.

30. The process of ecumenical hermeneutics also needs to ensure that the dialogue partners are able to articulate the method by which they have derived their particular interpretation of historical faith or practice. An example of this is the presence of widespread agreement among the witnesses to the Tradition.

31. Ecumenical hermeneutics, moreover, must enable the dialogue partners to declare their particular understanding of the relationship between "continuity" and "discontinuity" in the historic expression of the faith of the people of God.

32. Tradition is transmitted orally as well as through written texts. An important criterion for ecumenical hermeneutics, therefore, is that, wherever possible, oral sources as well as written sources need to be utilized. Contemporary emphases in historical studies have produced a number of relevant methodologies by which oral tradition may be identified and understood.

c) Symbols and practices

33. Meaning is encoded and conveyed in non-literary symbols as well as in text and oral tradition. Christian art and music, liturgical gestures or colours, icons, the creation and use of sacred space and time, the cross and crucifixes, and similar Christian symbols or signs, therefore, are important aspects of the way in which the various dialogue partners understand and communicate their faith. Ecumenical hermeneutics needs to be intentional about incorporating this rich, but often neglected, source material for interpretation, communication and reception.

34. As with symbols, Christian practices need to be taken into consideration by those engaged in ecumenical hermeneutics. Even when there is basic theological agreement on such issues as baptism or eucharist, the specific way in which a particular ecclesial community practises baptism and celebrates eucharist in its local and cultural context may be significant hermeneutically.

C. Producing and reading ecumenical documents

35. The criteria of ecumenical hermeneutics apply not only to ecumenical dialogue but also to the production of ecumenical documents which are frequently the result of such dialogue.

36. The production and reading of ecumenical documents, however, also focuses on the dimensions of communication and reception which are part of the hermeneutical process. Faith and Order's experience with BEM indicates that communication and reception is, to a large extent, dependent upon the level of success achieved in the interpretive dimension of ecumenical hermeneutics.

37. The issue of the language used in ecumenical documents is crucial for communication and reception. In respect of biblical terminology, lack of familiarity with a particular term does not appear to be as great a problem as terminology which for some churches has negative connotations.

38. Given that the goal of ecumenical hermeneutics is to facilitate Christian unity as part of the unity of all humankind, the language used in ecumenical documents needs to be as inclusive as possible. This applies especially to language which may marginalize various groups.

39. In light of the clarification made at Montreal regarding "Tradition" and "traditions", the consistent use of this distinction in the publication of ecumenical documents should be encouraged, although it is recognized that in languages which do not have letters in both upper case and lower case, this distinction is more difficult to show visually.

40. The dialogical perspective of ecumenical hermeneutics is operative both in the production and in the reception of ecumenical documents. It is important to recognize, however, that the dialogical perspective functions differently in these two spheres. Ecumenical documents are written jointly in the context of active discussion during which the dialogue partners may question each other with regard to their respective interpretations, challenging each others' positions and laying bare insights that point to convergence. On the other hand, ecumenical documents are read by people who must enter into the dialogue without having been part of the initial discussion and who did not

have the opportunity to present their own views in their own terms or to check their perceptions of the views being presented by others. Moreover, ecumenical documents are often produced through multilateral dialogue, whereas these documents are normally read from the point of view of a single tradition. Consequently, it is crucial that special care is taken by those who produce ecumenical documents to ensure that meaningful exchange is facilitated at all levels by adequate attention to those dimensions of ecumenical hermeneutics which result in accurate communication and reception.

RECOMMENDATIONS

1. We consider it important that the work on ecumenical hermeneutics be continued. As areas for further study we would especially name the following:
–   The interface between cultural diversity and confessional divisions needs further reflection. This could be done on a regional level.
–   The meaning of signs, symbols and practices as non-verbal expressions of the Christian faith should be further explored so that they can be better incorporated as source material for interpretation, dialogue and reception (cf. Part II, paras 33 and 34)
–   Methodologies inherent in traditional biblical interpretations and contemporary critical methodologies (cf. part I, paras 17, 18; part II, para. 23) should be brought into dialogue with each other.
2. Since part II "Working Principles for Ecumenical Hermeneutics" is a completely new draft more work will be necessary after further reflection on the present text. We therefore recommend that in view of the discussion and recommendations of the plenary commission, a small group be asked to redraft this part in order that the whole text may be presented to the board in January 1997. During this process a wider range of responses should also be asked from people who have been involved in various stages of this study.
3. We recommend that the plenary commission be invited to address especially the question as to how "working principles for ecumenical hermeneutics" may help to facilitate reception in the churches (part I, paras 39-42 and part II, para. 40).
4. The study on ecumenical hermeneutics has implications for the ongoing study on ecclesiology and should be taken into account as this study develops. Insights from the ecclesiology study should also be appropriated by the study on ecumenical hermeneutics. This is especially important since both studies deal with the question of authority in the church and how this is exercised. We therefore recommend that the above paper be received by the study group on ecclesiology, and that in the future the two study processes be carried out in correspondence with each other.
5. We recommend that, after the plenary commission has given further direction and the "working principles" have been revised, the whole text be published together with the two case studies on the BEM process by William Tabbernee and William Henn.

Bible Studies

Matthew 18:21-35

GEIKO MÜLLER-FAHRENHOLZ

Whenever the disciples have a fundamental question for Jesus, Peter is the one who asks it. So in Matthew 18, verse 21: "Then Peter came up and said to him: 'Lord, how often shall my brother sin against me, and I forgive him? As many as seven times?' Jesus said to him: 'I do not say to you seven times, but seventy times seven'."[1] This is frustrating. Peter poses a thoroughly sensible question, and the response from the Master is so radical that it borders on the absurd.

How often am I to forgive my brother or sister who sins against me? Is seven times enough? That is rather generous; for "normal" is something quite different. You should forgive at least three times, argued the rabbis of Jesus' time. Even that is quite different from what usually happens between us: I do to you what you do to me.

Is Peter's proposal not a fine example of the "fuller righteousness" claimed in the sermon on the Mount (cf. Matt. 5:20)? Is this not the special effort Jesus asks of his disciples? Surely the world would be a lot better off if this seven-times rule were heeded!

However, Jesus' answer transcends our efforts at a gradual improvement of our practice of forgiveness. The number Jesus uses, whether seven times seven or seventy times seven – I favour the latter – is not decisive. It is the numbering itself that is carried to the absurd.

Nonetheless, when Matthew uses the number seventy-seven, he means to indicate that the message of the Messiah throws a new light on the entire history of humankind. "77" – this number reminds of us Lamech's song of revenge in the mythical origins of time. "I kill a man for wounding me, a young man for a blow. Cain may be avenged seven times, but Lamech seventy-seven" (Gen. 4:23f.). So Jesus appears before us as the "anti-Lamech", the messianic messenger against this ancestor of all despots. Against the incalculable and brutalizing tendencies of retaliation, we encounter here the incalculable power of forgiveness.

This throws into relief the petition on forgiveness which in the Lord's prayer comes immediately after the petition for our daily bread. Why? As we need bread each day, so we need forgiveness each day. For hunger for bread and thirst for water is like hunger for revenge and thirst for retaliation. The ubiquity of revenge indicates how desperately this world needs forgiveness, and so the forgiving work of the Messiah belongs in our everyday life in the same way as daily bread.

"Therefore", in order to understand how incalculable forgiveness is, "the kingdom of heaven can be compared to a king who wished to settle accounts with his servants." So begins the parable we all know. And there we find this "wicked servant" who owes his king ten thousand talents and must now account for it.

We must remember that, in the days of Jesus, "ten thousand" was considered to be the highest number imaginable. And a talent was the highest monetary unit that existed. The entire tax yield of Judah and Samaria amounted to 200 talents. The annual budget of King Herod was 900 talents. Ten thousand talents equalled 50 million dinars, and one dinar was the average payment for a day's work. The king has given this fantastic sum as credit to his servant, and the amazing thing is that the servant has spent it all and has nothing left to pay his debt! The only thing is to fall to his knees and ask for respite, for some patience, because he will pay everything back. What a vain and totally unrealistic promise!

For some inconceivable reason, the king feels deep pity for this servant. He does not throw him into the debtors' prison but forgives him the entire debt. That man has wasted 50 million dinars – and walks away free!

This is a story that defies common sense. But it is *meant* to defy common sense. There is no such king on earth, only in heaven. The parable is there to open our eyes to the kingdom of God. It opens the horizon of mercy in the most fundamental, unfathomable, indeed heavenly way.

As faithful people we have learned that the mercy of God, Creator of heaven and earth, is unfathomable. Fifty million dinars are "peanuts" to the Almighty! But is it so easy to understand the omnipotence of God? I doubt it.

Before we examine this more closely, let us take a look at the servant. How on earth is it possible that someone – and this is not some spendthrift, just a Mr or Mrs Everybody – can waste such a colossal sum? How can someone consume 50 million dinars and stand there, on judgment day, with empty hands? If the attitude of the king gives us an idea of the immeasurable mercy of God, the conduct of the servant gives us an idea of the immeasurable need of each human being.

And now this man, unexpectedly pardoned, walks through the door and encounters a fellow servant who owes him a hundred dinars. He grabs him by the throat and demands the money. Immediately! The fellow asks for some patience, for a little magnanimity so he can have time to find the money. But no! Into prison with the man – there can be no pardon!

The king hears about this, summons his servant and asks him: "You wicked servant! I forgave you your whole debt because you pleaded with me; should you not have had mercy on your fellow servant, as I had mercy on you?" And the king gives him over to the jailers until he has paid his debt. Considering the size of the debt, this will take an eternity.

Then follows the summary which links this parable to Peter's question and the basic dilemma of all followers of Jesus: "So also my heavenly Father will do to every one of you, if you do not forgive your brother from your heart."

Again this throws light on the petition in the Lord's prayer. As the king forgives his servant, at his request, so his servant should forgive his fellow human being who requests forgiveness. What kind of relationship is this? The philosopher Hannah Arendt argues: "Human beings should not forgive because God forgives and because they should act likewise. Rather, it is the other way round. God forgives us our trespasses just as we forgive those who trespass against us."[2] Arendt thinks that human beings need forgiveness because, to quote the words of Jesus, we do not know what we are doing. In other words, we are not able to identify the hurting and "trespassing" aspects of our daily activities and therefore we always rely on the reality of forgiveness. What is called "trespassing" in the petition of the Lord's prayer must not be associated with crime and criminals, at least not primarily. How to deal with this kind of guilt is a different matter for Arendt. She concentrates on the daily offences which "are a consequence of the nature of our activities... All the time they require forgiveness, acquittal and forgetting; for human life could not go on if human beings did not release each other all the time from the consequences of what they have done without knowing what they are doing. It is only this capacity of forgiving which makes it possible for human beings who have been born with the gift of freedom to remain free in this world."[3]

Interesting though this reflection is, I don't think it holds true, and certainly not in the perspective of the parable we are discussing here. It does not speak of an equal relationship but of a profoundly unequal situation. The sum the fellow servant owes his colleague is the 500,000th part of the debt that the servant has to account for with regard to his king. The enormity of the "God-debt" reveals the smallness of human indebtedness. The greatness of the amnesty that the servant experiences makes a magnanimous renunciation of his fellow's debt obvious. This is the salient point of the parable – that the man who has been blessed beyond proportion should himself be so pusillanimous.

To express it classically, the vertical dimension of forgiveness, the mercy that comes from God, renders possible the horizontal dimension of forgiveness among human beings, in other words, the daily practice of mercy.

This way of connecting the vertical with the horizontal is common to many of us. And as we do so, the real challenges of this parable become visible in all their urgency. As I see it, we are faced with two.

Let me return to the 50 million dinars. This unimaginably large sum is to give us an idea of how unimaginably great is God's mercy. However, what happens with something that is unimaginable? It blows our mind and thus becomes unclear, unintelligible, and finally unreal. So are we blind in respect to God's mercy because it is too great, because it transcends the boundaries of our imagination? Like the air we take for granted, so that only when someone tries to strangle us do we realize how precious it is? As air is being polluted we are beginning to appreciate that it is the elixir of life and not a resource to be taken for granted. Likewise, is God's grace too great for our tiny hearts? At all times there have been mystics who have led us into the school of "God-attentiveness" (*Gottesachtsamkeit*). They have said that we must make ourselves naked and empty in our souls so as to provide a little more space for the grace of God that transcends all space. To quote a German mystic whose hymns appear in the hymnal of the Protestant churches, Gerhard Tersteegen says:

> Luft, die alles füllet, drin wir immer schweben,
> aller Dinge Grund und Leben,
> Meer ohn Grund und Ende, Wunder aller Wunder,
> ich senk mich in dich hinunter.
> Ich in dir, du in mir, lass mich ganz verschwinden,
> dich nur sehn und finden.[4]

"Let me disappear entirely"! It is an exercise in self-emptying and receptivity. There is so much we have to learn here! We need to develop the myriad of minutely balanced processes in our body instead of taking it for granted and mistreating it senselessly. Or we might be overwhelmed by the awe-inspiring vastness of innumerable galaxies that travel their course in the universe. They could make us receptive to the wonder of all wonders that surrounds us day by day.

And yet, this is not the decisive thing. If we were only to reflect with awe on the omnipotence of the Creator, we would come to the conclusion that God's forgiveness with regard to us tiny little earthlings would only be a matter of supreme amnesty, a gesture of magnanimity, a whim.

Just three words in the parable protect us from such a misunderstanding: "out of pity". The Greek word *splagchna* refers to the bowels as the place of feelings. Thus we could say: as the king sees his servant in all his helplessness, his stomach aches with love. His heart grieves with compassion. It is the pity of God which helps us understand the cross of the Son of God. It is Jesus dying on the cross which gives us an idea of the wounded mercy of God, of the grief our guilt causes God. It sounds blasphemous, but God suffers from our narrow-minded forgetfulness of God and contempt for our neighbour. We cannot grasp it, but Jesus, our brother and God's Son, understands. Therefore he prays as he is nailed to the cross: "Father, forgive; for they know not what they are doing."

It is the cross that reveals that God remains loving in God's suffering. Forgiveness comes from the pain of the victim, it is rooted in the messianic mercy.

Again, this throws new light on the petition of the Lord's prayer. Forgiveness must be asked for by the perpetrator, but it can only be granted by the victim. We are God's perpetrators, God is our victim. And as God forgives us, we get a glimpse of the immeasurable depth of God's love. And that creates within us the space to offer reconciliation to those who have victimized us.

It is important to note that the prayer of Jesus comes from the perspective of the victim while our common understanding of sin and guilt is oriented towards the perpetrator. To be sure, reconciliation is a tremendous challenge for the perpetrator because it implies the disarming confession of wrong and the denuding and shameful admission of guilt. But let us not overlook the other side! Reconciliation is an equally tremendous challenge for the victim because it entails the painful encounter with suffering endured and the return to the origins of hurt. Why have so many survivors of the Holocaust concealed from their children their years in the death camps? Or, to give a quite different example, why do so many women who have been sexually violated not go to court? Because they cannot bear the thought of returning again and again to the source of their humiliation and the origin of their nightmares.

Let me return to the parable and the second challenge it presents.

One hundred dinars – that is what is at stake between the two servants of the king. Three months' salary, in other words, a debt that can be settled relatively easily. The moral of this story seems obvious: Dear human beings! Compared to the astronomically high debts that you have to God, your earthly debts and liabilities are "peanuts" indeed! Compared to your "God-debts", guilt among humans is trivial.

If we understand the parable this way, does it not turn human injustices into trifling things in an unacceptable manner? There is of course a lot of everyday hurt and offence that might easily be forgiven if we could only be a little more magnanimous and a lot less obstinate. But what about the Shoah, this guilt which transcends all ways of counting? I do not want to use this parable in order to trivialize this guilt.

And what of the debt crisis that squeezes the very breath out of an increasingly larger number of nations, this social and political crime against the rights of coming generations – is this a trifling matter? And the devastation of nature, the destabilization of the climate and all the ecological crimes against the rights of plants and animals, rivers and oceans, land and air – everything or nothing but trifling things, *sub specie aeternitatis*?

To say this would be a wicked misunderstanding! It would turn us into wicked servants of another kind. I believe that the parable does not justify this generalization. It is important to pay close attention to the details. It speaks of a king and his servants, and this shows that it refers directly to the Christian community. This is further emphasized by the context, i.e. Peter's question about forgiveness which he poses on behalf of all the disciples, and the explicit reference to the community of disciples at the end of the parable: "So my heavenly Father will do to every one of you, if you do not forgive your brother from your heart." It is the practice of forgiveness in the community of Christ that is put to the test here.

This turns the parable into an extremely difficult one. There is much disunity among our churches that has become obsolete through theological convergences, for example, the Lima text on baptism, eucharist and ministry. Nonetheless, the divisions between the churches are being reinforced and restated by old historical differences in piety, liturgy and church life. Indeed, should we not ask ourselves how we – who want to be considered servants of one and the same God, as we stand united in our indebtedness to God – dare account for the trifling disputes on matters of doctrine, for church leaders defending their organizational integrity and financial sovereignty, for all the inflexibility regarding liturgical and spiritual forms? How dare we justify these things which burden our lives together and render our common witness to the world obscure and incredible? Should we not realize, with fear and trembling, that we are hurting each other over differences in doctrine and piety that are often centuries old, without finding the word of forgiveness? What is hindering us? What leads us to aggravate our daily differences and to disregard the very great guilt that unites us before the throne of God?

My impression is that we do not think highly enough of the grace of God. We are lacking in gratitude. We are not humble enough. That is why we have mistrusted our mystics again and again, and persecuted those who were – or should have been – our teachers in the awe of God and in humility. We are not sufficiently inspired by the daily grace of God; in other words, we do not train ourselves to live each hour in the Spirit of God, the pneuma of life, the air which fills all things.

Not seven times, but seventy-seven times, says Jesus. That is the messianic challenge. It does not concern a gradual improvement of our practice, but presents the alternative to the despotic reasonings about guilt that have become current since the days of Cain and Lamech's song of revenge. As Christians and churches we are faced with this messianic challenge. That is the yard-stick of our deeds.

Whoever keeps account of each act of forgiveness does not think highly enough of the messianic mercy of God. We are deeply indebted because we have received such abundance of grace. We should remember this each day, and celebrate it together. This would stimulate magnanimity in our dealings with each other. As we remember the pity of God, undeniably powerful in the cross, we would gather the strength to stretch out our arms and take to our hearts those who have sinned against us. Such a daily practice of forgiveness would reflect the sun that rises each day over the just and the unjust, the sun of the merciful justice of God. That would be the alternative for reconciliation in a world that is about to suffocate under Lamech's avenging curse.

I pray that we do our work here in Moshi with the gratitude towards God and the humility towards our fellow human beings that this part of the gospel teaches us. As our hearts are filled with the grace of God, our hands and feet will be ready for the work required of us: to further reconciliation, to resist all forms of hatred, and to manifest the bonds of peace that alone can heal the open sores of our churches and the bitter wounds of the nations.

NOTES

1 Quotes taken from the Revised Standard Version.
2 Hannah Arendt, *Vita activa oder Vom tätigen Leben*, Munich, Piper, 1981, p.234 (my translation).
3 *Ibid.*, p.235.
4 Literally: "Air that fills everything, in which we are floating all the time, ground and life of all things. Sea without ground and limit, wonder of all wonders, I drown myself in you, I in you, you in me, let me disappear entirely, only see and find you."

Luke 24:13-35

TURID KARLSEN SEIM

Christ Jesus, our faith reaches back for the authentic touch of your incarnation. We would touch your hands, look into your face, hear your voice, discover your meaning. We have not seen, O Lord our God, but we believe. Bless us and transform us with your living touch this day. Amen.

Two people are on their way home to their village, Emmaus. They have celebrated the Passover in Jerusalem but, despite the feast, they are sad as they try to come to terms with an event that means nothing but frustration and disappointment to them. We are told that there are "two of them", which means that they have been among the followers of Jesus of Nazareth. One of them is called Cleopas, the other remains unnamed. All we ever learn about them is through this story; they are not among the apostolic celebrities.

Their expectations of the prophet they had chosen to follow had been high. They had eagerly waited for the redeeming moment of victory; they had looked forward to seeing the enemies of their people slain and humiliated; they had hoped for their day of glory, the ultimate manifestation of God's preferential option for them, God's people. But reality had defeated them; their hero of promises had lost his case, and if hope was to survive they would have to look elsewhere. They are leaving Jerusalem, the place of power and glory now turned to misery; they are going home to Emmaus. This is the scream of their return, the hurt of misplaced trust, of faith no longer knowing what to believe.

Walking together

The Emmaus story is presented as a journey. The narrative language of mobility, walking, moving along, proceeding on one's way, learning on the road, reflects a fundamental theme of Luke's writings. In Acts, *he hodos*, "the Way" is a designation, a narrative symbol for the self-understanding of the early Christian community (9:2; 19:9,23; 22:4; 24:14,22). They are a movement, following the divine calling.

In the gospel the long story of what is called the Lukan travel account from 9:51 onwards portrays Jesus acting and teaching as he is constantly on the move from Galilee to Jerusalem, the city of his divine destiny. The disciples are called to be with him on the road towards Jerusalem (8:1-3). Jerusalem later represents a point of departure for the apostolic mission, as the disciples are told to move on to the ends of the earth (Acts 1:8). So there is no abiding place, or perhaps in the end every place becomes a place for his presence to be revealed.

However, the direction of the journey is never insignificant. In the Emmaus episode the two disciples are on the road again. But they are not moving on, following their teacher. They are leaving Jerusalem to return to where they once started. They are moving backwards, not forward, disillusioned and sad with heavy hearts and minds struggling to come to terms with what has happened.

As they search their minds for sense and reason, they talk together, the one not leaving the other to find out for himself. Is this one reason the disciples always travel two by two in Luke, so that they should have this taste of community, for reflection not to take place in isolation? There is in the story an emphasis on the exchange going on between the two, on their dialogue as a common struggle for meaning. They even welcome a stranger into their conversation as he overtakes them on the road. Initially he asks innocent questions, an outsider's questions, making them tell their story. They do so, assuming they possess knowledge he does not have.

A tale of many stories

Their story conveys their disappointment. It is intriguing to see how the three elements all start with hopeful statements. These statements reflect traditional material which elsewhere in the New Testament constitutes positive affirmations of Christian faith, but here leads to expressions of utter frustration. The wonderful life of Jesus is punctured by his tragic death; their hope that he was the one to redeem Israel is replaced by disillusion; the talk of some women that his grave is empty yet angels had proclaimed that he is alive, is undermined by the fact that Jesus himself they did not see.

This report of the two is a meticulous repetition of what has already been told earlier in the same gospel. But still it constitutes a major part of the dialogue in the Emmaus episode. Why is this? Are we likely to forget it? What are we being told that we did not already know? It has been suggested that the last part of their response is an interpolation that interrupts the original correspondence between the account of the disciples and Jesus' response. This may be so in terms of tradition history, but why does it still make excellent sense as it is?

The account of the two in its present form, especially in the last part, is certainly repetitive as it reiterates the morning's events, already reported just before. But it also reveals a confusion and a hesitation as to what and whom to believe beyond what they have experienced themselves and seen with their own eyes. Women may spread the word that he is no longer to be found among the dead but should be sought among the living – but does that change anything? Are not the fanciful imagination and loose tongues of women such that they are never really trustworthy? We know already from vv.10-11 that the eleven and all the other men did not believe what the women told them, dismissing it as idle talk. Even if Peter was sufficiently stirred to go and look for himself and was amazed at the empty tomb, nothing more happened. He went home again – as Cleopas and his friend now are on their way back home. What they have been told may have made them wonder, but it does not restore their faith and hope.

The story they tell their unknown companion on the road shows how they struggle to transcend their own experience by trusting the stories of others whose credibility was not readily accepted. They could always ask for more; they could always refuse to believe what they themselves had not witnessed. In this way the story addresses intriguing questions about how credibility is conceived and authority attained. It should make us re-question whom we are accustomed to trust or willing to believe. What does it take to convince us, to have our story adjusted or reinterpreted, to open our eyes? What does it take – or whom does it take? In the end it seems that only the recognition of the Lord himself brings restoration; he is the one verifiable teacher. But the Emmaus story implies that by his appearance he lends credibility to those whom they had been reluctant to trust. The retelling of the many stories within this one story is a remarkable way of bringing them together, of receiving each other's stories, of reconciling the multiple witnesses into the one witness of a restored and united community.

Return to a common belonging

It is interesting to note how the language of the Emmaus story again and again indicates subtly that both the two on the road and the persons to whom they refer are all part of the same larger group, how they together constitute a "we" (v.13: "two of them"; v.22: "some women of our group"; v.24: "some of those who were with us"). They are still characterized according to this belonging, but they are about to move apart, going to their separate destinations. The two have left the others in Jerusalem, utterly disappointed. When they reach their village they want him to stay with them. But what happens is that he makes them move. They have hardly settled, when they recognize Jesus and return to Jerusalem the very same day.

The road to Emmaus is no longer a one-way street. It becomes a continuation of their travel to Jerusalem; the journey to Emmaus is presented as a journey from Jerusalem and back again. Its geographical focus is Jerusalem, and that is why we are given an estimation of the distance, "about seven miles".

Back in Jerusalem, the two are reunited with the group they had left. Immediately and rather abruptly they learn that the risen Lord has appeared in Jerusalem as well – to Simon. And they respond by telling their story. In this manner both appearances, the Jerusalem story of his appearance to Simon Peter and the Emmaus story of his walk and meal with two otherwise unknown disciples, are merged with the story of the women into a common recognition of the resurrection and presence of the crucified Lord. There is no competition; there is no indication of their previous arguments over which is the greatest – as happened after Jesus had foretold his death in Luke 9:44ff., and similarly at the last meal in 22:24ff. They are mutually giving account, and they mutually receive each other's stories. For the remainder of the events of the gospel of Luke, the Lord appears to the entire community and none of its members are in a privileged position.

Receiving the presence of the Lord

Let us return to the two on their way to Emmaus, responding to the curiosity of an unknown companion. The whole episode so far portrays how they are searching for meaning. The irony of the story is that they cannot possibly understand – not yet. We are told that their eyes "were being kept" from recognizing that the stranger is Jesus himself. The gospels often display the blindness of people, including the disciples, their failure to understand Jesus and his teaching. But it is never expressed like this. This language is unique. It is also highly ironical: when he does appear, the one whom the women and others from their group, despite all the circumstantial evidence, had not seen, they are unable to recognize him. Not until their eyes are opened in the same way they were closed do they know him for who he is.

In the tradition of interpretation the blinding of the disciples has been a puzzle for many: Why are their eyes being kept and by whom? Why does Jesus need to teach his disciples without their recognizing who their teacher is? Some assume that the disciples are blinded by grief, others that they are spiritually blind to the transformed nature of the resurrected body of Christ. Jesus' reproach: "Oh, how foolish you are and how slow of heart to believe all that the prophets have declared", is therefore taken to refer to their closed eyes. But in this story their blindness does not seem to be their inability to get the message right. When the unknown traveller instructs them, there is no indication that they did not listen and learn. Indeed, they later say that their hearts were burning. The blindness affects only their recognition of who he is, and in his reproach Jesus is not holding something against them which is hardly their fault. The passive constructions make clear that their recognition is meant to be suspended; he is being concealed.

An element of suspended recognition and, in some cases, of doubt, even disbelief, occurs in some of the other appearance stories as well. These stories are remarkably devoid of what has been called apocalyptic stage props. There is neither smoke nor fire, not a hint of an earthquake, nothing to indicate a divine epiphany, no breathtaking transfiguration. Instead they tend to underscore ordinariness. However, the appearance stories and the stories of the empty tomb respond to slightly different questions which it is important to keep apart. The empty tomb is open to a variety of explanations, as the stories themselves reveal. But more importantly, the Emmaus story shows that even if they might accept that he is risen, the question of his "whereabouts", his presence, remains: "but they did not see him".

By the irony of their eyes "being kept", the Emmaus story calls off this search for the resurrected, living Christ. He is the one who finds them. The language of this story is undergirded by Luke's understanding of divine necessity (the divine "dei"). It is also consistent with the language of the appearance stories: He comes to them, he shows himself to them. They are not finders of his presence; they are receivers.

The deliberately delayed recognition in the Emmaus story can further be read as an illumination of the same theme as the Thomas incident in the gospel of John which concludes, "Blessed are those who have not seen, and yet have come to believe". The two who complain that the messengers from the empty tomb had not seen him are themselves deliberately kept from recognizing him when he is there. When in the end their eyes are opened to know him, he immediately vanishes from sight.

Revisioning meaning

As readers we are already in the beginning told what the two disciples cannot see, and we keep waiting for the moment when the disciples will discover what we already know. The disciples in the story are allowed an innocence we cannot claim, but this innocence entails confusion and despair and they have in the end to stand corrected. The consolation is in this correction, in the indication of new configurations of familiar material. The greater knowledge we are given as listeners/readers, no longer dealing with the raw facts but with "a connected account", compensates for our later role. At the same time the story constantly continues to confront our vain dreams about immediately convincing success, so that in the end we all stand corrected.

The discrepancy between the disciples in the story and the readers as the narrator's confidants, upon which St John of Damascus was among the first to reflect, is more than a clever literary device, more than the wisdom of hindsight. Theologically it helps to maintain, within the tradition, a permanent struggle for meaning, a glimpse of initial vulnerability and confusion when confronted with events that seemed to be the opposite of the fulfilment they had anticipated. It helps to maintain the search for divine purpose in what seemed to be nothing but disaster and defeat. It admits that multiple interpretations are possible, even reasonable. But it also insists that there are certain events with which we have to come to terms and which determine true meaning. This true meaning is not necessarily the obvious one, it is not readily received and believed. What is incontestably given is the divine imperative and ever puzzling paradox of Jesus' suffering and death as necessary to enter into glory. This represents the hermeneutical key by which doors may be opened.

There are two subtly connected hide-and-seek strategies in the Emmaus story. The identity of their fellow traveller is hidden from the disciples in the story, while we as readers have no excuse for not recognizing him from the beginning. But what is kept from us is a full account of what the two disciples learned from Jesus. The story shows a subtle connection between the unrecognized appearance of Jesus and the hidden meaning of texts.

Later interpreters have constantly tried to help the author out by providing the implied list of proof-texts. The summary style of the verse may be an invitation to do so, but there is no way of deciding whether the suggestions are correct or not. In fact, sometimes interpreters tend to spend more energy supplementing the text with what is not there rather than exploring what is. To listen to the silences of a story means to respect them, not to violate them. We should always recognize the importance of what the scripture text withholds, the artistry of suggestion and implication that deliberately refrains from stating a definitive and exhaustive meaning. When Jesus' speech at this point is curtailed and no longer direct, this may be an indication that there is no fixed solution to our interpretative efforts.

Travelling one day on the local bus in Chicago where I am living this year, I sat next to a little girl. She was solving biblical puzzles, and whenever she had finished one, she made sure she had it right by looking at the back of the book where the correct answers were given. I was impressed by her knowledge and would have liked my students, and indeed myself, to be equally knowledgeable. Indeed, if only it were that simple! We cannot excuse ourselves from accepting the invitation to become interpreters, to explore the scriptures again and again. But there is no complete answer book. The freedom to explore cannot be contained. It is indeed remarkable how comprehensive and therefore vague the reference to Moses and all the prophets is. The point is not the particulars of the evidence as the repeated "all" ("all the prophets and all the scriptures"); it is rather the conviction that in the suffering of Jesus the Messiah the witness of scripture is fulfilled and not contradicted.

The insistence on God fulfilling the promises God has made is a fundamental pattern in the writings of Luke. But it is not primarily a matter of proving exact correspondence so that no doubt is possible. No, the act or event of fulfilment is portrayed as something both old and new, predicted and yet unpredictable. There is not only correspondence, but also an effect of tension. Even for those who believe in the promise, the fulfilment does not necessarily carry self-explanatory and obvious conviction. Interpretative struggle and argument are needed, and the process of accepting fulfilment involves elements of surprise and of overcoming opposition and misinformed expectations, of human objections and prejudices – as, among many others, the story in Acts about Cornelius's conversion demonstrates. In the reception of fulfilment there is always a mixture of facing experience as well as reading scripture. Such reception is in the end only possible by the intervening guidance of the Spirit.

The undergirding concern in the need to make scripture and history meet is theological – in the real sense of that word. It has to do with our understanding of God, of how God remains faithful to Godself. Promise and fulfilment are not a matter of logical exercise, but of seeking a fundamental consistency in God's words and acts. It is an insistence on God's unswerving authority beyond all human manipulation. This is the struggle of Paul throughout Romans, and this is the struggle of Luke. This is our constantly ongoing struggle.

Walking on towards community

The attraction of the Emmaus story has often been its seemingly very simple conclusion: faith is restored because in the end the presence of the Lord is revealed in the breaking of the bread – stated in almost liturgical language. But this would not make sense in the same lasting way if there had not been a complexity already introduced, if the two had not been in dialogue as they were on the road, if the opening up of scripture had not given meaning to the contradictions of their experience, if the unknown traveller had not made their incongruent pieces come together. The risen Christ does not remain with them beyond the moment of revelation. As he vanishes, they move to join the others, to reaffirm community. They are left with the word of God potent with meaning and with the breaking of the bread. They took it as they were given – we may still receive it.

But will we allow it to heal the pain of our fragmented, disconnected witnesses and our competing voices? Will it stop our arguments about which is the greatest? Will we change our direction from moving apart to go to where the others are? Will we give account to each other and share our stories? Will we acknowledge that we are all part of one community as our eyes have been opened to recognize the divine gifts and presence among us – the gracious God being the host of all?

1 Corinthians 12:12-26

ABRAHAM KURUVILLA

There is a saying in India that when good people turn bad they are worse than the ones who were bad from the start. Good things turning bad is no different; a rotten egg gives off a foul smell. The Holy Spirit is God's precious gift to humanity; the gifts of the Spirit empower the church in mission. But the way some Christians exercised the gift of the Spirit in Corinth threatened the very foundations of the church. Paul tries in this text to help the Corinthians see that they have seriously misunderstood the Holy Spirit and its work, and this is at the root of their division. Paul's correctives are aimed at restoring the spiritual health of the Corinthian believers and restoring the unity of the church in Corinth.

There are four aspects of the Corinthian misunderstanding of the Holy Spirit.

1. The "gift" nature of the Holy Spirit and of the charismata was forgotten. Paul reminds the Corinthians that they have all been baptized into the same body by the Holy Spirit and that they have been granted the same Spirit to drink (v.13). The gift of the Holy Spirit is Christ's promise to the church and its fulfilment. It would appear that at least some Christians in Corinth understood this gift and its manifestations as a reward they had earned from God, possibly for the steadfastness of their faith. Others might have thought of it as a reward for their moral excellence. Like all aspects of the saving mystery of God the Holy Spirit is not "earned". The Spirit and its manifestations are granted to the church and its members despite our human frailties and not because we have overcome them. In terms of moral excellence, some at least in Corinth were guilty of "immorality not even the heathen would be guilty of" (5:1). If God were to wait till we had achieved moral excellence before he granted us the gift of the Spirit, we would never receive it. The fact is that he has touched us in our baptism through his Spirit and evoked a response in us. The good work he has started in us continues. Our struggle against sin continues on the strength of divine grace, and it is as we struggle that we are granted the Spirit as a gift to further the cause of God's kingdom and to testify to its power. Notions of earning the Spirit as a reward would make us proud and arrogant, lead us to belittle others and eventually to our own spiritual death. The acknowledgment that the Holy Spirit is a gift granted to us despite our frailties saves us from that.

2. Paul's presentation of the importance of every organ for the whole body is very interesting. The necessity of different organs and the impossibility of an organ standing apart from the body are very clearly portrayed in vv.14-20.

This argument is proof that some people in Corinth did not value their membership in the church. They had a sense of self-sufficiency; their baptism was a private affair between them and God. The gift of the Spirit was a personal gift which they could exercise as they pleased; for their growth and development as believers they did not feel indebted to anyone. In the exercise of the Spirit and in the daily discharge of their responsibilities they did not feel accountable to anyone. They were exhibiting a false sense of autonomy.

In fact we have no Christian existence apart from our belonging to the church. Most of us were born into Christian families. It is through careful nurture, Sunday school, youth groups, the ministry, etc. that we were enabled to confess Jesus as Lord. Our parents took us to church and we would have been encouraged to join in family prayers. It is in the faithful exercise of Christian nurture by the church and the family that faith is handed down through generations. Those of us who are first-generation Christians came to believe because we encountered the gracious love of God through the preaching, teaching or diakonia of someone. That someone had been sent by a church and belongs to a church. For our confession "Jesus is Lord" we are indebted to a whole lot of people across the world. For our continued confession of Jesus as Lord we will need the fellowship and support of other members of the body of Christ. For baptism into Christ and the receiving of the gift of the Spirit we need to be grateful to the church. Unfortunately in Corinth there were many who wanted to discard the church and say, "I believe because I have chosen to believe. I have received the Spirit because God is pleased with me."

We find predecessors in Corinth for the radical individualists of today. They, as well as we, are invited to see the truth, that for what we are today we are indebted to the community of believers, past and present. The exercise of our gifts today makes sense only as part of the body, the church.

3. As we read through verses 21-26 we notice that Paul is at pains to show that organs which seem unimportant are in fact very important, even indispensable. In the Corinthian church those who exercised less spectacular gifts seem to have been valued less, hence Paul's corrective. Once we understand the gifts as a merit the next logical step is to ask who has more merit. The gifts that God granted to fragile humans are being used to create a hierarchy. They have degenerated to become the source of competition and rivalry. The disciples of Christ during the days of Jesus began to argue as to who was greater among them. The Corinthian Christians in the apostolic tradition are carrying on the debate; the difference is that the cause of argument is the gift of the Spirit itself.

Once the hierarchy is set up Christians cease to see each other as brothers and sisters. As two believers encounter each other they soon learn to ask who is greater. For those who have not learned the primary lesson that human worth is in making ourselves available to others in service, even the gift of the Holy Spirit becomes a new source of jealousy and quarrel.

A church which sees the gifts of the Spirit hierarchically is a loser. Some think that they are more important and powerful than others, and thus they become insecure. Tomorrow someone else might become more important; a brother or a sister is no more a brother or sister – they are potential rivals to be controlled and managed. On the contrary, those who think that their gifts are less important move to the margins. They discount their gifts and discount themselves. Vast resources of the church remain unutilized or underutilized. Paul's invitation to all who think of themselves as greater than others is to stop attributing their gift to themselves and learn to give thanks to God for it. It is also an invitation to give up sleepless nights worrying about who is the greatest in the church. That would liberate us to love and serve the world. Paul is also inviting those who think of their gift as unimportant and hence of themselves as unimportant to recognize their gift. Not recognizing their gift amounts to not recognizing the giver, God himself. It is as we recognize our gifts and give thanks to God that we are liberated to love and serve the world.

4. We noted earlier that there was a false sense of sufficiency among believers in Corinth. This acted as a barrier to seeing themselves as part of a larger whole. In verses 14-20 Paul is at pains to help the Corinthians see that an organ of the body, however good and effective, is functional only as a part of the body; in isolation it has no worth or significance. Elsewhere Paul has also used the analogy of stones that form a building.

Each believer, while important in God's design, is incomplete without the others. However, the incompleteness will not be experienced without a vision of the larger whole. A brick would feel complete in itself in the absence of the vision of a building. In the creation of this larger whole there is need of diverse components, a need best illustrated in the metaphor of the body. In the body the diversity of organs is necessary for it to function properly. It is the loss of this vision of the larger whole that is a hindrance to the ecumenical movement. A large number of believers and churches are happily reconciled to the divided state of the church, because they have no sense of incompleteness within.

It is the vision of a larger whole and the sense of incompleteness within, which helps us welcome the differentness of the other. This differentness is then not a threat, but on the contrary opens up the possibility of completion and fulfilment. When God created Eve out of the rib of Adam and brought her before him, his immediate reaction was, "this is now the bone of my bones and the flesh of my flesh". She was certainly different; but that was not a threat to Adam for she complemented him and the two formed a larger whole, the human community. The invitation from Paul to the Corinthians is equally well an invitation to us. We are called to be aware of the incompleteness of the human person without a human community. The denominations are challenged to be aware of an inner poverty when isolated from the rest of the body of Christ. To seek and realize the wholeness we may have to give up some of our idiosyncrasies, some of our "individual freedom", or rework our sense of identity. When we discover the wholeness of the whole we would realize that the "freedom" and "liberty" we enjoyed were in fact an impoverishing slavery.

* * *

We have noted four misperceptions the Corinthians had about the Holy Spirit and the gifts of the Spirit, and also looked at some of the sad consequences of these misperceptions and the way out indicated by St Paul through the use of the metaphor of the body. We are indeed directed to the way of genuine communion in the body of Christ. In verse 26, Paul goes on to bring out two blessings of genuine communion.

First, when we are part of the body and aware of it the pain experienced by one organ is shared by the whole body; it is not merely the pain of one organ. In local congregations people may suffer from physical or mental illness. There may be pain due to family conflicts or divorce. In some parts of the world where Christians are a minority there may be prejudice towards and persecution of Christians. In some denominations there may be strife and conflict so bad that the public witness of the church is damaged. Paul reminds us that the pain of an organ is the pain of the body. There is consolation for the suffering part that it is shared by the body, the body as a whole activates itself to support and strengthen the suffering part. The degree to which we sense the pain of the parts is in fact a measure of our ecumenical commitment. It is one of our great privileges that we are called to share in the sufferings of the body of Christ. Through our preaching and teaching, social service and evangelism, we are responding to the needs of others. This response becomes most significant when we pray for those who suffer elsewhere and feel the pain of their suffering in our own psyche. This is the privilege of a church in koinonia with the church catholic.

The second blessing is that we are able to rejoice and give glory to God for the gifts bestowed on others. When we are guided by the spirit of self-sufficiency and the resulting competition, the gifts of the other are a threat to us. For we begin to worry whether he/she is going to outdo us. When we truly belong to the body the gifts granted to the other are a resource of the body in which every member of the body rejoices. The inward threat and insecurity are cast out. The freedom of recognizing the other without fear of losing one's place in the church is discovered. That discovery is indeed one in which we will wholeheartedly rejoice and give thanks to God: it is the cornerstone of koinonia.

We live in a fragmented world. In that world the spirit of unity granted to us is itself distorted to worsen the fragmentation. We are invited by Paul to be aware of what we in our sinfulness do to the most Holy Spirit. Inspired by the Spirit of unity he calls us to the one koinonia, the koinonia of the body of Christ within which we share in the sufferings of others, individual believers and believing communities. May we by the grace of God enter into the joy of that koinonia.

Acts 15:1-35

OLIVIA WESLEY

J.G. Saxe concluded his poem "The Blind Men and the Elephant" with these words:

> And so these men of Hindustan
> Disputed loud and long
> Each in his own opinion

Exceeding stiff and strong
Though each was partly in the right
And all were in the wrong.

There were six of them, all blind and each in his blindness giving verdict from his observation of a single part of what the elephant was. One came against the side, another the trunk, yet another the tusk, the knee, the ear and the tail. So indeed all were in the right partly and at the same time all were wrong. What would give a composite description if they were to stay blind would have been a synthesis of all their points of view; that would mean each man was making a compromise, because the elephant is not divided.

And so is Christianity. Christ is not divided but experienced at various levels. Hermeneutics should be a synthesis of our understanding of Christ's good news.

As we move around and interact, we come across people with different thoughts, experiences, ideas, opinions and backgrounds. We sometimes wonder when people with the same background, family ties, religious, ethnic backgrounds react to situations in quite a different way to what we would expect.

From time to time, Christians are faced with situations wherein they have to determine right from wrong. We set our own standards, forgetting the standards Christ himself has set. But "let every man be fully persuaded in his own mind" (Rom. 14:5).

It is in the light of this that I want us to look at the controversy that arose, which brought about the meeting of the Jerusalem council.

The problem arose between the Aramaic Christians from Jerusalem and Paul and Barnabas in Antioch. It all came as a result of Paul, Peter and other Christians baptizing uncircumcised Gentiles who had received the gospel. Apart from the problem of circumcision, there was heated debate as to whether Gentiles had to adopt Jewish Christian customs before they were baptized. The Jewish Christians believed it was right to impose their own customs and culture as well as their religion on the Gentile Christians.

We need to ask ourselves some questions: Is that what Jesus wanted? Does he impose his own culture and customs on we who follow him? Has he just taught us what the Christian life is all about? What is the road to salvation? These and many other questions come to mind when we think of our divided Christian community. Faith and Order is trying to bring about a visible unity – that is why we are all here.

Let us think, and with the vision that we have for the future strive to make that visible koinonia possible.

Despite the fact that there was a misunderstanding between the two groups, there was one common element which should have brought both groups together. The cohesive factor was the joy in knowing that Gentiles were turning to God. In the case of Cornelius, the whole house received the baptism of the Holy Spirit even before water baptism, and the people spoke in tongues. There was joy when Peter recounted to those of the circumcision party how God himself sent the Holy Spirit to the Gentiles.

So our God has the last say, not us. We have to give joy for those who turn to Christ. Jesus himself said "I came not to call the righteous but sinners to repentance", "for those who are whole need not a physician but those who are ill" (Luke 5:32,31).

It is a pity that that cohesive factor of joy in the Gentiles accepting Christ was missed, as that would have been a binding element for both groups. The koinonia would not have been lost. The Christian community, be it Hellenistic or Aramaic-speaking, should praise God for an extended Christian community. "There is joy in heaven for every sinner that turns to God."

Peter supports the action of Paul and Barnabas. Peter had reason to do this. God had made it known to Peter "not to call anything He had made common or unclean". The Gentiles therefore had a place in the salvation history of mankind.

Peter played a facilitating role to link both sides. He was to get them to understand each other and bring about a unity. Again this is our role in Faith and Order, in the ongoing dialogue – our interpretation of scripture. Just as the two groups understood the issue differently, so Christians in different denominations interpret scripture in different ways. Can we compare ourselves to the six blind men of Hindustan who described the elephant in different ways? They were not all wrong and at the same time not all right, but there is a linking factor.

At the end of their deliberations those present had agreed that Gentiles need not be circumcised. This was God himself welcoming the Gentiles. They were now part and parcel of God's people. Can you stop God from choosing those he wants? When God accepts he accepts unconditionally – so circumcision is not a condition.

But some conditions were eventually made – probably in order not to offend the Jewish Christians there. Gentile Christians were to keep some Jewish regulations: "they were to abstain from pollutions of idols, fornication, from things strangled and from blood" (Acts 15:20; for blood, see Lev. 17:8-13). This was a compromise. It had to be accepted for the work of the church to progress.

There are many times when Christians disagree but if we "preach Christ" and we believe in his headship, then we must disagree to agree. There must be a compromise – a visible unity.

In our interpretation of scripture, we need to be open to new truths. Whatever truth we may have is relative. Only God is absolute. Truth is like the horizon, the more you move towards it, the more it evades you. So no one person or a group of persons has a monopoly of the truth. One view can complement and enrich the other.

I pray that God will help us to understand his word and interpret with richness all that may exalt his name, bring unity and peace to all men.

Let us pray: "Help us Lord to have a better understanding of You, so that we may reach out to your people who do not know you, bring them into your fold, so that your Name may be glorified and your word spread throughout the world. This we ask for your Holy Name's sake. Amen."

Hebrews 9:22 and Ephesians 2:11-22

GEIKO MÜLLER-FAHRENHOLZ

You know the tragedy. The well-respected families of Capulet and Montague are divided by an old feud. No one remembers its origin, but there is "low-intensity warfare" between the two families, nourished by all kinds of mischievous provocations. But young Juliet Capulet and young Romeo Montague fall in love with each other. The enmity between their families prevents them from living out their love together, and drives them early to their graves. Their death reconciles the two families. As they look on their dead children Juliet's father says to Romeo's father: "O, brother Montague" – at long last he recognizes his hereditary foe as his brother! – "give me thy hand." The two fathers enter into a covenant with each other to build a monument for their children. They establish the memorial of that love which ended their enmity. The parents become reconciled once their children – "poor sacrifices of our enmity" (Capulet) – have met their death.

So it goes, again and again. Shakespeare's tragedy is a piece of world literature because what happened in Verona occurs everywhere in the world. The fathers' fury is the children's grave. It is the death of the innocent children which brings the violence of the guilty parents to an end.

On Sunday, 15 September 1963, four young girls died in 16th Street Baptist Church in Birmingham, Alabama. They were at Sunday school when white racists threw a bomb into their church. It was by no means the first bomb thrown into a church of black Christians. The death of these four innocent children, however, brought the nation to their senses. From that Sunday on large numbers of white Americans who had remained passive for so long realized that racism is an evil that needs to be combated.

But this raises the shocking question, must it take the death of innocent children to quiet the rage and hatred within us? Are we really prepared to offer the greatest sacrifice for the malice and violence of our hearts? Are we ready, again and again, to offer that which is dearest to us, our children, our own flesh and blood, at the altar of our enmities? Do we really need to make these sacrifices to satisfy our hidden fury? Will we only come to our senses when our latent violence is soaked with the blood of our children?

You may think these questions are abominable barbarism. We like to think we have gone beyond that level of primitive culture when warring people would sacrifice their prisoners, when innocent children, virgins or young men were offered up to placate the gods? Indeed, it would be hard to find this kind of sacrificial ritual these days. But does this mean that the time of sacrifices has ended? You know as well as I do that this it not the case.

Most nations are still prepared to send their young men – and sometimes their young women – to war against presumed enemies. In spite of today's technology military service carries with it an aura of sacrifice; at least, official patriotic rhetoric is very quick to infer this.

The search for scapegoats to be sent into the wilderness if need be is commonplace even today. The media feed on it. They elevate famous people – politicians, members of royal families, celebrities from film and sport – to the status of "stars", that is, they are placed above us in the heavens so that they can be sent to hell, should the need arise. We have seen this only recently at the European soccer championships and the Olympic games in Atlanta. In today's secularized world these sacrificial rituals take place in public, especially in the arenas of politics and entertainment, and not least in that of sports.

"Without the shedding of blood there is no forgiveness of sins", says the Letter to the Hebrews (9:22). So is the Bible confirming that people will not come to their senses until blood has been shed?

Among all the New Testament writings the Letter to the Hebrews is the most deeply rooted in the Jewish faith. Therefore it tries to show the uniqueness of God's revelation in Christ in reference to the sacrificial theology of Israel. There the concept of atonement plays a central role. Since human life cannot please God because it is disfigured by sin and aberration, it requires expiation. This can only be brought about by precisely described rituals at which appropriate means, in other words sacrifices, are offered, conducted by priests appointed for this purpose and endowed with specific privileges. This priestly group requires special expiating rituals for its own atonement; the more serious the transgression, the more important the atonement, and the purer the sacrifice. In this framework of concepts the Letter to the Hebrews describes Christ not only as the immaculate, unsurpassable offering, but at the same time as the immaculate, eternal and unsurpassable priest:

> For it was fitting that we should have such a high priest, holy, blameless, unstained, separated from sinners, exalted above the heavens. He has no need, like those high priests, to offer sacrifices daily, first for their own sins and then for the sins of the people; he did this once and for all when he offered up himself (7:26f.).

What is happening here? Is the fatal cycle of violence and sacrifice enforced because it is placed within God? Do we have here ultimate ratification or radical devaluation? I think Christ's self-offering on the cross is not the transcendental justification and sanctioning, but rather the transcendental cancellation of sacrifice. The very idea of sacrifice is carried to the absurd. Since it is impossible to think of a greater sacrifice for God than the Son of God, that is God-self, the possibility of further sacrifices is annulled. It makes no sense at all to want to please God with offerings of plants, animals or even human beings since God's Son is the ultimate sacrifice. Similarly the institution of priests has become obsolete; for it is no longer possible or indeed necessary to place special people with their rituals of expiation between human beings and God; the Son is at the right hand of God to intercede for us.

Thus the possibility of sacrifice is taken away from humans and lifted up to God. With the death of Jesus on the cross the time of sacrificing has ended. At least, that is our message, our raison d'etre in the discipleship of Jesus Christ.

Why has God put an end to the time of sacrificing? Because he has taken enmity and violence away from creation.

In order to understand that better, let us look at a passage from Ephesians (2:11-22). While the Letter to the Hebrews is addressed to Christians rooted in the Jewish faith, the Letter to the Ephesians speaks to people who are at home in the Greco-Roman world. They are "pagans"; they are separated from Jewish Christians by a decisive ritual fault, in that they are not circumcised. This indicates that they do not belong to the history of the covenant that God has made with Israel: they are strangers, excluded, exiled. They are "without God in the world" – a horrible phrase, for when you are without God, then you are God-less, you are far away from God, and no way and no offering will overcome this enmity.

So here we have the fundamental critique of all human attempt to secure the nearness of God through sacrifice. When God does not come to us, then we are without hope; for we cannot get close to God on our own behalf. When God does not enter into covenant with us, all our striving is in vain, even if we send countless sacrifices up to the heavens. When God is not with us we must remain without God in the world.

But now God is in the world. In Christ Jesus God has taken on our flesh and blood. Christ has authenticated this unconditional and uncompromising nearness to the point of sacrificing himself on the cross. And through this deed those who were far off have been brought near. Strangers have been turned into relatives, foes into friends. "In the blood of Christ", says verse 13. The blood of Christ has not acquired its saving strength because it placates an angry God. (What a concept of God it would be to think that God must saturate himself with the blood of his Son! It is true, however, that the atonement-theology of Anselm of Canterbury leaned in that direction.) No, the blood of Christ is the source of our salvation because it shows us that God does not need a sacrifice in order to love creation. God draws all and everything into God's covenant out of free love.

Therefore our text says tersely: "He is our peace." And unfolds it. He has abolished the law with all its commandments and ordinances. That means all the lofty religious concepts, the complicated rituals and rules, the taboos and cults, all the attempts of human beings to pave a way to God are rendered superfluous and unmasked in all their uselessness. All the attempts to overcome the enmity between the human being and God by way of bloody sacrifices have been revealed as what they have always been: absurd, futile, disastrous experiments in self-made salvation. He is our peace; for he has taken enmity itself away from creation. That is the best news we could have, not only in reference to our relationship with God, but also in our relationship as human beings and our community with all creatures. There are no more enemies! There is no more reason to be suspicious, to fight each other, to go to war, to fear and hate the other. There is no reason any more for violence.

Peace – four times this word is mentioned in those few verses. What is peace? Peace comes to us as liberation and as inhabitation. It is liberation from enmity and incorporation into the household of God. More precisely, we are called to become part of God's home, stones of the holy temple.

We are within the temple, not outside it. We need no high priests and no sacrifices, no scapegoats and sacrificial lambs. We are linked with God and reconciled "in the Spirit". And here we find a concept which has become for me central in recent years: *oikodomé*. In the pneuma God dwells in the midst of God's creatures. God builds a home, a *katoiketerion*, and we, God's creatures, are called to let ourselves be built into this household, to be remembered and incorporated into this building process. So we are talking about incorporation, integration, inhabitation.

There is no space here to unfold the relevance of this "oikodomical" approach for the ecumenical movement. We all know that our epoch is suffering greatly under the paradigm of domination which has been typical of our times. The domination of human beings over the earth is being revealed with increasing clarity as ecocidal and, therefore, suicidal. Ecological research has taught us what we should have learned a long time ago from indigenous peoples and their "nature religions", namely that we humans are but a part of the web of life on this planet and that our life as a species depends on our capacity to bring our life-forms and needs into equilibrium with the needs of all other species. In this context we realize the importance of the paradigm of inhabitation for the peace of the earth and all its creatures. It is this "ecodomical" approach that renders our movement genuinely ecumenical; it helps us to discover the relevance, not only as a means for interchurch relations, but in cosmic, political and economic contexts. At the end of this century which many have called "ecumenical" we are still very much at the beginning; for we are only beginning to explore the outline of a paradigm of inhabitation.

Why do we find it so difficult to take this road of inhabitation which God has paved for us in Christ Jesus, with joy and determination? The obstacles are not confessional constraints or other forms of "church politics", but are deeply rooted in our human nature and history. We are products of a history of violence, we are, to quote Ephesians, the children of "enmity". Is this an ontological judgment? Are we condemned to live out the potential of violence which accumulates within us outside times of war, or at least to seek satisfaction in sacrificial rituals?

At the end of his disturbing book *Violence and the Sacred*, René Girard summarizes his thesis:

> There is behind seemingly extreme differences a unity of all mythologies and all cultures, something encompassing all cultures be they religious or antireligious. This unity of all unities is dependent on one single mechanism, constantly disponible because constantly misunderstood, guaranteeing spontaneously the one-mindedness within community whenever it turns against the reconciling victim.[1]

So Girard's starting point is that wherever human beings have to live together violence builds up. This violence must be diffused in a process of catharsis if it is not to blow up human community. "The only task is to protect those who live together from their own violence," says Girard.[2] And since every catharsis needs its *catharma*, that is, the purifying and atoning medium, human communities need "cathartic or reconciling objects" time and again. In former times these were animal or human sacrifices. In the classic Greek period those rituals were replaced by acting out tragedy on stage. This is for me the first step in the process of transferring sacrificial rituals to the level of mimetic repetition, at the end of which we find it can be manipulated by the electronic media.

The cathartic victim plays an important, though often unacknowledged, role in criminal justice, too. Gil Bailie has written a disturbing and illuminating book, called *Violence Unveiled: Humanity at the Crossroads.*[3] In it Bailie describes the dangerous fascination of the execution of a criminal. The executed person may well be a heinous murderer, but it appears that for many people that criminal serves as a welcome sacrifice for the murderous violence they harbour within themselves.

To be sure, in our secularized societies no one seriously believes that the pure victim exists and hence that "sacred violence" could absorb and pacify the destructive violence in our cultures. But this does not mean that such mechanisms do not exist any more. "Cultural violence that does not climax in catharsis will result in mimesis," says Bailie,[4] in other words, it will be repeated constantly. The *katharma*, the medicine, turns into a "contagion", in other words poison. The cathartic object that was meant to liberate from violence is turned into the contagious object which intensifies violence.

We may well react with scepticism to Girard's rigid generalizations, but this should not prevent us from admitting that Girard and others subscribing to his approach, like Bailie, can help us achieve a clearer understanding of the power of violence in our midst. I find it perfectly acceptable to speak of the "mimetic fascination" of violence as a mechanism which characterizes our time and is re-enacted repeatedly in the media. It requires considerable courage to face this violence that is latent within us, and to acknowledge its unruly mimetic fury. However, this perception helps us to grasp the full meaning of the New Testament insisting on Christ as the "turning of the times" and the beginner of a new humanity. We understand more clearly the cosmic radiance and universal actuality of Christ. In the most radical manner he has done away with this widespread cultural mechanism of dealing with latent violence. Ephesians 2:16 says that he reconciles us with God and with each other in one body, through the cross, thereby bringing the hostility to an end (in literal translation: "thereby killing the hostility within himself"). How does this happen?

The mighty God does not claim an innocent sacrifice, but becomes the sacrifice in God-self. The death on the cross qualifies incarnation. God becomes a human being, but not just any sort of human being. Rather, God goes all the way to the most extreme loneliness, the loneliness of the victim. God empties himself and takes the form of a servant, as it is said in Philippians, all the way to the death on the cross (Phil. 2:7ff.). What we earlier called God's inhabitation in creation is now qualified more precisely. The ending of enmity is revealed as the devaluation of the spiral of violence and victimization.

That is what has entered the world in Christ: the most radical change of perspective imaginable. God does not claim to receive sacrifices, God claims to be the final sacrifice. That is the great mystery in God's revelation in Jesus as the Christ.

Therefore, the first words the crucified speaks from the cross, according to Luke's gospel, are: "Father, forgive, for they do not know what they do." They didn't know it then just as we don't know it today. Again and again we humans think that the Messiah should have the power to liberate himself from the cross, to step down. God's Son should be free from suffering. We don't know what we are doing. We think we understand God when we continue the ungodly game of violence and victimization. But the cross is the correction of a universal error: the man from Nazareth is God's Son because he accepts the cross, because he carries the pain, tolerates the shame, enters the death of the God-forsaken one.

In the light of this mystery Christians have with shock identified Christ in what they read in the book of Isaiah: "Yet on himself he bore our sufferings, our torments he endured, while we counted him smitten by God." But this is exactly the error. He is not smitten by God, rather God-self is smitten. That is the fundamental change, the end of all sacrifices: "The chastisement he bore is health for us and by his scourging we are healed" (Isa. 53:4ff.). That is what Ephesians is testifying: on the cross Christ kills the enmity, he kills death and death's violent might.

That is the basis for the gospel of peace for all human beings. In the last resort, this is the reason we are gathered here.

Let me end these reflections by addressing two aspects of our situation, our practical life and our worship life.

A few days ago I read that a church leader from the Pacific had said: "Each time I beat my wife, she should be grateful to me; for this brings her a step closer to salvation."[5] That is a cynical perversion of the cross! This fellow Christian from the Pacific makes his wife the object of his violence and gives this "ritual" Christological justification. No, Christ has not taken it on himself to be the victim of human violence in order for us to continue this ungodly game of victimization, but for us to have peace and make peace. So Christianity is challenged time and again to bear out in practical life what Christ has revealed: We are sisters and brothers, we are one family of God, we will not allow ourselves to be divided into rulers and vassals, lords and servants, priests and sacrifices. What Jesus has suffered on the cross he has suffered once and for all. That is the soteriological exclusivity of his death. And so Christians are once and for all restrained from making others the object of their violence and from beatifying innocent suffering. We are called to be a koinonia of the liberated, a community in which all have equal dignity and value; the gifts are different, but the dignity of being called God's children is indivisible!

Such a koinonia sees itself as an ecodomical community, a constructive, creative, edifying fellowship of friends in the service of life and in the struggle against the manifold forms of violence that turn so many people's lives into hell. Therefore we will belong to those who combat violence against women and children. The reports coming out of the Ecumenical Decade of Churches in Solidarity with Women testify to the amount of daily violence against women and children.

But that will not be enough. Clearly, domestic violence is a mimetic repetition of public and economic violence. We are in a time that no longer considers wars and warlike conflicts to be deplorable aberrations, but makes them presentable. And therefore we in Faith and Order will have to address ourselves more forcefully to these manifold forms of structural violence and the increasingly devastating victimization of the poor. The paradigm of inhabitation implies struggling against the fatal tendencies of "enmification" and for the "dehostilization" of our situations; for this determines not only the physical survival of humankind, but the future of the human being and the God-given dignity of creation.

And finally, what is the significance of overcoming victimization for our worship life? That is a tricky question; for all too often and for far too long Christian worship bordered on rituals of sacred violence in which the crucified was offered as the immaculate *katharma* for the sins of the world. However, when the message of the crucified consists in annulment of sacrificing then the central dimension of our worship life can be nothing else but the celebration of liberation and the feast of inhabitation, doxology and thanksgiving. In a word: *eucharistia*.

The Letter to the Ephesians emphasizes that for Christ's sake we are to regard ourselves as parts of the *katoiketerion* of God. So we are all part of the doxological community. That has profound ramifications for the significance we attribute to the various functions in worship. The functions must be understood as emanations of the koinonia of the *familia Dei*, not in opposition to the *laos Theou*.

The eucharistic dimension of our worship life is rooted in the anamnesis, that is, the constant remembering and appropriation of the mystery of God's love: "In the night he was betrayed, he took bread..." This act of remembering is the constant correction of our infidelity and the many forms of betrayal against the unity of God's children which we keep committing. What happens in the eucharist is the mimetic repetition of our liberation. Therefore, I am deeply convinced that we can only celebrate the eucharist together, as an expression of our humility and our gratitude. Since Christ has torn down the walls between us, we are not permitted to continue building walls in the eucharist. Since Christ is the end of our enmities, the eucharist must be the celebration of our uniting and the feast of friends. This is the way to become receptive for the energies of the Holy Spirit so that it can embrace us with the "bonds of peace", as stated in the famous fourth chapter of Ephesians. There we read:

> ...until we all attain to the unity of the faith and of the knowledge of the Son of God, to mature manhood, to the measure of the stature of the fullness of Christ; so that we may no longer be children, tossed to and fro and carried about with every wind of doctrine, by the cunning of men, by their craftiness in deceitful wiles. Rather, speaking the trust in love, we are to grow up in every way into him who is the head, into Christ, from whom the whole body is joined together... So the body grows and is built up in love (4:13-16).

NOTES

1 Page 441 (the German version), translation mine.
2 *Ibid.*, p.429.
3 New York, Crossroad, 1995.
4 *Ibid.*, p.91.
5 J. Jäger-Sommer, "Braucht der Christengott das Menschenopfer?", *Publik Forum*, 12, 1996, p.51.

Philippians 2:1-16

MANAS BUTHELEZI

The proposed theme for this passage in Philippians is "one church for the service of others".

When I speak of *liturgy*, I am referring to the type of text material used, rather than suggesting that Paul touches on the subject of liturgy as such. Part of this pericope, verses 6-11, is very often regarded as an extract from liturgical material. In his writings Paul seems to quote as freely from the Old Testament as he does from documents apparently used for confessional, catechetical and liturgical purposes. This passage is an example of the latter.

The worship of God *(leitourgia)* should be the point of departure for theology and ethics. Authentic theology and genuine ethics are the true works *(erga)* of the people of God *(laos tou Theou)*. They are the "liturgy after the liturgy". A theologian and political activist who is not motivated by the worship and adoration of God may just as well redefine himself as a philosopher of religion or a secular philanthropist. To what extent do worship texts and intensive worship experience play a role in some of what I would call *issue theologies*, e. g. Black theology, feminist theology, theology of development, theology of ecology, etc.? One can raise the same question for theology in general. Paul is teaching us a lesson here. The Christological and ethical elements of Philippians 2:6-11 are woven in liturgical material.

This whole passage includes one of the most famous New Testament hymns. In the original Greek the hymn appears as five three-line stanzas. Apart from the Psalms, we have no existing collection of such hymns. On the one hand, there are only references to a hymn which was sung on a particular occasion, without a record of the hymn itself, as appears in Mark 14:26: "And when they had sung a hymn, they went out to the Mount of Olives" (RSV). On the other hand, we find literary forms of the biblical text which suggest a hymn structure, as in verses 6-11 of our text. There seem to have been at least three types of liturgical music: psalms, hymns, and spiritual songs or odes. "Let the word of Christ dwell in you richly, teach and admonish one another in all wisdom, and sing psalms and hymns and spiritual songs *(psalmois hymnois odais pneumatikais)* with thankfulness in your hearts to God" (Col. 3:16). This has a parallel in Ephesians 5:18-19: "And do not get drunk with wine, for that is debauchery; but be filled with the Spirit, addressing one another in psalms and hymns and spiritual songs, singing and making melody to the Lord with all your heart."

It can safely be assumed that *psalms* here refers to the psalter which was part of the liturgical tradition of the early church. *Hymns* were musical texts specially composed for Christian worship. St Augustine gave one of the earliest definitions of a hymn: "A hymn is a song containing praise of God. If you praise God, but without a song, you do not have a hymn. If you praise anything, which does not pertain to the glory of God, even if you sing it, you do not have a hymn. Hence a hymn contains the three elements: song and praise of God."[1] The lyrics of the hymn were essentially summaries of the faith, similar to those used for confessional and catechetical purposes. The Philippian hymn is the best example of this. It is a summary of the cosmic history of salvation through Jesus Christ.

The obvious interpretation of *spiritual songs or odes* is that this refers to popular songs sung for general, spiritual edification; they are not necessarily crafted for liturgical purposes. Philo seems to suggest another meaning when, in one of his statements, he cautions that "praises and hymns should not be in actual sounds but sung in our minds". The spiritual odes were probably melodic alleluias and other chants of a jubilant or ecstatic character, richly ornamented.[2] There is also the suggestion of wordless jubilation. In this regard Augustine said: "One who rejoices does not speak words, but it is a sort of sound without words, since it is the voice of a soul poured out in joy and expressing, as best it can, the feeling, though not grasping the sense... Filled with too much joy, he cannot explain in words what it is in which he delights... and whom does jubilation benefit but the ineffable God."[3]

Ecclesiologically, Paul appeals for *church unity*: "So if there is any encouragement in Christ, any incentive of love, any participation in the Spirit, any affection and sympathy,..." (2:1). Already in the first chapter he has referred to signs of disunity within the congregation. Even though several people preached about the same Jesus Christ, the representatives of different factions in Philippi failed to manifest the spirit of unity, but displayed much rivalry and mutual jealousy in the process (1:15-18). The dispute between Eu-o'dia and Syn'tyche probably forms part of the background of Paul's concern. "I entreat Eu-o'dia and I entreat Syn'tyche to agree in the Lord. And I ask you also, true yokefellow, help these women, for they have laboured side by side with me in the gospel together with Clement and the rest of my fellow workers, whose names are in the book of life" (Phil. 4:2-3).

As far as *unity* is concerned, Paul argues that the Philippians are capable of satisfying his wish that they be one for four reasons.

First, encouragement *(paraklesis)* in Christ. No matter what their problems are, they have this resource for striving for unity. This *paraklesis* may be understood in two senses.

1. Paul, who was probably familiar with the Johannine tradition, may be referring to Christ's encouragement in the general sense of Christ's saving work, particularly to the promise that the Father will send the paraclete, the Holy Spirit. "And I will pray the Father, and he will give you another Counsellor, to be with you for ever" (John 14:16).

2. On the other hand, he may be referring specifically to Christ's high priestly prayer for the unity of his followers. He is saying to them: Be one: Christ is praying for you! "I do not pray for these only, but also for those who believe in me through their word, that they may all be one; even as thou, Father, art in me, and I in thee, that they also may be in us, so that the world may believe that thou hast sent me" (John 17:20-21).

Second, the incentive of love. The Philippians are able to draw from the resource of God's love which has been poured upon all who believe. "And hope does not disappoint us, because God's love has been poured into our hearts through the Holy Spirit which has been given to us" (Rom. 5:5).

Third, participation in the Spirit *(koinonia pneumatos)*. As we participate in the fellowship of the Holy Spirit, we attain fellowship with one another. He becomes the medium for our unity. "If the Spirit of him who raised Jesus from the dead dwells in you, he who raised Christ Jesus from the dead will give life to your mortal bodies also through his Spirit which dwells in you" (Rom. 8:11).

Fourth, affection and sympathy. Here he appeals simply to their tender, inner feelings as those participating in the Spirit (literally, *splagchna* refers to tender visceral organs). He concludes his train of thought by saying that all this, if fulfilled, will serve to complete his joy. Paul cannot possibly mean that his basic joy as a Christian is dependent on the behaviour of other people. All he means is that something will be added to the quality of the joy he has, if they witness about their unity. As he states in Philippians 4:4, true joy comes from the Lord, about which Christ said: "These things I have spoken to you, that my joy may be in you, and that your joy may be full" (John 15:11). His cup of joy, as it were, will be fuller if they manifest Christian unity in their daily conduct. He may also be thinking of those "who preach Christ not sincerely", but in order to frustrate him in his imprisonment (1:17).

With regard to *the fruits of church unity*, verses 2-4 of our text read: "Complete my joy by being of the same mind, having the same love, being in full accord and of one mind. Do nothing from selfishness or conceit, but in humility count others better than yourselves. Let each of you look not only to his own interests, but also to the interests of others."

"Being of the same mind" refers to the Christian frame of mind and mental outlook, and is reminiscent of what he has already said about different ways of preaching Christ. "Some indeed preach Christ from envy and rivalry, but others from good will. The latter do it out of love, knowing that I am put here for the defence of the gospel; the former proclaim Christ out of partisanship, not sincerely but thinking to afflict me in my imprisonment. What then? Only that in every way, whether in pretence or in truth, Christ is proclaimed; and in that I rejoice" (Phil. 1:15-18). I am reminded of the present-day differences of opinion on how to do theology or how to preach the gospel (e. g. mass evangelism, pulpit and Sunday-only evangelism, Sisters of Jesus, etc.).

Being of the same mind *(to auto phronete)* is facilitated by "thinking the one thing" *(to hen phronountes)*, that is, thinking about the same thing or focusing on one point. As Christians they must strive to have the same priorities when it comes to matters of faith, which form the content of their thought and discussion. For Paul the subject that occupied his mind is evident in what he said to the Corinthians: "But we preach Christ crucified, a stumbling block to Jews and folly to Gentiles, but to those who are called, both Jews and Greeks, Christ the power of God and the wisdom of God. For the foolishness of God is wiser than men, and the weakness of God is stronger than men" (1 Cor. 1:23-25).

Disunity is sometimes caused by the fact that people are not talking about the same issue of debate in the first place. On the other hand, there may be considerable satisfaction that unity is in being simply because people have been focusing on a topical, yet non-abiding issue. In South Africa we experienced church unity as we fought apartheid. Now that apartheid is gone, what next? What is *the one thing* we have to discover and zero in on together?

With "having the same love", Paul is probably thinking of the love which is a gift of God, and which qualifies us to be children of God and makes the interests of others paramount. This love is in contrast to other kinds of love, e. g. *philia* and *eros*. "And above all these put on love (agape), which binds everything together in perfect harmony" (Col. 3:14). This is a challenge to the current dispute around the identification of the genuinely Christian areas of social involvement (for example, Programme to Combat Racism).

"Being in full accord" *(sumpsuchol)* refers to souls that beat together in tune with Christ and with one another. Although the Book of Acts at several places uses a different Greek word, *homothumadon*, to describe the state of being of *one accord*, the basic connotation is the same. "All these with one accord *[homothumadon]* devoted themselves to prayer, together with the women and Mary the mother of Jesus, and with his brothers" (Acts 1:14). This probably included consensus in matters of faith and life, which was a level much deeper than the modern concept of "convergence".

The general principles of Paul's *ethics*, as enunciated in verses 2-4 of our text, are an extension of his understanding of the saving love of God, *agape*. Those who have been transformed by that love, by allowing themselves to die and rise with Christ, are expected to imitate Christ in their behaviour. "Do nothing from selfishness or conceit, but in humility count others better than yourselves. Let each of you look not only to his own interests, but also to the interests of others." Christ is portrayed as being more than just a moral example. It is assumed that there should be a correspondence of minds between ours and his. This is not just some practical exhortation about doing what Christ did. In him we become who we should be and then become able to do what he did.

Just as we, of the seed of the old Adam, have inherited sinful tendencies, Jesus Christ has started a new generation of human beings. "If, because of one man's trespass, death reigned through that one man, much more will those who receive the abundance of grace and the free gift of righteousness reign in life through the one man Jesus Christ" (Rom. 5:17-19).

There is a relationship between Jesus Christ and the baptized believer: Christ lives in the believer, and the believer lives in Christ. Paul has already referred to this in Philippians 1:21: "For to me to live is Christ, and to die is gain."

In Galatians 2:20 he says: "I have been crucified with Christ; it is no longer I who live, but Christ who lives in me; and the life I now live in the flesh I live by faith in the Son of God, who loved me and gave himself for me."

Paul is at pains to explain how the benefits of Christ's death and resurrection become ours, not only at the level of salvation, but also in relation to how we become enabled to produce the fruits of righteousness. We become imitators *(mimetai)* of Christ on the world stage, as it were, in the original theatrical sense of being mimics of Christ to those who only see similarity of out-ward mannerisms and habits. Paul meant it in a profound sense when he said: "And you became imitators of us and of the Lord, for you received the word in much affliction, with joy inspired by the Holy Spirit" (1 Thess. 1:6).

The semitic concept of corporate personality is probably the background of Paul's thinking. A member of a family unit or tribe stands and acts for the entire social unit of which he is a member. He is thus the centre of a psychic community which has a common will and a common responsibility. There are similarities between this and the African concept of spirituality.

Paul talks of a *life-style of obedience* in verses 12-13 of our text: "There-fore, my beloved, as you have always obeyed, so now, not only as in my pres-ence but much more in my absence, work out your own salvation with fear and trembling; for God is at work in you, both to will and to work for his good pleasure." The connecting word, *therefore* or *consequently*, implies that what has been said before should give rise to what is being said now. The unity among the believers is as important as the unity between Christ and the believ-ers in giving rise to unity in service. There is a link between ecclesiology and Christian ethics, on the one hand, and between Christology and Christian anthropology, on the other. Paul has taught us that a divided church has an ineffective ministry of outreach, and also that those who have died and risen with Christ are quality people who are able to live for others.

Christian obedience is an exercise in Christian responsibility rather than a matter of being pushed and forced from without. It is those who are truly free who can truly obey. Christian obedience has nothing to do with a life of bondage to rules and regulations. It is a liberated and an enlightened exercise of freedom. It is all a matter of Christian anthropology.

Christian obedience is a natural fruit of God working in us and making us will what is pleasant to him. Humanly speaking, incarnation means that God made himself small enough to dwell in us and work in us, and big enough for us to dwell in him and serve him. Hence Paul says: "I have been crucified with Christ; it is no longer I who live, but Christ who lives in me; and the life I now live in the flesh I live by faith in the Son of God, who loved me and gave him-self for me" (Gal. 2:20).

Christian obedience is a fulfilment of the prophecy of Jeremiah when he said: "Behold, the days are coming, says the LORD, when I will make a new covenant with the house of Israel and the house of Judah, not like the covenant which I made with their fathers when I took them by the hand to bring them out of the land of Egypt, my covenant which they broke, though I was their husband, says the LORD. But this is the covenant which I will make with the house of Israel after those days, says the LORD: I will put my law within them, and I will write it upon their hearts; and I will be their God, and they shall be my people" (Jer. 31:31-33).

Christian obedience is a life of total submission to the life of Christ to a point of being buried and risen with Christ. In Colossians 3:1-4, Paul says: "If then you have been raised with Christ, seek the things that are above, where Christ is, seated at the right hand of God. Set your minds on things that are above, not on things that are on earth. For you have died, and your life is hid with Christ in God. When Christ who is our life appears, then you also will appear with him in glory."

Paul also talks in the text of "the light of the world": "Do all things without grumbling or questioning, that you may be blameless and innocent, children of God without blemish in the midst of a crooked and perverse generation, among whom you shine as lights in the world, holding fast the word of life, so that in the day of Christ I may be proud that I did not run in vain or labour in vain" (vv.14-16). The actual phrase Paul uses can be freely translated as heavenly luminaries to the world *(hos phosteres en kosmo)*. That is reminiscent of John 17:15-16: "I do not pray that thou shouldst take them out of the world, but that thou shouldst keep them from the evil one. They are not of the world, even as I am not of the world."

In Matthew 5:14-16, Jesus uses the image of a lighting contraption *(phos tou kosmou,* cf. *luchnon* for *lamp* in v.15) which can be switched on and off according to specific need. In Philippians, Paul says that Christians are like stars, the sun and the moon, which are always there for all to see at any time. As luminaries for service, Christians act as sons of the "Father who is in heaven; for he makes his sun rise on the evil and on the good, and sends rain on the just and on the unjust".

In what way are Christians luminaries in the socio-ethical sense? Paul probably has in mind the moral principles which he listed in verses 3-5. Christians are to implement those principles not only among themselves, but also "in the midst of this crooked and perverse generation" (v.15).

Christians must seek to serve the interest of the community and society in general, because the church does not exist for itself, but for others in the spirit of its Lord. Since we are Christ's luminaries, "life in us becomes life in others and then there is life around".

Christians should set a public example in their mutual relationships and in how they solve internal problems. They must "do all things without grumbling *(choris goggusmon)* or questioning *(dialogismon)*" (v.14). The Greek onomatopoeic word suggests the sound of murmuring or grumbling.

Dialogue sessions, including those of Faith and Order, can very easily degenerate into parties of collective murmurings. The Pauline ethical principle of seeking the interest of the other is relevant there as well.

NOTES

[1] Quoted in Andrew Wilson-Dickson, *The Story of Christian Music*, Lion, 1992, pp.24ff.
[2] Gerald Abraham, *The Concise Oxford History of Music*, Oxford, New York, 1979, pp.55ff.
[3] *The Story of Christian Music*, p.45.

Romans 3:21-30; also Acts 9:1-19; Galatians l:13-17; 2 Corinthians 12:1-5

ANTOINETTE WIRE

Our Bible study theme for this meeting is conversion or change. We generally think of conversion as something required of others, of non-believers or of non-Christians, or at least of those not from our kind of Christianity. They need to convert and become like us. But the Bible most often calls for conversion of the insiders. It is to Israel that the prophets cry: Shuv! Repent! Return! What is conversion for us insiders? What change is needed in us?

Perhaps the most famous conversion story in the Bible is about a devout man named Saul on the way to Damascus with documents to wipe out a heresy threatening that city. Luke considers the story so important he tells it several times in the Acts of the Apostles, and it has recently been used as a challenge to us from South African Christians. Three things happen on the road to Damascus in Acts 9. First, a blinding light knocks Paul to the ground. As far as we hear, he has no vision. In fact, the sight he once had is taken away. Second, a voice says, "Saul, Saul, why are you persecuting me?" And when he asks, "Who are you, Lord?" the voice says, "I am Jesus whom you are persecuting." To this devout man abandoning the comforts of Jerusalem in defence of the Lord, the Lord is saying, "I am Jesus whom you are persecuting."

First a disabling light, second the voice of his Lord from the opposite direction. And third, not a divine revelation or secret mystery, but only, "Get up and go in the city and you will be told what to do." So he has to depend on his friends to lead him by the hand to Damascus, and he has to depend on a stranger named Ananias to take the risk to come and find him and bring him his sight and Holy Spirit and baptism, and the life-time task, as God put it to Ananias, "to bear Jesus' name before nations and kings and the children of Israel".

This is how Luke tells the story, as an event disrupting a confident religious life. But perhaps Paul in his own letters can give us who seek conversion a more intimate and inspiring view. As far as we can tell, Paul refers to his conversion only twice in all his letters, and that very briefly, both times where his credentials as an apostle of Jesus Christ have been called into question. Yet his conversion does not establish his own authority. People apparently arrived in Galatia after Paul left, coming from the apostles in Jerusalem who had lived with Jesus and asking where Paul got his authority, since he was not on good terms with the apostles. Later in his letter to Galatia Paul does argue that the Jerusalem apostles agreed with his gospel and then went back on their agreement, but he begins by rejecting all human authority. He says (Gal. 1:13-17) that he was more zealous of the ancestral traditions than all the others of his age when suddenly, as he puts it, "God was pleased to reveal his son in me, so that I might proclaim him among the nations". The point is that his stable religious life was undercut, not by the apostles' memory of Jesus, but by an encounter with the living Lord. What he discovered was that Jesus was God's chosen one, revealed to him, as he says, "so that I might proclaim him among the nations". His task was to make God accessible to people outside the ancestral tradition through this Lord Jesus.

The second mention of his conversion in 2 Corinthians 12 shows that it cannot be used by Paul to establish his authority or set an example for others. In Corinth people do share their visions and revelations to inspire each other, but Paul is wary of this. He claims that reciting divine encounters is nothing but a fool's boast and he tells his conversion almost as a parody of such claims of divine immediacy, intimacy and insight. He will only tell about "a certain person" who as long as fourteen years ago was caught up into heaven, but Paul says he doesn't know if the person's body was there or not. And what the person heard there was "unspeakable speech" so he cannot speak it. That is all he will say about his conversion experience. It has given him no advantage over others.

If we are to hear what Paul's conversion meant to him, it seems that we will have to look at the life his conversion led him into. He says clearly that "God was pleased to reveal his son in me so that I might proclaim him among the nations," and all of his letters are written about this work. Suddenly we have the problem of too much material to look at. I will focus on just one passage, Romans 3:21-30, which may be the heart of Paul's defence of his gospel to the nations. Some say that Paul is here preparing his oral defence for his trial in Jerusalem, that he anticipates in 15:30. In any case, Romans is Paul's most consistent effort to explain his work to the devout who insisted that God's integrity could not be honoured – or, as they put it, God's righteousness could not be established – apart from the ancestral traditions of Judaism. If we can listen to Paul today as devout people committed to the ancestral traditions of Christianity, we may be able to learn what conversion could mean for us.

Paul begins Romans by showing that no one has any advantage before God. God's righteousness reveals that all people have sinned, both those outside and inside of God's people, and no one, no matter how devout, measures up to God's righteousness. Then in 3:21-22 he says, "Now, quite apart from the principle of measuring up, God's righteousness attested by the law and prophets has been revealed, God's righteousness through the trust of Jesus Christ for all who trust." Paul does not stop to explain if he means it is Jesus who trusts God or others who trust Jesus or both, but instead he goes straight to his main point. "For there is no distinction. For all have sinned and do not measure up to the glory of God, being made righteous free of charge by a gift through the redemption in Christ Jesus." Then briefly Paul explains this in terms of ancestral atonement traditions, saying that God made Jesus a place of mercy through trust in his blood, so as to show God's righteousness by mercifully passing over former sins. The reason for this, Paul says, is not to undercut but to demonstrate God's righteousness, the one act both proving God-self to be righteous and making others righteous from the trust of Jesus.

But Paul returns quickly (3:27-28) to his main point about the distinctions between devout people and other people which are cancelled out by this. "Where then is the boast?" he asks, and answers, "It is excluded. On what principle? On the principle of measuring up? No, on the principle of trust. For we hold that people are made righteous by trust, apart from the principle of measuring up." Paul then puts this theologically, "Is God the God of God's people only? Is God not the God of the nations also?" And he answers, "Yes, God of the nations also, *since God is One* and will make the circumcized (that is, the initiated – we might read baptized) righteous by trust and the uncircumcized (the uninitiated – we might say unbaptized) righteous through trust." God can only be One – hence God of all – and will make all right with God in a process of trust.

Yet Paul says: the initiated *by* trust, and the uninitiated *through* trust? These different prepositions seem to be allowing for differences in the way God makes people righteous. We in our various Christian traditions and denominations are each quite convinced that we have the oldest and most solid tradition, that we administer the true initiation, that we know what is adequate trust in Jesus and what is not. Or perhaps in the ecumenical movement we are more generous with each other and think that by pooling all our strengths we can come to proclaim a gospel of Jesus Christ that preserves God's honour and draws all the nations to it.

This may seem like an advance over the past, a larger and more inclusive Christianity that can defend God's righteousness in a threatening world. But this is not yet to understand Paul. In his conversion Paul received a revelation of Jesus Christ outside the ancestral tradition – even apart from the Jerusalem apostolic tradition of his time. He was called to manifest God to the nations, the Gentiles, to those considered unclean and outsiders. He did this successfully, but in innovative ways that caused conflict wherever he went. His letters are witness to this. We do not have to agree with every means he used in order to have the highest respect for his drive to carry out his mission, that is, to reach outsiders not on the principle of "measuring up" but on the basis of the trust of Jesus Christ.

Paul's great problem was how to persuade the insiders that these outsiders truly could be God's people. By the time he completes Romans, traditional Judaism and traditional Christianity are rejecting his way of converting people. He argues on two fronts. First, he argues that these outsiders are included by trust, not that differently from how the insiders also were included. No person is righteous and God is not restricted to one righteous people but is the God of all, "since God is One and will make the initiated righteous by trust and the uninitiated righteous through trust". This told the Jews in Paul's time, and tells us today, that we insiders are not the apple of God's eye. God is indeed One, no less, and all people are equally God's. Such a God can make all right with God through trust.

Second, he argues that, as outsiders are being included, this cannot exclude the insiders with their stricter standards because the one God is faithful – that is, trustworthy – and will remain loyal to the insiders even if they foolishly rely on their own being righteous rather than on God. In Romans chapters 9-11 Paul tries to fathom how it is possible for these insiders, for the devout, to learn to trust God. He tries many proposals, ending up with the idea that insiders must somehow feel themselves to be outsiders in order to become jealous and learn to desire what they lack, so they can trust God to give it. Yet even this insight Paul presents as a mystery that he does not fully understand, and he ends chapter 11 with a doxology, "O, the depths of the riches and wisdom and knowledge of God! God's judgments are unsearchable! God's ways leave no trace!"

So what have we learned about how God converts those of us who are insiders? For one thing, we see that God is converting us by waking us up to the whole world that is God's, showing us that God, who is One, is already at work drawing all people into this relation of trust that we treasure. At the same time, God is converting us by destabilizing our own authority, so that we can trust God alone and not ourselves. Then we can perhaps begin to desire union with God through Christ as a union with all God's different people gathered by the work of God's innovative Spirit – a work that is, indeed, beyond our understanding.

"Where then is the boast? It is excluded. On what principle? On the principle of measuring up? No, on the principle of trust. For we hold that people are made righteous by trust, apart from the principle of measuring up. Is God the God of God's people only? Is God not the God of the nations also? Yes, God of the nations also, since God is One and will make the initiated righteous by trust and the uninitiated righteous through trust" (Rom. 3:27-30).

1 Corinthians 1:10ff.

FREDERICK SHOO

As a steward at the WCC's sixth assembly in Vancouver, I was fascinated by the breadth of the church of Christ. Today, thirteen years later, an important stream of the WCC is holding a major meeting here in my home town of Moshi. Is this not incredible?

It is an honour for me to conduct a Bible study at this meeting of the Faith and Order commission. I was given the freedom to choose any text, and I have taken one of the epistles of St Paul. I have done so because I believe, among the apostles, no other has dealt so extensively and sincerely with practical challenges facing the church. Despite all the controversies surrounding his name, we still have a lot to learn from this great servant of Christ.

Paul is writing from Ephesus to the church at Corinth, by then an important city. The church of Christ there was fairly large (Acts 18:8). As a Roman provincial capital, Corinth was enjoying commercial and political prosperity. People of different cultures and religions were attracted to come and live in this city. There were Greeks, Roman colonists and Jews: the city was multicultural. But Corinth was not only remarkable for its prosperity, but also for its vice; it was what we may call "a global village in miniature".

In this city there were scores of small Christian congregations, each under its own leadership, and Paul was aware of this. But he still addressed them as "the church of God at Corinth" (1 Cor. 1:2). He does not say, "to the congregations at Corinth". The unity of the church is something real to him. Despite all the differences, Paul speaks of the one church of God. "Now I plead with you brethren" (v.10). I see two important points in this verse. First, the careful choice of terminology in his approach. The issue he is about to address is a serious one, yet he does not simply recommend or prescribe, he does not condemn or accuse. He pleads with them. We have a lesson here: What kind of language do we use when we as brothers and sisters talk to each other? How do our committee reports sound? Are they only recommendations or is there this sincere spirit of passionate plea? I think it makes a difference. A passionate plea involves some degree of personal involvement, a deep feeling and a sense of commitment to what one is advocating. This does not, however, mean mere emotionalism.

The second thing is the driving force behind this passionate plea. Paul does not plead with them in the name of the pagan world which blankets the whole of life in Corinth. In other words, it is not the global situation or what the politicians are trying to do which moves him to plead with the brethren. It is a *name*, the person of the triune God! He does not say, I plead with you in the name of the changing global situation, or in the name of global neighbourhood. It is not that these are not important to him; they are very important indeed. Yet he invokes the name of our Lord Jesus Christ. Here speaks a man full of experience. He knows that by invoking the name of Jesus, the apostles healed (Acts 3:6 and baptized (Acts 2:38).

By invoking this name mountains were moved. What may have seemed impossible became possible. Paul is not simply reacting to a situation, he is acting responsibly. What he is about to say matters *for Jesus' sake* and hence for the sake of the city of Corinth, the church at Corinth, and indeed for the sake of God's creation. In the name of Jesus Christ, wounds that rend a church can be healed.

The problem facing the church at Corinth was not the Judaising tendencies like in other churches, for example at Ephesus (Eph 2:19). These tendencies were not causing the church at Corinth great problems; Paul mentions this only in passing (1 Cor. 7:18).

The problem in Corinth was the factions among Christians, which were not doctrinal but partisan in nature. Corinthian Christians were splitting into rival factions. Some were becoming fans of one teacher or another (v.12). Tensions were growing among Christians. Instead of acknowledging themselves to be members of God's own family and seeking fellowship with one another, Corinthian Christians were becoming mere groups, each living and functioning for itself.

It is this factious spirit among Christians which most disturbed the apostle. Why should Christians behave like soccer fans? We know that for soccer fans it matters a lot which team is playing. Here in Tanzania it matters whether it is Simba or Yanga, in England whether it is Aston Villa or Manchester United, in Germany Bayern Munchen or Borusia Dortmund, etc. All they do is partisan. Their reactions are highly emotional; their "devotions" to their teams are too uncritical.

Paul pleads with Corinthian Christians to be perfectly joined together in the same mind and in the same judgment without contention (v.11). This does not mean total uniformity. We know that Paul is quite aware of the different Christian communities at Corinth and elsewhere. He is also aware of different gifts even within one Christian community (1 Cor. 12). He also speaks of the church as one body of Christ with its members as its parts, each doing its share (Eph. 4:1ff.). Paul is without doubt an advocate of unity in diversity.

But what disturbs him is not the issue of unity and diversity: it is the threat to koinonia of partisanship. He is afraid that Christians are changing into mere fans. Partisanship is a threat to the visible unity of the church because it denies the complementarity of diversities.

Factions and not diversities are dangerous to the church of Christ because they are a stumbling block to its utmost call, i.e. to witness Christ in word and in deed until his parousia. This demands koinonia.

Koinonia is for the children of God: men and women who, having been freed from all bondage of sin and guided by the Holy Spirit, do honour koinonia as a gift of God. The freedom they receive through Christ enables them to come to terms with themselves, let alone their traditions and established power structure. Koinonia is possible for those who are filled with hope by the Holy Spirit, hence open and ready for something new – men and women of anticipation.

Paul is writing this letter to the Christians, realizing how weak a divided church will stand before the challenges to be faced in a city like Corinth.

As we face the new century, is it not time for church leaders and teachers to address all Christians a message like the one we have heard?

The unity of the church is not our choice, it is given. The visibility of this unity demands our readiness to work together for the complementarity of our diversities. This is a challenge to all of us.

John 4:5-42

KWAME JOSEPH A. LABI

My choice of this passage was somewhat accidental. I have read it several times, not only because I like St John's gospel, but also because at least once a year I have to read it, and even preach on it. It is the gospel reading for the fifth Sunday of Pascha (Easter) in the Eastern Orthodox lectionary. And so as I was still pondering what passage would be appropriate for what I had been asked to do, I found myself, once again, on the fifth Sunday of Pascha, reading this passage and paying fresh attention to it. I knew then that this was my passage.

The first thing that hit me with a kind of new freshness was the paschal implications of this passage. Why has the church been reading the story of the Samaritan woman in connection with Pascha, as a paschal event? What is paschal in this story? And yet it became clear to me, and increasingly so as I continued to ponder this passage, that the key to a fuller understanding of it, or should I say, the key to understanding the mind of the church on this passage was in recognizing its paschal significance.

The significance of water as a symbol of the new creation and its close relationship with the paschal event is still attested to in many of our traditions today. Significantly, three out of the six gospel readings of the paschal season in the Orthodox tradition have water as an element in the central theme – on the fourth Sunday, the paralytic (John 5:1-15), on the fifth Sunday, the Samaritan woman, and on the sixth, the blind man (John 9:1-38).

However, it seems to me that a contrast is being drawn, at least by the author of this gospel, between water and living water. I believe that in the ordinary sense, living water will denote water, flowing fresh from a spring as opposed to water from a man-made well or pond. I believe also that a certain significance was attached to this difference in Judaic culture and spirituality, a significance that I see carried over to the Christian tradition, at least that represented by mine. And so on Holy Friday, an Orthodox hymn, paraphrasing Jeremiah 2:12-13, says:

> Israel my first-born son
> Has committed two evil deeds
> He has abandoned me, the fountain of living water
> And dug for himself a broken well....

Living water, water of life: this is the link with Pascha. The significance of Pascha is that it makes possible a new life: true life from God as opposed to what passes in this life as life; a new life, not that given by the water and food that support this existence; a new life that can only be guaranteed by him who alone is himself and gives himself as the food (bread) of life and the fountain of the water of life (see also John 6:26ff.). Another Orthodox Paschal hymn emphasizes this distinction with this invitation:

> Come, let us drink,
> Not miraculous water drawn forth from a barren stone
> But a new vintage from the fount of incorruption
> Springing from the tomb of life...

What Pascha gives us is a new life, not a new lease on the old. The old is death, only the new is life. So it is life that all this is about. We are not just talking about some "tradition", who drank from what; who or what is greater or more important; we are talking about life – life and death.

This, and nothing else, is the premise of all our theological discussion. Viewed from this premise, theology is no longer an academic exercise, done by theologians, with no relationship to life. Theology is life. The discussions we engage in are about life, our life.

It is clear, however, that once we start talking in this way, we make no sense at all. What is life? I have heard that questions asked several times and endless discussions and debates about what constitutes "life in all its fullness" (John 10:10). The Samaritan woman's dilemma has been the church's dilemma in presenting the gospel. And very often the temptation is very strong to reduce this radical newness to the categories of the old. Or perhaps, is it our own lack of understanding, our failure to appreciate the full import of this newness that makes us do so? But this is a real dilemma: "Give me this water, that I may not thirst, nor come here to draw" (v.15). There is no doubt here that Jesus and the woman are on different wave-lengths. Obviously, Jesus was not making sense; and often theology, if it attempts to address this newness, the "one thing needed" (Luke 10:42) does not make any sense. Personally, I even feel a tone of ridicule in what the woman says, just as theology and our theological discussions are often ridiculed because they are not dealing, as it were, with "real life" issues – life, according to the categories of *this* world. This is the real dilemma. How do we make this mystery of the new life, this paschal mystery real? Is it by changing our priorities in order to fit what this world regards as relevant to its life? It is true that Jesus switches to the woman's wave-length in order to communicate with her. But it is just so that he can communicate with her and bring her, and others like her, "her people", to the mystery that is himself, to the acceptance of that mystery that is revealed only in himself. The essence of his message, the mystery, what he has been trying to say all along, remains the same, "... I am He". The woman's recognition of Jesus as a prophet is significant only in so far as it leads her and the others into this deeper mystery.

And so it seems as if this first part of the story of the Samaritan woman is preparing us in a way for the second part – the revelation of Jesus the Christ for who he really is and what that means for us and for our life in him.

Verses 20-25 establish a close link between our faith and our worship. In asking her questions about worship, the woman seems to be saying: "Since you seem to be a prophet, I guess you should know..." Our worship indeed expresses who we are, whom we understand our God to be and how we relate to him. Jesus' answer, like all his teaching, seems to be pointing in a new direction. He seems to be saying that unless we are willing to see the mystery of salvation in an entirely new light, we will continue to miss it. He seems to be saying that unless our worship is filled with a new content – a content that is Christ himself, in the power of the Spirit – unless the emphasis shifts from the where or even the how to the what, the *who* of worship, our discussions will continue to be academic and irrelevant, and many will continue to be led astray. Indeed, our life in Christ needs to be anchored in worship, but true worship is that which reveals Christ as he is and not as we want him to be. For true worship is worship of the Father, in the Son (the Truth) and the Holy Spirit. True worship is that whose content and meaning is the one undivided Trinity.

Verses 27-38 introduce another dimension to this life in Christ. The Lord says: "my food is to do..." (v.34). But then, immediately, he introduces the theme of the harvest. Is Christ saying that this is in essence his work? Well, at least he seems to be telling his disciples that "bringing the harvest home" is at the heart of what he expects of them. This is of the essence of the "will" of the Father and crucial to finishing "his work". Mission indeed is his food, and if we are members of his body, it is ours too. Mission is of the essence of our life in Christ; it is essential to our life. We shall return to this and other aspects of it shortly.

Finally, verses 39-42 show all this must necessarily lead to faith in Jesus as the Christ, the saviour of the world. For me what is important is that the crucial factor in bringing the Samaritans to acceptance of Christ as the awaited Messiah is no longer the woman's testimony but Christ's own word. It is what he teaches them, more than the miracle(s) he may have performed, that leads them to him. I believe that this is the work of theology – to bring people to God in Christ. Our theology will continue to be irrelevant if it does not seek primarily to bring people to Christ. The gospels are full of examples where good deeds and accepted teachings, by themselves, are not enough to give us the life that we seek.

However, it is verses 36-38 that I believe introduce the most relevant element for us today: i.e. our part in this overall scheme of things. What we are doing today is part of God's overall scheme. Many have laboured before us, and we cannot fail to see the fruit of their labour. Many have toiled so that the "fields are already white for harvest". We cannot let their labour go to naught or the fruits of their labour go to waste. We must go to the harvest and gather fruit for eternal life. For this is what it is all about: eternal life. Our theological discussions, even arguments, are about eternal life. Our seemingly endless discussions about worship, about creeds, about mission are about eternal life. Our seemingly irrelevant debates about ministry, the ordination of women and their role in the church are about eternal life. Our often painful discussions about communion and intercommunion are about eternal life. The never-ending, often frustrating bilateral and multilateral dialogues are about eternal life, because the unity of the churches is about eternal life, our life. That is why we cannot give up. But this is also why it is even more important that we do not destroy or ignore what work has already been done. That is why it is even more important that we accept this work, reap and appropriate its fruit. I believe that this is what these verses are trying to say to us today.

I believe that the harvest is ripe today. Many are today looking for something different. This, I believe, is the cause of the emergence and multiplication of new religious movements throughout the world. There is a search for something, and I cannot believe that Christianity no longer has that something. But the world needs to hear us and believe. Unfortunately, the world will not continue to hear and believe our divided voice. The world needs to hear us in a fresh, new way in order to receive this gift of God, this mystery of life – life that the world cannot give.

By-laws of the Faith and Order Commission

1. Meanings in these by-laws:

1.1 Faith and Order means the plenary commission and the board hereinafter defined.

1.2 The plenary commission means the plenary commission on Faith and Order of the Council.

1.3 The board means the board of Faith and Order of the Council.

1.4 The officers means the moderator and vice-moderators of the plenary commission and the board, the executive director of Unit I and the director of the Faith and Order secretariat.

1.5 The *secretariat* means the secretariat of Faith and Order.

2. Introduction

Faith and Order represents an historic, founding movement of the Council. There is a need for it to have a continuing, identifiable visibility and structure in order to maintain its ability to incorporate the participation of the Roman Catholic Church and other non-member churches of the Council in the organizing and staffing of its activities within the overall framework of the Council and in particular of Unit I.

3. Aim and functions

3.1 The *aim* of Faith and Order is to proclaim the oneness of the church of Jesus Christ and to call the churches to the goal of visible unity in one faith and one eucharistic fellowship, expressed in worship and in common life in Christ, in order that the world may believe.

3.2 The *functions* of the plenary commission and the board are:
   a) to study such questions of faith, order and worship as bear on this aim and to examine such social, cultural, political, racial and other factors as affect the unity of the church;
   b) to study the theological implications of the existence and development of the ecumenical movement and to keep prominently before the Council the obligation to work towards unity;

c) to promote prayer for unity;

d) to study matters in the present relationship of the churches to one another which cause difficulties or which particularly require theological clarification;

e) to study the steps being taken by the churches towards closer unity with one another and to provide information concerning such steps;

f) to bring to the attention of the churches, by the best means available, reports of Faith and Order meetings and studies;

g) to provide opportunities for consultation among those whose churches are engaged in union negotiations or other specific efforts towards unity.

In pursuing these functions the following principles shall be observed:

i) Faith and Order in seeking to draw the churches into conversation and study, shall recognize that only the churches themselves are competent to initiate steps towards union by entering into negotiations with one another. The work of Faith and Order is to act, on their invitation, as helper and adviser.

ii) It shall conduct its work in such a way that all are invited to share reciprocally in giving and receiving and no one shall be asked to be disloyal to his or her convictions nor to compromise them. Differences are to be clarified and recorded as honestly as agreements.

4. Organization

4.1 The Faith and Order plenary commission and board are constitutionally responsible to the central committee through the commission of Unit I.

4.2 The plenary commission shall have as its primary task theological study, debate and appraisal. It will initiate the programme on Faith and Order, lay down general guidelines for it and share in its communication to the churches.

4.3 The board will be responsible for implementing the programme, guiding the staff in the development of Faith and Order work and making administrative decisions on behalf of Faith and Order, supervising the ongoing work and acting on behalf of Faith and Order between meetings of the plenary commission. It shall represent the work of Faith and Order in relation to the commission of Unit I and, through it, to the Council generally.

4.4 The plenary commission shall consist of not more than 120 members (including the officers and other members of the board).

4.5 The board shall consist of not more than 30 members (including the officers).

4.6 The plenary commission, before each assembly, shall appoint a nominations committee to prepare a list of names for the election of the new board by the central committee at its first meeting after the assembly. The members will hold office until the next assembly.

4.7 The board, at its last meeting before each assembly, shall propose a person as moderator of Faith and Order for election by the central committee at its first meeting after the assembly. The moderator will hold office until the next assembly.

4.8 At its first meeting after the assembly, the board shall elect not more than four vice-moderators from among its members. The vice-moderators will hold office until the next assembly.

4.9 At its first meeting after the assembly the board shall prepare a list of names additional to the moderator and members of the board, for the election of the new plenary commission by the central committee at its next meeting. The commissioners will hold office until the next assembly.

4.10 Vacancies on the plenary commission and the board shall be filled by the central committee on the nomination of the board.

4.11 Since the size of the plenary commission and the board and the provisions of by-law 4.12 preclude full representation of all member churches of the Council, appointment shall be made on the basis of personal capacity to serve the purposes of Faith and Order. At the same time, care shall be taken to secure a reasonable geographical and confessional representation of churches on the plenary commission, board and among the officers and secretariat. The membership of the plenary commission shall include a sufficient number of women, young and lay persons.

4.12 Persons who are members of churches which do not belong to the Council, but which confess Jesus Christ as God and Saviour, are eligible for membership of the plenary commission and the board.

4.13 Before any candidate is nominated for appointment by the central committee, steps shall be taken to ensure that his or her name is acceptable to the church to which he or she belongs. A member should be willing to accept some responsibility for communication between Faith and Order and his or her church and ecumenical bodies in his or her country.

5. The secretariat

5.1 The Faith and Order secretariat shall be the members of the staff of Unit I who are assigned to the work of Faith and Order.

5.2 The staff will be appointed in accordance with the normal procedure for the appointment of Council staff. The general secretary shall, after due consultation with the officers of Faith and Order and of Unit I, nominate for appointment or re-appointment members of the executive staff of the secretariat by the central committee or the executive committee of the Council. Prior to the submission of names to the central committee or the executive committee the board will make its views known on the nominations to the appointing body.

5.3 The secretariat shall be responsible for ensuring the continuation of the work of Faith and Order in accordance with the policy agreed at meetings of the plenary commission and the board and approved by the central committee. The secretariat will keep in regular contact with the officers and members of Faith and Order.

6. World conferences

6.1 World conferences on Faith and Order may be held when, on the recommendation of the board, the central committee so decides.

6.2 The invitation to take part in such conferences shall be addressed to the churches throughout the world which confess Jesus Christ as God and Saviour.

6.3 Such conferences shall consist primarily of delegates appointed by the churches to represent them. Youth delegates, special advisers and observers may also be invited.

6.4 Careful attention shall be given to the communication of the reports and recommendations of the world conferences to the churches.

7. Faith and Order meetings

7.1 The plenary commission shall normally meet once between assemblies, but may be convened at any time by the board with the approval of the executive committee of the Council.

7.2 The board shall normally meet every year, but may be convened at any time by the moderator in consultation with the other officers of Faith and Order or at the request of not less than one third of the members of the board.

7.3 The secretariat shall be responsible for giving due notice of meetings of both the plenary commission and of the board, for keeping its minutes and other records and, in consultation with the moderator, for preparing its agenda.

7.4 A member of the plenary commission, by advance notice in writing to the secretariat, signed by both the commission member and the appropriate representative of the member's church, may name a proxy to represent the member at any meeting at which the member is unable to be present.

7.5 A member of the board may name a person to represent him or her at any meeting at which the member is unable to be present, but such a person may not vote.

7.6 Other persons may be invited to be present and to speak, if the moderator so rules, but not to vote. In particular, in order to secure representation of its study groups, members of these may be invited to attend either body as consultants.

7.7 In the absence of the moderator, one of the vice-moderators shall preside at such meetings. In the absence of any of these officers, the meeting shall elect one of its members to take the chair. One third of the total membership (including proxies) shall constitute a quorum.

7.8 Faith and Order shall normally conduct its business according to the rule of procedure of the central committee. Questions arising about procedure shall be decided by a majority vote of those present and voting.

7.9 If, at any time when it is inconvenient to hold a meeting of the board, the moderator and secretariat shall decide that there is business requiring immediate action by the board, it shall be permissible for them to obtain by post or fax the opinions of its members and the majority opinion thus ascertained shall be treated as equivalent to the decision of a duly convened meeting.

8. Faith and Order studies

8.1 The board, giving due attention to the general guidelines laid down by the plenary commission (see 4.2), shall formulate and carry through the study programme.

8.2 The secretariat, as authorized by the board, shall invite persons to serve on the study groups and consultations. They shall pay particular regard to the need to involve members of both the plenary commission and the board in the study programme, whether by membership of a study group, consultations or by written consultation. Due regard shall be paid to special competence in the fields of study concerned and to the need for the representation of a variety of ecclesiastical traditions and theological viewpoints.

8.3 Study groups shall normally include both those who are and those who are not members of the plenary commission or the board. They may also include persons who do not belong to members churches of the Council.

8.4 In planning such studies all possible contacts shall be sought or maintained with allied work already in progress under such auspices as those of regional or national councils or of individual churches or of ecumenical institutes and theological faculties or departments.

8.5 Study groups shall prepare reports, as requested, for discussion in the plenary commission and the board, at world conferences on Faith and Order or at assemblies. Any such reports should bear a clear indication of its status.

8.6 The publication of such reports and of other Faith and Order papers shall be the responsibility of the secretariat, provided that adequate financial resources are available.

9. Finance

9.1 The financing of the work of Faith and Order will be undertaken in the normal way as part of the work of Unit I. The secretariat, in close consultation with the board, shall be responsible for working with the executive director and finance officer of the Unit in preparing a budget for the activities of Faith and Order.

9.2 The board will receive reports on the budget and funding of the work of Faith and Order and will provide oversight of the detailed planning and policy in relation to the funding of programmatic activities (e. g. studies) and projects of Faith and Order within the overall policies and budget of the Unit approved by the central committee.

9.3 The board will assist in developing the financial resources available for the work of Faith and Order.

10. Communication with the churches

The plenary commission and the board shall be concerned to facilitate communication with the churches. They shall make generally available results of studies where such studies are formally communicated to the churches through the central committee. In certain studies the churches may be invited to make a formal response.

11. Revision of the by-laws

Proposals for the amendment of these by-laws may be made by the board or by the central committee in consultation with the board and the unit commission. Any proposed amendment must be circulated in writing to the members of the plenary commission not less than three months before the meeting of the board at which it is to be considered for adoption. A proposed amendment requires the approval of two-thirds of the members of the board present and voting, before final approval by the central committee.

Participants

Moderator of the Faith and Order Commission
*Dr Mary TANNER (Church of England), Council of Christian Unity, Church House, Great Smith Street, London SW1P 3NZ, England

Vice-moderators
*V. Rev. Prof. Emmanuel CLAPSIS (Greek Orthodox Archdiocese of North and South America/Ecumenical Patriarchate),39 Arcadia Road, Westwood, MA 02080, USA

*Rev. Dr Paul A. CROW, Jr (Disciples of Christ), Council on Christian Unity, P.O.Box 1986, Indianapolis, IN 46206, USA

*Rev. Araceli ROCCHIETTI (Methodist Church), Julio Cesar 1264, Apt 702, Montevideo, Uruguay

*Mrs Veronia SWAI (Evangelical Lutheran Church in Tanzania), Women's Work, P.O. Box 195, Moshi, Tanzania

Commission members and observers
Ms Ilina ABADJIEVA (Bulgarian Orthodox Church), P.O. Box 484, Lexington, MA 02173-0005, USA (younger theologian)

Deaconess Bella ADEMOLA (Methodist Church), 17A Okotieboh Close, S.W. Ikoyi, Lagos, Nigeria

Rev. Dr Hilarion ALFEYEV (Russian Orthodox Church), DECR, St Daniel Monastery, Danilovsky val 22, 113 191 Moscow, Russia (proxy for Nicolas Lossky)

Ms Roula ALKHOURI (National Evangelical Synod of Syria and Lebanon), c/o Presbyterian Church (USA), 1044 Alta Vista Road, Louisville, KY 40205, USA (proxy for Najla Abou-Sawan Kassab)

Rev. Dr Dan ANTWI (Presbyterian Church of Ghana), Principal, Trinity College, P.O. Box 48, Legon, Ghana

---

* Faith and Order board member

Dr Kamol ARAYAPRATEEP (Church of Christ in Thailand), Church of Christ in Thailand,14 Pramuan Road, 10500 Bangkok, Thailand

Rev. Dr Sebastian BAKARE (Church of the Province of Central Africa, Diocese of Harare [Anglican]), University of Zimbabwe, Box MP 167, Mount Pleasant, Harare, Zimbabwe

Rev. Alyson BARNETT-COWAN (Anglican Church of Canada), Anglican Church of Canada, 600 Jarvis Street, Toronto, Ontario M4Y 2J6, Canada

Dr Silke-Petra BERGJAN (Evangelical Church of Germany [Reformed]), Gustav-Müller-Strasse 31,10829 Berlin, Germany

Rev. Prof. Dr Wolfgang A. BIENERT (Evangelical Church in Germany [United]), Hahnbergstrasse 5, 35043 Marburg, Germany

Prof. André BIRMELÉ (Evangelical Church of Augsbourg Confession of Alsace and Lorraine), 87, rue Strohl, 67520 Wangen, France

Metropolitan BISHOY of Damietta (Coptic Orthodox Church), Midan Sorour - Coptic Church, Damietta, Egypt

Prof. Dr Klauspeter BLASER (Swiss Protestant Church Federation), Université de Lausanne, Faculté de théologie, 2 Dorigny, 1015 Lausanne, Switzerland

Rev. Hugh Blessing BOE (Church of the Province of Melanesia [Anglican]), P.O. Box 19, Honiara, Solomon Islands

Sister Cecily BOULDING (Roman Catholic Church), Dominican Sisters, 7 Montpelier Avenue, Ealing, London W5 2XP, England (press)

Ms Farida BOULOS (Syrian Orthodox Patriarchate of Antioch), Syrian Orthodox Archbishopric, P.O. Box 4194, Aleppo, Syria (proxy for Metropolitan Ibrahim)

Rev. Fr Martin BOURGINE (Roman Catholic Church), Monastero di Bose, 13887 Magnano (BI), Italy (younger theologian)

Rev. Fr Frans BOUWEN (Roman Catholic Church), Sainte Anne, B.P. 19079, 91190 Jerusalem, Israel

Rev. Dr Sven-Erik BRODD (Church of Sweden), Uppsala University, Faculty of Theology, P.O. Box 1604, 751 46 Uppsala, Sweden

Rt Rev. Dr Manas BUTHELEZI (Evangelical Lutheran Church in South Africa), ELCSA Central Diocese, P.O. Box 1210, Roodeport 1725, South Africa

*Rev. Neville CALLAM (Jamaica Baptist Union), 8 Haining Crescent, Kingston 5, Jamaica, West Indies

Rev. Manuel Pedro CARDOSO (Presbyterian Church of Portugal), Rua de D. José I, 37-1o Dto, 3080 Figueira da Foz, Portugal

Metropolitan CHRYSANTHOS of Limassol (Church of Cyprus), P.O. Box 6091, Limassol, Cyprus

Rev. Keith CLEMENTS (Baptist Union of Great Britain) Conference of European Churches, 150 Route de Ferney, 1211 Geneva 2, Switzerland

Rev. Tony COATES (United Reformed Church), San Michele, Friar's Close, Shenfield, Brentwood CM15 8HX, England (interpreter)

Mr David COBB (Disciples of Christ), 3724 North Versailles Avenue, Dallas, TX 75209, USA(younger theologian)

Dr Pamela COUTURE (United Methodist Church), Candler School of Theology, Emory University, Atlanta, GA 30322, USA (proxy for Roberta Bondi)

*Rev. Dr Janet CRAWFORD (Anglican Church in Aotearoa, New Zealand and Polynesia), St John's College, Private Bag 28 907, Remuera 1136, Auckland, Aotearoa New Zealand

*Rev. Martin CRESSEY (United Reformed Church), 147 Thornton Road, Girton, Cambridge CB3 0NE, England (also observer for World Alliance of Reformed Churches)

*Dr Sophie DEICHA (Archdiocese of the Russian Orthodox Parishes in Western Europe/Ecumenical Patriarchate), 50, rue de Mareil, 78100 Saint-Germain-en-Laye, France

Mrs Christiane DIETERLÉ (Reformed Church in France), 6 Clos du Marquis, 07300 Tournon s/Rhône, France

*Rev. Dr Peter DONALD (Church of Scotland), St Serf's Manse, 1 Denham Green Terrace, Edinburgh EH5 3PG, Scotland

Rt Rev. Sigqibo DWANE (Church of the Province of Southern Africa [Anglican]), P.O. Box 46803, Glosderry 7702, Western Cape, South Africa

Mme Marguerite FASSINOU (Methodist Church) P.O. Box 571, Porto-Novo, Bsenin

Mr Alfer C. FIAFERANA, P.O. Box 76657, Nairobi, Kenya (interpreter)

Prof. Kyriaki FITZGERALD (Greek Orthodox Archidocese of North and South America/Ecumenical Patriarchate), 43, ch. Moïse-Duboule, 1209 Geneva, Switzerland

V. Rev. Prof. Thomas FITZGERALD (Greek Orthodox Archidocese of North and South America/Ecumenical Patriarchate), Unit I Executive Director, World Council of Churches, Geneva, Switzerland

Ms Olga GANABA (Russian Orthodox Church), Department of External Church Relations, St Daniel Monastery, 22 Danilovsky val, 113 191 Moscow, CIS

Rev. GAO Ying (Christian Council of China), c/o Christian Council of China, Nanjing Office, 17 Da Jian Xiang, Nanjing 210 029, China

Sister Dr Donna GEERNAERT, SC (Roman Catholic Church), 90 Parent Avenue, Ottawa, Ontario K1N 7B1, Canada

Rev. Dr J.W. GLADSTONE (Church of South India), Principal, Kerala United Theological Seminary, Kannammoola, Trivandrum 695 011, Kerala, India

Rev. Marc GOERTZ (Reformed Church in France), 6 rue Alexandre Dumas, 06100 Nice, France (interpreter)

Prof. S. Mark HEIM (American Baptist Churches), Andover Newton Theological School, Department of Christian Religion, 210 Herrick Road, Newton Centre, MA 02159-2243, USA

Prof. Susanne HEINE (Lutheran Church in Austria), Buchfeldgasse 9, 1080 Vienna, Austria

Rev. Prof. William HENN OFM Cap. (Roman Catholic Church), Collegio Internazionale S. Lorenzo, C.P. 18382, GRA km 65.050, 00163 Rome, Italy (proxy for Frank Matera)

Prof. L.A. (Bert) HOEDEMAKER (Netherlands Reformed Church), Gorecthkade 1-30,9713 BA Groningen, Netherlands

Prof. Hristov Stojanov HRISTOV (Bulgarian Orthodox Church), ul. Stefan Karadja 8,1000 Sofia, Bulgaria

Rev. Prof. Viorel IONITA (Romanian Orthodox Church), Conference of European Churches, P.O. Box 2100, 1211 Geneva 2, Switzerland (observer for CEC)

Rev. Prof. Vladimir IVANOV (Russian Orthodox Church), Wiedensteiner Strasse 10, 10318 Berlin, Germany (proxy for Alexy Osipov)

Sister Dr Margaret JENKINS CSB (Roman Catholic Church), Yarra Theological Union, P.O. Box 79, Box Hill, Vic. 3128, Australia

Rev. László KALLAY (Reformed Church in Romania), str. Calvin Nr. 1, 3700 Oradea, Romania

Rev. Charles KAMALEKI (Christian Council of Tanzania), I.D.M. Mzumbe, P.O. Box No. 1, Morogoro, Tanzania (observer)

Rev. Prof. Kenji KANDA (United Church of Christ in Japan), 5-1-36-301, Kamikotoen, Nishinomiya-shi, Hyogo-ken 662, Japan

Rev. Pam KERR (Uniting Church in Australia), 8 Fillipin Court, Werribee, Vic. 3030, Australia (proxy for Dorothy Lee)

Mr Elekiah A. KIHALI (Greek Orthodox Patriarchate of Alexandria), Holy Cross Greek Orthodox School of Theology, 50 Goddard Avenue, Brookline, MA 02146, USA (younger theologian)

Rev. Gabriel KIMIREI, (Evangelical Lutheran Church in Tanzania), P.O. Box 519, Arusha, Tanzania

Mgr Prof. Aloys KLEIN (Roman Catholic Church), Johann-Adam-Möhler-Institut, Leostrasse 13a, 33098 Paderborn, Germany

Rev. Bruno KNOBLAUCH (Evangelical Church of the River Plate), Sucre 2855 - 2o piso,1428 Buenos Aires, Argentina (observer for CLAI)

Rev. Dr Symond KOCK (Presbyterian Church), Trinity Theological College, 7 Mount Sophia, Singapore 228458, Republic of Singapore (proxy for Yeow Choo Lak)

Rev. Arthur KO LAY (Myanmar Baptist Convention), Myanmar Baptist Convention, 143, Minye Kyawswa Road, Lanmadaw, P.O. Box 506, Yangon, Myanmar

Rev. Fr Johns Abraham KONAT (Malankara Orthodox Syrian Church), Pampakuda PO, via Muvattupuzha, Kerala 686 667, India

Rev. Dr Abraham KURUVILLA (Mar Thoma Syrian Church), T.M.A. Counselling Centre, Amalagiri P.O., Kottayam, Kerala 686 036, India

Rev. Fr K. Joseph LABI (Greek Orthodox Patriarchate of Alexandria), Orthodox Church - National Secretariat, P.O. Box 274, Legon, Ghana

Dr Nadia LAHUTSKY (Disciples of Christ), Department of Religion, Texas Christian University, Box 298100, Ft Worth, TX 76129, USA (proxy for Beverley Gaventa)

Deacon Elpidophoros LAMBRINIADIS (Ecumenical Patriarchate), Rum Patrikhanesi, Fener-Haliç, 34220 Istanbul, Turkey (younger theologian)

Dom Emmanuel LANNE OSB (Roman Catholic Church), Monastère Bénédictin, 5590 Chevetogne, Belgium

*Prof. Kyung Sook LEE (Methodist Church of Korea), 9-201 Chungwha Apt, Itaewondong, Yongsan-ku, 140 200 Seoul, Korea

Dr Lars LINDBERG (Mission Covenant Church of Sweden), Torsgatan 2, 3ter, 753 15 Uppsala, Sweden

Dr Barnabas MAHUNJA (Roman Catholic Church), Dar es Salaam, Tanzania

Rev. Harald MALSCHITZKY (Evangelical Church of Lutheran Confession in Brazil), ECLCB, Caixa Postal 2876, 90001-970 Porto Alegre RS, Brazil

Rev. Dr Marcello MAMMARELLA (Roman Catholic Church), 1 via Raffaello, 65124 Pescara, Italy

Rev. Michael MARKERT (Evangelical Church in Germany), Auenstrasse 28, 04105 Leipzig, Germany (proxy for Gunther Wenz)

Sr Claudia MSHAMBO (Roman Catholic Church), Tanzania (younger theologian)

*Rev. Dr Melanie MAY (Church of the Brethren), Colgate Rochester Divinity School, 1100 South Goodman Street, Rochester, NY 14620, USA

Rev. Prof. Nestor MIGUEZ (Evangelical Methodist Church of Argentina), ISEDET, Camacua 252, 1406 Buenos Aires, Argentina

Rev. Albert L.D. MONGI, (Evangelical Lutheran Church in Tanzania) General Secretary, Bible Society of Tanzania, P.O. Box 175, Dodoma, Tanzania (observer for Bible Society of Tanzania)

Rev. Aidan MSAFIRI (Roman Catholic Church), St James Seminary, P.O. Box 1927, Moshi, Tanzania (younger theologian)

Rev. Dr Geiko MÜLLER-FAHRENHOLZ (Evangelical Church of Germany), Oberblockland 6,28357 Bremen, Germany

Dr Joel MUSVOSVI (Seventh-Day Adventist Church), Ministries Secretary, Eastern Africa Division of SDA, P.O. Box H 100, Highlands, Harare, Zimbabwe (observer for SDA General Conference)

Rev. Robert MUTTA (Baptist Convention of Tanzania), General Secretary, Baptist Convention of Tanzania, P.O. Box 273, Iringa, Tanzania (observer)

Rev. Dr Samuel MWANIKI (Presbyterian Church of East Africa), c/o Presbyterian Church of East Africa, P.O. Box 48268, Nairobi, Kenya

Rev. Fr Felix NEEFJES OFM (Roman Catholic Church), Rua Pernambuco 880 - Funcionários, Belo Horizonte - MG 30130-151, Brazil

Rev. Bernard NTAHOTURI (Episcopal Church of Burundi), Episcopal Church of Burundi, B.P. 2098, Bujumbara, Burundi (observer for Anglican Communion)

Rev. Dr Elizabeth NORDBECK (United Church of Christ), Dean, Andover Newton Theological School, 210 Herrick Road, Newton Centre, MA 02159-2243, USA

Rev. Alexander J. OCHUMBO SJ (Roman Catholic Church), Jesuit Community, P.O. Box 1140, Dar-es-Salaam, Tanzania (younger theologian)

*Sister Dr Mary O'DRISCOLL (Roman Catholic Church), Convitto San Tommaso, 20, Via degli Ibernesi, 00184 Rome, Italy

*Most Rev. John ONAIYEKAN (Roman Catholic Church), Bishop's House, P.O. Box 286, Garki, Abuja, Federal Capital Territory, Nigeria

Dr Evelyn PARKER (Christian Methodist Episcopal Church), 5013 E. Seminary Avenue, Apt 1, Richmond, VA 23227, USA (proxy for Thomas Hoyt)

Rev. Prof. Martin F. PARMENTIER (Old Catholic Church), Burg. Lambooylaan 19, 1217 LB Hilversum, Netherlands

Ms Margaret PATER (Methodist Church), Lange Strasse 33, 17489 Greifswald, Germany (interpreter)

Rev. Dr Juha PIHKALA (Evangelical Lutheran Church of Finland), Sotkankatu 18 B 57, 33230 Tamperere, Finland

Rev. Rogelio PRIETO (Spanish Episcopal Reformed Church), Seminario Evangélico Unido de Teología, c/ Beneficencia 18bis, 28004 Madrid, Spain

Mgr John RADANO (Roman Catholic Church), Pontifical Council for Promoting Christian Unity, 00120 Vatican City, Europe

Rev. Dr Konrad RAISER (Evangelical Church in Germany), General Secretary, World Council of Churches, Geneva, Switzerland

Rev. Zoé RAMISARIVELO (Church of Jesus Christ in Madagascar), c/o Rev. Lala Rasendrahasina, B.P. 623, 101 Antananarivo, Madagascar (proxy for E. Razafimahefa)

Rev. Dr Cecil M. ROBECK (Assemblies of God), Fuller Theological Seminary, 135 N. Oakland Avenue, Pasadena, CA 91182, USA

*Rt Rev. Barry ROGERSON (Church of England), Bishop of Bristol, Bishop's House, Clifton Hill, Bristol BS8 1BW, England

*Rev. Dr William G. RUSCH (Evangelical Lutheran Church in America), NCCCUSA/Faith and Order, 475 Riverside Drive, Room 870, New York, NY 10115-0050, USA (also observer for the Lutheran World Federation)

Rev. Fr Jorge SCAMPINI OP (Roman Catholic Church), Convento Santo Domingo, Defensa 422, 1065 Buenos Aires, Argentina

Rev. Dr Barbara SCHWAHN (Evangelical Church of Hesse-Nassau), Martin-Luther-Strasse 24, 56203 Höhr-Grenzhausen, Germany (younger theologian)

Rev. Dr Werner SCHWARTZ (Evangelical Church in Germany [United]), Gartenstrasse 6, 67227 Frankenthal, Germany

*Prof. Turid Karlsen SEIM (Church of Norway), Det Teologiske Fakultet, Universitet i Oslo, Postboks 1023, Blindern, 0315 Oslo, Norway

Rev. Dr Matthias SENS (Evangelical Church in Germany [United]), Evangelisches Konsistorium, Postfach 1424, 39004 Magdeburg, Germany

Rev. Dr Hermen SHASTRI (Methodist Church in Malaysia), No. 1, Lorong Putri 5/9E, 46000 Petaling Jaya, Selangor, Malaysia

Rev. Dr Frederick SHOO (Evangelical Lutheran Church in Tanzania)

Rev. Drijandi L. SIGILIPOE (East Java Christian Church [Reformed]), Greja Kristen Jawi Wetan, Jl S. Supriadi 18, Malang 65147, Indonesia (proxy for Wismoady Wahono)

Rev. J. SIMALENGA (Anglican Church), St Mark's Theological College, P.O. Box 25017, Dar-es-Salaam, Tanzania (observer)

Rev. Rudolf von SINNER (Swiss Protestant Church Federation), Richenstrasse 23, 4058 Basel, Switzerland (younger theologian)

Rev. G.L. SYAMBWA (Moravian Church), MOTHECO, P.O. Box 1104, Mbeya, Tanzania (observer)

Rev. Dr Péter SZENTPETERY (Lutheran Church in Hungary), Rákospatak utca 9, 1142 Budapest, Hungary (proxy for Eva Geröfi)

Dr Constance TARASAR (Orthodox Church in America), 40 Beaumont Circle, Apt. 4, Yonkers, NY 10710, USA

Rev. Livingstone THOMPSON (Moravian Church in Jamaica), Trinity Moravian Church, 35 Montgomery Avenue, Kingston 10, Jamaica, Caribbean

Rev. Dr Michael TITA (Romanian Orthodox Church), Department for Foreign Church Relations, Bd Regina Maria 1, 70 461 Bucharest IV, Romania (proxy for Metropolitan Daniel of Moldavia and Bukovina)

Rev. Lucretia VAN OMMEREN (Evangelical Lutheran Church in Surinam), Evangelisch Lutherse Kerk, Waterkant 102, P.O. Box 585, Paramaribo, Surinam

Mr Valentin VASETCHKO (Russian Orthodox Church), Department for External Church Relations, St Daniel Monastery, 22 Danilovsky val, 113 191 Moscow, CIS (younger theologian)

Rev. Dr Gerhard VOSS OSB (Roman Catholic Church), Abtei Niederaltaich, 94557 Niederaltaich, Germany (press)

Rev. Olivia WESLEY (Methodist Church), The Methodist Church, 4 George Street, P.O. Box 64, Freetown, Sierra Leone

Dr Catrin WILLIAMS (Presbyterian Church of Wales), School of Theology and Religious Studies, University of Wales, Bangor, Gwynedd LL57 2DG, Wales, Great Britain

Rev. Dr Monrelle WILLIAMS (Church of the Province in the West Indies [Anglican]), Caribbean Conference of Churches, P.O. Box 616, Bridgetown, Barbados, West Indies (observer for Caribbean Conference of Churches)

Prof. Dr Antoinette Clark WIRE (Presbyterian Church [USA]), San Francisco Theological Seminary, 2 Kensington Road, San Anselmo, CA 94960, USA

Dr Chong-Gyiau WONG (Presbyterian Church of Taiwan), Tainan Theological College and Seminary, 117 Sec. 1 East Gate Road, Tainan, Taiwan

*Rev. Prof. YEMBA Kekumba (Church of Christ in Zaire – Methodist Community), Africa University, P.O. Box 1320, Mutare, Zimbabwe

Members of the secretariat

Rev. Dr Thomas F. BEST (Disciples of Christ), executive secretary

Dr Peter BOUTENEFF (Orthodox Church in America), executive secretary

Rev. Dr Alan FALCONER (Church of Scotland), director

Rev. Dr Dagmar HELLER (Evangelical Church in Germany; United), executive secretary

Mrs Carolyn McCOMISH (Swiss Protestant Church Federation), administrative assistant

Mrs Renate SBEGHEN (Evangelical Church in Germany: Lutheran), administrative assistant

Apologies

Dr Charles AMJAD-ALI, Pakistan (no proxy)

Rev. Christobella BAGH, India (no proxy)

Prof. Roberta BONDI, USA

*Metropolitan DANIEL of Moldavia and Bukovina, Romania

V. Rev. Prof. George DRAGAS, USA

Prof. Pavel FILIPI, Czech Republic (no proxy)

Prof. Beverley GAVENTA, USA

Rev. Eva GERÖFI, Hungary

Ms Justina HILUKILUAH, Namibia (no proxy)

*Bishop Thomas HOYT, Jr, USA

*Metropolitan Dr G. Yohanna IBRAHIM, Syria

Metropolitan JOHN of Pergamon (Zizioulas), Greece (no proxy)

Ms Najla Abou-Sawan KASSAB, Lebanon

Rev. Dr Dorothy LEE, Australia

*Prof. Nicolas LOSSKY, France

Rev. Dr Frank J. MATERA, USA

Dr Kirsten Busch NIELSEN, Denmark (no proxy)

Prof. Alexy OSIPOV, Russia

Rev. Edmond RAZAFIMAHEFA, Madagascar

*Rev. Raquel RODRIGUEZ, USA (no proxy)

Dr David T. SHANNON, USA (no proxy)

*Prof. Evangelos THEODOROU, Greece (no proxy)
*Rev. Prof. Jean TILLARD, Canada (no proxy)
Rev. Rhee Timbang, Philippines (no proxy)
Rev. Dr Wismoady WAHONO, Indonesia
*Prof. Dorothea WENDEBOURG, Germany (no proxy)
Prof. Gunter WENZ, Germany
Rev. Dr YEOW Choo Lak, Singapore

Members of the local committee	**Stewards**
Rev. Eliisonguo A.J. KIWIA	Mr Basil GWEGA
Mr Seth KITANGE	Rev. A. KAJEMBE
Rev. Andrew MADOLE	Rev. G. KITOMARI
Mr Ellison MALEKIA	Rev. Anna MAKYAO
Mrs Eunice MSHOMI	Mr Thomas MAMBO
Col. E. J. MSHOMI	Ms Naeli MPUNGO
Rev. Nigel ROOMS	Rev. D. MNANKALY
Mrs Veronica SWAI	Ms Rose MOSHA
Rev. Paul URIA	Ms Justine MSAIYE

Contributors

André Birmelé (Lutheran) teaches systematics at the University of Strasbourg and is a member of the Strasbourg Institute of Ecumenics, France

Manas Buthelezi is bishop of the Central Diocese of the Evangelical Lutheran Church of South Africa

Neville Callam is a pastor of the Kingston Baptist Union, Jamaica and member of the board of Faith and Order

Keith Clements (Baptist) is general secretary of the Conference of European Churches, Geneva

Janet Crawford (Anglican) teaches church history and liturgics in the College of St John the Evangelist, Auckland, Aotearoa New Zealand

Alan Falconer (Reformed) is director of the secretariat of the commission on Faith and Order, World Council of Churches

Thomas FitzGerald (Orthodox) is the executive director of Unit I, Unity and Renewal, of the World Council of Churches

Olga Ganaba (Orthodox) is on the staff of the Department of External Church Relations of the Russian Orthodox Church in Moscow

Donna Geernaert, SC (Roman Catholic), is on the staff of the Canadian Conference of Bishops

J.W. Gladstone (CSI) is principal of Kerala United Theological Seminary, Trivandrum, India

S. Mark Heim (Baptist) is professor of theology at Andover Newton Theological School, USA

Susanne Heine (Lutheran) is professor of practical theology and the psychology of religion, in the University of Vienna, Austria

William Henn, OFA, Cap. (Roman Catholic) is professor of systematic theology of the International College of S. Lorenzo, Rome, Italy

Yemba Kekumba (Methodist) is dean of the faculty of divinity of the African University, Mutare, Zimbabwe

Abraham Kuruvilla (Oriental Orthodox) is director of the TMA Counselling Centre, Kottayam, India

Erasto N. Kweka is bishop of the Northern Diocese of the Evangelical Lutheran Church in Tanzania (ELCT)

J. Kwame Labi is a priest of the Greek Orthodox Patriarchate of Alexandria, in Ghana

Kyung Sook Lee (Methodist) is professor of Old Testament, Ewha Women's University, Seoul, Korea

Melanie May (Church of the Brethren) is dean for women and gender studies at Colgate Rochester Divinity School, USA

Nestor Míguez (Methodist) is on the staff of ISEDET, Buenos Aires, Argentina

H.E. Benjamin William Mkapa (Roman Catholic) is president of Tanzania

Victus Mrosso is a church historian in Tanzania

Geiko Müller Fahrenholz (Lutheran) is a theological author and consultant

Mary O'Driscoll, OP (Roman Catholic) is professor of systematic theology, Anselmiana University, Rome, Italy

John A. Radano (Roman Catholic) is an executive of the Pontifical Council for Promoting Christian Unity, Vatican

Konrad Raiser (Lutheran) is general secretary of the World Council of Churches, Geneva

Cecil Robeck (Assemblies of God) is dean of Fuller Theological Seminary, USA

Jorge A. Scampini, OP, is a Roman Catholic priest in Buenos Aires, Argentina

Turid Karlsen Seim (Lutheran) is professor of New Testament at the Theological Faculty of the University of Oslo, Norway

Frederick Shoo (Lutheran) is principal of Zonal Theological College and Lutheran Bible School, Mwika, Tanzania.

Mary Tanner (Anglican) is general secretary of the Council on Christian Unity of the General Synod of the Church of England

Jean-Marie Tillard, OP (Roman Catholic) teaches at the Dominican Faculty, Ottawa, Canada

Olivia Wesley (Methodist) is a pastor of the Methodist Church in Freetown, Sierra Leone

Antoinette Wire (Presbyterian) is professor of New Testament, San Francisco Theological Seminary, USA